A HISTORY OF THE
AFRICAN
AMERICAN
PEOPLE

AFRO-AMERICAN MONUMENT.

A HISTORY OF THE AFRICAN AMERICAN PEOPLE

The History, Traditions & Culture of African Americans

Consultant Editors: James Oliver Horton, Professor of History and American Civilization, The George Washington University
Lois E. Horton, Associate Professor of Sociology and American Studies, George Mason University

SMITHMARK

This edition published in 1995 by
SMITHMARK Publishers,
a division of U.S. Media Holdings, Inc.,
16 East 32nd Street,
New York, NY 10016.

1 2 3 4 5 6 7 8 9

SMITHMARK books are available for bulk purchase for sales promotion and premium use.
For details write or call the manager of special sales,
SMITHMARK Publishers,
16 East 32nd Street, New York,
NY 10016; (212) 532-6600.

ISBN 0-8317-5514-8

Printed in France

CREDITS:
Project Editors: Will Steeds and Christopher Westhorp
Designer: John Heritage
Color photography: Don Eiler, Richmond, Virginia (© Salamander Books Ltd) and Gregory A. Linder, Normal, Illinois (© Salamander Books Ltd)
Editor: Nikky Twyman
Picture Research: Kym S. Rice
Map: Janos Marffy (© Salamander Books Ltd)
Filmset: SX Composing Ltd, England
Color reproduction: Pixel Tech Ltd, Singapore

Printed in France by Partenaires

Prelim captions:
Endpapers: The Moses Speese family near Westerville, Custer County, Nebraska, in 1888 after moving West.
Page 1: A heavy set of slave leg irons dating from the eighteenth century.
Page 2: 'Afro-American Monument,' a large chromolithograph published for the Tennessee Centennial Exposition in Nashville in 1897, consists of 11 vignettes surrounding a central arched medallion which show the history of African Americans from 1619 to 1897.
Page 3: These objects are all from the 10th Cavalry and date from the 1870s: a drum and drumsticks, a document case, a holster, and a belt.
Page 5: A collection of pins from the 1960s covering the civil rights groups and radical movements.
Page 7: A symbolic image of southern, rural poverty.

Introduction note
[1] Nicholas Lemann, *The Promised Land: The Great Black Migration and How It Changed America,* New York: Vintage Books, 1992, p.54.

CONSULTANT EDITORS

James Oliver Horton (Introductions and Consultant, and The Exodusters: Moving West, and Motown) is Professor of History and American Civilization at The George Washington University and Director of the African American Communities Project, National Museum of American History, Smithsonian Institution. His books include *Black Bostonians* and *Free People of Color.*

Lois E. Horton (Introductions and Consultant, and The Harlem Renaissance, Motown, and Black Hollywood) is Associate Professor of Sociology and American Studies at George Mason University. Her work includes the book *Black Bostonians.*

CONTRIBUTING AUTHORS

Daniel C. Littlefield (Africans in America) is Professor of History and Black Studies at the University of Illinois at Urbana. He is author of *Rice and Slaves: Ethnicity and the Slave Trade in Colonial South Carolina.*

Gary B. Nash (The Bittersweet Cup of Freedom) is Professor of History at the University of California, Los Angeles. He has written a number of books, including *Forging Freedom* and *Race and Revolution.*

Ira Berlin (The Slaves' Changing World) is Professor of History at the University of Maryland. His books include *Slaves Without Masters* and *Free at Last.*

Leslie M. Harris (A Limited Freedom) is Assistant Professor of History at Emory University and is currently working on a book entitled *Creating the African-American Working Class in New York City, 1785-1863.*

David W. Blight (The Age of Emancipation) is Professor of History and Black Studies at Amherst College. His books include *Frederick Douglass' Civil War* and *When This Cruel War is Over.*

James R. Grossman (A Certain Kind of Soul) is Director of the Dr. William M. Scholl Center for Family and Community History, Newberry Library, Chicago. He is the author of *Land of Hope: Chicago, Black Southerners and the Great Migration.*

Joe William Trotter, Jr. (From Hard Times to Hope) is Professor of History at Carnegie Mellon University. His books include *Black Milwaukee* and *Coal, Class and Color.*

Clayborne Carson (A Season of Struggle) is Professor of History at Stanford University and Director of the Martin Luther King Papers Project. His books include *In Struggle, Malcolm X: The FBI File,* and *Eyes on the Prize Civil Rights Reader.*

Roger Wilkins (Race, Culture, and Conservatism) is a Pulitzer-Prize winning journalist and Clarence J. Robinson Professor of History and American Culture at George Mason University. His books include *Quiet Riots* and *A Man's Life.*

ADDITIONAL CONTRIBUTORS:

Thomas J. Davis (The Stono Rebellion), Department of History, State University of New York at Buffalo, is the author of *A Rumor of Revolt: The "Great Negro Plot" in Colonial New York* (1985).

W. Jeffrey Bolster (African-American Seamen), Department of History, University of New Hampshire, is the author of '"To Feel Like a Man": Black Seamen in the Northern States, 1800-1860,' *Journal of American History* 76, 4 (March 1990), 1173-1199.

John M. Vlach (Slave Housing), Department of American Civilization, The George Washington University, is the author of *Back of the Big House: The Architecture of Plantation Slavery* (1993).

Adele Logan Alexander (Women in Slavery), Department of History, The George Washington University, is the author of *Ambiguous Lives: Free Women of Color in Rural Georgia, 1789-1889* (1991).

Marie Tyler McGraw (Henry 'Box' Brown), Department of American Civilization, The George Washington University, is the author of *At the Falls: Richmond, Virginia and its People* (1994).

Douglas Henry Daniels (The Blues Comes North), Department of Black Studies, University of California at Santa Barbara, is the author of *Pioneer Urbanites: A Social and Cultural History of Black San Francisco* (1979).

Spencer Crew (Albert Crew), Director of the National Museum of American History, Smithsonian Institution, is the author of *Black Life in Secondary Cities: A Comparative Analysis of Camden and Elizabeth, NJ, 1860-1920* (1993).

Lonnie Bunch (The African American in Professional Sport), National Museum of American History, Smithsonian Institution, is the author of *Jacob Lawrence: The Migration Series* (1993).

Raymond Arsenault (Bayard Rustin and the 'Miracle in Montgomery'), Department of History, University of South Florida, is the author of *St. Petersburg and the Florida Dream, 1888-1950* (1988).

Robin D.G. Kelley (Hip Hop: An Urban Mix), Department of History, New York University, is the author of *Race Rebels: Culture, Politics and the Black Working Class* (1994).

CONTENTS

INTRODUCTION

THE MISSISSIPPI DELTA was an unforgiving place, especially for black people. Before freedom, most were slaves; after freedom, they were sharecroppers, and few could hope for anything better. Long, backbreaking days spent in the hot southern sun, picking cotton for shares of the profit with the white landowner holding the books, figuring the expenses, and parceling out the shares. Uless Carter grew up there in the early twentieth century. At the end of one sharecropping year, after keeping meticulous accounts, the Carter family discovered they would not be paid their share. Their boss had decided to use their money to send his own son to college. Black labor had supported planters and their children, had financed white education, for hundreds of years. Uless Carter was virtually powerless in the face of this injustice in the South where the laws favored the economically and politically powerful whites, but he was not passive. Carter protested as he could; he abandoned the Delta for the 'promised land' of Chicago.[1]

Over their long history in America, Africans and African Americans used migration and escape, guile and cunning, powerful and persuasive rhetoric or violence, to gain freedom or confront injustice. This is their story, their active resistance to the aims of slavery, segregation and the other manifestations of racial injustice, and their role in the making of American history and culture.

The essays, short features, and excerpts from documents, literature, and biographies in this volume do not constitute a survey of African-American history, although they do cover a broad range of that history. Rather, they describe and analyze the African-American experience and the struggle for freedom and equality. They are written by eminent scholars engaged in the most pathbreaking work in their respective fields, and have an expansive focus on society, politics, and culture. Included are individual stories, family life, organizations, and broader social relations, plus African-American cultural traditions in music, literature, art, and religious and political institutions.

The presence of Africans in America profoundly affected the nature and development of all aspects of American society. Their labor made European settlement possible, sustained an expanding economy, and encouraged geographical expansion. Their cultures flavored the unfolding American cultures in the western hemisphere, and their role and treatment raised questions regarding tolerance, and equality and freedom, continually confronting professions of the American belief in liberty. As individuals and in organized groups, African Americans participated in the exploration of the American continent, fought to establish national independence, pressed for the realization of Constitutional guarantees, helped build America's towns and cities, schools and businesses, and played a part in molding the character of the nation. African Americans have given the nation a distinctive look and sound, helping to create those things that are now recognized as American. Telling the dramatic story of black America is telling a different tale; one sometimes tragic and sometimes inspiring for its revelation of human triumph in the face of great adversity. This story discloses the diversity of experiences that have constituted the American experience.

James Oliver Horton

Lois E. Horton

JAMES OLIVER HORTON, PROFESSOR OF HISTORY AND AMERICAN CIVILIZATION
THE GEORGE WASHINGTON UNIVERSITY
LOIS E. HORTON, ASSOCIATE PROFESSOR OF SOCIOLOGY AND AMERICAN STUDIES
GEORGE MASON UNIVERSITY

Chapter 1

AFRICANS IN AMERICA

Africa provided many of the earliest laborers for European settlement in America. Africans possessed the skill and experience necessary to establish European-initiated agriculture, and used their cultural traditions, combined with those of Europe and Native America, to create a new American culture. Bound labor in the Old World knew no racial boundaries; American variations shaped by region, climate, and agricultural-labor demands evolved into a system of chattel slavery based on race. Tens of millions of people on both sides of the Atlantic suffered in the process of slavery's development, a process shaped by decisions made in Europe, Africa, and America. Yet the story is not simply one about victims. Slaves resisted their captivity overtly or surreptitiously, using passive resistance as an effective weapon and taking advantage of the vulnerability of their slaveholders whenever possible. Even those who suffered most while building European-dominated America established communities which sustained them and helped form the social and political institutions of the new culture which became the nation.

Many objects made by early African Americans reflected, naturally enough, West African styles and usage. This is an Akan drum from The Gold Coast and it is almost identical to a drum made by African Americans in Virginia using deerskin and cedar (now in The British Museum). The sea grass basket (upright) and carpet are of recent African design, the basket plate was made by the Mandingo people, and the carved staff is from the Ewe people.

DANIEL C. LITTLEFIELD

AFRICANS WERE AMONG the earliest voyagers to the New World and among the first settlers in Hispaniola. Unlike the Europeans seeking wealth and adventure, most Africans came as bound servants, destined to secure wealth for others. Some might have come voluntarily, for there was a significant black presence in fifteenth- and sixteenth-century Iberia, and not all of these blacks were slaves. Free blacks and slaves, many born on the peninsula, adopted and contributed to the Iberian languages and culture – some popular sixteenth-century Iberian dances had a distinctly African flavor. Initially, the Spanish Crown, in order to preserve religious conformity, insisted that slaves sent to the New World be Christians.

Most blacks did not come to America by way of Iberia, however, but directly from Africa as part of the Atlantic slave trade. They went primarily to sugar-producing regions in the West Indies or Latin America to fill the insatiable demands of Brazil (from the sixteenth to nineteenth centuries), Barbados (in the seventeenth century), Jamaica and St. Domingue (in the eighteenth century), and Cuba (in the nineteenth century). Before the 1830s, four times as many Africans as Europeans came to the Americas; it wasn't until the 1840s that European migration permanently surpassed African migration. 'In terms of immigration alone, then,' one scholar comments, 'America was an extension of Africa rather than Europe until well into the nineteenth century.'[1]

Africans fed an Atlantic economy based largely upon the production of tropical and semitropical staples for European consumption. Sugar was most important, but rice, indigo, and coffee, and other crops like cotton and tobacco, were included. Grown on large plantations, these crops united West Africa, western Europe, and the Americas in an economic and social-symbiotic relationship. This 'plantation complex' reached from Portuguese Brazil to the English colonies on the Chesapeake Bay. French, English, Spanish, and Dutch islands in the Caribbean were focal points, but the system's grasp extended throughout the New World, even to those areas where most labor was free. Even free labor economies, like New England and the British middle colonies, contained slaves. These were not slave societies, but the presence of slaves stood as mute testimony to their participation in the slave-labor system.

Spanish Domination of the New World

Within 50 years of Columbus's discovery, most of the tropical New World was under Spanish control. Blacks were part of many Spanish expeditions, and 200 blacks accompanied the expedition of Pedro de Alvarado in 1520 to conquer Guatemala. By the beginning of the sixteenth century, numerous blacks

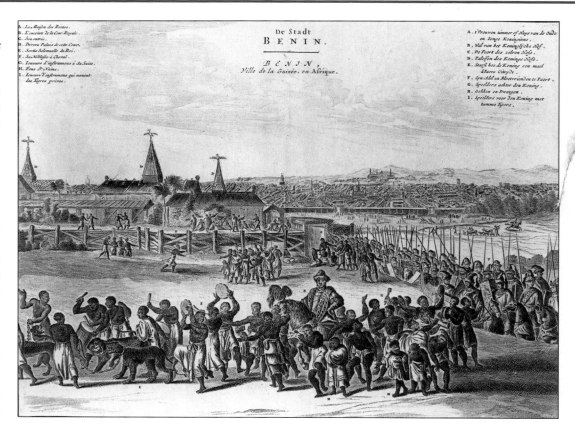

were scattered throughout Spanish possessions in the Caribbean and on the mainland. As early as 1503 the governor of Cuba complained that black slaves were running away and encouraging Native Americans to revolt.

Despite the prior existence of blacks in the Spanish New World, the responsibility for black importation is usually attributed to the Spanish monk Bartolomé de las Casas. He was with Columbus in Hispaniola in 1495 when Native Americans revolted against Spanish exploitation. This threat to Spanish authority was one that Columbus could not permit, and he suppressed it ruthlessly. 'What followed,' as one historian describes the scene, 'was simply a massacre. The riders killed until their horses could no longer be coaxed into a trot. Later the survivors were hunted down with hounds and put to work in the mines. Many of them died within a few days, totally unable to stand captivity.'[2]

Las Casas was horrified, and he devoted the rest of his life to the service of the Indians, appealing for more Africans to be sent in order to spare Native Americans. Although he may not have envisioned the exploitation that slavery eventually became, he obviously expected most of the work to be done by blacks. In answer to his appeal, Emperor Charles V authorized the beginning of the *asiento*, a license or contract to import African slaves into the Spanish New World. In the 10 years between 1520 and 1530, 9,000 blacks were brought to the New World, some of them directly from the coast of Africa. But what really spurred the importation of blacks was the decline of Native American populations. The native Mexican population in 1519 – estimated at about 28 million – was reduced almost by half (to 17 million) within 13 years. By 1580, according to one source, there were

only 2 million full-blooded Indians left.

Meanwhile, the African population increased. In 1570, Mexico (Viceroyalty of New Spain) had a black slave population of about 20,000, outnumbering whites by 25 percent. About 2,000 slaves became fugitives and the free colored population numbered about 2,500. The mixed population was the most numerically important, however. The Africans' greater resistance to European and other diseases, and their closer contact with Native Americans, facilitated the rapid growth of a mixed population – either zambo (black/Indian) or Afro-mestizo (black/white/Indian). By the middle of the seventeenth century, this group was the largest and fastest-growing single new population. So Africans and Spaniards gave birth to a new people, who blended the genes and cultures of Africa, Europe, and America.

Portugal, Sugar, and the Black Labor Force

Columbus brought sugar cane to Hispaniola during his second voyage in 1493. By 1526 there were reported to be 25 sugar plantations on the island, each employing 80–100 African and Indian slaves. Sugar is a very labor-intensive crop and extremely taxing to grow: many believed that only blacks could do it well. Indians were often used but they were generally considered to be too weak.

Blacks also performed skilled tasks connected with sugar production. They sometimes filled the role of sugar master, supervising all operations of the mill. Other

Above: An early eighteenth-century engraving of a ceremony being conducted outside Benin City on the Guinea coast. The picture hints at the kingdom's wealth and a highly developed system of government, trade and culture.

sion of Madeira (in the Atlantic) and São Tomé (in the Gulf of Guinea) was already the world's leading sugar producer. Moreover, in the Gulf of Guinea, it had already established a plantation system based on African labor. So when they discovered Brazil, the Portuguese considered producing sugar there. The presumably 'natural' source of labor in Brazil was the Native American but the Tupinambá Indians along the coast, accustomed to a 'hunting and gathering' culture, could not long be induced to labor voluntarily for the Portuguese colonists. Moreover, Tupinambá males considered cultivation women's work. The colonists resorted to slavery, raiding villages, and inciting intertribal (or interethnic) wars. But this policy failed and some priests argued in favor of protecting the Indians and, as in Spanish colonial America, the bettering of their condition was closely related to the increased importation of African labor.

The Portuguese established a connection between sugar and black slavery in the Old World and, early on, considered transporting this combination to the Americas. Although by the eighteenth century plantation labor had come to mean slave labor (and that meant African labor), the connection had not always been so close. The heritage of Roman slavery lingered in southern Europe during the Middle Ages and never quite expired. This was especially true in the Iberian peninsula after its conquest by the Moslems in the eighth century. As an important institution in Moslem Africa, slavery was carried into the peninsula with the conquerors. The resulting conflict between Moslem and Christian gave slavery a new lease on life and it became an important institution in both Christian and Moslem spheres, the slaves generally being prisoners of war.

Above: *Kingdoms such as Benin were built on trade and had developed metallurgical technologies based on the working of gold, copper, bronze, iron, and even steel. Benin was renowned for elaborate artistry in brass, and this hip mask was probably an insignia of rank for a military or palace official.*

Right: *A sixteenth-century woodcut showing African slaves – and, no doubt, indigenous Indians too – being worked intensively in a sugar mill in Hispaniola.*

slaves were cartwrights, blacksmiths, press operators, carpenters, sugar refiners, and sugar boilers, but these jobs were also among the most rigorous and dangerous. It was not unusual for slaves to have their arms broken or cut off by catching them in the sugar mill. A viceroy complained in 1586 about the use of Indians in these jobs, and in 1601 the Crown prohibited the use of Indians on sugar plantations in any capacity whatsoever. The planters were to rely exclusively on black slaves.

When the Portuguese voyager Pedro Cabral was blown off course and stumbled upon Brazil in 1500, Portugal, through its posses-

Mediterranean Slaves

At the same time, a slave trade existed in the Mediterranean, controlled after the eleventh century by Italian city-states. They dealt particularly in Slavic peoples (from which the word 'slave,' *sclavus*, derived – the Roman word was *servitus*) along the Black Sea and eastern Mediterranean where they set up slave trading posts. Armenians, Bulgarians, Circassians, Greeks, Georgians, Jews, and Tartars, and others, were part of this traffic. After the middle of the fifteenth century, when Ottoman Turks closed off the Black Sea, Italian operations shifted west, towards North Africa, and blacks were brought to the Mediterranean.

Black slaves served a domestic and prestige function in southern Europe and had additional tasks in Iberia, where many were traded or captured in warfare. Others, however, served with European bondsmen, free peasants, and local serfs on sugar plantations on Mediterranean islands. Practically unknown in Europe before the Crusades, sugar was produced by Venice in regions of the Middle East taken from the Moors in the twelfth century. European sugar production moved from there to Cyprus and, during the thirteenth to fifteenth centuries, spread to Crete, Sicily, and southern Iberia. Bound as well as free labor was associated with it, and black as well as white bondspeople – Christians and Moslems – worked to produce it. In this period, blacks were not uniquely associated with either slavery or the slave trade. Initially, they may not even have formed the majority of its victims.

By the dawn of the European Age of Discovery this situation was already changing. The first sizeable group of blacks was brought to Lisbon directly from the Atlantic coast of Africa in 1444. Later, the Portuguese established the first plantation system under European control to depend entirely on African slave labor off Africa's western coast. These were sugar plantations, and the link between sugar cane and the African slave was then firmly made. The slave society that developed there became a prototype of the Portuguese plantation structure that developed in Brazil, and Brazilian plantations demanded enslaved Africans for most of the next four centuries.

There was thus a continuous progression in the institution of slavery in Iberia from the time of the Roman empire to the modern era. Slaves from the Roman empire were gradually replaced by Moslem and Christian slaves, mostly white, and these slaves eventually were displaced by blacks. In the Mediterranean, meanwhile, blacks were increasingly, though not uniquely, involved in sugar production. During the transition, however, philosophical and technological changes brought about a change in the rationale of slavery in Europe, ending it for whites. Arguments used to justify the use of prisoners captured in warfare were difficult in situations where slaves were neither originally enemies nor necessarily infidels. Increasingly slavery and the slave trade consisted of technologically more advanced people enslaving those materially less advanced. New arguments rationalized an old institution, using both religion and technology: 'To take the black man from the wilds of Africa was a humanitarian and Christian task for it transformed a savage and a heretic into a person capable of benefiting from the fruits of Western Civilization.'[3]

Below: *An early eighteenth-century engraving showing the king of the Kongo receiving foreign visitors to his throne in about 1650. Note the close presence of the Christian missionaries.*

Colonization by Northern Europe

Northern Europeans, coming late to discovery, found most of the tropical New World in Iberian hands. Spaniards were the only European settlers in the Caribbean before the seventeenth century, and they located selectively, principally in the Greater Antilles (Cuba, Hispaniola, Jamaica, and Puerto Rico), with a view to protecting and supporting their interests on the mainland. In the early seventeenth century, Dutch, English, and French colonization efforts succeeded in the Lesser Antilles, a chain of islands stretching south from Puerto Rico toward the Venezuelan coast. They raised minor crops like cotton, tobacco, and pimento.

The English and French began their plantations with white indentured servants, whose numbers were supplemented by condemned criminals and war prisoners. French policy until the 1680s was to depend on white bondsmen to populate the Antilles. But the English began a transition to sugar in Barbados in the 1640s and simultaneously switched to African slaves. In a generation, with the aid of Africans supplied by Dutch traders, Barbados went from a settlement based on white labor (6,000 Africans and 19,000 Europeans in 1643) to one where (by 1680) blacks outnumbered whites by a ratio of 2:1.

Once the switch was made, Europeans argued that Africans were superior laborers, able to stand the tropical clime where white men could not. They conveniently forgot the viable, though not as remunerative, agricultural regime that preceded sugar's sway. The physical advantage that Africans offered was their greater immunity to tropical disease, *not* their superior resistance to the sun. They offered the practical advantage that, bought and sold as chattels, they could be made to perform tasks that white men could not be compelled to do.

In fact, sugar planters forced Africans to labor far beyond the normal expectations of traditional society. West India plantations were capitalist enterprises, regarding slaves as units of production. They did not value stable, slave family life and seldom attempted to establish or maintain an equal sex ratio on their estates. They normally requested two men for every woman and viewed raising young slaves to adulthood as being bad business. Consequently, they neither encouraged women to reproduce nor supported them or their children when they did. As a result, sugar regions usually suffered a net annual slave population decrease and had to depend on the slave trade to maintain their labor force.

There were exceptions in the West Indies, but not generally until sugar production decreased or the slave trade was threatened. The big exception was North America. Africans had greater susceptibility to pulmonary diseases like pneumonia and influenza there, and in early Virginia, for example, the death rate for both black and white people was high. Nevertheless, blacks thrived on the

BASKETRY

Africans transported to America brought with them not only crop cultivation skills but also a host of other everyday craft skills, such as pottery, carving, and basketry, to mention just a few. The African methods and designs not only survived the Middle Passage, they continued to be used by plantation slaves and can still be seen today among some of their descendants.

These baskets are modern, but all are based on West African-derived designs. They are made from coiled sea grass from the South Carolina low country; other crops, however, were also used, such as rush and sweetgrass. Rice was once the area's principal plantation crop, its production included the use of a specialized coiled basket created by African Americans for winnowing known as a 'fanner.'

In the Sea Islands of South Carolina, rice was a favored food of the slaves rather than merely just a commercial crop; similarly, however, it meant basketry was therefore much practiced as a craft. These baskets (below) are all from the Sea Islands. Clockwise, from top left, they are: a 'lamp basket' of sweetgrass, pine straw, and palmetto palm leaf; a corrugated-sided 'picnic basket' with a steeple top and V-shaped groove, all made of sweetgrass, pine straw, and palm leaf; a 'bottle basket' of seagrass sewn with colored ribbons; a 'sewing basket' of grasses and reeds; a 'fruit basket' of rushes, sweetgrass, pine straw and palm leaf; and a small, oval-shaped basket to hold sewing items.

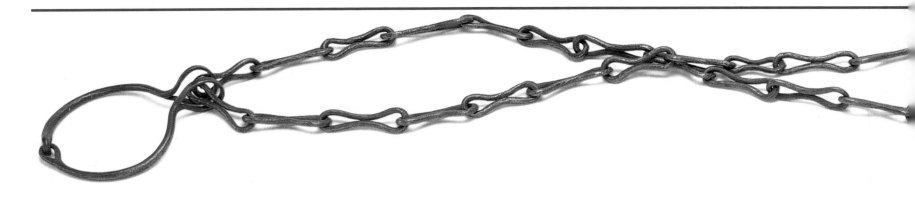

continent in a way that they did not under slavery in the islands, because the economics of production did not permit the same thoughtless waste of life. Neither cotton, nor tobacco, nor rice was as remunerative as sugar, and planters could not totally replace their labor force every few years as they might in the Caribbean. Consequently, they learned to depend on slave conservation and reproduction. The North American slave population was the only one in the New World's major slave societies to reproduce itself.

Origins

Most imported Africans came from an area stretching from Senegambia to Angola, within a few hundred miles (300–400km) of the western coast. Venture Smith, for example, was captured as a 6-year-old in the West African interior by an African enemy who raided his country. He recalled traveling 'about four hundred miles' (approximately 600km) before approaching the slave port of Anamaboo on the coast of modern Ghana.[4] Long-distance trade along the river systems of West and Central Africa meant that some captives traveled through vast regions of varying ethnicities, languages, cultures, and climates.

Western African cultures were shaped in part by the climate which, although varying, does not experience the wide temperature range common to Europe or North America. A true tropical climate, characterized by high daily temperatures of around 80°F (27°C) and heavy annual rainfall, is limited to within a few degrees of the equator, and tropical rain-

forests stretch along the southern coast from eastern Zaire to Gabon and the Cameroons, and in West Africa from the Niger Delta to Sierra Leone. Savanna regions, north and south of the equator, traditionally supported sedentary populations of agriculturalists. The western Sudan also supported nomadic pastoralists. Savanna agriculturalists cultivated millet, sorghum, watermelon, tamarind, kola, and sesame, to which they added the American complex of maize, manioc, groundnuts, and sweet potatoes after the sixteenth century. Forest agriculturalists raised maize, manioc, yams, and bananas. Rice is grown in various northern and southern savanna regions, particularly in the western Sudan, and along the Upper Guinea coast often dry rice, or rice using natural ponds or flooding. But in coastal Senegal and Sierra Leone, the Baga use intensive irrigation to reclaim mangrove swamps for sophisticated methods of rice cultivation. Domesticated chickens, goats, and dogs exist throughout West Africa, plus there are sheep in some places, cattle in the savanna, and horses in the western Sudan. Throughout the region, agriculturalists practice shifting hoe cultivation, and, in places, crop rotation and fallowing

Trade systems and Iron-Age technology facilitated the development of complex African states. Trans-Saharan trade spurred empires among Mande-speaking peoples (Soninke, Malinke, Bambara) in the western Sudan and among Kanuri-speakers farther east. Atlantic trade after European contact, together with trans-Saharan and other internal

trade in some cases, initiated or strengthened kingdoms along the leeward coast of Guinea, including those formed among the Akan, Gã, Ewe, Fon, Yoruba, and Edo. The same combinations of internal and external exchange encouraged state formation among Bantu-speaking peoples in Central Africa, particularly among the Vili, Matamba, Kongo, and Mbundu. The early Sudanic states sometimes reached considerable size: the sixteenth-century empire of Songhai, for example, was larger than the modern United States. But most African polities were significantly smaller. Moreover, unlike European structures, they were relationships of peoples rather than of land.

Whether or not there was a state system, the local lineage to which people belonged was most important, with villages governed by a clan head or village chief who exercised local authority. State systems consisted of a second level of lineage relationships, the leaders of one group establishing hegemony over others but exacting feudal-like obeisance and obligations rather than a structural reorganization of society. Local authority remained much the same. Thus the kidnaped African Olaudah Equiano, describing life in his Ibo village after its conquest by a larger political structure, commented: 'our subjection to the king of Benin was little more than nominal; for every transaction of government . . . was conducted by the chief or elders of the place.'[5] Descent tended to be patrilineal in western Africa, and matrilineal in south-central Africa. There were exceptions to these rules, and a few African societies were bilateral. Most practiced polygyny.

Complex social organization encouraged

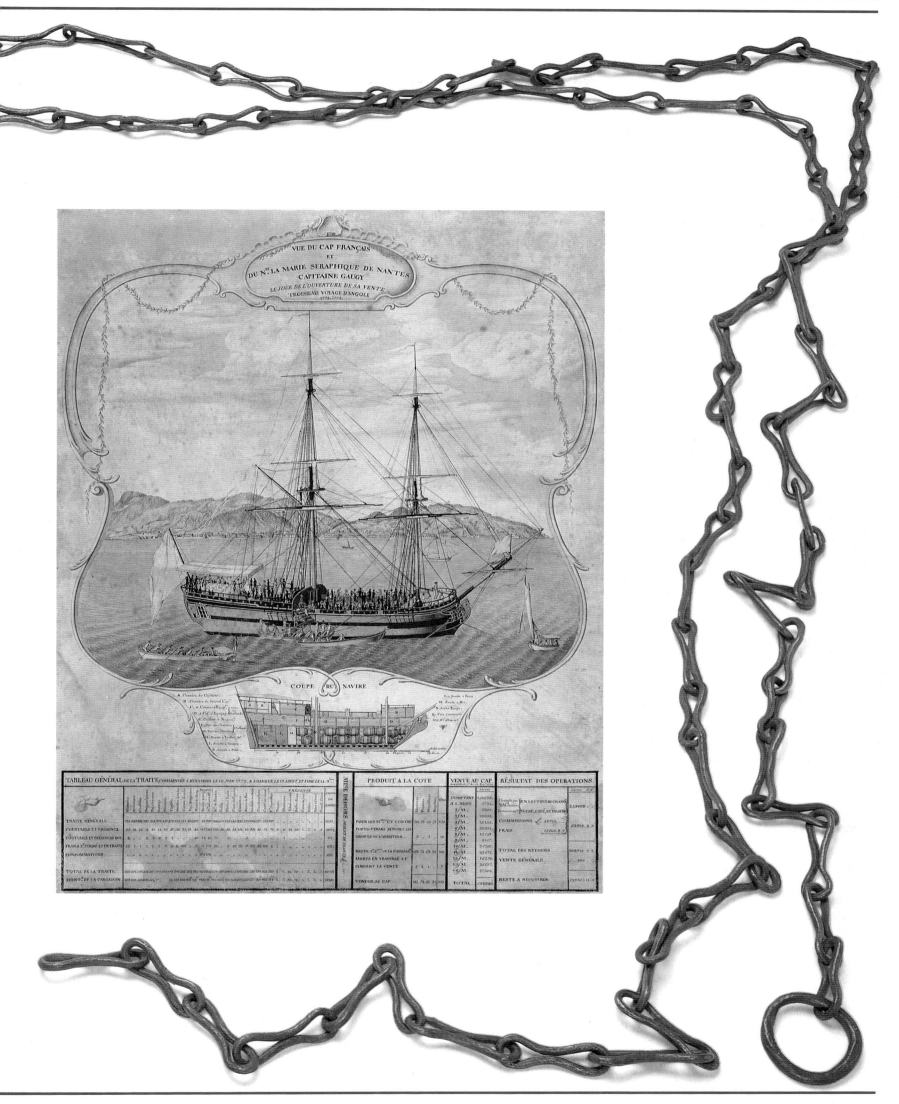

artisanal specialization, and various Africans were skilled in gold, copper, bronze, and iron work. African steel, created through a process that prefigured techniques not developed in Europe until the nineteenth century, equaled or exceeded that made anywhere in the fifteenth-century world. Basket-weaving, pottery-making, cotton-spinning, and cloth-weaving flourished in their regions, and everywhere craftsmen routinely generated works of great artistic value. There was commonly no separate class of artists, however, for African societies did not usually separate the functions of artisan and artist. They nevertheless placed great emphasis on artistic expression and professional creativity. Indeed, skill in a performing art was sometimes a prerequisite to high rank – as among the Yoruba and Asante, for instance, where a chief or priest might have to be a good dancer. The fifteenth-century kingdom of Benin, in southwestern Nigeria, is fabled for its art work, which extended from lost-wax-method brass-and bronze-casting to wood- and ivory-carving of distinctive style and attraction. Much of the art was used to record historical events and commemorate favored rulers or other ancestors. But sometimes artifacts were carved simply as decoration. Powerful people used woodcarvings on doors, doorposts, and furniture for their houses in Benin City to empha-

size their position or authority. Yet many of the finely sculptured African masks and figurines had a ceremonial role. So an Ibo sculptor, asked to produce a mask to be taken to America as an example of his work, produced a sculpture of a man wearing a mask, explaining that the beauty of the mask was not in the mask alone.

Although fewer Africans than Europeans had experience with the sea, Africans were accomplished boatmen, well-versed in the intricacies of riverine travel or ocean voyages along the coast, a skill invaluable for North American river navigation. Experience with watercraft enabled many bondsmen to master American river systems, readily assimilating Native American boat-building techniques and geographical information. They sometimes – in South Carolina, for example – dominated colonial, inland water travel. African long, shallow-drafted craft were well-suited to inland waterways and – being driven by oar-power rather than by the wind – were more maneuverable than the larger, wind-driven European vessels.

Justifying Slavery
Early European observers frequently justified enslaving Africans on the grounds that Africans engaged in their *own* form of indigenous servitude and that the European version

was preferable. In fact, argues historian John Thornton, African slavery derived from a different social and legal structure from that in Europe. African societies did not recognize private property in land, an essential ingredient of European social and political organization; Africans claimed people instead. 'Slaves,' Thornton avers, 'were the only form of private, revenue-producing property recognized in African law.'[6] Consequently, slavery was ancient and widespread. Its existence said nothing about African social development on a European model, however, for Africa used an entirely different value system. When Europeans gave up slaves, they surrendered an important labor source, but land, a basic cornerstone of society, remained. When Africans gave up slaves they surrendered something more basic. This is not to argue in favor of African bondage systems or to suggest that they were better or worse than (or even essentially different from) such systems elsewhere, but rather to point out that they were part of a different way of looking at the world.

African institutions of slavery were more than labor systems; they were related to the issue of kinship. African lineage-based societies and state systems increased their wealth and strength by adding members to the group. This accretion could occur in a number of ways, perhaps most often by marriage – women and children being particular assets. But it could also occur in the involuntary service of war captives or other unfortunates who worked for or were adopted by the state or individual families in 'patron-client' relationships, thus according them social existence. As members of an extended family, they might in many ways be treated like other family members and yet not achieve absolute equality, based on their status as historical outsiders. The longer they were part of a community, the closer they came to absorption, even though their origin might never be forgotten. They would obtain many rights and privileges, secure land for cultivation, and be free from the threat of sale. They might achieve great wealth and political power, exceeding even that of free people. They might even acquire slaves of their own.

Trade slaves, those most likely to be sold to Europeans, were often older war captives who were perceived as a threat to the host community. They might never adjust and always posed the risk of running away. Their greatest value to the community was the return from their sale. Their position was closest to that of chattel slaves in the Americas, though they often had more privileges, were not distinguished permanently from their masters by skin color as an unquestioned mark of degradation, and did not perform chores that sepa-

rated them from free men. Younger people, especially women and children, had value beyond the simply pecuniary and were more often kept – adopted – to become part of the local society. Olaudah Equiano, who experienced both African and American slavery, spoke almost wistfully of the Old World experience:

With us, [slaves] do no more work than other members of the community, even their master; their food, clothing and lodging were nearly the same as theirs, [except that they were not permitted to eat with those who were free born]; and there was scarce any other difference between them, than a superior degree of importance which the head of a family possesses in our state, and that authority which, as such, he exercises over every part of his household.[7]

Indigenous African servitude, therefore, had similarities as well as significant dissimilarities with institutions of bondage elsewhere.

Because the technological distance between Africa and Europe was not as great as it was later to become, the slave trade was a collaborative effort; for Africans, not Europeans, controlled the African coast. European merchants trading in Africa had to be fairly precise about where in Africa they planned to trade. Not only did trading systems differ, but so did the goods desired – commodities suitable for one part of the coast were often unsuited to another. Even the currencies were disparate and Europeans had to adapt to African practices. Thus Africans in Senegambia used iron bars as a medium of exchange and the British, who had a trading post in the Gambia River, kept accounts there in bars and pence; on the Gold Coast, Africans used gold and Europeans kept accounts in ounces; on the Slave Coast the cowry, a type of shell, served as money and accounts were kept in cowries. Slave prices varied with the region, the season, and economic, social, or political conditions.[8]

Below: *The European slave traders possessed slave compounds on the Guinea coast which were maintained for them by powerful native kings whom they rewarded for their work with Western goods and currency. Once supplied with Western weapons, tribal warfare was exacerbated to the benefit of the slave trade.*

Above: *Equiano's frontispiece portrait.*

THE MIDDLE PASSAGE

Olaudah Equiano, a young Ibo boy, was kidnaped from his home in Benin (now Nigeria) in West Africa and brought to America as a slave. The following is his account of the Middle Passage.

'The stench of the hold [where the slaves were kept below deck] while we were on the coast was so intolerably loathsome, that it was dangerous to remain there for any time, and some of us had been permitted to stay on the deck for fresh air; but now that the whole ship's cargo were confined together, it became absolutely pestilential. The closeness of the place, and the heat of the climate, added to the number in the ship which was so crowded that each had scarcely room to turn himself, almost suffocated us. This produced copious perspirations, so that the air soon became unfit for respiration, from a variety of loathsome smells, and brought on a sickness amongst the slaves of which many died, thus falling victims to the improvident avarice, as I may call it, of their purchasers. This wretched situation was again aggravated by the galling of the chains, now become insupportable; and the filth of the necessary tubs, into which the children often fell, and were almost suffocated. The shrieks of the women, and the groans of the dying, rendered the whole scene of horror almost inconceivable.'[1]

Note

[1] Olaudah Equiano, quoted in Thomas R. Frazier (ed.), *Afro-American History: Primary Sources*, New York: Harcourt Brace and World, Inc., 1970, p. 20.

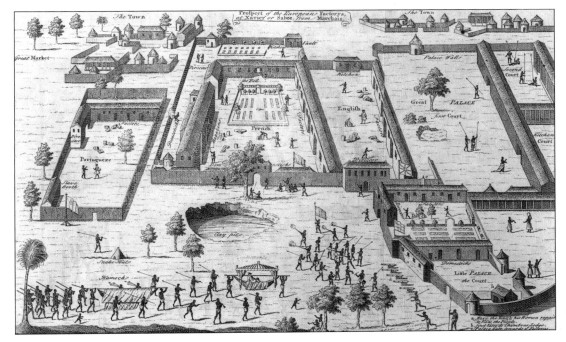

Naturally there was a need to collate the period of trade on the African coast with that at the port of debarkation. Sometimes this worked to the trader's advantage. A Liverpool company advised their ship captain in 1797:

> We do not wish you to arrive in Jamaica before the end of October that you may escape the Hurricane Season and avoid all the disadvantages attending the Sale of Slaves in those months, do not therefore be in too great a hurry in Bonny; propose to the leading Traders very low Barrs to begin with, and if they do not comply therewith, seem indifferent as to the length of your stay, nay you may even shew them a disposition to go to New Callabar, and thus you will most likely bring them to moderate terms and avoid the hurry and confusion which always attends the receiving great numbers of Negros on board at the same moment.[9]

On the other hand, when in November 1764 William Davenport and Company directed their ship to trade in Gambia for 120 Negroes 'Suitable for ye Carolina Markett,' they cautioned the captain not to 'stand with the Trader for four or five Barrs a Head in ye Latter end of your Purchase in order to gett Dispatched out of ye River that you may be one of the Earliest Ships at So Carolina.'[10] They admonished him, however, not to arrive before 1 March.

The demand for labor was greatest in the cropping season, when prices were likely to be highest. In North America this period extended from about April to November. Since North American temperatures were colder and generally more variable than anything experienced in tropical latitudes, the slave trade there was largely seasonal. In the southern colonies, the optimum period of trade was between March and September, to avoid the extra expense of winter clothing for slaves and the increased chances of slave mortality. Moreover, slaves brought lower prices in winter than in the spring or summer because they could not be put to immediate use.

The Middle Passage

The trip from West Africa to the Americas, the notorious 'Middle Passage,' took an average of 62 days and was horrifying and costly. Initially, regular merchant vessels were converted to slave ships, especially fitted to hold the human cargo. By the second half of the eighteenth century, however, vessels were constructed specifically for the trade. They were sleek, narrow vessels, with special grates and portholes to direct air below deck. The space between decks was normally 4–5ft (1.2–1.5m) and slaves could not stand – and occasionally could not even sit – upright. In one remarkably objectionable and presumably atypical case, the space between decks was a mere 14in (35cm). Crowded and unsanitary conditions, poor food, inadequate supplies, insufficient drinking water, epidemic diseases, and long voyages conspired to make slave ships legendary for their foul smell and high death rate.

Seventeenth-century ships of the Royal African Company averaged a death rate as high as 24 percent. These rates decreased in the eighteenth and nineteenth centuries, reaching an average range of 10–15 percent. Of

Below: The movement of slaves from Africa to the New World (shown in red below) was a new development in an older trade from Africa to Europe and the Middle East (shown in blue). A three-way trade evolved which became known as the 'triangular trade': European goods (guns, alcohol, and cloth) were traded in Africa for slaves; these were shipped to the Americas and sold to the plantation-owners; the slave-labor products (rum, cotton, tobacco, and sugar) were then carried to Europe on the home-leg.

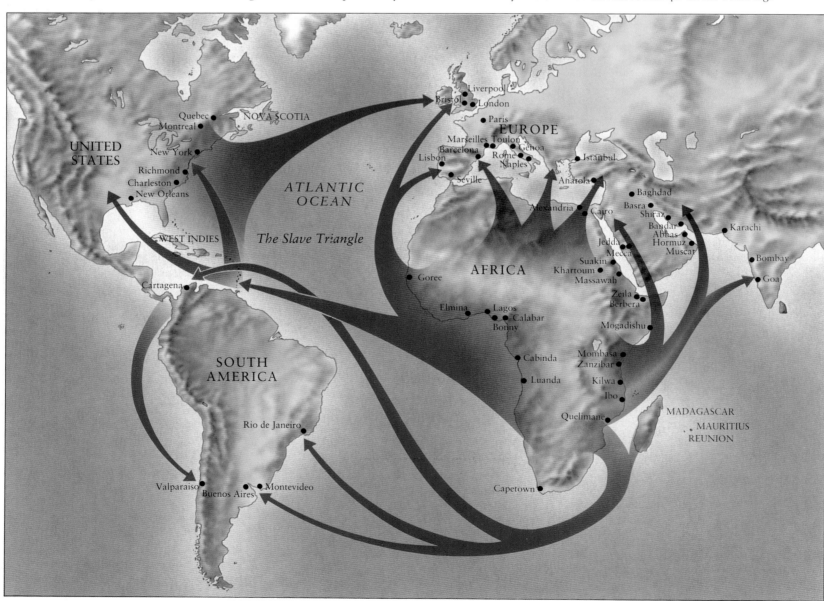

course the death rate for white sailors engaged in the trade was high too. In the second half of the eighteenth century sailors' deaths frequently exceeded that of slaves: one study found, for example, that whites died at a rate of 169 per 1000 compared to a black rate of 152 per 1000. Still, the crews, in the business for profit, had a choice, whereas the slaves did not. Because they had to care for slaves and guard against insurrection, slavers carried larger crews than merchant ships. A common measure was 1 sailor for every 10 slaves.

Despite harsh conditions, the economics of trade encouraged ship captains to have reasonable consideration for their cargo, as often their wages and commissions depended on the number of slaves delivered safely to port. They tried to obtain sufficient food for them, and of the type preferred by their particular African group. They sometimes carried peas and beans from England but usually secured food on the African coast: rice in Upper Guinea, yams or plantains in the Niger Delta, corn in Angola. They also learned to carry limes to reduce scurvy.

European profits ranged enormously, from as low as 3 percent to as high as 57 percent in the eighteenth century. Comparing the price of slaves on the coast with those in South Carolina amply illustrates this point. A slave costing £9.43 sterling in Africa in the 1720s fetched £15–18 in South Carolina at the same period. Prices rose over the century and the same slave in the 1760s cost £14.10 in Africa and was sold in South Carolina for £35. Of course, these costs did not represent a simple one-to-one relationship in money, but included the price of wares used in trade and incidental charges required to grease the wheels of commerce, including customs, tolls, and taxes paid to African potentates.

Profits depended upon many things going well, and there was a great deal of luck involved. Some people made much money, but there could also be great loss. Depending on the cost of goods dispensed, the rate of mortality in passage, and the demand in America, slave voyages could be hazardous. A 10 percent return seemed to be average for the eighteenth century.

Regional and Sex Preferences

Planters generally preferred male slaves over females for particularly heavy work, but North American slaveholders in particular placed a more equal valuation on men and women because the crops they produced could be worked by either. Men and women often commanded different prices, but the variance was not as large as is sometimes assumed. Slave cargoes generally contained twice as many men as women, partially because African sellers were reluctant to part with women and children whom they could easily absorb into their own societies. They were more willing to sell men, who could prove dangerous to have on hand. But African traders in some regions of the coast sold

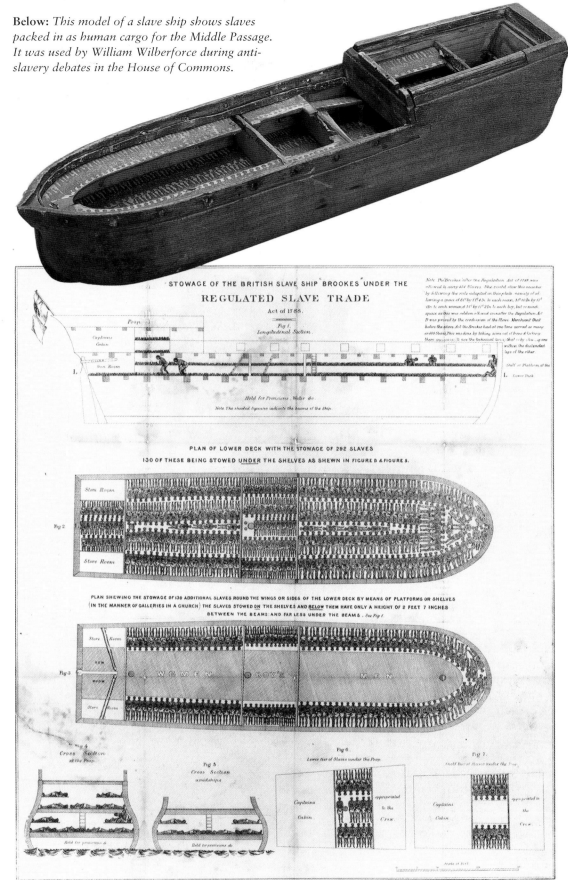

Below: This model of a slave ship shows slaves packed in as human cargo for the Middle Passage. It was used by William Wilberforce during anti-slavery debates in the House of Commons.

women more often than those in other regions. A British official wrote in the 1780s that 'few Women are allowed to be had on the Gold Coast & those never Approved in the West Indies, being Old. Eboe Women (from Bonney & New Calabar) are very fine and may be had.' He later wrote that more 'and better' women could be had at those two ports than anywhere else on the coast.[11]

Colonial planters also expressed regional

Above: This plan from 1788 shows the Liverpool vessel Brookes and was used by pro-abolitionist Member of Parliament William Wilberforce to argue for the end of the trade. He compared the plan's legal stowage allocation of 482 with the actual numbers of slaves carried, which he had gleaned from slave merchants' records. These showed that some 609 had been squeezed on board, many of them chained men forced to lie on top of one another, others kept on the open deck.

preferences for slaves, based on their perception of a particular African national or ethnic character and their knowledge of local African skills. Seventeenth-century Brazilians preferred Angolans, though these fashions shifted in the eighteenth century towards Akan-speaking peoples along the so-called Mina or Mine coast of modern Ghana. In South Carolina, planters preferred slaves from Angola and Upper Guinea. Equiano, with an exaggerated ethnic pride, generalized the preference, writing that 'The West India planters prefer the slaves of Benin or Eboe, to those of any other part of Guinea, for their hardiness, intelligence, integrity, and zeal.'[12] Distinctions that planters made among slaves militated against – though they did not entirely prevent – the kind of stereotyping of blacks that characterized the nineteenth-century United States. In particular, African expertise in boat-making and riverine travel, not to mention cattle-raising, all of which were important to early South Carolinians, prevented the blanket assumption that slaves were in need of minute direction from their masters. Englishmen may have had the advantage on the seas but they did not always maintain it on Carolina's rivers and swamps.

Because Britain's North American colonies did not grow sugar, they were economically less important to the mother country than her West India colonies and commanded less of the slave trade. The region that became the United States absorbed only about 5 percent of Africans brought into the New World. Jamaica alone absorbed more than that. South Carolina was an exception, however, and by 1715 her black population exceeded her white population by about 40 percent. In that respect, South Carolina looked more like Barbados or Jamaica than it did Virginia or Maryland. Accordingly, eighteenth-century South Carolina was the continent's leading importer of slaves.

Unlike Virginia, where slavery was developed gradually, in South Carolina slavery was envisioned from its inception in the 1660s. And while Virginia's plantation system was established and worked for most of the seventeenth century largely by white indentured servants, black slaves were important in South Carolina from the start. The proprietors provided that every settler who brought a black, male slave to the colony would get 20 acres (8 hectares) of land for each and 10 acres (4 hectares) for every black female brought there. Perhaps as many as a third of early South Carolina settlers were black. They contributed African methods of cattle-raising, modified by practices developed in the islands. These included grass-burning to clear pastures, free-grazing and nighttime penning for protection. They helped to develop exports in naval stores – especially pitch and tar. Most importantly, they helped to generate South Carolina's rice industry and were largely responsible for teaching Englishmen, who had no prior experience, how to grow the crop successfully. As

The first blood in the deadliest slave revolt in colonial British North America was spilled on Sunday 9 September 1739, at a Stono River crossing about 20 miles (30km) southwest of Charleston, South Carolina. A group of black men assembled by plan close to sunset and killed two white men working at Hutchenson's store. Seizing small arms, gunpowder, and shot from the stock, they outfitted themselves with whatever else they could carry by hand and burned the remainder. Then numbering about 20, the rebels attacked Godfrey's place, killed him, his daughter and son, and burnt the house.

The band then headed south. Ninety miles (145km) away sat Savannah. Another 150 miles (240km) away stood Spain's headquarters

Left: *South Carolina was the most highly evolved slave importer during the early period of European settlement. This advertisement of a cargo from 1753 reveals that people sought slaves from certain areas of West Africa.*

in Florida. Between them lay a no man's land of channels, inlets, lagoons, and the great Okefenokee Swamp. Many had made the trek since 1733 when Britain founded Savannah, and Spain retaliated by proclaiming protection and liberty for African Americans who escaped to St. Augustine. Carolina slaveholders complained bitterly about their losses. Their consternation was especially great as the Stono rebels struck, for just 10 months earlier the Spanish had welcomed a group of about 25 black fugitives.

At daybreak the rebels pounced on a succession of places along the main road. They appeared ready to repay selected whites for abuse or kindness. They spared a slaveholding tavernkeeper named Wallace because he was reputedly a good man who treated slaves kindly. In contrast the rebels marked a slaveholder named Rose for death, but some of his slaves hid him and he escaped. Bullock also managed to escape, although his house was burned. The whites caught at Lemy's, Hext's, Sprye's, Sacheverell's, and Nash's fared less well: they were killed and their houses burned.

The rebels sent South Carolina Lieutenant Governor William Bull scampering for his life too that morning, for they chanced upon him as he was on horseback toward Charleston. He barely escaped, but as luck would have it, his deliverance proved crucial. Until Bull spread an alarm that both warned whites of the approaching danger and called them to arms,

the rebels had surprise on their side. They had struck quickly with the soothing night and drowsy dawn covering their attacks and advance. Their trail of burned houses and dead whites was bound to be discovered sooner or later as work-week traffic began that Monday. And survivors such as Wallace, Rose, and Bullock were sure to sound an alarm, but they were behind the rebels. Bull could block them.

A shift occurred then. The rebels' ranks had swelled to about 90 and become more brazen. Shows of force replaced stealth as the troop hoisted makeshift banners, beat drums, and paraded farther south. Slower and less disciplined than at the start, they were no longer attackers.

Midway between Charleston and Savannah, the militia mustered by Bull located the rebels

Above: *Nat Turner's rebellion, a century after Stono, confirmed the worst fears of whites.*

Below: *The conical-roofed houses on the Mulberry plantation are reminiscent of Africa.*

in a field and charged, routing the larger band. But as some slaves fled, a bold hard core fought their way clear. A week later and 30 miles (50km) farther south whites caught and killed 10 from the core of 30.

News of the declaration of the War of Jenkin's Ear between Spain and Britain deepened the dread that the Stono rebels were part of a broader uprising. Word that the rebel core was Portuguese-speaking – perhaps Catholic, and not long imported from Angola – fanned rumors of a Spanish-slave alliance.

Outnumbered by blacks who were more than 60 percent of South Carolina's population, the colony's whites resolved to suppress the rebellion with vengeance. The manhunt for every possible rebel lasted almost a year. Two of the band were reported apprehended and executed in March 1740. And as late as August 1740 a black identified as 'one of the slaves that was concerned in the Insurrection at Stono' was also said to have been apprehended.

Between 10 and 20 blacks remained unaccounted for in the end. Whether they reached freedom, or died trying, long excited curiosity, as did the uncertain death toll of the uprising and its aftermath. The 40–60 blacks killed topped the 31 executed in New York's so-called Great Negro Plot of 1741. And no other colonial encounter came close to the (at least) 23 whites the rebels killed in their initial raids and in battle on 10 September: the New York Uprising of 1712 killed about half that number. In North America only the toll of more than 50 whites killed in Virginia in Nat Turner's Rebellion of 1831 surpassed South Carolina's Stono Rebellion of 1739.

Thomas J. Davis

early as 1698, though, the colonial government expressed alarm at the number of blacks brought in and urged that they be balanced by settlement of more whites. But well into the eighteenth century and beyond, depending on locale, South Carolina continued to look, in the words of one visitor, 'more like a negro country than like a country settled by white people.'[13]

Virginians embraced African slavery more slowly. Determined to build an English society, they did not encourage large numbers of foreigners – even those from Scotland or Ireland – to settle in their midst, much less the exotic African. Moreover, tobacco cultivation in a temperate climate was readily accomplished by white labor. So the black population grew slowly, trickling in as the colony involved itself in the Atlantic economy: in 1625 there were only 23 blacks in Virginia, and by 1650, no more than 300. With the absence of sufficient white workmen, Englishmen sometimes attempted to coerce the labor of Native Americans, but those in Virginia were not used to the sustained, regimented field work colonists desired. Virginia Indians raised their own crops but most of that was women's work which men found distasteful. If captured and forced to labor, they either sickened and died or managed to escape to their compatriots, a feat much easier for them than for disgruntled English servants or African slaves. An expanding economy by the mid-

century attracted many English bondsmen to the colony, often young people in search of a better life who sold their service for the price of passage. Conditions did not always meet their expectations, however: their 'seasoning' to the new disease environment was taxing and often fatal; work was harsher than they were normally used to in England; and, from the master's point of view, they were frequently troublesome. Neither had much choice. For servants, alternative destinations were limited; for planters, the high death rate meant that even had they changed their preference from English servants to African slaves, the initial higher outlay for a slave who might not survive made slavery an uneconomical choice. Not until the end of the century did better survival rates in the Chesapeake and an increase in slaving make African labor a viable alternative. Simultaneously, falling birth rates and greater opportunity in England produced fewer British emigrants, while acquisition of New York and Pennsylvania gave them more choice of destination in America. These conditions, and others, made African slavery more practical in the Chesapeake.

Below: *This watercolor by Benjamin Henry Latrobe shows a late eighteenth-century barbering scene in Norfolk, Virginia. It is set on a Sunday, the traditional 'day off' for slaves. This was one of the service-related occupations open to African Americans in white-dominated society.*

The Nature of Seventeenth-century Slavery

Meanwhile, blacks in the colony gained a measure of acceptability. While the first Africans to arrive in Virginia in 1619 were clearly bought as slaves, slavery was not yet an established institution, and, whatever their legal status, blacks quite likely were treated little differently from the English servants alongside whom they toiled. Racial attitudes in English culture encouraged a negative reaction to blacks and they were clearly distinguished in colonial records. But Virginia did not forbid manumission for meritorious or other service, and blacks could make legal contracts with their masters to work their way out of slavery. Francis Payne, for example, contracted with his mistress in 1643 to purchase his freedom for a sum equal to the price of three English servants. He gained his freedom in 1649, then set about freeing his wife and children, a task completed in 1656. Other blacks did likewise, and Virginia's free black community grew, living in relative equality with their white neighbors, acting to all intents and purposes like English people. Francis Payne, evidently after the death of his first wife, or perhaps it was a son of the same name, married a white English woman. Free blacks did not forget their heritage, however, which some memorialized in personal and place names. They also benefited from their African agricultural experience which doubtless contributed to their success before and

after freedom. Tensions were greater along class than racial lines until social unrest boiled over into Bacon's Rebellion in 1676, which pitted slaves, white servants, and free black and white farmers against local Indians and the colonial government. The fact that the last rebellious group to surrender consisted of black slaves and white servants convinced the ruling elite that such an alliance could destroy the colony. They then moved to separate the two by passing laws that privileged whites and derogated blacks, accelerating moves already begun. Moreover, by the 1680s, black slavery had become viable and laws and attitudes hardened; black people increasingly replaced white people in the tobacco fields and the position of free blacks became tenuous. Still, in Virginia, the percentage of blacks who were free in the late seventeenth century was greater than in any other period during the era of slavery.

By the end of the seventeenth century, then, Africans worked plantations from Brazil to the Chesapeake. In regions where there were no plantations, particularly in the Spanish empire and in English colonies north of Maryland, they worked in the country and in towns as domestic servants, farm hands, and commercial laborers. Many had gained their freedom but most were bound in an evolving system of slavery which provided the basis for economic development in an unfolding Atlantic society. Their relationships with Europeans and Native Americans produced a New World culture in which their contribution was pervasive. They brought brains as well as brawn, and African knowledge and expertise secured the survival and success of European enterprise that might otherwise have failed.

Notes

[1] David Eltis, 'Free and Coerced Transatlantic Migrations: Some Comparisons,' *American Historical Review* 88 (April 1983): 255.

[2] Daniel P. Mannix and Malcolm Cowley, *Black Cargoes: A History of the Atlantic Slave Trade, 1518–1865*, New York: Viking Press, 1962, p. 2.

[3] Luis M. Diaz-Soler, *Historia de la esclavitud negra en Puerto Rico, 1493–1890*, Madrid: 1953, p. 2.

[4] Quoted in Thomas R. Frazier (ed.), *Afro-American History: Primary Sources*, New York: Harcourt Brace and World, Inc., 1970, p. 10.

[5] Olaudah Equiano, *The Life of Olaudah Equiano*, reprint New York: Negro Universities Press, 1969, p. 9.

[6] John Thornton, *Africa and Africans in the Making of the Atlantic World, 1400–1680*, Cambridge: Cambridge University Press, 1992, p. 38.

[7] Equiano, *Life*, p. 20.

[8] Daniel C. Littlefield, *Rice and Slaves: Ethnicity and the Slave Trade in Colonial South Carolina*, Urbana: University of Illinois Press, 1991.

[9] *Ibid.*, p. 51.

[10] *Ibid.*, p. 52.

[11] *Ibid.*, p. 72.

[12] Equiano, *Life*, p. 17.

[13] Quoted in Peter Wood, *Black Majority*, New York: Alfred A. Knopf, 1972, p. 132.

Above: *While some black people now lived freely in America, many more in Africa continued to suffer the indignity of enslavement. This nineteenth-century image shows yoked and chained captives still being brought into market.*

Below: *Justus Englehardt Kuhn's portrait of Henry Darnall III from 1710 is interesting because of the black attendant. It suggests the unequal relationship of the races and is the earliest American depiction of an enslaved person.*

THE BITTERSWEET CUP OF FREEDOM

During the eighteenth century, Africans and Europeans were becoming Americans; most Native Americans were being evicted from their eastern homes and were pushed westward across the Appalachian Mountains. The country began its experiment with liberal democratic government bearing a heavy burden, a continuing irritant that would prove increasingly dangerous. Its democracy coexisted with a slave labor system. At the grassroots level, the society was multiracial, black, brown, and red. It was sustained by the work and sacrifice of women as well as men, the poor as well as the rich. Yet those who designed the political and economic system and its controls were all white men of economic and social standing. Some of the Founding Fathers saw the evil that slavery brought to the emergent nation, but in the end their choice was to tolerate and even defend it. Bearing this inherent contradiction from its inception, through many compromises, racialism and its most extreme manifestation, slavery, remained the nation's fundamental flaw. This critical period laid the foundation for the new nation's institutional and cultural life and for its multiracial society.

'Liberty Displaying Arts and Sciences' by Samuel Jennings was painted in 1792 for Philadelphia's Library Company whose membership included many abolitionists. It provides the perfect symbolism for the heady times of American liberty and freedom, while at the same time attacking slavery. The goddess of Liberty is the white woman bestowing, as an act of goodness, charity and enlightenment, gifts of knowledge to the newly freed African Americans who seem eager and thankful to receive it.

GARY B. NASH

L IKE BRITISH COLONISTS in other cities, Philadelphians expressed their outrage at Parliament's Stamp Act of 1765 – not a punishing tax but a clear signal of the new British policy of regulating the colonies more forcefully after the Seven Years' War. On 5 October 1765, two black drummers 'beat thro all parts of the City with Muffled Drums' as the bells pealed at Christ Church and the State House.[1] Responding to the black drummers' beat, a huge assembly of Philadelphians gathered in the State House yard to intimidate the stamp distributor from taking up his office. Within a few months, such protests would convince Parliament to repeal the Stamp Act. But the wick of the lamp of liberty had been trimmed and the spark of Revolutionary consciousness had been touched. Before blood was shed 10 years later in the small farming communities of Concord and Lexington, west of Boston, an acrid debate, often punctuated by violence, obliged Americans of all kinds to examine their beliefs about freedom, equality, and natural rights. These self-probings were personal, communal, and eventually national. Moreover, they leaped over racial, gender, and social lines, carrying the Americans onto new terrain that had not been contemplated when the argument over the stamp taxes imposed by Parliament initiated a tumultuous decade that ended with the American Declaration of Independence in 1776.

Yearning for Liberty

For the half-million African Americans in the British colonies, overwhelmingly enslaved, revenue stamps, sugar duties, or tea parties affected them little. Nonetheless, they were politicized by the language and modes of protest against the English. Their yearning for freedom was as old as their presence in the colonies, but they began to see new opportunities for securing their freedom amidst the

Below: *This view of the Van Bergen plantation in the lower Hudson River Valley region of New York state includes the presence of black slaves or servants. Emancipation in the North began in 1777 and by 1825 most northern slaves were free.*

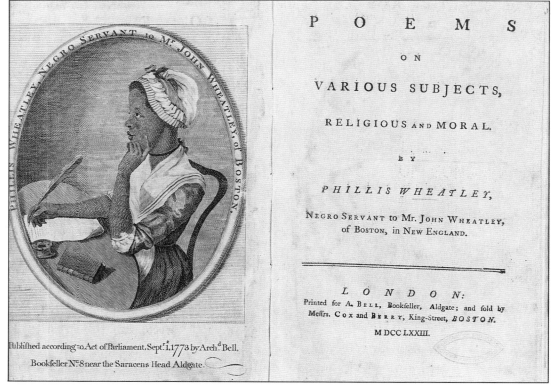

disruptions of a society in rebellion. Eavesdropping on their masters' dinner-table conversations, working in taverns and coffeehouses where Revolutionary politics were hatched, and reading or hearing about pamphlets containing white protests against slavery, many black Americans imbibed the ideology of inalienable rights and fit the ringing phrases of the day to their own situation. 'In every human breast,' wrote the young black Phillis Wheatley in Boston, 'God has implanted a Principle, which we call love of freedom; it is impatient of Oppression, and pants for Deliverance; and by the leave of our modern Egyptians I will assert, that the same Principle lives in us.'[2] The reference to Egyptians was an apt allusion because the liberty-craving white Americans, since the founding generation in New England, had seen themselves as oppressed Israelites fleeing into Canaan. No less than white Americans, African Americans began to see themselves as a 'chosen people' for whom God had special purposes.

When the language of protest overflowed its initial boundaries and confronted the relation-

Above: *The frontispiece from Phyliss Wheatley's 1773 book. Brought to Boston from Africa as a child, she was taught by her owners to read and write. Her abilities were used as evidence of African-American intellectual abilities.*

ship between American liberty and domestic slavery, African Americans must have talked passionately among themselves. In every northern seaport, writers were pointing out the hypocrisy of arguing for God-given natural liberties while cruel, life-draining, perpetual slavery flourished everywhere and was growing rapidly. A few Quakers had been launching attacks on slavery for several generations, but the scorn they had been subject to gave way to a recognition of the grotesque contradiction between arguing for American freedoms which were being infringed by their English masters while American masters were denying freedom to thousands of Africans. 'With what consistency' could American slaveholders 'complain so loudly of attempts to enslave them,' wrote the newly arrived Tom Paine in 1775, 'while they hold so many hundred thousand in slavery?'[3]

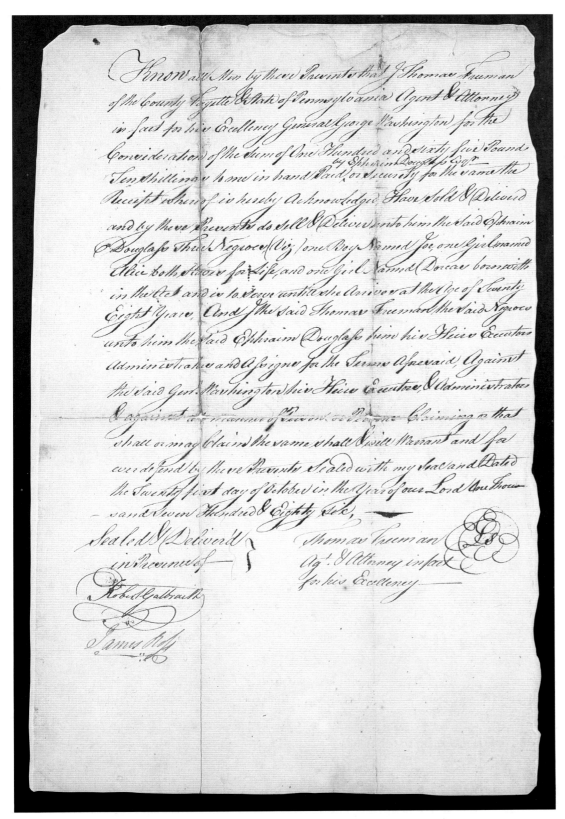

Left: A slave bill of sale dating from 21 October 1786. Despite the Declaration of Independence and the espousals of liberty, slaves remained property to be bought and sold. Ironically, this bill was signed by Thomas Freeman, the agent of George Washington.

One can only imagine how the spirits of enslaved Africans might have been lifted by hearing from white writers that 'the flame has spread north and south, and every breast now pants for Liberty . . . ,' so that the colonists must ban further slave importations, 'emancipate the whole race' of Africans, and restore 'that liberty we have so long unjustly detained from them.'[4] What is certain is that many slaves acted on their hatred of oppression to petition for their freedom in ways calculated to prick further the conscience of the master class. Their petitions were couched cautiously at first but became bolder as the war began. They made it clear that they did not regard their requests for freedom as appeals to a merciful master class but as a demand for the restoration of inherent rights unlawfully wrested from them. 'We expect your house [the legislature] will . . . take our deplorable case into serious consideration, and give us that simple relief which, as men, we have a natural right to,' remonstrated four slaves in Thompson, Massachusetts, in 1773. Six years later in Connecticut, blacks echoed these demands: 'We do not ask for nothing, but what we are fully persuaded is ours to claim,' for 'we are the Creatures of that God, who made of one Blood, and Kindred, all the Nations of the Earth'; hence, 'there is nothing that leads us to a Belief, or Suspicion, that we are any more obliged to serve them, than they us, and . . . can never be convinced that we were made to be Slaves.'[5] In the same year, a group of slaves in Portsmouth, New Hampshire, argued that 'the God of nature gave them life and freedom' and that freedom 'is an inherent right of the human species, not to be surrendered but by consent.'[6]

The Revolutionary War Begins

By its very nature, the Revolutionary War created wholly new situations for slaves. With the gigantic movement of both civilian and military populations in and out of nearly every

Above: *William L. Breton's watercolor 'The Old London Coffee House' depicts a slave auction on the porch. Slavery was gradually abolished in Philadelphia, and the African-American community there became one of the nation's most important.*

major seaport from Savannah to Boston between 1775 and 1781, urban slaves had unprecedented opportunities for making their personal declarations of independence and for destabilizing the institution of slavery. Similarly, in the countryside, as Tory and Whig militia units crisscrossed the terrain, plundering the estates of their enemies, slaves found ways of tearing gaping holes in the fabric of slavery.

A turning point in the calculation of enslaved Africans came in November 1775 when the royal governor of Virginia, Lord Dunmore, issued a dramatic proclamation that guaranteed freedom to slaves and indentured servants who would escape their masters and reach the king's forces. Against this concrete offer of perpetual freedom, slaves had to calculate the chance that the American patriots would respond to calls for abolition and follow the urgings of the first abolition society, established in Pennsylvania in 1775. Waiting for possible freedom as a white gift at some indeterminate point turned out to be a poor substitute for immediate freedom. For some, offers of freedom for blacks who would serve in place of their masters led to service in the American Revolutionary army. But a far greater number fled to the British, whenever the British army or navy was within reach. By December 1775, Dunmore's Proclamation had thrown white Virginians into a frenzy of

Left: *General Marquis de Lafayette, hero of Washington's Revolutionary forces, attended to by his valet James Armistead who became a vital double-agent working within the camp of the traitor Benedict Arnold.*

fear, and enough slaves had reached his troops to form the Black Regiment, 'whose soldiers wore on the breast of their uniform the chilling inscription "Liberty to Slaves."'[7] In the North, where the war centered for most of the first five years, a general sympathy for the British cause quickly took hold. As the German Lutheran leader Henry Melchior Muhlenberg noted, blacks 'secretly wished that the British army might win, for then all Negro slaves will gain their freedom. It is said that this sentiment is almost universal among the Negroes in America.'[8] Even in the budding capital of American abolitionism, and where many believed that the city's slaves were docile and relatively contented, white Philadelphians were shocked when a white 'gentlewoman,' walking near Christ Church, was insulted by a black man only a few weeks after Dunmore's Proclamation. When the woman reprimanded him, he shot back, 'Stay you d[amne]d white bitch 'till Lord Dunmore and his black regiment come, and then we will see who is to take the wall.'[9]

Although the number can never be exactly calculated, the flight of slaves to the British lines was very large and at times strained the British army's ability to provision them. Thomas Jefferson reported that 30,000 slaves fled their masters during the British invasion of Virginia in 1781. More than half of Virginia's slaves were in situations that would have made flight nearly impossible because they were young children, women with infants, physically depleted men and women over 45, and men whose flight would have left their families at the mercy of revengeful masters. Thus, 30,000 slaves fleeing their masters could have represented about half of those who may be considered eligible escapees, predominantly male. In South Carolina and Georgia, a similar proportion of adult males probably fled to the British during the southern campaigns between 1779 and 1781.

SLAVES' PETITION FOR FREEDOM

The contradictions between the demands of those crying out for liberty and freedom from the oppressive British, and the real-life situation of bondage which existed for thousands of African Americans 'owned' by those same people demanding freedom from supposed tyranny was clear to many people, black and white, in eighteenth-century America.

This paradox, of a nation being born due to demands for freedom and consensual government but simultaneously seeking to deny these rights to a substantial section of its own population, was not lost on the black community and its nascent leadership. Quick to appreciate their position as citizens being denied their rights, black Americans lobbied their state legislatures and filed suits to have their freedom recognized from the mid-1760s onward. The petition below was typical in this regard and did not necessarily fall on deaf ears.

Boston, 20 April 1773
Sir, The efforts made by the legislative of this province in their last sessions to free themselves from slavery, gave us, who are in that deplorable state, a high degree of satisfaction. We expect great things from men who have made such a noble stand against the designs of their *fellow-men* to enslave them. We cannot but wish and hope Sir, that you will have the same grand object, we mean civil and religious liberty, in view in your next session. The divine spirit of *freedom*, seems to fire every humane breast on this continent, except such as are bribed to assist in executing the execrable plan.

We are very sensible that it would be highly detrimental to our present masters, if we were allowed to demand all that of *right* belongs to us for past services; this we disclaim. Even the *Spaniards*, who have not those sublime ideas of freedom that English men have, are conscious that they have no right to all the services of their fellow-men, we mean the *Africans*, who they have purchased with their money; therefore they allow them one day in a week to work for themselves, to enable them to earn money to purchase the residue of their time . . .

In behalf of our fellow slaves in this province, and by order of their Committee.
Peter Bestes
Sambo Freeman
Felix Holbrook
Chester Joie[1]

Note
[1] Printed leaflet, quoted in Herbert Aptheker (ed.), *A Documentary History of the Negro People in the United States*, 2 vols, New York: Citadel Press, 1951, vol. I, pp. 7–8.

While thousands of black Americans saw the British as liberators, the British themselves were less interested in humanitarian release of captive fellow humans than in a strategy for weakening the American southerners by depriving them of a considerable part of their labor force. The British never succored the slaves of Loyalists and promptly returned any Loyalist slaves who fled to the British lines. How cold-blooded the British could be was demonstrated dramatically at the Franco-American siege of British-occupied Yorktown. When the British found themselves surrounded and growing short of provisions, General Charles Cornwallis expelled from his encampments several thousand black Virginians who had claimed freedom under Dunmore's Proclamation. An embarrassed Hessian officer wrote that the British

> drove back to the enemy all of our black friends, whom we had taken along to despoil the countryside . . . We had used them to good advantage and set them free, and now, with fear and trembling, they had to face the reward of their cruel masters. [10]

Northern Hunger for Freedom

In the North, where only about 10 percent of the half-million enslaved Africans lived, the hungering for freedom was also intense. In eastern Pennsylvania, where slavery existed in a milder form than in the South, African

Above: *James Armistead looks on as the British surrender at Yorktown. After his role against Arnold, Armistead had worked within General Lord Cornwallis's camp, becoming privy to crucial information. As reward he gained his own freedom in 1786 and took the name Lafayette.*

Americans proved no less likely to flee to the British. 'By the invasion of this state, and the possession the enemy obtained of this city and neighbourhood,' wrote a wartime leader in Philadelphia in 1779, '[a] great part of the slaves hereabouts were enticed away by the British army.'[11] In New York City and its surrounding hinterland, slave flight burgeoned. The slave of Quaker John Corlies is illustrative. Named Titus by his master, this 21-year-old fled his owner in 1775 and headed south to join the black regiment being formed by Lord Dunmore. Renaming himself Colonel Tye, he was soon back in northern New Jersey organizing other slaves and free blacks to fight against the Americans. For five years, he served as the leader of a local guerrilla band that terrorized the patriot farmers of northern New Jersey. Known as 'one of Lord Dunmore's Crew,' Tye fought for five years before dying from battle wounds and lockjaw.[12] Known all over New Jersey, Tye stood as a symbol of black rebellion, a testimony to the fact that the American Revolution was the greatest slave rebellion in the long history of North American slavery.

Tye and thousands of other enslaved blacks show that the high-toned rhetoric of natural rights and moral rectitude that accompanied the onset of the Revolution had only a limited power to soften the hearts of American slave masters. To be sure, several thousand masters manumitted their slaves; but as a proportion of all slave owners, these manumitters were insignificant compared to those who finally could not give up their investment in human property. The American Revolution brought to the fore a sharp collision between human rights and property rights; the latter became ascendant among the majority of slave owners, confirming Adam Smith's hard-nosed proposition that morality could rarely, if ever, transcend economic interest.

While the Colonel Tye's were numerically dominant among the half-million black Americans in choosing the British side, many free blacks and a small number of slaves fought for the American cause. These were the minority celebrated by William C. Nell, the first black American historian, who in the 1850s held high the abolitionist banner by pointing to the blood shed for the 'glorious cause' by black Americans in the time of the nation's birth. Among those whom Nell celebrated in his *Colored Patriots of the American Revolution* was Prince, the slave of a New Hampshire soldier who had pulled one of the oars carrying George Washington across the Delaware River in a piercing snow and sleet storm on Christmas night, 1776. Another was James Armistead, a Virginia slave whose master gave him permission to enlist under Lafayette, the French general who came to fight with the Americans. Armistead played a dramatic role as a double-spy, infiltrating the British lines at Yorktown while posing as a runaway Virginia slave and bringing back to the American forces crucial information that gave the Americans the upper hand in the climactic battle of the war. In 1786, the General Assembly of Virginia emancipated Armistead (who would call himself James Lafayette thereafter).

Another who fought with the Americans was a man who became the new nation's wealthiest free black, a considerable essayist, an eloquent abolitionist, and the progenitor of a talented family of children and grandchildren. James Forten's great-grandfather had been brought in chains from Africa to the Delaware River and had been one of the first slaves in Pennsylvania to buy his freedom. Forten's father, born free, was a sailmaker, and he sent his son James to Anthony Benezet's school where he learned to read and write and imbibed many of the kindly Quaker's principles about the universality of humankind. In 1781, at age 15, Forten signed on Stephen Decatur's 22-gun privateer as a powderboy and began a career of heroic acts that would gain him fame in Philadelphia. 'Scarce wafted from his native shore, and perilled upon the dark blue sea,' wrote Nell, 'than he found himself amid the roar of cannon, the smoke of blood, the dying, and the dead.'[13] This purplish passage referred to the bloody engagement of Decatur's *Royal Louis* with the British ship *Lawrence*, in which Forten was the only survivor at his gun station. But Forten's colors showed even truer on the next voyage, when the British captured his ship after a battle at sea. The British captain's son befriended Forten, who was offered free passage to England and the patronage of the captain's family. 'NO, NO!' replied Forten, 'I am here a prisoner for the liberties of my country; I never, NEVER, shall prove a traitor to her interests.'[14] His offer spurned, the British captain consigned Forten to the *Old Jersey*, the rotting deathtrap prison ship anchored in New York harbor where thousands of Americans died. Released seven months later as the war was drawing to a close, the 16-year-old Forten made his way shoeless from New York to Philadelphia. At the time, however, his exploits were notable primarily for their atypicality, for few American blacks had reason to be infected by the patriotic fever.

Exodus of Pro-British Slaves

For the thousands of American slaves who fought for 'life, liberty, and the pursuit of happiness' on the British side, the end of the war in 1783 ushered in a new perilous chapter. There could be no staying in the land of the victorious American revolutionaries, for the new United States was still slave country from North to South, and the blacks who had fought with the British were particularly hated and subject to reenslavement. But where would England send the American black loyalists? The West Indian sugar islands were built on slave labor and had no place for a large number of free blacks. England itself wished no influx of ex-slaves because London and other major cities already felt themselves burdened by growing numbers of impoverished blacks demanding public support. The answer to the problem was Nova Scotia, the easternmost part of the Canadian wilderness that England had acquired at the end of the Seven Years' War. Here, amidst the sparsely scattered old French settlers, the British could relocate the American blacks who had been their military supporters.

Thomas Peters came to symbolize the exodus of the pro-British American blacks in 1783. Kidnaped from the Yoruba tribe in what is now Nigeria and brought to North America by a French slave trader, Peters had been purchased in Louisiana about 1760. He resisted enslavement so fiercely that his master sold him into the English colonies. By 1770, Peters belonged to an immigrant Scots planter on North Carolina's Cape Fear River. Here he toiled while the storm brewed between England and the colonies.

Peters' plans for his own declaration of independence may have ripened as a result of the rhetoric of liberty he heard around his master's house, for William Campbell had become a leading member of the Sons of Liberty in Wilmington, North Carolina. When 20 British ships entered the Cape Fear River in March 1776 and disembarked royal troops, Peters seized the moment. Redefining himself as a man, instead of William Campbell's property, Peters escaped. After fighting with the British-officered Black Pioneers, he was evacuated from New York City by the British, with several thousand others, to disembark in Nova Scotia. The whims of international war and politics had destined him to pursue the struggle for survival and the quest for freedom in this unlikely corner of the earth.

Below: Normally a symbol of justice, these scales and weight evoke the injustice of measuring out the meager living allowance alloted to individual slaves by the owner. The ledger is from Virginia and covers the period 1747-85. It was used to record the supplies and the amounts.

The reception by the white Nova Scotians, including several thousand disbanded British soldier-settlers looking for a new lease on life, was decidedly frigid. White Nova Scotians were no more willing than the Americans had been to accept free blacks as fellow citizens and equals. Attacks on free British black citizens convinced Peters and other black leaders after six years of travail in Nova Scotia that they must pursue their dream of freedom and equality elsewhere. Carrying a petition from several hundred black families, Peters made his way to London in 1790. There he was able to work out details of a plan to transport the Nova Scotian blacks to the west coast of Africa, where English abolitionists were planning a refuge for England's poor free blacks.

This extraordinary mission to England – undertaken by an uneducated ex-slave who dared to proceed to the seat of British government without any knowledge whether he would find friends or supporters there – proved a turning point in black history. Peters returned to Nova Scotia in the fall of 1791 with a promise that a fleet of ships would arrive the next spring to carry the ransomed sons and daughters of Africa back to their homelands. Peters traveled on foot from village to village, spreading the word that the Sierra Leone Company had been chartered to launch a new society of those wishing to return to Africa from scattered parts of the British empire. On 15 January 1792, under sunny skies and a fair wind, a fleet of British ships stood out from Halifax harbor, laden with several thousand Africans who fervently desired to 'kiss their dear Malagueta,' the Malagueta pepper or 'grains of paradise' which grew prolifically in the region for which they were heading. After a difficult voyage, Thomas Peters, according to legend, led his shipmates ashore in Sierra Leone singing, 'The day of jubilee is comme; return ye ransomed sinners home.'[15] In less than four months he died of fever and was buried in Freetown, the aptly named capital of the new African nation. Although the British compatriots led by Peters were only a fragment of the black Americans of the Revolutionary era, they were the advance guard of the emigrationists who sporadically in the first half of the nineteenth century would give up hope for freedom and equality in the United States and return to Africa in one small wave after another.

Top: *This brutal iron slave collar was used to control and suppress the unwilling captive and render them more manageable. The interlocking iron ring is hinged on one side and the protruding spike was used to prevent the slave's head from being turned.*

Above: *A slave whip consisting of a crudely carved wooden handle and a leather strap. Such routine punishments as whipping – and the horrible scarring that resulted – were one of the evident evils of slavery, captured so powerfully in this nineteenth-century painting (right) by Verdier.*

The War Comes to an End

At the end of the Revolutionary War, a small percentage of black Americans had gained their freedom from conscience-stricken masters. Some superannuated slaves had masters who chose to free them rather than support them in their unproductive, declining years. Most who had been manumitted were in the North or in the Chesapeake region of the upper South. In the North, they could look to certain states for hope that the end of slavery might soon come. Pennsylvania passed a gradual abolition law in 1780; in Massachusetts, slavery was abolished by judicial decision in 1783; in Vermont, the constitution of 1777 declared slavery illegal. All states except South Carolina and Georgia halted the importation of slaves. Yet in New York and New Jersey, where thousands of slaves were still trapped in slavery at the end of the war, gradual abolition laws would not be passed for another generation.

Yet most of the Revolutionary generation, even in the North, drank very cautiously from the wells of republicanism while keeping track of their economic interests. By the end of the war in 1783, it was becoming clear to vast numbers of black Americans that much of the early Revolutionary rhetoric about natural rights had been exhausted. Reform-minded white Americans confronted two main problems. The first was economic: how would slave owners be compensated? The second was social: how would freed slaves fit into the social fabric of the new nation? Solutions to these two thorny problems hinged, in turn, first on a willingness to make economic sacrifices, and second on an ability to envision a biracial republican society. Northerners as well as southerners lost the abolitionist fire and would never rekindle it in their own generation. By the time they were in their graves the best opportunity for abolishing slavery had been lost.

For some half-million black Americans who saw the flame of freedom flickering out at the end of the war, the road ahead was confused and discouraging. Slavery was ebbing in the North, but it was surging in the South – the result of a rising birthrate that made further importation of African slaves almost unnecessary. Moreover, those who remained consigned to slavery had to struggle ahead after suffering the exodus of a great many of the most physically vigorous, psychologically aggressive, and politically able. Emerging from the war, the African-American population must have included a disproportionate number of older slaves, women with small children, and those physically broken or emotionally paralyzed by the slave experience.

Leaders of the Free Blacks

Yet in spite of the heavy losses of black males in the prime of life, vigorous and visionary free black communities began to form throughout the North. The largest were in the maritime towns because that was where work and companionship were most available. But hardly any sizeable town between Maine and Maryland failed to develop a subcommunity of free blacks, each with men and women who emerged as leaders. By looking at several of these leaders we can see some of the pathways that led from the denial of autonomy under slavery to creative, though often obstructed, roles under freedom.

Jupiter Hammon of Long Island exemplifies the cautious, tentative yearning for freedom among slaves who could not make a clean break from their masters – and from the detested institution of slavery. Born in 1711 into the possession of the prominent Lloyd family of merchants and manorial landlords,

Hammon served as a valued house servant. Early converted to Christianity, Hammon wrote poetry filled with ecstatic yearnings for salvation in the afterlife. When the Lloyds fled Long Island after the British occupied New York City in 1776, Hammon, already 65 years old, willingly stayed at their side. He continued to preach the gospel of the redeeming salvation that would come to those, black and white alike, who accepted Christ. 'If we are slaves it is by the permission of God; if we are free it must be by the power of the most high God . . .'[16]

Even in this quiescent house servant, sparks of the freedom fighter smoldered. His *A Winter Piece* in 1782 urged the moral reformation of African Americans and exhorted them to retain their African identity while remaining within the white-dominated young American nation. After the war, Hammon adopted a gradualist approach to the abolition of slavery. In his last written piece, *An Address to the Negroes in the State of New-York*, published as the Constitutional Convention was gathering in Philadelphia, Hammon 'hoped that God would open their eyes [i.e., those of white Americans], when they were so much engaged for liberty, to think of the state of the poor blacks, and pity them.'[17] Hammon had imbibed much of the conservative message in Christianity that urged the dispossessed to look for release in the afterlife; but even this black minister had edged his way toward using his literary gifts for the cause of black independence.

In the new nation, the human material out of which postwar black society would have to be constructed included thousands who were less cautious than Hammon. Yet some of them had played their hands carefully during the war because already they had secured a small stake in American society. Such a man was Prince Hall of Boston. The slave of a Boston merchant and a worshiper at School Street Church shepherded by the New Light revivalist Andrew Crosswell, Hall was about 40 when the war broke out. He received his freedom in 1770, and very quickly played a role in the five petitions that Boston's blacks placed before the legislature just before the war. Several of these remonstrances against slavery came from a group of 14 black Masons, Hall among them, who had joined a Masonic lodge formed by one of the British regiments that was occupying the Massachusetts capital. 'We expect great things from men who have made such a noble stand against the designs of their *fellow-men* to enslave them,' read one petition. Another petition declared that 'we have in common with all other men a natural right to our freedoms . . . as we are a freeborn people and have never forfeited this blessing by any compact or agreement whatever.'[18]

Hall might have joined the British forces before they retreated from Boston in March 1776. But instead, he cast his lot with the land of his birth. After the war, the fires that burned in Hall never subsided. But Boston's small

PAUL

CAPTAIN

CUFFEE

1812.

ENGRAVED FOR ABRM. L. PENNOCK, BY MASON & MAAS.

Three leagues offshore, where Virginia's plantations appeared as just a smudge on the horizon, HMS *Leopard* brazenly opened fire on the United States frigate *Chesapeake* during the afternoon of 22 June 1807, before forcibly impressing four men. A provocation for the War of 1812, the incident became whitewashed in popular memory: few Americans recollected that two of the sailors violently plucked from the *Chesapeake* that day were black.

The routes to the sea which William Ware and Daniel Martin followed, before their rendezvous with history, were typical and speak for men of their generation as long-gone yarns once did. Ware's youth epitomized the shadowy world between slavery and freedom characteristic of many northern and border-state blacks. Born in western Maryland, he took to teaming on the Baltimore Road in his teens, and then lit out for sea. According to his master, Ware in 1807 was 'in reality my slave yet, having never been liberated by me, but

merely *permitted* to go at large.' Martin's life story captured another kind of movement by footloose youth within the black diaspora. Born in Bonaire, Dutch West Indies, and apprenticed as a servant at age seven by his mother to Captain William Howland, of Westport, Massachusetts, he had spent much of his young life at sea. He fled from Howland's widow at age 15, and found a niche in the restless waterfront world of masterless men. No master, no families, no land, no trade: Ware and Martin were incarnations of the rootless and often unruly free black Ishmaels that so disturbed white citizens.

Mariners of color sailed before the mast from the earliest days of Europeans' plunder and settlement along the Spanish Main, and their numbers increased dramatically during the eighteenth century. Ware and Martin, along with tens of thousands of other African-American seamen, did not hoe tobacco or ditch rice, but kept the New World plantation system

Left: *Paul Cuffe was a free black who had made his money as a shipping entrepreneur. He participated in the American colonization movement by transporting 38 African Americans to Sierra Leone in 1815.*

afloat. African Americans sailed on lofty clippers and homely coasters; they sailed in the navies, protecting commerce, and as pirates, preying on it; they sailed in whalers and privateersmen, as cooks and seamen – but rarely as officers. Masters forced some slaves to work on vessels, but multitudes of others fled to the wharves, seeking anonymity and liberty aboard ship.

Prominent from London to Barbados to Boston, in every seaport and roadstead washed by Atlantic tides, those itinerant seafaring men bound together the struggling Atlantic community of color with their stories and news. Nothing suggests their significance and worldliness so dramatically as the fact that six of the first seven narratives published by blacks in English were written by sailors. Black leaders later emerged from the Church, but prestigious African Americans in the late eighteenth and early nineteenth centuries (including Olaudah Equiano, Paul Cuffe, James Forten, and Denmark Vesey) emerged from the swirling eddies of maritime labor.

Crew lists deposited in customs houses by outbound captains reveal a two-sided coin: black labor contributed fundamentally to maritime enterprise, and free black men depended on seafaring wages, far more in fact than did whites. Between 1803 and 1822, African-American men filled between 15 and 22 percent of the seafaring jobs in New York, Baltimore, New Orleans, and Rhode Island. Given their relative strength in the population, these numbers suggest that free black men were about seven times as likely as whites to go to sea in this era, a result of their lack of property and limited opportunities. Facing daunting obstacles to most employment, men of color esteemed maritime work a sheet anchor for economic survival. While African-American seafaring is one of the great untold stories of maritime history, it speaks as well to the tenacity and perseverance with which the first generations of freed blacks seized every financial opportunity to build families and enduring institutions.

Black sailors were more likely than whites to have families. But they lived a paradox: to have a home (i.e., not to live under a white master's

Below: *A dockside scene at the Arch Street Ferry in Philadelphia. Many black men found work in the maritime trades.*

roof), black males often had to ship out, estranging themselves from families left behind.

Seafaring posed worse threats. All sailors faced the captain's lash and nature's fury. Blacks alone confronted unscrupulous officers and boardinghouse keepers who sold thousands of free black seamen into southern and West Indian slavery. 'My Captin has put me in the Chan gan,' lamented John Tidd from New Orleans; 'he want to sall me.' Thousands more languished in filthy jails, victims of Negro Seamen Acts that, after 1822, demanded incarceration of free black sailors in slave territory to prevent them from spreading freedom's heresy. Challenged by hemispheric slavery at every turn, black seamen retaliated. Politicized sailors smuggled slaves to freedom. 'After we had got into the ocean,' remembered escapee William Grimes, 'the sailors gave three hearty cheers, and gave me to understand that I was clear.'

Black history has been strangely silent regarding sailors, and maritime history, like the *Chesapeake* affair, has been whitewashed in popular imagination. For men like Ware and Martin, however, seafaring remained a powerful antidote to slavery, and a linchpin in the daily struggle through which they defined themselves.

W. Jeffrey Bolster

black community of several hundred had much to suffer. While a judicial decree abolished slavery in 1783, black freedmen and freedwomen soon learned that freedom came only by degrees. Black Bostonians found only ill-paid work and deep prejudice against them. In 1786, when the Shaysite Rebellion swept Massachusetts, Hall tried to offset white hostility by offering what he called the Commonwealth's 'meanest members in this time of trouble and confusion' to fight against the agrarian insurgents.[19]

Spurned by the governor and discouraged at their plight, Hall led Boston's free black community in an entirely different direction. Hardly six weeks after offering to march against the Shaysites, Hall petitioned the legislature on behalf of the city's African Americans to support a plan for returning to Africa. Believing that they would never escape the racism that hobbled them, they wished 'earnestly. . . to return to Africa, our native country. . . where we shall live among our equals and be more comfortable and happy, than we can be in our present situation . . .'[20] This was probably the first colonization impulse – an early form of black nationalism – to emerge in the new American republic, an indication that the republic was seen by black citizens as a flawed, racially divided society.

When Hall's colonization plan failed, he continued to organize, protesting the exclusion of black children from tax-supported free schools, protesting against the kidnaping of free blacks into slavery, and calling for the end of the slave trade. Death silenced his voice in June 1807, just six months before the slave trade legally ended.

In Richard Allen's way of grappling with his identity and with the future of black Americans we can see a different postwar strategy at work. Allen, 24 years younger than Prince Hall, had grown up as a slave to the family of Benjamin Chew, a wealthy, conservative lawyer and proprietary officeholder in Pennsylvania. Chew sold Allen's family to a Delaware farmer in the early 1770s, and it was here in about 1777 that Allen experienced a religious conversion at the hands of itinerant Methodists. Allen's master also fell to the power of the Methodist message, and, nudged along by economic necessity, became enough convinced of the sin of slaveholding to allow Allen and his brother to purchase their freedom. In 1780, with the war still raging, Allen, age 20, began a six-year religious sojourn, interspersing work as a sawyer, wagon driver, and shoemaker. Stints of itinerant preaching carried him by foot over hundreds of miles to black and white audiences in dozens of villages, crossroads, and farms. In the mid-1780s, Allen received the call to preach in Philadelphia to a small group of free blacks who were worshiping at St. George's Methodist Church, a rude, dirt-floored building in the German part of the city.

Allen soon increased the black Methodist flock with his hortatory skills and steady

demeanor. He soon joined another recently released slave, Absalom Jones, in launching the Free African Society of Philadelphia, the first black mutual aid association in the new nation. This led to a desire for an independent black church. Allen's fervent Methodism brought him into conflict with other emerging black leaders who wished for a nondenominational or 'union' church. Thus, within a few years, two black churches took form. In both cases the guiding idea was that black Americans emerging from slavery required independent black churches because, as the Philadelphia black leaders phrased it, 'men are more influenced by their moral equals than by their superiors' and 'are more easily governed by persons chosen by themselves for that purpose than by persons who are placed over them by accidental circumstances.'[21] In this quietly radical message, the seed of black

Left: Jarena Lee was the first female to preach in the African Methodist Episcopal Church created by Richard Allen in 1816. She was 60 years old in 1844 when this image was produced, and an inspiration to other black women.

autonomy was planted at the capital city of American abolitionism.

The autonomous black churches founded in Philadelphia only a decade after the war ended were critically important in furthering the social and psychological rehabilitation of recently freed slaves. The desire 'to worship God under our own vine and fig tree,' as Allen put it, was in essence a desire to stand apart from white society, avoiding both the paternalistic benevolence of its racially liberal members and the animosity of its racially intolerant members.[22] It was this distancing from whites that allowed former slaves to strike out on independent courses in other areas of concern. From Allen's church, Mother Bethel, flowed petitions and sermons against slavery and the slave trade, plans for black schools and mutual aid societies, protests against race discrimination in the city of brotherly love, and, on occasion, emigrationist schemes.

Hammon, Hall, and Allen represent the different forms taken by the quest for place and self-definition as African Americans emerged from the Revolution. Between the 1780s and the 1820s, during the life span of the Revolutionary generation, black Americans by the thousands wrestled to find an identity, trying to reconcile their consciousness of being African with that of being American. For the most part, they had to solve this problem by living a double existence, maintaining a dialectical relationship between the two parts of their identity. This is what W. E. B. DuBois called 'two unreconciled strivings; two warring ideals in one dark body, whose dogged strength alone keeps it from being torn asunder.'[23]

Charges of Inferiority

By creating alternative institutions, the founding generation of free black Americans was able to maintain its dialectical existence as both Africans and Americans. In creating a sense of peoplehood, nothing was more important than the construction of autonomous black churches. Both as places of refuge and citadels of strength, the emerging independent black churches were vital in giving free blacks, and slaves within reach of their influence, a sense of peoplehood within a white republic that was increasingly hostile to the free black presence. The 'coming out' from white churches, as the decision to leave white churches was expressed, involved a painful and sometimes dangerous process of rebirthing. At the heart of this process of being reborn was the psychologically crucial step of rejecting white definitions of black people's place. It was in challenging the right of white churches to govern them in the area of religion that free blacks took their most important step toward self-determination in a white republic that was determined, for the most part, to give them no self.

Ironically, part of the rising feeling against free blacks in the North and upper South was in fact caused by this psychologically vital move toward self-determination. 'Their aspirings and little vanities have been rapidly growing since they got those separate churches,' sneered a white Philadelphia Methodist in the 1820s. 'Thirty or forty years ago, they were much humbler, more esteemed in their places, and more useful to themselves and others.'[24] Daniel Payne, bishop of the African Methodist Episcopal Church, wrote on the opposite side of the same coin some years later that the 'unpardonable crime' that free blacks had

committed in forming independent churches 'was that they dared to organize a Church of men, men to think for themselves, men to talk for themselves, men to act for themselves.'[25]

Thus arose a great and tragic paradox: as free blacks removed themselves from white paternalist influence by founding and sustaining their own institutions for guiding the religious, moral, and educational lives of their people, white charges about insurmountable black inferiority intensified. The first period of creative institution-building by recently freed slaves was accompanied in the early nineteenth century by the revival of earlier patterns of racist thought that insisted on innate black inferiority. Antislavery sentiment among white Americans was declining, private manu-

Below: *Pavel Svinin's watercolor 'Worldly Folk' was painted early in the nineteenth century. This scene of Philadelphia represents the city's different groups, from unskilled chimney sweeps to affluent, fashionable urbanites.*

missions were slowing, and the radical wing of Revolutionary republicanism was ebbing by the end of the eighteenth century.

Black leaders vigorously answered such charges of inferiority in the early nineteenth century. Far from inferior, they saw themselves as 'the people of God,' 'a chosen generation,' 'a holy nation,' to use the phrases of Daniel Coker of Baltimore, the Methodist leader of the fastest-growing, free black urban population in the South. Coker gave biblical sanction to the passage from slavery to freedom by likening it to the Hebrew Exodus from Egypt. Wherever black preachers testified, black Christians heard the message that, contrary to white belief, God had not made them inferior to whites, but indeed they were superior to white Christians who were mired in the sins of slaveholding and racism and had trapped themselves in the logical contradiction of trying to build a republic of slaveholders. In one of the hymns that echoed through Richard Allen's Mother Bethel Church in Philadelphia, black worshipers sang out:

What poor despised company
Of travellers are these
That's walking yonder narrow way,
Along that rugged maze?

Why that are of a royal line,
They'r children of a King;
Heirs of immortal Crown divine,
And loud for joy they sing.

Why do they then appear so mean,
And why so much despis'd?
Because of their rich robes unseen
The world is not apprized.[26]

Just as their personal emancipations from slavery had involved a psychological rebirth, the collective emancipation of black churches from white ecclesiastical authority signaled a political maturation. When it became clear that the new nation was to be defined as a republic for white men only, free blacks who earlier had attempted to adapt to white society and live quiet lives by white, middle-class norms became thoroughly politicized. The need for direct and less reserved action was becoming clear by the late 1780s when the Constitutional Convention in Philadelphia drafted the famous document that was then ratified by the states. The Convention buried the issue of abolishing slavery; indeed, through the fugitive slave clause and the counting of three-fifths of all slaves in determining seats in the House of Representatives, the Convention solidified the institution of slavery. Thus, the mild-mannered Absalom Jones, founder of the first African Protestant Episcopal Church, carried a petition to Congress through the streets of Philadelphia in 1797. He had written it on behalf of four North Carolina refugees from slavery whose freedom was imperiled because the harsh Fugitive Slave Law passed by Congress in

Gabriel Prosser, a 24-year-old slave, had devised a plan to arm 1,000 slaves for an assault on the city. A drenching downpour delayed the attack, giving time for several black house servants to sound the alarm before the conspirators struck. Blacks paid a heavy price as alarmed whites exacted their revenge. Prosser and his allies built their defense on the same contradiction between slavery and republicanism that the white Revolutionary leaders had spoken of repeatedly. As one of the defendants said,

> I have nothing more to offer than what General Washington would have had to offer, had he been taken by the British and put to trial by them. I have adventured my life in endeavouring to obtain the liberty of my countrymen, and I am a willing sacrifice in their cause. [30]

With the end of the slave trade in 1807, at a time when white abolitionism was fading rapidly, northern black clergymen who had created independent black churches began to use annual New Year's Day celebrations to keep alive the call for slavery's abolition. By now, their gospel was one of social deliverance as well as a theology of salvation. From their pulpits, 'God spoke out in thunder tones against chattel slavery and sharply condemned other forms of injustice inflicted upon any of His children.'[31] They repeatedly invoked the elevated phrases of Revolutionary ideology, confronting white Americans with the misalignment between their sacred texts and their continued adherence to slavery. God had surely been listening, wrote Peter Williams Jr. in New York City in 1808,

> when the sons of 76 pronounced these United States free and independent; when the spirit of patriotism, erected a temple sacred to liberty; when the inspired voice of Americans first uttered those noble sentiments, 'we hold these truths to be self-evident, that all men are created equal; that they are endowed by their Creator with certain inalienable rights.

How long would it be, then, until 'the sun of liberty shall beam resplendent on the whole African race?' queried Williams.[32] From Boston, in the same year, came another chiding of white Americans who presumed, in defiance of their own Revolutionary principles, to exercise authority over blacks 'by depriving us of our freedom, as though they had a command from heaven thus to do.'[33]

Striving for Occupational Independence

While keeping alive the Revolutionary hopes for the abolition of slavery, free African Americans had to tend to the realities of daily life. Among the thousands of northern blacks, who were becoming predominantly an urban people, the struggle for skilled positions was intense. Black urban dwellers were largely excluded from the budding industrializing tex-

1793 gave virtual hunting licenses to southern agents intent on seizing free blacks in northern cities. Could African Americans not expect 'public justice' from the national government? When would the government end the 'unconstitutional bondage' that was a 'direct violation of the declared fundamental principles of the Constitution?' Attempting to direct the moral compass of the government back to the sacred texts of the Revolutionary era, Jones, with a hint of irony, addressed the petition 'To the President, Senate, and House of Representatives of the – most free and enlightened nation in the world!!!'[27]

Boston's black residents also kept the fires of antislavery protest burning. In 1797, Prince Hall condemned slavery in an address at the African Masonic Lodge. Celebrating the black rebellion in St. Domingue, Hall denounced 'the daily insults' suffered by the city's black citizens 'on public days of recreation.'[28] Two years later, Philadelphia's free blacks petitioned the government again, and this time it was the recently politicized James Forten who shepherded the petition to Congress. Steadfast to the Revolutionary credo, he wrote: 'Though our faces are black, yet we are men, and . . . are as anxious to enjoy the birth-right of the human race as those who [are white].' Forten knew that the 55 delegates at Philadelphia who framed the Constitution had been unwilling to advertise their abandonment of Revolutionary principles by specifying that slaves had no natural rights; thus they had omitted all mention of the word 'slave.' Now Forten put this omission to good use. The petition went on:

> In the Constitution and in the Fugitive bill, no mention is made of Black people or Slaves – therefore if the Bill of Rights, or the decla-

Above: *These simply-made everyday items – hooks, a ladle, plate and spoon, broom, and cauldron – are representative of those which would have been owned by poor black people – or poor whites – living in one-room, dirt-floor houses in the Chesapeake region of the United States.*

> ration of Congress [i.e., the Declaration of Independence] are of any validity, we beseech that as we are men, we may be admitted to partake of the Liberties and inalienable Rights therein held forth . . . [29]

Slave Rebellions – 1791 and 1800

The struggles for freedom carried on by black Americans were made all the more difficult by two slave rebellions that generated intense alarm about black militancy. In 1791, panic-stricken French planters fleeing the Caribbean island of St. Domingue carried word to the North American mainland of the black Haitians' successful rebellion against a French colonial army of 25,000. The news spread terror through the South, where rumors abounded that Haitian incendiaries would soon be landing. In the northern cities, hundreds of French slaves arrived in the grasp of their fleeing masters. Many of them obtained their freedom in cities such as Philadelphia, New York, and Baltimore, but many white urbanites believed the flood of black migrants would overwhelm them. With southern states barring the entry of free blacks from the West Indies and calling for the deportation of slaves previously brought in from the Caribbean, northern whites imagined their communities being invaded by unacculturated blacks bent on racial revenge.

A second shock followed in the summer of 1800, when another rebellion just outside Richmond, Virginia, was nipped in the bud.

PLANTATION ARTIFACTS

Most of the pieces here are items recovered from plantation sites as a result of archaeological excavations. All are similar to European-designed pieces of the period. the exceptions are the bowl (bottom left) from the Combahee River region and the jar (top right) from the Cooper River region, South Carolina. Both are examples of Colonware, so-called because it was made by African Americans and Native Americans during the Colonial period.

The salt-glazed chamber pot (top left), was found at the slave quarters of Kingsmill plantation, near Williamsburg, Virginia. The remaining pieces, including the clay pipe, were found at the slave quarters at Mount Vernon, family home of George Washington.

The blue and white porcelain pieces (center) are interesting, as well as important in showing how family traditions have preserved African-American history. They belong today to Loretta Carter Hanes of the Quander family which traces some of its ancestors to Mount Vernon.

As far back as can be remembered, family members have used blue and white porcelain tableware which has been passed from one generation to the next. They trace the tradition to their forebears at Mount Vernon. It is possible that these nineteenth-century pieces might have originally belonged to the Washington family and then come into the possession of the resident slaves, perhaps as gifts. Other excavated possessions have added to the evidence that the Mount Vernon slaves had a high level of material comfort.

tile, shoe, and metal sectors of the economy. Indeed, the majority toiled at common labor – as stevedores on the wharves, as cellar, well, and grave diggers, chimney sweeps and ash haulers, construction laborers, ragpickers, bootblacks, stablehands, sawyers, and white-washers. Yet in every city, skilled black artisans could be found, and many others held positions as barbers, servants, teachers, carters, and oystermen. It would have been rare in any seaport to see a ship enter the port without black mariners scrambling the decks.

In every city and town, the search of African Americans for self-employment was notable, originating in the same impulse that had led to the creation of independent black churches – the desire to live on one's own terms and to reduce, insofar as was possible, dependency on whites. At the top of the pyramid of independently employed free blacks stood a small but influential number of black doctors, ministers, teachers, and other professionals. In Philadelphia, black doctors practiced as early as 1784, and by the turn of the century Samuel

Wilson was so highly regarded for his skill in treating cancer that white Philadelphians readily went to him. The first black teacher in the city was Eleanor Harris, an African-born former slave, described after her death in 1797 as a 'woman of character' and a 'well qualified tutoress of children.'[34]

Providing personal service for both whites and blacks was another main area of employment. Every seaboard city, from Boston to Baltimore, had dozens of barbers, seamstresses, hairdressers, coachmen, nurses, gardeners, cooks, and waiters. Often such pursuits involved a dependency relationship with whites, as in the case of cooks or coachmen who resided in the white household, but in many other cases the washerwomen, cooks, and barbers maintained their own residences

Below: 'The Banjo Man' *is by an unknown artist and dates from the early nineteenth century. The* banza, *or banjo, was brought directly to the Americas from Africa by enslaved Africans. Here, it is being used to entertain children.*

and contracted their labor on their own terms.

At gala gatherings, free African Americans were also pioneering entrepreneurs. Philadelphia's Robert Bogle, a former slave who began as a waiter, was the first to hatch the idea of contracting food services at funerals, weddings, and parties. By the 1820s in Philadelphia, the famous catering firm of Augustine and Baptiste, founded by two of the French slaves brought to Philadelphia during the St. Domingue rebellion, were serving foreign dignitaries and wealthy Philadelphians at lavish balls and fetes. At such gatherings, black fiddlers often provided the music. By 1820 in Philadelphia, the city's most famous musician, Frank Johnson, was in demand everywhere. The French-speaking black from Martinique who had arrived in the city in about 1809 had soon become the leader of a dance orchestra, a celebrated keyed-bugle, trumpet, and violin player, and a prolific composer of dance and martial music, ballads, operatic arrangements, and minstrel songs. In 1819, Johnson was described as 'leader of the band at all balls public and private; sole director of all serenades . . . inventor-general of cotillions.'[35]

Though many free blacks were frozen in unskilled jobs at the bottom of the urban work forces of the early American republic, hundreds of them created their own work roles, thus providing themselves with decent material rewards, and, equally important, space to operate autonomously. Even the poor ragman made daily decisions with existential meaning that we can only guess at – which streets to walk, when to set out, when to quit work. Though he had to endure poverty, the ragman did not have to withstand the insulting comments of a boss or maintain a schedule set by somebody else.

While pursuing livelihoods, free African Americans sought family lives. The great disruption of slave family life during the Revolution, the dislocation in the war's aftermath, the postemancipation migration from plantations and farms to towns and cities, and the constraints placed on family formation by poverty: all these factors made the creation of black households a complex and difficult process. Emancipated African Americans first extricated themselves from white households; then they often combined households with relatives, friends, and boarders intermingling; finally, as they were able, they established nuclear households.

This process could be seen in every city. In Boston, for example, the first Federal census in 1790 revealed that more than one of every three blacks lived in a white household; 30 years later all but 16 percent of Boston's blacks resided in autonomous black households. By 1820, in the major northern seaports, the federal census-takers collected data that shows that more than three-quarters of these black households contained at least one adult male and one adult female – evidence that the matrifocal black family associated

Right: *Count Rumford and family in 1785 – the black servant an integral part of the household.*

with slavery had been replaced by the two-parent family of black urbanites.

The War of 1812

During the War of 1812 with Great Britain, northern free blacks tried to earn respect by volunteering for service. In New York City, for example, on 2 August 1814, nearly 1,000 'of the hearty and patriotic sons of Africa' turned out to work on the fortifications on Brooklyn Heights guarding the approach to the city. A month later, black Philadelphians formed brigades for refortifying the west bank of the Schuylkill River south of the city. But throughout most of the North, free blacks were exempted from military service, which largely prevented young males from proving their patriotism and civic responsibility. Nonetheless, northern African Americans fought valiantly on Great Lakes ships, and, at the anticlimactic Battle of New Orleans, several units of Louisiana's black Americans fought with General Andrew Jackson. It would be the last war in which black military personnel would fight in integrated units until the Korean War. The free blacks of the early American republic made strenuous efforts to create families, carve out occupational niches in local economies, and build institutions to sustain religious strivings and political agendas as they drank from a bittersweet cup of freedom.

Notes

[1] John Hughes to John Swift *et al.*, 5 November 1765, Miscellaneous MSS Collection, Box 1, Library Company of Philadelphia.

[2] Wheatley to Samson Occom, 11 February 1774, in Julian D. Mason, Jr. (ed.), *The Poems of Phillis Wheatley*, Chapel Hill: University of North Carolina Press, 1989, pp. 203–4.

[3] Thomas Paine, 'African Slavery in America,' in Philip Foner (ed.), *The Complete Writings of Thomas Paine*, 2 vols, New York: Citadel Press, 1945, vol. II, p. 18.

[4] *Pennsylvania Chronicle*, 21–8 November 1768.

[5] 'The Petition of the Negroes in the Towns of Stratford and Fairfield in the County of Fairfield Who Are Held in a State of Slavery,' in H. Aptheker (ed.), *A Documentary History of the Negro People in the United States*, 2 vols, New York: Citadel Press, 1951, vol. I, p. 78.

[6] Quoted in Benjamin Quarles, 'The Revolutionary War as a Black Declaration of Independence,' in Ira Berlin and Ronald Hoffman (eds.), *Slavery and Freedom in the Age of the American Revolution*, Charlottesville: University of Virginia Press, 1983, p. 290.

[7] *Pennsylvania Evening Post*, 5 December 1775.

[8] *The Journals of Henry Melchior Muhlenberg*, 3 vols, Philadelphia: 1942–58, vol. III, p. 78.

[9] *Pennsylvania Evening Post*, 14 December 1775.

[10] Quoted in Sylvia R. Frey, *Water from the Rock: Black Resistance in a Revolutionary Age*, Princeton, NJ: Princeton University Press, 1991, p. 170.

[11] *Pennsylvania Packet*, 12 December 1779.

[12] Graham R. Hodges, *African-Americans in Monmouth County During the Age of the American Revolution*, Lincroft, NJ: 1990, pp. 13–23.

[13] William C. Nell, *Colored Patriots of the American Revolution*, New York: 1862, p. 167.

[14] *Ibid.*, p. 170.

[15] Quoted in Gary B. Nash, 'Thomas Peters: Millwright and Deliverer,' in David G. Sweet and Gary B. Nash (eds), *Struggle and Survival in Colonial America*, Berkeley and Los Angeles: University of California Press, 1981, p. 83.

[16] Quoted in Phillip M. Richards, 'Nationalist Themes in the Preaching of Jupiter Hammon,' *Early American Literature* 25, 2 (1990): pp. 123–38.

[17] Quoted in Gary B. Nash, *Race and Revolution*, Madison, WI: Madison House, 1990, p. 63.

[18] Quoted in Sidney Kaplan, *The Black Presence in the Era of the American Revolution, 1770–1800*, Greenwich, CT: New York Graphic Society, 1973, p. 12.

[19] *Ibid.*, p. 184.

[20] *Ibid.*, p. 186.

[21] 'Address of the Representatives of the African Church [of Philadelphia],' quoted in Gary B. Nash, *Forging Freedom: The Formation of Philadelphia's Free Black Community, 1720–1840*, Cambridge, MA: Harvard University Press, 1988, p. 113.

[22] *The Life Experience and Gospel Labors of the Rt. Rev. Richard Allen, to Which is Annexed the Rise and Progress of the African Methodist Episcopal Church in the United States of America*, Nashville: 1960, p. 26.

[23] W. E. Burghart DuBois, *The Souls of Black Folk*, New York: New American Library, 1970, p. 3.

[24] John F. Watson, *Annals of Philadelphia, and Pennsylvania, in the Olden Time . . .*, 3 vols, Philadelphia: 1830; reprint 1900, vol. II, p. 261.

[25] Daniel Payne, *History of the African Methodist Episcopal Church*, 1891; reprint New York: Arno Press, 1969, pp. 9–10.

[26] Richard Allen, *A Collection of Hymns and Spiritual Songs from Various Authors*, Philadelphia: 1801, p. 17. Quoted in Gary B. Nash, *Race and Revolution*, Madison, WI: Madison House, 1990, p. 74.

[27] Quoted in Gary B. Nash, *Race and Revolution*, Madison, WI: Madison House, 1990, p. 78.

[28] Quoted in James Oliver Horton and Lois E. Horton, *Black Bostonians*, New York: 1979, pp. 29–30.

[29] Petition of the free blacks of Philadelphia to the President and Congress of the United States, 31 December 1799, excerpted in Kaplan, *Black Presence*, pp. 237–9.

[30] Robert Sutcliff, *Travels in Some Parts of North America . . .* York, England: 1815. Quoted in Leon Litwack, 'Trouble in Mind: The Bicentennial and the Afro-American Experience,' *Journal of American History* 74 (1987): p. 318.

[31] Quarles, 'The Revolutionary War as a Black Declaration of Independence,' p. 296.

[32] Peter Williams, Jr., *An Oration on the Abolition of the Slave Trade . . .*, New York: 1808, excerpted in Aptheker, *Documentary History*, p. 51.

[33] *The Sons of Africa: An Essay on Freedom . . .*, Boston: 1808, excerpted in Aptheker, *Documentary History*, p. 52.

[34] *American Mercury*, 6 March 1797.

[35] Bernard, *Retrospections of America, 1797–1811*, New York: 1887, pp. 189–90.

Chapter 3

THE SLAVES' CHANGING WORLD

Slavery defined a complex set of dynamic relationships and expectations. Slaves and slaveholders constantly struggled over responsibilities and rights within this system of inordinately unequal power. The same trans-Appalachian expansion celebrated for its democratizing effect on American free society changed the lives of slaves, but seldom for the better. Nineteenth-century slavery was significantly different from the eighteenth-century institution as the center shifted westward. Slaves became more isolated, had fewer alternatives to field labor, and were wrenched from more stable family and community surroundings. In the deep South, they produced a culture that was substantially different from that of the Chesapeake or the Atlantic Coast eastern South of pre-Revolutionary America. This deep-South region with its cotton-based economy came to dominate southern culture in the decades before the Civil War.

'A Southern Cornfield' by Thomas Waterman Wood, painted in 1861, shows slaveworkers near Nashville, Tennessee, as they labor in the sun to maintain the cornfields. Whereas some crops were specifically tied to a particular area – tobacco, sugar, and rice, for example – cereals were grown almost everywhere. In the antebellum period, slaves accounted for just under half of Nashville's unskilled labor force.

IRA BERLIN

On 1 JANUARY 1800, Americans turned the page on the calendar and marked the start of a new century.[1] Almanacs, magazines, and newspapers trumpeted the end of one era and the beginning of another. In the previous century, independence had been won, the republic secured, and the continent opened to American exploration and settlement. The new century offered the opportunity to fulfill the promise of the old: most Americans embraced it enthusiastically, celebrating the possibilities.

For at least one group of Americans, however, the possibilities presented by the centennial were constrained and somber, if not dispiriting. Black people had arrived on mainland North America some 200 years earlier. By the beginning of the nineteenth century, most were second-, third-, or perhaps even fourth-generation Americans. Their forebears had suffered the wrenching process of enslavement in Africa, the nightmare of the Middle Passage, and the inexorable transformation that accompanies the meeting of two cultures. Once in the New World, transplanted Africans grew the great staples of Atlantic commerce – tobacco, rice, and indigo – under the lash of European and European-American slave owners.

There were glimmers of hope. The War for American Independence divided white Americans and left slavery vulnerable. Seizing the moment, thousands of slaves escaped bondage, and the opponents of slavery – white and black – assailed the institution openly. Eventually, they liquidated slavery in the northern states and freed large numbers of slaves in the southern ones. By the beginning of the nineteenth century, more than 10 percent of the black population had secured its liberty. But the same War for Independence also liberated slave owners from the oversight of their colonial overlords, elevated them to a place of primacy in the new republic, and allowed slavery to expand as never before. Thus, the dawn of the new century saw most black people locked in bondage, with little chance of escape. For most slaves, liberation would not come for another 60 years when another massive war again divided white Americans and allowed black Americans to seize their freedom.

But, if bondage remained the fate of the vast majority of African Americans in the years between the turn of the century and the ratification of the 13th Amendment, slave life did not remain unaltered. Instead, the same powerful forces that propelled free Americans across the continent reshaped the American economy, and transformed American society, also remade the lives of black people in slavery.

The story of African-American life in the 60 years before the Civil War was the story of

Below: *Savannah, Georgia, in a painting by Fermin Cerveau dating from 1837. The street scene shows blacks and whites going about their daily business. At the time, about one-third of the city's population were slaves, usually employed as domestic servants.*

change. In 1800, the great mass of slaves lived along the Atlantic seaboard, cultivated tobacco or rice, and practiced a variety of religions derived from Africa. On the eve of emancipation, most slaves resided in the interior of the South, grew cotton or sugar, and professed some variant of Christianity. These massive demographic, economic, and cultural changes combined to reweave the fabric of African-American society.

The Second Great Migration

First and most important of these transformations was the movement of black people from the eastern seaboard to the interior of the South. In 1800, more than 80 percent of the slave population resided between the Delaware and the Savannah Rivers in Maryland, Virginia, and the Carolinas. By the beginning of the Civil War, only a third of the slave population lived in Maryland, Virginia, and North and South Carolina. Instead, most slaves resided in the lower South: Georgia, Alabama, Mississippi, Louisiana, and the states to the west. Indeed, the most dynamic portions of the slave population could be found on the Arkansas and Texas frontier.

Within the lower South, slaves were even more concentrated. A rich ribbon of dark alluvial soil that stretched from Georgia to Mississippi – the so-called 'black belt,' named for the color of the soil and the color of the people who worked it – became the primary site of African Americans in slavery. A second and equally formidable concentration of slaves could be found along the Mississippi River, especially between New Orleans and

Memphis. Smaller river systems – the Savannah, Alamaha, Flint, Chattahoochee, Tennessee, Tombigbee, and Yazoo – sheltered additional agglomerations of slaves. Although the preponderance of the slave population in the black belt and river bottoms seldom reached the levels that had been achieved in low-country Carolina during the eighteenth century, where slaves composed upward of 90 percent of the population, slaves made up a substantial majority in these areas.

The movement of some 1 million slaves from the seaboard to the black belt and the river bottoms of the interior deeply disrupted the civilization that black people had established in the aftermath of their forced exodus from Africa. In the almost two centuries of settlement along the seaboard, African and African-American slaves had created complex communities, linked together by ties of kinship and friendship and resting upon a foundation of shared values and beliefs. Those communities became increasingly self-contained with the closing of the slave trade, which had ended in the lower South by constitutional mandate in 1808 and a generation earlier in the upper South. The westward movement of plantation culture, whether it was driven by individual planters who accompanied their slaves or by professional slave

Above: *'After the Sale: Slaves Going South from Richmond' by Eyre Crowe, painted in 1853. By the antebellum period there was an active slave trade between the states in which Richmond was one of the principal centers.*

traders who speculated in human flesh, tore the seaboard society asunder, exiling hundreds of thousands from their birthplace and traumatizing those who remained. Families and sometimes whole communities dissolved under the pressure of this Second Great Migration.[2]

Changes founded on the seaboard resonated in the interior. Generally, it was the young who were the first to be sent west, as frontier planters needed both the muscle of young men and women to clear the land and their reproductive capacity to assure a steadily expanding labor force. On the frontier, slaves, many of them children, reconstructed African-American life from the memories of the older seaboard civilization, much as their ancestors had refashioned their lives on the western side of the Atlantic from memories of Africa.

Still, in many ways, the Second Great Migration differed from the first, not only dwarfing it in size, but also presenting a distinctive demographic outline. The forced transatlantic migration had been heavily

weighted toward men, while men and women moved to the interior of the South in roughly equal numbers. Additionally, Africans who arrived in mainland North America in the seventeenth and eighteenth centuries had been linguistically and culturally estranged from one another, talking a variety of tongues, practicing a host of different customs, and articulating a variety of different beliefs. They knew little of their owners' language or culture, and what they knew, they knew imperfectly. In the nineteenth century, African Americans who were carried into the interior of the South spoke the same language and shared a common culture. Differences between African Americans originating in the Chesapeake and in the Carolina low country paled in comparison to differences between Africans derived from the Senegambia and Angola. And, if Africans hardly knew the Europeans who had enslaved them, African Americans knew the ways of their owners all too well.

Migration and Cultural Reconstruction

But if there were differences between the transatlantic and the mainland migrations, the process of cultural reconstruction was the same. Families had to be reconstituted, leadership reasserted, and culture refashioned in new circumstances, so a generation which would know its parents' homeland only through dim recollections could be tutored in the ways of the old country. In many ways, the memory of Virginia and Carolina, kept alive by the continued influx of newcomers to the West, became as important for black people in the nineteenth-century black belt as the memory of Africa had been for black people in the seventeenth- and eighteenth-century seaboard. 'You may readily suppose that I was not fool enough to marry a Texas girl,' a former slave who had been sold from Virginia as a boy assured his sister some 20 years later.[3]

The forcible extraction of thousands of African-American slaves from the seaboard states also reshaped the lives of those left behind. Molding hopes and expectations to the relentless reality of the westward movement, those who lived under the ever-present threat of sale 'down the river' also reformulated African-American life. Among the new truths was the sad fact that many could not expect to see their children grow to maturity. During the nineteenth century, more than a third of the children in the upper South were separated from their parents by the process of sale to the interior. Parents, too, were separated from each other, as husbands and wives could be sold at any time. If African-American society on the frontier was a culture of youth, slave society on the seaboard was weighted toward the aged, often bereft of children, and sundered by the separation of spouses and siblings. Few slave parents could expect to nurture their children to maturity, watch their grandchildren grow up, and succor their own elderly parents. Slavery played havoc with African-American family life in the new frontier and the old settlements.

Whatever the effects of the Second Great Migration on southern slave society at its terminal points, the movement west was neither direct nor linear. Those who traveled west with their owners in family groups or entire plantation populations, rather than with traders in coffles of strangers, enjoyed a measure of security. But it was a short-lived consolation. Few pioneering owners stayed in one spot for long, as they searched for the cheap land in the wake of Indian evictions and government land auctions, first in Georgia, then Alabama, and finally Mississippi or even Arkansas or Texas. With little cash on hand and few ties to reliable sources of credit, aspiring planters were vulnerable to the wild swings of a boom-and-bust economy. When the catastrophe struck, slaves were ruined with their owners. But, even in the best of times, slaves might be sold or traded anywhere along the way, as each stop provided the occasion for yet another division. Separated from friends only recently acquired, transplanted slaves were forced again to reconstruct their lives.

Passing from owner to owner, slaves caught in the interstate trade learned to make a strange world familiar in quick order. Just as shipmates in the transatlantic journey had frequently became fast friends, slaves who moved west together forged bonds with hopes of creating a modicum of social stability. But the massive disorganization that accompanied the forced migration from the seaboard to the interior broke many men and women. Realizing that friendships struck along the route were in all likelihood doomed, they capitulated to the social chaos that accompanied the movement west. Observers captured their demoralization in the 'downcast look' that characterized many new arrivals. For such men and women, the task of reestablishing shattered ties of kinship and friendship was impossible when transiency was the only certainty.

The Plantation

The movement to the interior helped democratize American society, giving many free Americans a chance to participate in the wealth of the continent. True to the peculiari-

ON THE AUCTION BLOCK

Above: These tags identified the wearers as urban slaves and the type of work they did.

ties of American democracy, the number of slaveholders grew steadily as the nation marched west. Most of these newly minted masters and mistresses owned only a few slaves. But most slaves lived on plantations, by common consent defined as a unit of 20 or more. More than a quarter of the slave population – some 1 million slaves in 1850 – dwelled on great plantations of 50 or more slaves. In the states of the lower South, where plantations were concentrated, the proportion was even higher. On the eve of the Civil War,

Above: Slaves on the auction block in St. Louis in the last sale to take place there shortly before the Civil War. The auction presented a grave threat to African-American families with little notice taken of their wish to remain together. Many were split up and dispersed.

Below: A notice advertising a sale of 30 slaves in Jackson, Mississippi, in late December 1841, the property of a deceased man's estate. Slaves were often sold as part of such settlements, with little regard for their family structure.

'The crowd collected round the stand, the huddling group of Negroes, the examination of muscle, teeth, the exhibition of agility, the look of the auctioneer, the agony of my mother – I can shut my eyes and see them all.

My brothers and sisters were bid off first, and one by one, while my mother, paralyzed by grief, held me by the hand. Her turn came, and she was bought by Isaac Riley of Montgomery county. Then I was offered to the assembled purchasers. My mother, half distracted with the thought of parting forever from all her children pushed through the crowd, while the bidding for me was going on, to the spot where Riley was standing. She fell at his feet, and clung to his knees, entreating him in tones that a mother could only command, to buy her *baby* as well as herself, and spare to her one, at least, of her little ones. Will it, can it be believed that this man, thus appealed to, was capable not merely of turning a deaf ear to her supplication, but of disengaging himself from her with such violent blows and kicks, as to reduce her to the necessity of creeping out of his reach, and mingling the groan of bodily suffering with the sob of a breaking heart?. . . I must have been then between five and six years old . . .'[1]

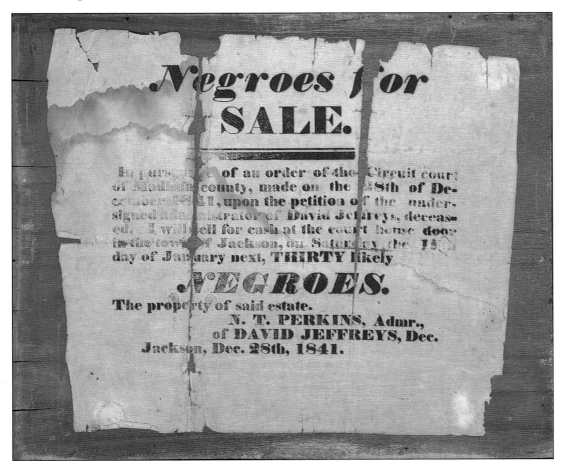

Negroes for SALE.

In pursuance of an order of the Circuit court of Madison county, made on the 28th of December 1841, upon the petition of the undersigned administrator of David Jeffreys, deceased. I will sell for cash at the court house door in the town of Jackson, on Saturday the 15th day of January next, THIRTY likely *NEGROES.*

The property of said estate.
N. T. PERKINS, Admr.,
of DAVID JEFFREYS, Dec.
Jackson, Dec. 28th, 1841.

Note
[1] Josiah Henson, *Truth Stranger than Fiction, Father Henson's Story of his Own Life*, Boston, MA: J. P. Jewett & Co., 1858, pp. 11–13.

more than one-third of the slaves in the lower South resided on plantations of 50 or more. Thus, although slaves could be found in a variety of different venues – towns and cities, farmsteads and mill runs, iron forges and turpentine camps – the plantation was the crucible of nineteenth-century African-American life in slavery.

The plantation was many things – a unit of capitalist production and the site of a precapitalist community – but for slaves plantation life meant work, unrelentingly hard work that began at sunup, paused only slightly at sundown, and frequently continued long into the night. Most plantation slaves engaged in the meanest sort of labor, from which they derived few tangible benefits. But the same work was also a source of personal satisfaction and of political self-assertion. The act of creation, which even the most onerous and exploitative labor entailed, allowed slaves to affirm the humanity that chattel bondage denied. By making something where once there was nothing, slaves discredited the masters' shibboleth that they were simply property, countered the daily humiliations that tested their self-esteem, and laid claim to the fruits of their labor for themselves and their posterity.

Because work was both a source of the slaves' oppression and a seed of their liberation, it became the terrain upon which slaves and their owners battled for the wealth that the slaves produced. The conflict took many forms, involving the organization of labor, the pace of work, the division of labor, and the composition of the labor force. If slave owners wielded the lash – for slavery never ceased to rest upon brute force – slaves employed an array of weapons of their own, feigning ignorance, slowing the line, maiming animals, breaking tools, disappearing at critical moments, and, as a last resort, confronting slave owners directly and violently.

Agricultural Diversity
The character of these workplace struggles rested, to a considerable degree, on the productive processes themselves, which differed throughout the South. Here, too, change was the watchword, as many slaveholders abandoned the great staples of the colonial era and introduced new ones. During the seventeenth and eighteenth centuries, most plantation slaves grew tobacco and rice, with indigo being a secondary crop in low-country Carolina and in Louisiana. While the cultivation of tobacco and rice remained important in the nineteenth-century South, indigo fell to the vagaries of international politics and trade; the crops grown by plantation slaves changed. The American government's purchase of Louisiana during the first decade of the nineteenth century placed a major sugar-producing area within the bounds of the United States. Many planters, particularly in the upper South, grew less tobacco and expanded cereal production. They introduced new crops like hemp, all the while diversifying their out-

SLAVE HOUSING

Above: *The interior of a slave cabin in Virginia shows women drying their laundry at the fire. Note the presence of four children, the care of whom was a collaborative communal effort.*

The houses in which slaves were confined are generally seen as nothing more than just one of the indignities that African Americans were forced to endure as a condition of their bondage. Many commentators agreed with the 1783 observation of German traveler Johann David Schoepf who found slave quarters to be 'badly kept cabins of wood . . . of the structure and solidity of a house of cards.'[1] The structures to which he was referring were rarely more than small, one-room, boxlike pens expediently constructed with roughly hewn logs. They often had dirt floors, only small holes in the walls for windows, and fireplaces and chimneys made out of mud and sticks. While it is not surprising to find repeated complaints about such buildings in the testimonies of former slaves, some slave owners also concurred with their negative assessments. As late as 1856 a Mississippi planter wrote in a letter to the *Southern Cultivator* that because 'negro houses are "knocked up" in a very careless, bungling manner – always too small and too low' they were, in his view, 'well-calculated to generate disease.'[2]

Given the deplorable conditions in which most slaves were forced to live, a number of 'scientific' planters decided that their old, dilapidated houses should be replaced. Though motivated perhaps by altruism or a sense of moral duty, more significant for these men was their realization that the loss of labor due to frequent slave illness would lead quickly to a decline in their profits. Thus they deemed it prudent and a sign of sound management to see that their work force was well housed. Consequently, around 1820, a little-reported reform movement was launched. There were repeated calls to replace decrepit slave cabins,

and numerous standing buildings all across the South from this period illustrate that the suggested reforms were actually carried out. By the 1850s, frame buildings covered with siding were replacing the older log huts. New dwellings, even when built with logs, were usually outfitted with wooden floors, masonry fireplaces, glazed windows, and were raised a few feet (around 1.5m) off the ground on blocks to enhance ventilation and occupant comfort. Average room sizes increased from 12 x 12ft (4 x 4m) to 18 x 18ft (6 x 6m), more than doubling the amount of floor space. On some estates, rows of cabins were constructed with brick, stone, or tabby concrete, and occasionally even decorated with flourishes of stylish ornament. While the one-room cabin remained a commonplace feature of plantations, by the middle of the nineteenth century the repertoire of slave houses had been considerably expanded. New plans provided for between two and four rooms in a variety of different configurations that might be built both one and two stories high.

Improved housing was but one of a series of benefits that slaves were able to negotiate for themselves by using effective strategies for day-to-day resistance. By employing modest acts of defiance, such as work slowdowns, feigned sickness, petty theft, or the destruction of property – the so-called 'weapons of the weak' – slaves found that they could significantly interrupt the work routines of plantations. Armed with these tactics, they were able to

earn certain 'privileges,' including – in addition to improved housing – better rations, regular medical care, plots of land to be used for their own gardens, and permission to travel off the plantation. New slave housing should be seen, then, as one of the tangible results of successful protest, as something that slaves won for themselves rather than something they were given. Planters, no doubt, hoped that their actions would make their workers more complacent and accepting of their captive status. However, each newly negotiated benefit only heightened expectations among slaves and led to further acts of protest.

The modest domestic benefits that slaves were able to secure for themselves clearly encouraged some to develop a sense of symbolic ownership over, at least, their

Above: *These brick cabins were built on the Belair plantation near New Orleans to house the many families which were needed because of the labor-intensive sugar industry.*

portions of the plantation landscape. The quarters community came to be seen as slave space; a domain not merely allowed to slaves, but one claimed by them. Others went further by expanding their sense of dominion to include the plantation's fields, crops, livestock, machinery, and other buildings: South Carolina planter J. Motte Alston noted with some irritation that his slave foreman Cudjoe 'looked

Below: *Everyday items excavated from slave homes, including bone buttons, a brass buckle and pins, beads, a thimble – even cufflinks.*

upon my property as belonging to him.'[3] Improved conditions in the quarters not only helped to stabilize the slave community but, it seems, also enkindled desires for greater authority and autonomy.

John Michael Vlach

Notes

[1] Johann David Schoepf, *Travels in the Confederation 1783–1784*, trans. Alfred J. Morrison, New York: Bergman Publishers, 1968, pp. 32–3.
[2] 'Omo,' quoted in James O. Breeden (ed.), *Advice among Masters: The Ideal in Slave Management in the Old South*, Westport, CT: Greenwood Press, 1980, p. 127.
[3] Quoted in Charles Joyner, *Down by the Riverside: A South Carolina Slave Community*, Urbana: University of Illinois Press, 1984, pp. 42–3.

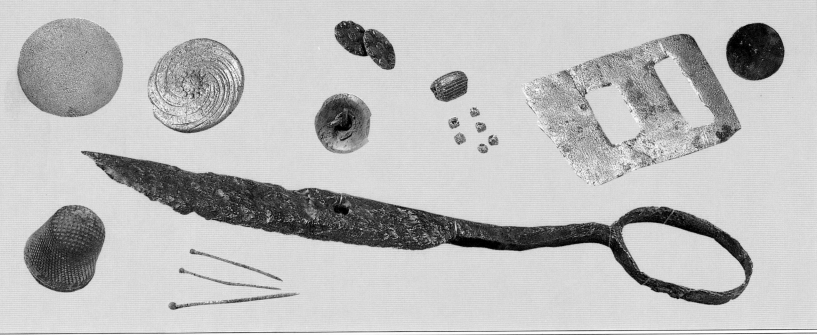

allowing slaves to set the pace of their labor and giving them a small measure of time to work independently for their own benefit. Tobacco planters, preoccupied with care of the broad-leafed weed – the tedious process of worming, topping, suckering, and priming through the summer until the mature plant was cut, stripped, cured, and packed in hogsheads in the winter – organized their slaves in yet another configuration. Tobacco slaves labored in closely supervised squads rather than gang-sized units.

The organization of tobacco, rice, and sugar production, as well as that of wheat and other small grains, had been established in the eighteenth century. But it did not remain unaltered in the new era. Planters throughout the South, alive to the spirit of agricultural reform, introduced new tools, experimented with new work regimens, and inaugurated new systems of management in an effort to squeeze more profit from their slaves' labor. Thus the plow supplanted the hoe in much of tobacco cultivation, steam-powered rice mills replaced the winnowing house and the mortar and pestle in hulling rice, and giant vacuum pans provided a vast new technology for processing sugar. Innovations in technology, organization, and work routine jolted slave workers in much the same way they transformed the lives of free workers during the nineteenth century. Although some of these innovations eased the slaves' burden, mostly they provided occasions for slaveholders to increase the pace and intensity of work, expand the number of hours slaves spent in the field, and enlarge the quotas slaves were expected to meet.

As planters placed new demands on already overburdened men and women, slaves searched for ways to reduce their obligations, to restore the old balance, and even to roll back new demands. The introduction of new technology, new methods, and new systems of supervision set in motion new conflicts between slave owners and slaves, keeping the plantation in perpetual turmoil. But no tool or method, no matter how revolutionary, had as powerful an effect on nineteenth-century slave life as the changes set in motion by the 'Cotton Revolution.'

The Cotton Revolution

Few mainland slaves grew cotton prior to American independence. But that changed dramatically in the last decade of the eighteenth century as the first stirring of the Industrial Revolution increased demand for the fiber. Along the Georgia and Carolina coast, planters quickly expanded production of long-staple cotton, whose smooth black seeds were easily separated by hand from its luxuriant, silky strands. But the long-staple variety grew well only in unique environs of the low country, and attempts to expand production of a short-staple variant were obstructed by the difficulty of removing the sticky green seeds. Once that obstacle was overcome by the invention of a mechanical

put by combining traditional crops with dairying and herding under the rubric of so-called mixed agriculture.

Each of the great staples had evolved a particular regimen, which both reflected and shaped the demography, economy, and society of the region in which it was grown. Around the Chesapeake, for example, slaves grew tobacco on independent satellite farms called 'quarters' that were organized around a single large estate. At the home quarter, resident planters presided over what observers characterized as small villages with the Big House nestled among artisan shops, barns, an icehouse, laundry, and occasionally even a small infirmary; buildings denominated, with a nice sense of the plantation's social order, as 'dependencies.' A tutor on Robert Carter's estate observed that the home plantation was 'like a town, but most of the Inhabitants are black.'[4] Rice, on the other hand, was produced on large unitary plantations carved out of the swamps of the South Carolina and Georgia lowlands. Production was directed by planters residing in Charleston, Savannah, or the lesser rice ports rather than on-site. Urban-based absentees governed through a long chain of command, at the base of which stood slave

Above: *Having worked hard all day until sunset, the field laborers would line up and carry back their day's load on their heads for weighing. Note the woman carrying a small child in her arms.*

foremen or 'drivers.' In southern Louisiana, sugar production presented yet another spatial and organizational schema. Estates encompassed both agricultural production and industrial process – the fields, where the cane was grown and the mill, where it was transformed into sugar and molasses. Farm and factory surrounded the Big House, whose owner also spent much time in a New Orleans or Natchez townhouse.

The diverse economic geography of plantation life reflected an equally diverse occupational structure, managerial hierarchy, and work regimen within the plantation. Although sugar was grown by large gangs of field hands supervised by white overseers, it required a small army of slave artisans to process the cane, pack the liquid and crystalline precipitates into hogsheads (which they constructed), and transport them by wagon and boat. Rice planters, operating from their urban command posts, eschewed gang labor and instead organized field work by the 'task,' thereby

'gin,' production soared as cotton cultivation spread quickly to the uplands and then across the southern interior.

During the first decade of the nineteenth century, the Cotton Revolution began in earnest. Halted briefly by Jeffersonian and Madisonian commercial policies, it gathered momentum in the prosperity that followed the War of 1812. Cotton production moved west into the interior of the South, sinking its deepest roots in the black belt.

The creation of the vast empire of cotton was the work of a generation of slaves, who cleared the land, broke the soil, 'chopped' the cotton, picked the tufts of fiber from the prickly bolls, separated the seeds from the fiber, packed the fiber into bales, and sent it off to Europe and the North where it fueled a revolution of still greater magnitude. In 1800, the South produced less than 100,000 bales of cotton; 60 years later, production stood at over 4 million bales – the vast majority grown by slaves. On the eve of the Civil War, some 3 million slaves, three-quarters of the southern slave population, were directly involved in the production of cotton.

Since cotton was grown almost everywhere in the lower South, and portions of the upper South as well, and since its cultivation occupied the vast majority of slaves, its special requirements and seasonal rhythms shaped the development of slave culture. Its most distinguishing characteristic was its utter simplicity of production and the general absence of special supporting crafts. Unlike sugar – whose production was as much industrial as agricultural – or even tobacco and rice, cotton required almost no refining beyond ginning. Once the seed was removed from the fiber,

cotton needed no special handling, and since, unlike sugar or tobacco, it was not perishable, it required no special packing in barrels or housing in specially designed barns or sheds. Squeezed mechanically into bales, cotton could sit under a tarpaulin on a plantation landing for months, even years, awaiting transit to some point of export.

The occupational structure of the cotton plantation thus displayed none of the diversity and complexity of estates devoted to tobacco, rice, or sugar. With the exception of a blacksmith or carpenter on a great plantation, virtually all slaves were field hands who did pretty much the same work. The slave coopers, wheelwrights, harness-makers, and tanners who serviced the plantation economy during the eighteenth century, and whose presence was so visible on the great sugar estates in the nineteenth century, were almost totally absent from the cotton plantation. Cotton planters sometimes promoted a particularly adept slave to the head of a gang with hopes that he or she would set a fast pace, or distinguished between those who plowed and those who hoed. But, in general, the uniformity of the processes associated with planting, cultivating, and harvesting cotton reduced the significance of such a division of labor to differences of age and sex. The movement from seaboard to the interior, from tobacco and rice to cotton, occasioned a sharp decline in the need for skilled slaves.

Moreover, since there was no special

Below: *An 1850's engraving of cotton being compacted into transportable bales at a large cotton press in Louisiana gives an idea of the numbers of workers needed in this simple industry.*

urgency in moving cotton to market, and since the lower South was a particularly well-watered region, with plantations often located by some river or bayou, the wagoners and the hostlers, along with blacksmiths, wheelwrights, harness-makers, and tanners who served them, were also much reduced in number. As boatmen and wagoners disappeared from the plantation roster, the number of slaves who regularly traversed the countryside – thereby gaining knowledge of the world beyond the plantation – also declined. Even those who traveled off the great estates had little opportunity to visit a seaport, and, amid the forest of masts and a farrago of strange tongues, the chance to rub elbows with blue-water sailors who knew directly of Africa and its place in the large Atlantic world. In many ways, nineteenth-century slaves were less cosmopolitan than their eighteenth-century forebears.

The growth of cotton culture also reduced the proportion of slaves, almost always men, in managerial positions. In the eighteenth century, urban-based rice planters relied upon drivers to mediate between themselves and their plantation slaves. In the Chesapeake, tobacco planters frequently placed trusted slaves in charge of individual quarters. Indeed, many quarters took the name of the slave foreman. While slave drivers and foremen continued to reign in the older plantation areas, they were rare in the cotton South where the white overseer became a plantation fixture. As cotton came to dominate southern agriculture, the proportion of slave men who could aspire to managerial positions declined.

The Cotton Revolution altered slave life in other ways as well. Slaveholding planters

seized control of rich soils of the black belt and the river basins, relegated yeoman farmers to the margins, and dominated the production of the staple. But cotton plantations rarely grew so large, or became so profitable, as to support the quasi-absenteeism of either rice or sugar production, where slave owners maintained an urban residence at least part of the year. Only a few cotton planters could afford to single out more than one or two adult slaves for special duties in the house. Indeed, most servants were children. Those few adults who worked in and around the Big House often labored in the field part of the time, and, if they did not, they had kinfolks and friends who did. The distance between house and field was small, physically and socially, in the cotton South, creating a fluidity of movement between the Big House and the quarter.

The few slave men and women who had a permanent place in the Big House – as cooks and carriage drivers, seamstresses and valets, housekeepers and gardeners – had scant opportunity to pass their special place in the plantation hierarchy to their children. Such a hereditary class had begun to emerge in the seaboard South during the late eighteenth century, as planters elaborated their great estates. The movement west had severed such lines of occupational descent, and the advent

Above: An unknown artist painted this chained and imploring slave. The slogan underneath is that of the Anti-Slavery Society. Slavery was abolished in Britain's colonies in 1833 and by the 1830s the movement was growing in the United States.

of cotton culture stymied their reformation. The absence of a hereditary retinue of house servants or a corps of body servants in the cotton South, like the absence of a large number of plantation-based tradesmen, promoted solidarity within the slave community, creating an intraplantation unity that was unique among the plantation slaves of the New World.

Plantation Social Order

With the resident planter as its beau ideal, life on the cotton plantation became increasingly insular during the nineteenth century. Cotton planters sealed the borders of their estates and claimed the right to regulate visitors to the quarter. They denounced marriages outside of the plantation and became chary about slaves traveling off the plantation for any reason. Such practices had been common in the eighteenth-century seaboard South and continued into the nineteenth century in the upper South, where the small size of agricultural units made visiting and interplantation marriages a neces-

sity. To curb the mobility of their slaves, some cotton planters constructed their labor force in a manner calculated to provide every marriageable hand a partner within the estate. A few even purchased slaves for this very reason. Planters were never entirely successful in closing their estates to the outside world, as patterns of sociability and the necessity of production continued to breach the barriers they created. Indeed, by any measure, the planters' aspiration to confine slaves to the limits of their plantation was a dismal failure. Nonetheless, plantation borders became less permeable in the nineteenth century than they were in the eighteenth.

Within the boundaries of the plantation, southerners, both black and white, came to identify themselves with the land, its singular beauty, and its ancient mysteries. Although the reality of southern life belied this image of ageless stability, slaveholding planters found much to like in this seeming timelessness. From it, they inferred an immutable relationship between subordinate and superior.

Planters understood this relationship in terms of the patriarchal ideal. Emphasizing that, like their wives and children, their slaves were fed and clothed out of the household larder, slaveholders celebrated their special responsibility for the workers they owned, whom they called 'family.' Planters draped themselves in the cloak of *paterfamilias* and consigned their slaves to an eternal childhood, often denominating them 'girls' and 'boys' until age transformed them into 'uncles' and 'aunts.' The slaveholders' assault fell particularly heavily on slave men. Equating manhood with control over an independent household, the masters of the great plantation contested the right to choose a wife and discipline children, thus consigning slave men to lesser roles within their own families.

The incorporation of slaves into what planters called their larger family, 'our family black and white,' enhanced the slaveholders' sense of responsibility for their slaves and encouraged slave owners to improve the material circumstances of plantation life. Slaves were generally better fed and housed in the nineteenth century than they had been in the seventeenth and eighteenth. However, along with these material improvements came a deepening intrusion into the most private portions of life in the quarter. Aspects of slave life which slaveholders had largely ignored during the eighteenth century, everything from child-rearing to religious practices, came under intense scrutiny during the nineteenth, as planters became increasingly self-conscious about their responsibilities. Still, like all ideologues, slaveholders violated their own principles when it suited their purposes. And, like all paternalists, slaveholders emphasized their people's responsibility to them, rather than their responsibility to their people. Indeed, the paternalist ideology provided slaveholders with a powerful justification of their systematic expropriation of the slaves' labor.

Recreating the Social Order

Slaves viewed relations with their owners from a different perspective. While subject to their owners' overwhelming power, slaves struggled to increase their independence in all areas of their lives, asserting that in all ways they were full human beings. They pressed for nothing more relentlessly than control over their own labor, the denial of which constituted the very essence of chattel slavery. Conceding what they could not alter or deny, slaves worked without direct compensation but claimed a right to a predictable portion of what they produced. Slaves expected their owners to feed, clothe, and house them in accordance with customary usage, but, whereas they welcomed the regular allotment of rations and played their part in the charade surrounding Christmas gifting, they did not rest satisfied with the dole.

Through a continuous process of contest and negotiation with slaveholders, often playing off the slaveholders' recognition of their humanity implicit in paternal ideology, slaves established the right to control a portion of their lives. They used these small grants of free time to cultivate gardens, hunt, and fish; raise poultry, pigs, and cattle; make baskets, weave cloth, and practice other handicrafts; hire themselves to neighboring farmers and arti-

Above: A slave family's domestic scene: the women clean the clothing while one man plays with a child; another looks on at the camera.

sans; and receive payments for overwork. Charles Ball, a Maryland slave sold South early in the nineteenth century, described himself as 'a kind of freeman on Sunday,' and he used his free time 'to provide himself and his family, with many of the necessaries of life that his master refused to supply.'[5] The property that slaves accumulated had no standing at law; but it gained recognition in practice, enabling slaves to accumulate small and generally perishable resources. The slaves' self-directed economic activities – what historians have called 'the slaves' economy' – and the owners' recognition of those activities, fostered a vision of an independent life and the institutional basis for the partial realization of that vision.

The Second Great Migration and the Cotton Revolution threatened to unravel the century-old customs that had been established through a process of hard bargaining and continuous struggle. Access to gardens and provision grounds, free Sundays and half-Saturdays, the right to visit friends, market produce, and keep small earnings from work done outside the owners' ken were all put at

risk by the creation of a new plantation order. Slaveholders used the new circumstance of life and labor in the interior and the isolation – and perhaps naiveté – of transplanted slaves to ratchet up labor demands. They increased time spent in the field, enlarging the stint or the task for which slaves were responsible; reduced the slaves' free time, cutting the number of holidays; denied the right to travel abroad; constricted the slaves' internal economy. Although the new circumstances of the interior sometimes created opportunities to limit the authority of the owner, generally it was the master who gained from starting anew. Indeed, many slaveholders transported their slaves west, precisely to undo the boundaries slaves had set and to begin plantation life anew. Customary practices, established in the years of hard bargaining, withered in the shadow of the Second Great Migration and dissolved in the heat of the Cotton Revolution.

The Slave Family

Against the slaveholders' assault, slaves drew upon their memory of the past and the array of powerful institutions they had created for their own benefit. The most important of these was the African-American family. Since the mid-eighteenth century, African and African-American slaves on mainland North America had been a self-reproducing population with births exceeding deaths. Mainland slave owners, who were often marginal to the larger Atlantic plantation system, grasped the possibility of a self-reproducing labor force and turned from the transatlantic slave trade to natural growth as a source of workers. By the late eighteenth century, the growth of an indigenous African-American slave population allowed mainland slaveholders to close the African trade or acquiesce to the constitutional mandate to end African importation.

Playing upon the slaveholders' dependence on the slaves' natural increase, slaves gained control of the reproductive processes. They secured the right to choose their marriage partners and control the birthing process, served by slave midwives or 'grannies.' Only rarely, and then in dire emergencies, did slaveholders and their agents usher slave infants into the world. Slaves challenged their owners' right to name their children, so that, while slaveholders might claim symbolic paternity for the entire plantation family, few children were named by or after their white owners, many being named after their black fathers.

The hallmark of the slave's domestic life was a nuclear family enmeshed in an all-encompassing network of kin relationships. Courting, and sexual activity, between young slave men and women began in their late teens. Sometimes these relations begot children, but, during the nineteenth century, southern slaves generally did not marry until their early twenties, when they settled down in long-term monogamous relationships that lasted until they were disrupted either by sale or death. Although women bore primary responsibility for child-care, the slave family was not a matriarchy, and men played an important and visible role in supporting their households, raising children, and, upon occasion, protecting wives and children from the overwhelming power of the master and his minions.

A web of distinctive customs and beliefs sustained those lifelong relations and separated the family life of African-American slaves from that of other southerners. For example, nineteenth-century slaves rarely married kin. Indeed, marriage between slaves as distantly connected as second cousins was so unusual as to suggest the existence of a powerful proscription that some scholars have traced back to Africa. Such endogamy distinguished slaves from their owners, who constantly intermarried among themselves. Indeed, cousin marriage was one of the distinguishing features of the domestic life of the planter class.

Plantation slaves also underpinned their family life with intricate patterns of cross-generational naming that kept alive the memory of ancestors separated by sale or death. Thus, for example, of the 17 slave men who fathered children on the Sterling plantation in Louisiana's sugar country, seven had sons named after them, and 10 had grandsons named after them. Such patterns of paternal naming also had African roots.[6]

WOMEN IN SLAVERY

Above: *This portrait of 'Mammy' Sally Brown, slave of a Virginia planter, was painted in 1825 by Robert Matthew Sully. Nurses could be very influential figures in white households; that this portrait exists at all reflects that.*

Slavery in the United States, though a destructive and inexcusably demeaning condition for both sexes, was uniquely different for women. Although the early demographic imbalance heavily favored males, several women were among the first 'Negars' arriving at Jamestown, Virginia in 1619. Most southern black women remained chattel from that time through the Civil War.

White men's oppressive controls over *all* women included black women, but racist presumptions combined with brutal laws and realities severely circumscribed the lives of female slaves. Because slavery denied their black spouses any authority, and because some African traditions did not repudiate female autonomy as did most European gender conventions, within the family, black women often were not as disempowered as were white women. And in contrast to most white women, slave women's 'husbands' did not define them. Black women, however, faced harsh punishment administered by whites just as often as did black men. They also sometimes experienced violence at the hands of enslaved men, reflecting the men's own frustrations. Although slavery attempted to emasculate black males, it certainly did not empower black females in their stead.

State laws officially denied enslaved blacks the right to marry, and plantation practices undermined the permanency of conjugal relationships. Nonetheless, many devoted, long-lasting 'marriages' did survive within the slave community. Also, female bonds of friendship and extended, intergenerational family networks were often as significant as conjugal unions. Ties between black women and their children were usually stronger than those between the sexes. Slave women, of course, knew that economics or a master's whim could separate them from their spouses, parents, friends, and even children.

Sexuality was a central reality for enslaved

women. Despite widespread antimiscegenation laws, white men essentially had free sexual access to them, and the enforced intimacy of the 'peculiar institution' often stimulated such liaisons. Torn from the familial and communal fabric of their lives in Africa, black women were subject to rape on slave ships, at auction, and on plantations. Pervasive beliefs among whites that all black people were inferior, bestial, and erotically motivated, and the characterizations of black women as sexually insatiable, were used to excuse white men's misconduct. The added risk of reprisals from the white men's jealous wives often resulted in dire consequences for enslaved women and their mulatto children. Because the condition of servitude in the United States always derived from the status of the mother, however, having a white father did not legitimize any potential claims of freedom.

Although black women had no acknowledged rights of refusal, and consent concerning carnal relations was essentially irrelevant, they often vigorously resisted sexual coercion, thus endangering themselves and their loved ones. They also talked back, snitched food, feigned illness, slowed down or deliberately botched their work. Running away, however, was much more prevalent among male than female slaves, who usually bore the primary responsibility for their offspring.

After federal law officially ended the importation of slaves early in the nineteenth century, black women became increasingly valued for their procreative capacities. Therefore, although slave marriages were never legally recognized, some masters encouraged marital relationships in the slave quarters, and black women became human incubators as well as workers. The more fertile a woman, the greater her value as a 'breeder' to the owner, for whom she might provide a continuing supply of future laborers.

Masters expected female slaves to work in the fields as long and as hard as did men. That often conflicted with family demands, and in many ways rearing black children became a communal responsibility. After a full day devoted to production, women still had household chores to complete, plus the charge of transmitting moral values and culture to another generation.

Slave women sometimes received work assignments which were different from men, and other jobs supplemented their field labor.

Below: *A painting by Christian Mayr of a servants' wedding (the couple are in white) celebrated in the kitchen of a resort hotel at White Sulphur Springs, Virginia, in 1838.*

Owners and overseers required black girls to run errands and perform chores by the time they reached five or six, and old age brought them little respite. Older women, however, became the plantations' spinners, weavers, and seamstresses. Some worked as cooks or nursemaids for white children, and as midwives who provided traditional healing skills for other slaves and sometimes even for whites. Only a minority of enslaved women were servants in the Big House. They occasionally received the household's cast-off clothes and kitchen scraps, had to juggle around-the-clock demands of white families with the needs of their own kin. Nonetheless, domestic work sometimes was judged less onerous than picking cotton or steering a plow. Some slaves believed that proximity to whites enhanced their status and they hoped that trust and intimacy might lead to special privileges and favors – possibly even to emancipation.

In the fields, laundries, and slave quarters, women learned to work cooperatively. Perhaps the most important things slave mothers could impart to their daughters in a society where race, class, and gender all tragically combined to try to establish their inferiority, were responsibilities to kin, the importance of community, and the skills necessary to survive.

Adele Logan Alexander

MUSIC

Music was one of the most useful and important forms of expression available to a people in bondage. It was ubiquitous in African-American life, providing opportunities for pleasure in a generally oppressive existence, and allowing expressions of both joy and pain.

As it had in Africa, music played an integral role in the life of the community. It was a means for education, an art, and a language of sacred expression. It regulated the work process, was an emotional release, and provided entertainment. Through music, African Americans communicated with each other in ways unintelligible to slave owners, controlled the pace of their work, and strengthened the bonds of sentiment and experience which united their communities.

As music shaped the rhythms of African-American life, black music helped shape the musical traditions of American society. African instruments, such as the banjo, recreated by slaves in America, became American instruments.

Black musicians, both slave and free, held places of honor in their society and were often sought out as performers at social gatherings for whites and for blacks. They created many of the musical forms, popularized syncopated rhythms, and pioneered techniques which came to be characteristic of American music.

The instruments seen here are all nineteenth-century pieces; from top to bottom, they are: a gourd fiddle and bow from a Maryland plantation, an African lyre from Zaire, and a Congo stringed instrument.

Although known to their owners by only a single name, most slaves in fact had surnames or, as they called them, 'titles,' which they maintained clandestinely. Titles stretched back to Africa upon occasion but, more commonly, slaves reached for the most distant genealogical marker, perhaps the name of the first owner that could be identified. Slave surnames, although derived from the owning class, distinguished the slaves who adopted them from their present owner and established a separate lineage, heritage, and identity that contradicted masters' claims to a 'family, black and white.' 'My daddy,' recalled a former slave, 'was Aleck Trowell. After freedom he was called by his own name, Aleck Gillison . . . My father was sold from a Gillison, first off.'[7]

Slaves nurtured these generational connections in violation of laws that denied their existence and legitimated the power of their owners. Drawing on their small accumulations of property, slaves covertly developed their own system of inheritance, whereby one generation of slaves gave the next 'a start.' Inheritance practices differed from place to place, but they became more deeply entrenched as slaves elaborated their internal economies.

Although the property that slaves passed from generation to generation was often nothing more than a few sticks of furniture, some cookware and tools or a few barnyard animals, generational exchanges had deep emotive and psychological meaning. And they were not without material significance: they helped to maintain customary practices in the face of the slaveholders' continual reformulation of the plantation regimen. In practical ways, the slaves' system of inheritance both helped knit slaves together across generational lines and provided the material basis for a modicum of independence. It directly contested the masters' paternal claims based upon control over the household. A pig gifted to a newly established slave family not only enriched the couple's diet but also represented a degree of independence from the owner's dole. While the slaveholders' contribution to the slaves' competency was essential and recognized as such, it was the small product of the slaves' own economy – garden produce, the provision-ground crops, handicraft items, overwork payments, and the largess of hunting and fishing expeditions – which slaves viewed as the source of what independence they could wrestle from their owners.

Slave Religion

No less important than the family was the slaves' religion. Whereas the dense network of kin that stood at the core of the slave community in the nineteenth century had evolved along lines established in the seventeenth and eighteenth centuries, the religion of the quarter emerged from a new set of circumstances. Prior to American independence, most slaves knew little of Christianity, and most slave-

holders were indifferent – and frequently antagonistic – to their slaves imbibing the teaching of Jesus. Despite the heroic efforts of the Society for the Propagation of the Gospel in the Foreign Parts and other missionary organizations, few slaves converted, and most of them remained unchurched. Indeed, a powerful strain of African Christianity, derived from the sixteenth-century conversion of the Kongo's royal house, seems to have disappeared by the nineteenth century, as had a variety of Islamic practices.

A series of evangelical awakenings that accompanied the American Revolution and continued into the nineteenth century changed

Below: *One of the best known works of the black artist Henry Ossawa Turner is 'The Banjo Lesson' which depicts an elderly man instructing a young child on how to play the instrument.*

that radically. To the evangelicals, nothing more fully validated the power of God's grace than the conversion of the lowly slave. Indeed, evangelical Christians not only welcomed slaves into the fold as brothers and sisters in Christ, but also openly criticized slavery and, on occasion, accepted the leadership of black preachers and ministers.

The egalitarianism of the evangelical revivals waned in the late eighteenth century and had been all but extinguished among slaveholders by the first decade of the nineteenth century. However, the determination of many slaveholders to convert their slaves grew, not so much as Christian egalitarians seeking a oneness in Christ, but as Christian stewards bringing their God to heathens and as slaveholding paternalists bringing their civilization to savages. That the promise of a better life in the afterworld might make for

greater subordination in the slave quarter only made the new missionary spirit more compelling, at least to some members of the slave-owning class. Drawing upon the Pauline dictum that slaves should obey their masters, slaveholders built plantation chapels, invited itinerants to preach to their slaves, and, taking up the paternalist role directly, led their slaves in prayer.

For their part, slaves were increasingly receptive to the possibility of joining their owner's church. For some, it meant the surety of a day away from the fields or a chance to win the slave owner's confidence. But it also was an opportunity to practice a religion which, by the story of Moses, promised liberation from earthly bondage and, by the story of Jesus, promised eternal redemption and divine justice.

During the nineteenth century, tens of thousands of slaves converted to Christianity, and many thousands more were born into a faith their eighteenth-century forebears knew not or had consciously rejected. In its polity, the slaves' new religion did not differ markedly from that of their owners. Seated in the back rows and balconies, most slaves subscribed to Baptist, Methodist, or Presbyterian denominations. A few were Episcopalians and Lutherans, and slave Catholics abounded in Louisiana and parts of Maryland and Florida.

But if they shared church buildings, polity, and a variety of religious rituals with their

Above: This 1860 painting by John Antrobus shows the significance of the funeral ritual within the plantation slave community. The preacher is conducting the religious service which is also a communal event, excluded are the overseer (left, with horse) and the white owners (right).

owners, the belief and practice of African-American Christianity stood apart. African-American Christianity did not grow in virgin soil. Slaves incorporated Christianity into the diverse African religious practices, some of them polytheistic, some of them Islamic, and some of them Christian, that had evolved during the first 200 years of American captivity into a religion that was itself a syncretic amalgam. The creation of this Christianity was as much the creation of a new faith as the expansion of the white man's religion.

Slave owners had dished out Christianity in carefully measured portions, but slaves were equally selective in what they accepted and how they incorporated it into an existing cosmology. Patience and obedience may have loomed large in the slaveholders' message, but slaves found other themes more to their liking. Theologically, slaves had little truck with the doctrines of Paul and, instead, maintained the egalitarianism of the eighteenth-century revivals, emphasizing the basic unity of mankind and the irrelevance of earthly status for immortality. They identified particularly with the people of the Old Testament and their

heroic exodus from bondage. The message of the fundamental equality of all in the eyes of God and, when the master was out of range, in the eyes of man, remained a central tenet of African-American Christianity long after it ceased to echo in the slaveholder's church. But the theology of the black church did more than affirm the slaves' humanity, worth as a person, and life itself. The black church provided surety that the Day of Judgment – 'settling-up time' – would include a rebalancing of the scales. The wicked would be punished.

So, too, with the matter of salvation, a flexible metaphor that offered both earthly liberation and otherworldly redemption. Slave preachers wielded the promise of salvation skillfully so that, depending on the inclination of the listener, the message could be understood as either deeply conservative of the slave regime or utterly subversive of it. 'Free At Last' could speak both to the release from earthly tribulations and the release from chattel bondage. How the message was received by the congregants was left to the antiphonal repartee of preacher and his flock. It was communicated by gesture and emphasis, long-winded Biblical exegeses and significant silences, so that onlookers, particularly the masters, found it all but inaccessible.

African-American Christianity as it evolved in the nineteenth century thus had many parts, and slaves made use of all of them. Although Christian slaves drew strength from those elements which distinguished their religion from that of their owners, they often found it useful to underline the similarities. Just as slaveholders employed the Bible to bend slaves to their will, slaves did the same, holding their owners accountable to the ethical standards embedded in the Ten Commandments and the Sermon on the Mount.

Over time, the distinctive theology and practices embodied in African-American Christianity gained an institutional independence. As the white congregations outgrew their churches and moved to larger, more sumptuous quarters, black members took possession of the old buildings which they promptly renamed the 'African' church. Sometimes these edifices arrived as a gift worthy of the paternalists who donated them. More often, slaves purchased their churches with their own small accumulations earned from the produce of their gardens, provisions grounds, hunting expeditions, and overwork. Although slaves held no legal title to the buildings, there was no doubt that these were their churches. And, although they remained under the nominal supervision of the ministers or deacons of the white congregations, in practice black preachers and lay leaders exercised considerable control.

As they did, the African-American origins of the slaves' religion boldly asserted itself. The Old Testament mixed with the inheritance of Africa strained through the experience of the eighteenth-century evangelical awakenings. The antiphonal call-and-response that had connected African chieftains with their people in the Old World joined African-American preachers with theirs in the New. By its style alone, slaveholders sensed the differences between their own sedate worship and the religion of the quarter. Much of it had to do with sound – the groaning, gesticulating, stomping, and clapping that emanated from the black church (although similar sounds could also be heard in churches of white nonslaveholders). Slaves incorporated music and dance into their religion, mixing the sacred and the secular. The raw passions that accompanied conver-

sion and the dancing and singing that attended prayer scandalized the missionaries who claimed they had brought Christianity to the slaves. But the ecstasy of conversion, the staccato movements of the juba, and the rhythmic combinations that linked field shouts and sacred chants into solemn spirituals were as much a part of African-American Christianity as the Lord's Prayer.

There were other differences as well. Slave preachers mixed folk beliefs with their Christianity. Although slaveholders denounced conjuring as relics of African barbarism and worked to eliminate it, magic and conjuring had a powerful hold on plantation slaves who were certain it provided protection from the harshest and most arbitrary aspects of slavery, as well as the means of settling scores among themselves. Witchcraft and sorcery were less evident in the African churches of the urban South, pointing to the diverse evolution of African-American experience in the city and the countryside. While it was easy to distinguish African-American Christianity from the European-American variant, the differences between the services in the Old Brick Church on Edisto Island, South Carolina, and the First African Baptist Church in Richmond could be as profound as any distinctions between white and black religion.

African-American Christianity also supported the slaves' desire for independence by providing recognized avenues for ambitious slaves to realize their aspirations. Slave preachers and deacons became significant figures on the plantation and the larger community, often leading the service within the plantation chapel and organizing yet more independent meetings in brush arbors. The church became a particularly important path of social advancement to men and women who were cut off from the possibilities even the most disadvantaged of free people were

allowed. This was particularly true, as the Cotton Revolution constricted opportunities for slave men to rise into managerial and artisan positions within the plantation hierarchy and for slave women to take a permanent place in the Big House. The absence of a large corps of black foremen and drivers, artisans and tradesmen, and a distinct class of house servants threw the weight of African-American leadership to the African church. It elevated the black preacher into an unrivaled position of leadership in the plantation South.

The domestic and spiritual life of African-American slaves thus provides a model for the conflicting and contradictory evolution of the relationship between European-American slaveholders and African-American slaves. Slaves found shards of independence in the very same domestic and religious institutions that slave owners saw as evidence of the slaves' acquiescence to their rule and acceptance of the superiority of their 'white' culture. Indeed, what slaveholders often took as confirmation of their domination often became a source of self-assertion for slaves and the basis of opposition to the master's hegemony. What was true of family and church was equally true of art, architecture, cuisine, dance, language, and technology. The fullness of both African- and European-American culture was connected in ways which belied the shifting balance of power between master and slave.

By the way they worked, in the families they created, and in the churches where they worshiped, nineteenth-century slaves remade their lives to conform to the changes that accompanied the Second Great Migration, the Cotton Revolution, and the advent of African-American Christianity. Together, these changes set the stage for the transit to freedom when, some 60 years after the last northern state legislated emancipation, civil war again divided white Americans and again gave slaves the opportunity to seize their freedom.

Below: *The Sabbath might be one of the few times when slaves got a whole day to themselves. They would attend services and see to their domestic chores as well as play, sing, dance, and socialize.*

Notes

[1] I would like to thank Steven F. Miller and Sarah Russell of the University of Maryland for helpful suggestions.
[2] Although the 'Second Great Migration' has sometimes been used to describe the northward movement of black people that accompanied World War I, it is more appropriate to describe the forced march from the seaboard to the interior of the South that came directly after the close of the Atlantic trade.
[3] Hawkins Wilson to Sister Jane, enclosed in H. Wilson to Chief of the Freedmen's Bureau, at Richmond, 11 May 1867, Letters Received, ser. 3892, Bowling Green, VA Asst. Superintendent, Bureau of Refugees, Freedmen, and Abandoned Lands, RG 105, National Archives.
[4] Quoted in Edmund S. Morgan, *Virginians at Home: Family Life in the Eighteenth Century*, Charlottesville, VA: 1963, p. 53.
[5] Charles Ball, *Fifty Years in Chains*, NY: 1970 [1837], pp. 187, 273.
[6] Herbert G. Gutman, *The Black Family in Slavery and Freedom, 1750–1925*, NY: Pantheon, 1976, Chapter 5, and especially pp. 188–90.
[7] Quoted in Gutman, *Black Family*, p. 249. Italics added.

Chapter 4

A LIMITED FREEDOM

Slavery defined the lives of all black people in the decades before the Civil War, even those who were nominally free. As slavery was abolished in the northern states, social customs, black codes, state constitutional provisions and other exclusionary measures kept African Americans' rights limited and their citizenship in doubt until the Supreme Court negatively settled the question, temporarily at least, in the late 1850s. In the South, freedom and blackness were supposed to be nearly mutually exclusive, and free blacks faced racial restrictions often little different from those placed on slaves. Despite the limitations, free African Americans formed complex communities and organizations which profoundly affected the politics of the period, leading the way in social reform activism. Culturally, they adapted their African heritage and the cultural forms they developed in slavery to their circumscribed freedom, continuing to add variations to American culture. They were some of the most outspoken advocates of liberty and equality, and their demands for equal treatment placed them among the most tenacious advocates of liberal democracy in America.

Freedom for some, did not mean the elimination of prejudice. Most African Americans had a marginal role in white society, or were valued for their services. This watercolor from 1820 by John Lewis Krimmel is typical in that it shows a barroom dancing scene with the white people at leisure and enjoying the musical entertainment provided by the lone black fiddler.

LESLIE M. HARRIS

SOON AFTER THE CLOSE of the War of 1812, it became clear that attempts by blacks to achieve full citizenship during and after the Revolutionary War had not succeeded. The formation of the American Colonization Society in 1816, with its goal of removing blacks from the United States, as well as the wave of legal restrictions imposed on free blacks North and South in the 1820s, struck a blow to those who had hoped that northern emancipation and black participation in the Revolutionary War and the War of 1812 would convince the nation that blacks were worthy of political and social equality.

Urban Freedom

Despite the fact that economic and political opportunities were being closed off for many throughout the 1800s, free blacks were active participants in American cultural, social, political, and economic life. They created organizations and institutions which provided the basis for a vibrant political activism against slavery and for black equality. Although the majority of free blacks lived in rural areas, urban centers provided the greatest opportunities for the development of the free black community. By 1830, Baltimore held the largest free black community in the South and the nation, with 14,790 free blacks. New Orleans held the second-largest free black community in the South at 11,562. The cities of Philadelphia and New York held the largest concentrations of free blacks in the North, at 9,795 and 13,960, respectively.

In urban areas, freedom often meant that black men, women, and children all sought wage work to support families. Free black men in the South found a broader range of labor open to them than those in the North, where native white and immigrant workers kept blacks from skilled jobs. In New York City, only 12.5 percent of black men were engaged in skilled trades such as carpentering and painting. But in Richmond, Virginia, 32 percent and in Charleston, South Carolina, 76 percent of black men were skilled workers. In urban areas, many black men were unskilled laborers on the docks of port cities; in personal-service occupations such as domestic servants or waiters; or they worked as street cleaners, porters, or ragmen. A disproportionate number of black men were mariners in coastal areas and on inland waterways from Rhode Island to Louisiana. Black men worked on cargo boats on the Mississippi and on whalers from New England. Black sailors spent months or even years on transatlantic voyages to Europe, Africa, or the West Indies. They were relatively well paid, and gained greater respect at sea than they and their working-class counterparts did on land. However, months away from home could wreak havoc on family relations. Black sailors stayed at sea longer than white sailors, and were generally older and married. Wives and children could only partly depend on wages from a husband or father who was away at sea for months at a time.

A lack of steady work for black men meant that women and children in the family also worked. Black women worked as maids or cooks in hotels and boardinghouses; took in laundry; peddled food in urban markets; or scavenged trash piles, searching for discarded clothing and other items that might be used or sold for a meager profit. Black women, particularly in the North, might also work in dancehalls or as prostitutes. A lucky few in northern cities worked as seamstresses or in factories, where the work was more reliable and better paid, but such jobs were usually reserved for single white women.

Black children obtained jobs as soon as they were old enough, perhaps running errands at the same hotels or boardinghouses where their parents worked, assisting in the preparation of food to be peddled, or helping to scavenge. Black boys aged four to eight were also apprenticed, and sometimes bound out by desperate parents, to black and white chimney sweeps, who used the children to crawl down chimneys and scrub off the accumulations of

Right: *Forlorn looking chimney sweeps in Charleston just before the Civil War – dangerous work for young urban apprentices.*

soot. This dangerous work often resulted in cancer, lung problems, and broken or misshapen bones among young children.

Black Businesses

A small proportion of African-American men and women owned their own businesses. Black men in the North and South achieved middle-class status as barbers, restaurateurs, tailors, shoemakers, and the like, whereas black women owned restaurants, boardinghouses, and dressmaking establishments. Mulattoes in the lower South tended to be overrepresented at the higher end of the national black income and occupational structure. As descendants of their white owners, some were given opportunities – not available to the average slave – to learn skills which enabled them to hire themselves out and earn their own money. Masters who manumitted such slaves might also provide education, capital, land, or tools, with which a free black might support himself or establish business enterprises.

Through a combination of connections to the white community and hard work, a few free African Americans, mostly mulattoes, became a wealthy elite. Their property holdings and businesses rivaled white fortunes, even if they were unable to parlay their financial success into full political and social equality. Robert Purvis was born in South Carolina in 1810, the son of a white cotton broker and a mulatto woman. The family moved to Philadelphia when Purvis was nine. When his father died in 1826, Purvis was left a wealthy young man. He completed his education at Amherst College in Massachu-

setts, and traveled in Europe before returning to Philadelphia. His and his children's experiences with racism led him to become part of the struggle against slavery and for black equal rights.

In the North, blacks without connections like Purvis's managed to obtain education through liberal colleges and seminaries, or to save enough money to open their own businesses. As a result, a politically active elite composed of ministers, teachers, and businessmen grew in the 1820s and 1830s. Northern religious leaders – like New York's Samuel Cornish, founder of the Colored Presbyterian Church; Philadelphia's Richard Allen, founder of the African Methodist Episcopal Church;

Above: 'Three Sisters of the Coplan Family' by W. M. Prior in 1854. The three are Eliza, Nellie, and Margaret, daughters of a wealthy black businessman in Boston. Their dress and demeanor reflect their middle-class status.

and Boston's Thomas Paul, founder of the African Baptist Church – joined businessmen like Thomas Downing, owner of a famous New York oyster bar, and Philadelphia's black sailmaker James Forten, in creating political and social organizations. Their wives and daughters, such as Charlotte and Sarah Forten, were teachers or headed women's auxiliaries to the men's organizations. These men and women formed the leadership base of black movements for the abolition of slavery and for equal rights.

Wealthy black and mulatto men and women in the deep South were less likely to become abolitionists or advocates for black equal rights. Many sought to preserve their own freedom by separating themselves politically and socially from the struggles of poorer free blacks and slaves. A few even owned slaves themselves. The Ellison family of rural South Carolina was one of a small number of black families in the South whose fortunes were built on slave labor. The slave April Ellison purchased his freedom in 1816. Changing his name to William, he continued the work he had learned as a slave, making customized cotton gins for planters in the rural areas of South Carolina and beyond. By 1860, he owned over 100 slaves on a plantation in Sumter District, South Carolina. Ellison's reputation and wealth softened the hard edges of racial prejudice for his family. Both of his daughters married white men.

Most free black slave owners in the South owned only one or two slaves, who assisted

Below: This scene shows New York's notorious Five Points district, one of the poorest in the city and home to many African Americans and Irish. Although poverty and crime were rife, the northern cities also provided opportunities.

them on their farms or in their businesses as hoteliers, barbers, or blacksmiths. Further, the vast majority of black slaveholders were so only in the legal sense, 'owning' spouses and children in order to keep families together in states which required freed slaves to be removed from within their borders. But the most affluent African-American slaveholders identified closely with influential white patrons. Feeling little racial responsibility, many of these slave-owning blacks treated their slave property no better than did slave-owning whites. William Ellison was known not only for his wealth, but also for the frequency with which his slaves ran away from his strict rule.

Generally, relations between free blacks and whites, North and South, were mixed, at best. Racism was endemic. In the North, white workers, fearing low-wage competition from blacks, kept most of them from skilled employment. In most states, free blacks were denied the right to vote, to sit on juries, or to testify against whites in court. Public schools were segregated or nonexistent for blacks. In some midwestern states, free blacks were prevented from settlement. In southern cities, the civil rights of free blacks were restricted increasingly during the antebellum period, and their employment opportunities suffered. In the 1830s, Frederick Douglass observed that white workers in Baltimore 'began to feel it degrading' to work with blacks in the shipbuilding industry. Such feelings often escalated to physical violence against black workers, with the result that, by the Civil War, blacks North and South were forced out of many occupations they had dominated or shared with whites.[1]

There were exceptions. Blacks and whites sometimes shared the same neighborhoods, socialized together, and even married. Black and white workers who lived in the same buildings or blocks might go to grogshops or dance halls together after work. In New Orleans, a newspaper editor lamented the aid given by white men to female runaway slaves: 'Almost every day it is noted on the police records, that May, Jean, Jenette, Lucy, Susan, or some other refugee from service is caught in the premises of Mr. so and so, and that Mr. so and so has been arrested for harboring and concealing her.'[2] But blacks most often turned to each other for economic and political assistance and social life.

Black Self-help Groups

Urban self-help networks and community organizations helped free blacks withstand white aggression and enabled black migrants to support themselves and their families as they adjusted to city life. Extended family and neighbors took care of younger children when both parents worked outside the home. When death befell one or both parents, family and neighbors often informally adopted the orphans. Blacks also created more formal methods of dealing with economic uncer-

tainty. One of the first actions of free blacks in urban areas was the formation of mutual-relief organizations. Soon after the passage of the 1799 Gradual Emancipation Act in New York, black men formed the New York African Society for Mutual Relief. In Philadelphia, black women formed the Daughters of Africa. These organizations, predecessors of today's workers' compensation or insurance funds, addressed a multitude of needs. Black workers in these sex-segregated organizations paid monthly dues of several cents, which funded their work of providing for widows, orphans, and general poverty relief. The membership of relatively affluent blacks in some of these groups reflected both the economic fragility of the black middle class, and the desire of black ministers, teachers, and businessmen to encourage morality among blacks. Membership in the New York African Society for Mutual Relief might be terminated for a member who was jailed. Members of Boston's African Society could be removed for drunkenness. Other organizations, such as the Benevolent Daughters of Zion in New York, or the Sons of Africa in Philadelphia, were composed primarily of poorer workers, for whom membership might forestall a stay in the municipal almshouse. By 1830, there were several hundred such organizations in urban centers North and South.

Other black organizations reflected regional, social, and political differences. In Boston, Prince Hall's Negro Masonic Order addressed economic and political issues which affected all blacks. In contrast, southern black organizations such as the Brown Fellowship Society of Charleston tended to be exclusionary. The Browns limited their membership to 50 lighter-skinned 'free brown men' and their descendants. Their color elitism was challenged by the formation of the Society of Free Dark Men. However, both the Browns and the

Above: *The owner of this Richmond barbershop was a free black who occupied one of the most typical niches in the skilled labor market. With shoemaking and building, barbering accounted for 80 percent of the city's skilled, black labor.*

Free Dark Men drew their membership from middle- and upper-middle-class black men.

The Black Church

The founding of separate black churches provided a place where class and color divisions among blacks might be muted or forgotten. Such potential was lost in the South, however, where independent black churches became the target of whites, who saw them as the instigators of unrest among slaves. In Charleston, Morris Brown attempted to bridge class lines and boundaries between slaves and free blacks through the establishment of a branch of the African Methodist Episcopal Church in 1817. A man of property, Brown was popular with slaves and poorer free blacks as well as with members of the black elite. However, the church was destroyed and Brown was expelled from the state in the wake of the Denmark Vesey affair of 1822 (see page 66). Such was the fate of many independent black churches founded in the South during this period, leaving religious blacks to worship in the segregated pews of white churches.

In the North, however, the black church became the center of black political leadership. Richard Allen, Samuel Cornish, and Thomas Paul, and their clerical descendants, used their churches as bases for activism throughout the antebellum period. Such churches also built Sunday schools that were among the earliest educational facilities for blacks. Because northern blacks were excluded from most public schools, Quakers and educated blacks built independent black day and evening schools. The existence of day, evening, and

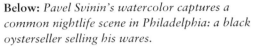

Left and right: John and Mary Jones were free blacks who moved to Chicago and became wealthy with a tailoring business. He campaigned successfully to abolish the Illinois Black Laws.

Free black workers helped shape urban culture through work songs derived from their African roots and their experiences in America. Dockworkers and boatmen often sang as they worked. In New York, sweep cleaners called rhythmically 'Sweep o-o-o-o' during the early morning hours. In the early evenings 'tubmen,' workers responsible for cleaning out the city's privies, sang bawdy songs to cheer them through the malodorous work. In the markets of Norfolk, Virginia, and other cities, vendors hawked their wares: 'Here's yer nice vegables – green corn, butter beans, taters, Irish taters, new jess bin digged; come an' get 'em while dey is fresh.'[4]

Below: Pavel Svinin's watercolor captures a common nightlife scene in Philadelphia: a black oysterseller selling his wares.

Sunday schools, and blacks' interest in education, meant that northern blacks often had surprisingly high literacy rates.

Street Life, North and South

Sometimes at odds with the formation of churches was the growth of a street and night life among urban blacks. From Providence to New Orleans, free blacks transformed cultural traditions developed under rural slavery and transferred them to urban dance halls, theaters, grogshops, oyster cellars, and brothels. Northern free blacks continued the ceremonies of Pinkster and Election Day that some had celebrated under slavery, and added parades and other street activities. Often excluded by whites from Fourth of July parades and other civic festivities, blacks celebrated their own holidays, such as Haitian Revolution Day and British Emancipation Day. Black Masons in Philadelphia and Boston celebrated the anniversaries of the founding of their organizations with elaborate processions through the streets of their cities. In 1825, the Wilberforce Society in New York City paraded in celebration of the law promising full emancipation in the state by 1827. In these parades, blacks rode on horseback and wore military uniforms, or carried large banners as they marched in procession, 'with a slow, majestic pace, as if the universe were looking on.' Middle-class whites often caricatured such processions in magazines, while working-class whites jeered or attacked them in the streets. Recalling the decision to brave such derision and worse, John J. Zuille, historian of the New York African Society for Mutual Relief, wrote that the society's members paraded 'though death stare[d] us in the face.' Such parades were an important confirmation of the black presence in the cities in the years immediately following northern emancipation.[3]

Social Life

Blacks also created places of amusement for themselves and for whites willing to share in their culture. In grogshops and dance halls, North and South, they danced to fiddle, banjo, and bones; drank rum; and ate oysters. In such places, prostitutes might loiter as they waited for customers, and frequent fights broke out between those who had imbibed too heavily. For black entrepreneurs, such spaces were a mixture of commercial enterprise and lawlessness in a society which limited the range of occupations to which blacks might aspire.

Blacks also ran more respectable establishments. In 1821, Allan Royce opened the African Grove Theater in New York City, America's first black theater. Performances ranged from ballet, opera, and Shakespearean drama to elaborate musical productions. The African Grove Theater was home to black dramatist Henry Brown's African Company, which in 1823 performed the first play by a black writer, Brown's *The Drama of King Shotaway*, based on a slave insurrection on the Island of St. Vincent in the West Indies. The African Grove was also the first school for a number of black actors who achieved international fame during the antebellum period, including the most famous antebellum black actor Ira Aldridge, internationally renowned for his interpretation of Othello.[5]

Concomitant with this flowering of black arts, however, was the growth of minstrelsy. By observing black dance halls and work songs, white performers learned the songs and dances that they caricatured in blackface minstrel shows beginning in the 1830s. Minstrel shows allowed whites to admire the skill of black music and dance without acknowledging blacks' claims to equality. White minstrels removed black performers from the stage and excluded them from creative control and profits. The early success of Royce's African Grove Theater ended in 1829 when New York City officials closed it because of the danger of 'civil discord.'[6]

Middle-class and elite blacks did not always support black cultural forms. Increasingly in the 1820s and 1830s, they disapproved of the dance halls, colorful clothing, loud music, and theater favored by poorer blacks. Concerned with the effects of such behavior on their efforts to obtain economic, political, and social equality, northern middle-class blacks urged black laborers towards a quieter urban demeanor throughout the antebellum period. Despite middle-class threats of withdrawal of patronage and education, however, the mass of blacks continued to express themselves publicly, viewing freedom of expression as part of the struggle for equal rights.

In the South, lack of approval for black street life was less politically or religiously motivated. In Natchez, Mississippi, the wealthy black barber, landowner, and slave owner, William Johnson, stopped attending the theater after a near-riot occurred in the segregated black balcony. Johnson and other wealthy blacks were disdainful of and embarrassed by the social and cultural life of poorer urban free blacks, who socialized with slaves and poor whites. Wealthier southern free blacks often attempted to differentiate themselves from poorer blacks in order to maintain their own social position.

For southern whites, urban life among free blacks during the 1820s raised fears of slave insurrections. Such fears were confirmed in an 1822 incident in Charleston, South Carolina, in which Denmark Vesey, a free black carpenter, was accused of plotting a slave rebellion involving 126 slaves and free blacks. During the trial, the role of free blacks as agitators was fully drawn out: 'Vesey being a free man encountered none of those obstacles which would have been in the way of a slave . . . [He had] . . . qualifications and advantages absolutely necessary for the Chief in a Conspiracy.' Vesey encouraged dissension among blacks: 'if his [black] companion bowed to a white person he would rebuke him, and observe that all men were born equal.'[7]

Following the conviction of Vesey and his alleged co-conspirators, restrictions on free blacks in Charleston and throughout the

Above: *William Wilberforce was a leading figure in the British abolitionist movement and he was honored in the United States in 1856 by having a black university named after him in Ohio.*

South greatly increased. The African Methodist Episcopal Church in Charleston was destroyed and its founder, Morris Brown, expelled from the state. South Carolina strictly enforced its Black Seamen's Acts, prohibiting black sailors from disembarking while their ships were in port. Black codes were adopted in other southern cities.

Colonization and the ACS

Some whites sought a more permanent solution to the problem of free blacks. In 1816, Charles Mercer, a Federalist legislator from Virginia, suggested that the Federal government fund the colonization of blacks in West Africa. Although unsuccessful, his suggestion attracted the support of Robert Finley, a New Jersey clergyman. The two formed the American Colonization Society (ACS) in Washington, DC. The organization, which attracted influential men like Andrew Jackson, Henry Clay, and Francis Scott Key, lobbied Congress to appropriate funds for black colonization. It also funded missionaries and established the settlement of Liberia. Although its plan of federal funding for large-scale colonization was never implemented, the ACS, through its newspaper, the *African Repository*, and through campaigns North and South, became an important voice for the belief that blacks could never achieve equality in the United States. Its position was a mixture of genuine concern for blacks in light of what it saw as unchangeable white racist attitudes and an underlying belief in black inferiority. The ACS encouraged southern states to emancipate their slaves through gradual manumission, and to send the freed slaves to Liberia. Free blacks were urged to obtain a Christian education and emigrate to Africa as missionaries. They would civilize and Christianize Africa and increase their own opportunities, while America would avoid a racial revolution as had occurred in Haiti.

Such arguments initially appealed to a wide spectrum of Americans. Southern slaveholders who were uncomfortable with the idea of slavery, but unwilling to increase the free black population, saw colonization as a solution to their dilemma. Quakers and others who had led the northern emancipation movement, dismayed by the increasing restrictions on free blacks' civil and political rights and by continued black poverty, pledged their support. Among free blacks, support for colonization was strongest in Massachusetts and Rhode Island – where the black communities were among the smallest in the nation – and among African-born blacks. As early as 1780, blacks in Newport, Rhode Island, had formed the Free African Union Society to encourage emigration to Africa. In Massachusetts, black sea captain Paul Cuffe became the most well-known supporter of African colonization. When the American Colonization Society brought greater resources and popularity to the idea after the War of 1812, many blacks in Newport, Providence, and Boston responded enthusiastically. In 1815, Cuffe transported a number of black families to the British West African colony of Sierra Leone.

Black supporters of colonization were disillusioned by the failure to eradicate southern slavery and viewed with increasing alarm the reluctance of whites to maintain or extend political and social equality. Black Philadelphians James Forten, the wealthy sailmaker, and Richard Allen, founder of the African Methodist Episcopal Church; New Yorker John Russwurm, the second black college graduate in the United States and co-founder of the first black newspaper, *Freedom's Journal*; and George Creighton, the wealthy black barber and slave owner of Charleston, all initially supported colonization. Russwurm left New York for Liberia in 1829, never to return to the United States. Creighton sold his business and offered to emancipate any of his slaves who would join him in Liberia.

But the vast majority of blacks opposed

Above: *With percussion instruments for blacks sometimes banned by slave owners, they had developed many other forms of beating out rhythms; one of them was the bones as shown here in this 1856 oil painting 'The Bone Player' by William Sidney Mount.*

Below: *The* Amistad *incident in 1839 – when slaves mutinied on a Spanish ship off the coast of Long Island and were then captured and imprisoned in the United States – was taken up by American abolitionists who used the case to illustrate the evils of slavery.*

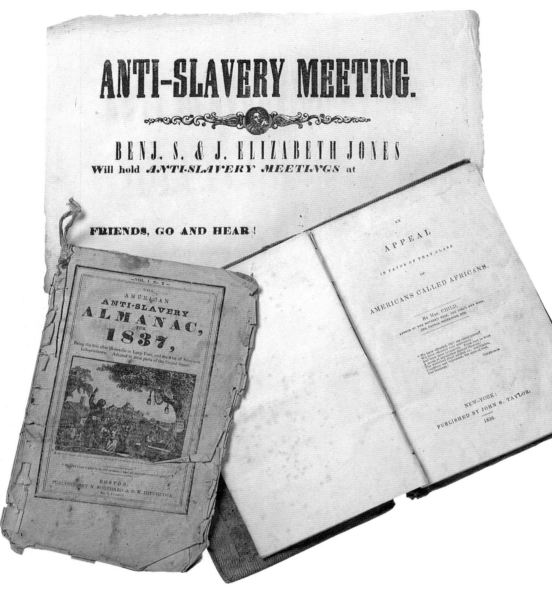

Left: *The abolitionist movement was prolific in its production of antislavery literature. In 1835 they distributed a million pieces. This handbill advertises a meeting; the book and almanac date from 1836 and 1837 respectively.*

Significantly more successful initially was emigration to Haiti. In 1824, Haiti's president, Jean Pierre Boyer, sent agents to the United States to recruit skilled black workers. That same year, over 6,000 blacks, encouraged by a black-led emigration movement to a black-ruled country, left Boston, New York, Philadelphia, and Baltimore for Haiti. However, by 1827, thousands had returned, disappointed by the state of the new nation, uncomfortable with the climate, unable to speak the language, and unprepared for rural life there.

Abolitionist Action and the AASS

For those free blacks who resolved to stay in the United States, two events in 1829 focused their attention on issues of antislavery and equal rights. Cincinnati whites, fearing an increasing black population, rioted for three days, driving many blacks out of the city to Canada. In Boston, David Walker, a free black from North Carolina, published his *Appeal to the Coloured Citizens of the World*, setting off a storm of fear among whites in southern states as his fiery call for slaves to free themselves turned up in the hands of free blacks and slaves there.

Both Walker's *Appeal* and the events in Cincinnati spurred free blacks to action. Sailors smuggled copies of David Walker's *Appeal* south, risking their lives in doing so. In Boston in 1832, Maria Stewart, a black woman inspired by Walker's religious message and her own readings of the Bible, became the first American woman to speak before mixed audiences of men and women in the United States. She spoke against slavery, encouraged free blacks to obtain education, and urged black women in particular to cease to 'bury their talents in performing mean, servile labor.'[9]

For several years prior to 1829, blacks in New York, Philadelphia, and Baltimore had considered holding a national convention to address the pressing issues of the day: antislavery, colonization, education, moral uplift, and economic improvement for blacks. The events in Cincinnati spurred them to action. In 1830, the first Convention of the Free People of Color was held in Philadelphia, with the majority of the delegates from Philadelphia and New York City. However, free blacks as far south as Washington, DC watched the convention with interest. The goals of these antebellum conventions reflected those of black middle-class leaders, but also served as a

colonization. At a meeting in January 1817, over 3,000 black Philadelphians crowded Bethel Church to vote against it with 'one long, loud, tremendous "No". . . which seemed as it would bring down the walls of the building.' They feared 'that all the free people would be compelled to go' to Africa, and they believed that colonization would not encourage emancipation, but would soothe slaveholders, who 'want to get rid of [free blacks] so as to make their property more secure.' The vehemence of the mass of the black community against colonization forced black leaders such as Allen and Forten to withdraw their support.[8]

Problems in Liberia further eroded black support. In South Carolina, over 100 free blacks sailed for Liberia on the *Jupiter* in 1835. These included wealthy blacks as well as slaves promised their freedom if they left the United States. However, when the *Jupiter* again departed for Liberia a year later, not one black person was aboard. Word had reached Charleston that the climate, disease, and scarcity of food made Liberian settlement dangerous. Only after 1850, when American free blacks experienced another wave of legal restrictions, did emigration regain popularity.

Left: *William Lloyd Garrison cofounded the American Anti-Slavery Society in 1833 and was its president for 25 years, from 1840 to 1865.*

forum for critical discussions of these goals by the black community as a whole.

Inspired by the new black activism, white New Englander William Lloyd Garrison founded the radical antislavery newspaper the *Liberator* in 1831 and two years later helped to form the American Anti-Slavery Society (AASS). The work of the AASS focused on the immediate abolition of southern slavery and racial prejudice, publicizing these causes through speeches, pamphlets, sewing bees, fairs, and other activities. The American Anti-Slavery Society constitution prominently linked the antislavery struggle to improving the condition of free blacks by 'removing public prejudice' and 'encouraging their intellectual, moral, and religious improvement' so that blacks might 'share an equality with the whites, of civil and religious privileges.'[10]

Free blacks flocked to the support of the AASS. Garrison's willingness to heed the advice of blacks encouraged them that a new day of interracial cooperation was dawning. Most of the blacks who participated in the leadership of the AASS during the 1830s were middle-class blacks. Laboring blacks contributed monetary and other support to the Society.

Fugitives and Kidnapings

Many blacks who did not participate in the formal abolition movement found informal ways to aid the cause. The abolitionist issue which concerned most free blacks was the

Below: *This branded hand (SS for slave stealer) belongs to Jonathan Walker, an abolitionist who tried to smuggle seven slaves to freedom in 1844 but was caught, jailed, fined, and branded.*

issue of fugitive slaves and kidnapings. Urban areas in the North and South contained substantial numbers of fugitive slaves who had attained freedom through their own ingenuity. Henry 'Box' Brown was one of several slaves who had friends seal them in boxes marked 'Fragile' and then ship them north. Ellen and William Craft, wife and husband, escaped slavery by having the light-skinned Ellen pose as the white male employer of the darker William. Fugitive Harriet Tubman not only escaped slavery herself, but returned many times to the South to help others escape. Because it was more difficult for families to escape, the majority of runaway slaves were single or married men who left families behind.

Once fugitives were in cities, they relied on neighbors and friends for day-to-day assistance and protection. Police officers, agents hired by southern masters to recover wayward property, or poor whites paid to find fugitives, searched black enclaves in urban areas for escaped slaves. They accosted black men, women, and children in their homes or as they walked to their jobs. Such invasions were threats to free blacks as well as fugitives. The color of a person's skin was enough to cast doubt on his or her freedom, while the confirmation under oath of a black's slave status by a white desiring a new slave, a quick lucrative sale, or a handsome cash reward could be enough to send almost any black person south into bondage. In a few cases, blacks, too, turned to capturing fugitives for reward money. But most blacks assisted and sheltered fugitives.

Formal and informal networks among blacks and sympathetic whites, known as the

SOJOURNER TRUTH

I have as much muscle as any man, and can do as much work as any man. I have plowed and reaped and husked and chopped and mowed, and can any man do more than that? I have heard much about the sexes being equal; I can carry as much as any man, and can eat as much too, if I can get it. I am as strong as any man that is now.

As for intellect, all I can say is, if woman have a pint and man a quart – why can't she have her little pint full? You need not be afraid to give us our rights for fear we will take too much – for we won't take more than our pint'll hold.

The poor men seem to be all in confusion and don't know what to do. Why children, if you have woman's rights give it to her and you will feel better. You will have your own rights, and they won't be so much trouble.

I can't read, but I can hear. I have heard the Bible and have learned that Eve caused man to sin. Well if woman upset the world, do give her a chance to set it right side up again. The lady has spoken about Jesus, how he never spurned woman from him . . . And how came Jesus into the world? Through God who created him and woman who bore him. Man, where is your part?

But the women are coming up blessed be God and a few of the men are coming up with them. But man is in a tight place, the poor slave is on him, woman is coming on him, and he is surely between a hawk and a buzzard.[1]

Note
[1] *Anti-Slavery Bugle*, Salem, Ohio, 21 June 1851, quoted in Charleton Mabee with Susan Mabee Newhouse, *Sojourner Truth: Slave, Prophet, Legend*, New York: New York University Press, 1993, pp. 81–2.

Underground Railroad, provided food, shelter, and other assistance against slave-catchers. In 1842, the slave Harriet Wilson escaped to New York City. After reuniting with her daughter and other friends there, she found employment as a nursemaid. Although Wilson kept her fugitive status secret from her white employers, she participated in the 'many impromptu vigilance committees' established for fugitives in New York:

> Every colored person, and every friend of their persecuted race, kept their eyes wide open. Every evening I examined the newspapers carefully, to see what Southerners had put up at the hotels. I did this for my own sake . . . I wished also to give information to others, if necessary; for if many were 'running to and fro,' I resolved that 'knowledge should be increased.'[11]

Some abolitionists tried to connect these grassroots methods of protecting fugitives to the formal abolitionist movement's legal skills. In 1835, black New York City grocer David Ruggles founded the New York Vigilance Committee. An executive committee of about eight, including Ruggles, black Presbyterian ministers Samuel Cornish and Theodore S. Wright, and the ex-slave and restaurateur Thomas Van Rensellaer, forged ties with white abolitionist lawyers who fought in the courts on behalf of those accused of being fugitive slaves. Vital to the work of the executive committee was the 'effective committee' of 100 men and women, each of whom was responsible for collecting money from 10–12 friends and for informing the executive committee of anyone who needed aid. In this way, the organization involved a large portion of New York City's black community, which then numbered between 13,000 and 16,000.

The New York Vigilance Committee prevented almost 1,400 blacks from being returned to slavery during its seven-year tenure. Abolitionists in Philadelphia, Boston, and other cities also formed such committees. However, abolitionist leaders did not approve of all grassroots efforts. In 1837, when black New Yorkers learned that the fugitive William Dixon had lost his case for freedom, they mobbed the courthouse and attempted to whisk Dixon away from the authorities, giving him a dirk and a knife with which to make his escape. Dixon was soon recaptured, but later won his case on appeal. Although David Ruggles lauded the mob actions, most abolitionist leaders decried the violent effort. Black Presbyterian minister Samuel Cornish urged the 'ignorant part of our coloured citizens' to stay away from such trials, leaving efforts to aid fugitives to the New York Vigilance Committee's 'eminent lawyers.'[12]

Despite such internal conflicts, abolitionists during the 1830s were successful in establishing the importance of abolishing slavery and achieving full equality for blacks. Such success carried a price, however. In the North, the

HENRY 'BOX' BROWN

THE RESURRECTION OF HENRY BOX BROWN AT PHILADELPHIA.
Who escaped from Richmond Va. in a Box 3 feet long 2½ ft deep and 2 ft wide

On Main Street in Richmond, Virginia, near the tobacco factories that employed so many hired-out slaves, Samuel Smith set up his shoemaker's shop under the sign of the Red Boot. Henry Brown, a slave born and raised in Louisa County, worked in one of those factories. In Virginia's state capital, industrial and commercial growth meant an expansion of the long-time local practice of hiring slaves, many from the countryside, for work in factories, stores, and households. Rural and urban slaves joined artisans from the American North, Britain, and Germany in providing labor and services for the tobacco factories, iron foundries, flour mills, and print shops of the bustling southern city.

Hired-out slaves could often acquire overtime pay, and Henry Brown managed to hire his wife from her owner and set up a home with her and their children, his wife taking in laundry to maintain the household. The domestic world they created ended abruptly when, with no warning, she and the children were sold south by the wife's new owner. When he realized that he could neither follow nor retrieve them, Brown began to plan an escape.

Slave runaways from Richmond were common, and most left the city hidden in some cramped and dark part of a ship pointed north. The city fathers legislated and fulminated, but both formal and ephemeral networks of assistance continued to aid runaways. The scheme that Brown concocted with the help of free black James C. A. Smith and northern-born white shoemaker Samuel Smith in 1848 was more complex than most. Brown

Above: *Henry Brown emerges from his box to see his friends and freedom. He was one of several slaves that escaped in this manner. It became a cause célèbre, however, and led to songs, pamphlets, and so on such as that below.*

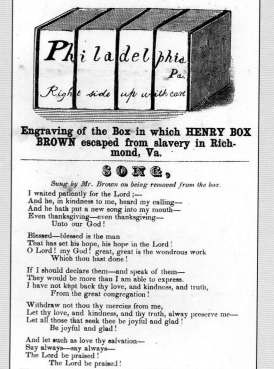

Engraving of the Box in which HENRY BOX BROWN escaped from slavery in Richmond, Va.

SONG,

Sung by Mr. Brown on being removed from the box.

I waited patiently for the Lord ;—
And he, in kindness to me, heard my calling—
And he hath put a new song into my mouth—
Even thanksgiving—even thanksgiving—
    Unto our God !

Blessed—blessed is the man
That has set his hope, his hope in the Lord !
O Lord ! my God ! great, great is the wondrous work
    Which thou hast done !

If I should declare them—and speak of them—
They would be more than I am able to express.
I have not kept back thy love, and kindness, and truth,
    From the great congregation !

Withdraw not thou thy mercies from me,
Let thy love, and kindness, and thy truth, alway preserve me—
Let all those that seek thee be joyful and glad !
    Be joyful and glad !

And let such as love thy salvation—
Say always—say always—
The Lord be praised !
    The Lord be praised !

Laing's Steam Press, 1 1-3 Water Street, Boston.

persuaded a black carpenter to make him a box – the largest one permitted on the railroad cars. With a pig's bladder filled with water and a few hard biscuits, Brown climbed into the 2ft x 2ft

(60cm x 60cm) box, drilled with three holes for air, and was nailed in by Samuel Smith. Despite directions which said, 'This side up with care,' Henry Brown was carted to the express office upside down. By railroad car and steam-boat, he traveled to Philadelphia where agents of the Underground Railroad cut the hickory hoops of the box and pried open the lid. Liberated, Brown stood and sang a hymn of praise.

Henry Brown became celebrated as 'Box' Brown and toured England for the abolitionist cause. The shoemaker he paid to help him was caught by the police in a later attempt to box up and send slaves to the North. Samuel Smith served eight years in the state penitentiary while James 'Boxer' Smith came North and joined Brown on his English tour. Their tour deteriorated as the two men quarreled,

Right: *The tobacco industry is depicted on a contemporary label.*

Below: *The Oberlin Rescuers, punished for helping fugitive slaves, are pictured at Cuyahoga Co. Jail in 1859.*

and 'Boxer' Smith claimed that 'Box' Brown was not sufficiently pious nor serious in his efforts to buy his wife and children out of slavery. The sober men who directed the movement for the abolition of slavery desired completely circumspect behavior from runaway slaves on the lecture circuit, and they stopped sponsoring Brown.

By that time, with the publication of a book, *The Narrative of Henry Box Brown*, and the widespread distribution of a lithograph depicting his escape, Brown's courage and ingenuity had made an important and permanent contribution to abolitionist literature and to the American iconography of the antislavery movement. The account of Brown's dramatic escape helped turn northern public opinion against slavery, but the price of celebrity was high. Henry 'Box' Brown, the protagonist of political theater, disappeared from the public stage when he used his freedom to quarrel with 'Boxer' Smith over money, to drink ginger beer, and to talk of finding another wife.

Marie Tyler McGraw

1830s was a time of intense rioting. In the summer of 1834, antiabolitionist mobs in New York City and Philadelphia singled out the homes and businesses of abolitionists and blacks for attack. In New York, mobs expressed fear of 'amalgamation,' or interracial marriage. In Philadelphia, they attacked churches and other institutions seen as symbols of growing black political, social, and economic power.

In the South, the abolitionist movement exacerbated whites' fears about free blacks' disruptive influence on southern society. Although unable to organize politically, free blacks in the South individually challenged whites by assisting runaway slaves. Beginning in 1835, in one of the most dramatic episodes of southern free black resistance, fugitive slaves fought the U.S. Army in the Seminole Indian War in Florida. Although many runaway slaves sought out urban areas, others found refuge in the swamps and wooded areas of the South. In Florida, as in other places throughout the South, some fugitives joined with Indian tribes. The federal government fought the Florida Seminole and black alliance for seven years in an effort to remove the Native Americans west and to re-enslave their fugitive slave allies. In 1842, the war ended as the government captured the last Seminole chiefs and moved the Native Americans west. However, the army was unable to re-enslave the black fugitives, who journeyed west with their Native-American allies. Although Native Americans and blacks were removed from the land, the war demonstrated the potential of black struggles for freedom.

Problems in the AASS

The difficulties whites had in accepting the goals of black freedom and equality were evident even within the ranks of the radical American Anti-Slavery Society. Despite the society's stated emphasis on achieving equality for blacks, many black individuals were not treated equally within the organization. Sarah Forten, daughter of black abolitionist James Forten, said of the white antislavery activists she met in her father's house, '[prejudice] obscure[d] their many virtues and chok[ed] up the avenues to higher and nobler sentiments' regarding blacks. New York black Presbyterian minister Theodore S. Wright agreed that many white abolitionists had not 'annihilate[d], in their own bosoms, the cord of caste.'[13] White abolitionists' unwillingness to address the problem of racism within the ranks of the AASS hindered black efforts to take greater leadership roles in the abolitionist movement in the 1830s. Further, the AASS was slow to address the economic problems of poorer blacks. It put little money towards establishing schools or fighting the job discrimination that black workers faced; many white abolitionists refused to hire blacks in their own businesses.

By 1840, the AASS had splintered over the issues of women's rights and political

Above: *Frederick Douglass hard at work in his study. His contribution to the African-American cause was immeasurable.*

activism. Although the issue of racism was not a direct cause of the split, the division of the organization resulted in greater freedom and independence for blacks who wished to work in the antislavery cause. For example, Garrison had opposed the participation of abolitionists in the formal politics of voting and running for governmental offices. Thus, none of the AASS's energy had been devoted to lifting voting restrictions for blacks. After the schism of 1840, however, obtaining the vote was one of the first issues that northern black leaders addressed, forming state conventions on the model of the black national convention movement, and petitioning state legislatures, with the aid of sympathetic whites.

Black Activism and Antislavery Lectures

Also after 1840, a new group of highly visible black activists appeared. These men and women drew on their experiences as slaves, fugitives, and free people to illuminate for the American and international public the plight of blacks in America. Frederick Douglass, Sojourner Truth, and William Wells Brown were among the most famous of this new group of black leaders. Autobiographical writings such as Frederick Douglass's *Narrative* (1845) and *My Bondage and My Freedom* (1855); the Presbyterian minister James W. C. Pennington's *The Fugitive Blacksmith* (1849); and William Wells Brown's *Narrative* (1847) all sold in the hundreds of thousands in the United States alone. Black lecturers such as Douglass, William and Ellen Craft, Sojourner

Truth, and Henry 'Box' Brown spent years on the road, speaking at antislavery rallies throughout the northern United States and Europe. Audiences had a seemingly insatiable hunger for stories of the brutality of slavery and the bravery of fugitives' escapes. After Frederick Douglass completed the delivery of a two-hour speech in Philadelphia to a standing-room-only audience, his listeners cried, 'Go on! Go on.' He took a five-minute break to allow anyone who wished to leave to do so. No one did, and he continued speaking for another 75 minutes to the packed house.[14]

Despite their popularity, few black antislavery lecturers were able to survive on the money derived from their lecture tours. Male lecturers depended on the additional income of their spouses at home. Douglass's wife Anna Murray Douglass worked as a shoebinder and laundress while he traveled and infrequently sent money home. According to the Douglasses' daughter, Rosetta, Anna took pride in perfecting her role as the wife and caretaker of Frederick Douglass, particularly after rumors began circulating that he was having an affair with Julia Griffiths, a British antislavery activist he met while on tour in England. Anna treated Frederick as her 'honored guest' when he was at home, and took pride in the fact that 'when he stood up before an audience . . . his linen was immaculate and that she had made it so,' even to the point of sending him a fresh supply when he was on the road.[15] William Wells Brown was not so fortunate. While away on tour, his wife began an extramarital affair which resulted in the breakup of their marriage.

For female antislavery lecturers, life on the circuit created different problems. Most Americans believed that women's place was at home, not giving speeches in front of mixed audiences of men and women. When white proslavery listeners at a rally in Indiana in 1858 refused to believe that Sojourner Truth was a woman, saying that 'your voice is the voice of a man,' she exposed her breast to the crowd to prove her womanhood. Maria Stewart left her native Boston due to the hostility directed at her resolve to speak in public, but not before citing Biblical examples of female leaders: 'Did [God] not raise up Deborah to be a mother and a judge in Israel? Did not Queen Esther save the lives of the Jews?'[16]

Dred Scott and the Fugitive Slave Law

Regardless of such difficulties, the international success and visibility of black male and female leaders was greater than at any previous time. In contrast, the 1840s and 1850s were years of increasing difficulty for the black masses. In northern cities like Boston and New York, blacks lost the competition for low-paying unskilled employment to the influx of Irish immigrants. The 1850 Fugitive Slave Law and the 1857 Dred Scott Case endangered black freedom across class lines. The 1850 law rewarded those who captured fugitives, and stiffened the penalties for those who protected them. The law signaled that black enslavement in the South was acceptable, and forced northerners to participate in that enslavement. When the slave, Dred Scott, brought his case for freedom before the Supreme Court, claiming that he had a right to his freedom because he had been brought by his master into free territory, he was not only refused his freedom, but he and the nation were informed that blacks were not citizens.

The Fugitive Slave Law and the Dred Scott decision helped to create a new black nationalism. In the North and South, and across class lines, free blacks made plans to emigrate to separate black communities. For many, such emigration meant movement out of urban areas targeted by slave-catchers, into the relative anonymity of the countryside. Such moves were encouraged by black and white abolitionists who had for years urged blacks to leave what they viewed as immoral urban areas. In 1843, the wealthy New York State abolitionist Gerrit Smith promised 40 acres (16 hectares) of land to black males and their families who wished to leave urban areas and create black farming communities. Over 1,000

black men, women, and children took advantage of Smith's offer. Other blacks moved west, or to communities in Canada. For some, even Canada was not far enough. Martin Delany, Alexander Crummell, and Henry Highland Garnet became the leaders of a new emigration movement which encouraged removal to the black states of Liberia and Haiti. They argued that blacks in these countries would serve as an example of success that would prove the possibility of black equality in the United States.

Although few blacks emigrated to Liberia or Haiti, many did move to Canada, as well as to rural areas in the western United States. As a result, the growth rate of the black population slowed in urban areas for the first time in many years. New York City and New Orleans actually lost population: New York's black population fell from a high of over 16,000 in 1840 to 12,472 in 1860; and New Orleans went from just over 15,000 in 1840 to under

10,000 by 1860. Not until after the Civil War would urban black populations achieve the growth rate of the 1830s. But by the eve of the Civil War, rural and urban free blacks – North and South – had carved out a precious and precarious political, social, economic, and cultural space between slavery and freedom.

Notes

[1] Frederick Douglass, *My Bondage and My Freedom*, ed. William L. Andrews, 1855, reprint Urbana: University of Illinois Press, 1987, p. 187.

[2] Ira Berlin, *Slaves Without Masters: The Free Negro in the Antebellum South*, New York: Pantheon, 1974, p. 263.

[3] Shane White, 'It Was a Proud Day: African Americans, Festivals, and Parades in the North, 1741–1834,' *Journal of American History* (June 1994): 13–50, 44, 45; John J. Zuille, *Historical Sketch of the New York African Society for Mutual Relief*, New York: 1892, p. 7.

[4] For chimney sweeps, see Samuel Wood, *The Cries of New-York*, 1808, 1814, reprint New York: 1931, p. 45; on tubmen, see Paul A. Gilje and Howard Rock, *Keepers of the Revolution: New Yorkers at Work in the Early Republic*, Ithaca, New York: Cornell University Press, 1992, pp. 218–21; on vendors' cries, William Wells Brown is quoted in Dena Epstein, *Sinful Tunes and Spirituals: Black Folk Music to the Civil War*, Urbana: University of Illinois Press, 1977, p. 181.

[5] Roi Ottley and William Weatherby, *The Negro in New York: An Informal Social History*, New York: New York Public Library, 1967, pp. 72–3.

[6] *Ibid.*, p. 73.

[7] Marina Wikramanayake, *A World in Shadow: The Free Black in Antebellum South Carolina*, Columbia, SC: University of South Carolina Press, 1973, p. 140 and Berlin, *Slaves Without Masters*, p. 250.

[8] Gary Nash, *Forging Freedom: The Formation of Philadelphia's Free Black Community, 1720–1840*, Cambridge, MA: Harvard University Press, 1988, pp. 238–9.

[9] Dorothy Sterling (ed.), *We Are Your Sisters: Black Women in the Nineteenth Century*, New York: Norton, 1984, pp. 153–4.

[10] Article 3, 'Constitution of the American Anti-Slavery Society,' in *Second Annual Report of the American Anti-Slavery Society, with the Speeches Delivered at the Anniversary Meeting, Held in the City of New-York, on the 12th of May, 1835, and the Minutes of the Meetings of the Society for Business*, New York: William S. Dorr, 1835, reprint New York: Kraus Reprint Co., 1972, p. 74.

[11] Harriet Jacobs, *Incidents in the Life of a Slave Girl, Written by Herself*, ed. Jean Fagan Yellin, 1861, reprint Cambridge, MA: Harvard University Press, 1987, pp. 164–70, 191–2, 223–5.

[12] Cornish, quoted in Jane Pease and William Pease, *They Who Would Be Free: Blacks' Search for Freedom, 1830–1861*, New York: Atheneum, 1974, pp. 209–10.

[13] Forten and Wright, quoted in Pease and Pease, *They Who Would be Free*, p. 83.

[14] On nineteenth-century rallies and the response to Frederick Douglass, see John Blassingame, 'Introduction to Series One,' in Blassingame (ed.), *The Frederick Douglass Papers*, New Haven, CT: 1979, Ser. One, vol. I, pp. xxviii–xxix.

[15] Account of Frederick and Anna Douglass in Sterling (ed.), *We Are Your Sisters*, pp. 133–7.

[16] Sterling, *We Are Your Sisters*, pp. 157, 135–7.

Below: *Martin Delany was an early advocate of black nationhood, either in the West or Africa. In the Civil War he was the first black commissioned officer and he rose to the rank of major.*

THE FIFTEENTH AMENDMENT.

CELEBRATED MAY 19th 1870.

Chapter 5

THE AGE OF EMANCIPATION

The American Civil War was the costliest war in American history in terms of the loss of human life and the destruction of property. For black people, it was a war of liberation, a struggle that ended the long nightmare of slavery, even though it did not bring complete freedom. More than 600,000 Americans died in the struggle that ended slavery, but slavery had taken millions of lives over the course of its more than 250-year presence in America. The war and emancipation brought new clarity to the constitutional issues of state's rights, citizenship and human freedom, but political terrorism facilitated the erection of new instruments of racial control. The end of Reconstruction ushered in legal segregation in the South and confirmed for the nation a racial system characterized by separation and inequality. This system denied political rights, an adequate education, and economic opportunities to most black Americans and would persist for almost a century.

This lithograph from 19 May 1870 commemorates the 15th Amendment passed in February 1869. This was a guarantee of equal suffrage, forbidding states to deny the right to vote on the grounds of race or previous condition of servitude. It followed the extension of citizenship enacted by the 14th Amendment of 1866, and the crucial 13th Amendment of 1865 which freed blacks from enslavement. Lincoln called emancipation 'the central act of my administration and the greatest event of the nineteenth century.'

DAVID W. BLIGHT

ON 12 APRIL 1864, three years to the day after the Civil War began, George W. Hatton, a sergeant in Company C, First Regiment, United States Colored Troops, encamped near New Bern, North Carolina, and sat down to write a letter. Hatton, his fellow soldiers, and their families had lived for generations as slaves. Now they were part of a liberating army and serving a government that waged total war to destroy slavery. Hatton struggled to find the right words:

> Though the Government openly declared that it did not want the Negroes in this conflict, I look around me and see hundreds of colored men armed and ready to defend the Government at any moment; and such are my feelings, that I can only say, the fetters have fallen – our bondage is over.

A month later, Hatton's regiment was encamped near Jamestown, Virginia, when several black freedwomen entered their lines showing evidence that they had been whipped. Members of Hatton's company managed to capture 'a Mr. Clayton,' the man who had allegedly administered the beatings. The white Virginian was stripped to the waist, tied to a tree, and given 20 lashes by one of his own former slaves, Union soldier William Harris. In turn, each of the women Clayton had beaten was given her chance to lay on the lash, in Hatton's words, 'remind[ing] him that they

were no longer his, but safely housed in Abraham's bosom, and under the protection of the Star Spangled Banner, and guarded by their own patriotic, though once down-trodden race.' He was overwhelmed by the transformation: 'The day is clear, the fields of grain are beautiful, and the birds are singing sweet melodious songs, while poor Mr. C. is crying to his servants for mercy.'[1]

Such acts of violent retribution by ex-slaves against their former masters were rare in the wake of emancipation. Most freedpeople simply sought land and security; some had mixed feelings about the white families who had owned them. The Civil War had many meanings in African-American history. It was the extraordinary time when blacks came to identify their own fate with that of the United States 'Government,' and its military and political fortunes. The war to save the Union became the war to free the slaves, with thousands of former bondsmen serving as Union soldiers and sailors. The Civil War and black emancipation became inextricable parts of the same epic event. Because the sectional balance of political and economic power was fundamentally altered for a century; and because, simply put, the conflict would not have happened were it not for the presence of over 4 million slaves and the array of contradictions

Below: *War always creates fear, uncertainty, and refugees. In the Civil War it provided an opportunity to flee from servitude. Thousands took to wagons, or just walked, and headed for the Union lines and liberation.*

they caused for the meaning of America, the Civil War may rightly be considered the 'Second American Revolution,' and emancipation the historical pivot by which blacks took a giant stride into the modern age.

Onset of War

The drama of emancipation is all the more striking because for black leaders the 1850s had been a decade of discouragement, division, and unpredictable political crisis. The coming of the Civil War tested more than the future of America's national existence; the crisis would determine whether African Americans had a future at all, with human rights, on the North American continent. After the election of Abraham Lincoln in 1860, the secession crisis the following winter, and the outbreak of war in the spring of 1861, African Americans could take heart that the 'jubilee' of black freedom that they had sung and written about for years might now happen. Somehow disunion might boil into strife sufficient enough to compel the federal government to destroy slavery. Although prophecy might never overtake reality, most blacks, with anxiety and hope, would have agreed with Frederick Douglass that, 'The contest must now be decided, and decided forever, which of the two, Freedom or Slavery, shall give law to this Republic. Let the conflict come!'[2]

Black responses to the outbreak of war in 1861 ranged from ecstasy to caution and resistance. Across the North, free black communities organized militia companies, and offered their services. In one resolution after another

black Bostonians declared their support. 'Our feelings urge us to say to our countrymen,' they announced, 'that we are ready to stand by and defend the Government with "our lives, our fortunes, and our sacred honor."' From Pittsburgh came the offer of a militia company called the 'Hannibal Guards,' who insisted on being considered 'American citizens.' Although 'deprived of all our political rights,' this group understood the moment as a historic main chance: they wished 'the government of the United States sustained against the tyranny of slavery.' From Philadelphia and New York came the news that the sizeable black populations of those cities would raise full regiments of infantry. In Albany, Ohio a militia company organized, calling itself the 'Attucks Guards,' and flying a handmade flag presented to them by the black women of the town. In Detroit a full military band sought to enlist, while from Battle Creek, Michigan, a physician, G. P. Miller, wrote to the War Department asking for the privilege of 'raising from 5,000 to 10,000 freemen to report in sixty days to take any position that may be assigned to us (sharpshooters preferred).'[3]

Before war's end both black musicians and marksmen would see action, but initially their services were rejected. During the first year of the war most states explicitly denied blacks participation in their militia. The official policy of the federal government reflected public opinion: the war was for the restoration of the Union, not against slavery. Amid confusion and bravado, many northerners believed that 'the rebellion' would be quelled in one

summer. Despite the history of the Revolution and the War of 1812, some Americans feared that white men simply would not shoulder muskets next to black men. Soon the necessities of war would compel them to act above their prejudices.

Black Reactions to the War

A vigorous debate about support for the war ensued among blacks during 1861. Spurned by the early rejection of enlistment, some blacks turned away in anger declaring, as did a man in Troy, New York, that 'we of the North must have all the rights which white men enjoy; until then we are in no condition to fight under the flag which gives us no protection.' An 'R. H. V.' from New York City was even more explicit in opposing black participation. 'No regiments of black troops,' he said, 'should leave their bodies to rot upon the battle-field beneath a Southern sun, to conquer a peace based upon the perpetuity of human bondage.' Black newspaper editors divided over the issue. New York's *Anglo-African* joined the *Douglass Monthly* of Rochester in vehemently urging support for a crusade against the slaveholding South. The exclusion policy angered Frederick Douglass deeply, and, by September 1861, he attacked the Lincoln administration's 'spectacle of

Below: *Black recruits to the Union forces in New York. African Americans were not encouraged to join until 1863 onward; more than 180,000 then did so, of whom nearly 40,000 died. The Confederacy tried not to take black prisoners.*

blind, unreasoning prejudice,' and accused it of fighting with its 'white hand' while allowing its 'black hand to remain tied.' Philadelphia's *Christian Recorder* dissented, concluding that, 'To offer ourselves now is to abandon self-respect and invite insult.' Blacks should not fight in a war where 'not only our citizenship, but our common humanity is denied.'[4] The war was not yet the social revolution it would become; and the end was not apparent from the beginning.

In the South, most African Americans soon found themselves living in a society under siege and invasion. The prospects for black freedom now depended on the scale of the war, and the slaves understood the stakes. One of the few economic strengths in the Confederacy's war-making capacity was its huge supply of black labor. Tens of thousands of slaves were pressed into service by the Confederacy to build fortifications and to work in army encampments. Slaves were 'hired out' by their owners to work in ordnance factories, armories, hospitals, and on military transport. In Georgia an estimated 10,000 blacks worked on Confederate defenses. In some 29 hospitals across northern Georgia in 1863, blacks comprised 80 percent (nearly 1,000 people) of the workers, especially the nurses, cooks, and laundresses. Confederate regulations authorized commanders to employ black fifers, drummers, and buglers, and pay them at a rate comparable with that of white military musicians.[5] As the conflict endured, and the displacement of peoples became ever more chaotic, many

owners began to 'refugee' their slaves to safer havens in the interior rather than hire them out to the army.

Huge numbers of slaves were set in motion by these removals. Families separated as men were forced into Confederate labor gangs; women and children were left to their own devices back on the home place, or were caught up in refugee movement as Union armies advanced. Especially for males, this social flux provided enormous opportunity for escape to Union lines; some joined Union forces in the wake of decisive battles. For slaves the war was about their freedom. As one slave 'war song' explained, 'I got my breast-plate sword and shield and I go marching thro' the field, Till the war is ended.'[6] Thousands were 'employed' (not always with compensation) as military laborers for the Union army. Wherever Union forces advanced, blacks were important as foragers, wagon masters, cooks, and construction workers for fortifications and bridges. Ex-slaves familiar with the southern countryside also served as spies and sources of military intelligence. Harriet Tubman, famous for her earlier career as a 'conductor' on the Underground Railroad, was one of the many blacks who served the Union cause as guides and spies. She was formally commended by the Secretary of War and at least five high-ranking Union officers for her two years' work in the sea islands as a nurse and a daring scout.

Congress Moves Toward Emancipation

Driven by human will and military necessity, a Union emancipation policy took shape simultaneously with this exodus of liberation. The black Union soldier and later historian, George Washington Williams, observed both motivations: 'Whenever a Negro appeared with a shovel in his hands, a white soldier took his gun and returned to the ranks.' During the first year of the war, Union military forces operated on an official policy of 'denial of asylum' to escaped slaves. The war was to restore the Union, but not to uproot slavery. Events quickly overtook such a policy. At Fortress Monroe, Virginia, in May 1861, General Benjamin F. Butler declared the slaves who entered his lines 'contraband of war.'[7] The idea of slaves as confiscated enemy property eventually caught on. In early August 1861, the federal Congress passed the First Confiscation Act, allowing for the seizure of all Confederate property that aided the war effort. Although slaves were not technically freed by this law, an inexorable process toward legal black freedom took root.

By the spring and summer of 1862, Congress led on the issue of emancipation,

Below: *These plantation workers were pictured in 1862 on Edisto Island, South Carolina. The men appear to be wearing elements of Union uniforms. Slaves in crucial theaters such as this were significant contributors to Union intelligence.*

abolishing slavery in the District of Columbia, with monetary compensation for former owners, and authorizing a large sum of money for the possible colonization of freed blacks abroad. The Lincoln administration, indeed, pursued a variety of Central American and Caribbean colonization schemes into 1863; this old idea of the removal of blacks from America died hard in the nineteenth century. But Lincoln, like many who would vote for him again in 1864, rose to the moral and military imperatives of emancipation. Frederick Douglass was greatly encouraged by an evolving emancipation movement in early 1862, whatever its motives. 'It is really wonderful,' he wrote, 'how all efforts to evade, postpone, and prevent its coming, have been mocked and defied by the stupendous sweep of events.'[8]

Those events moved now, as Julia Ward Howe described them in the 'Battle Hymn of the Republic,' with the 'fateful lightning' of a 'terrible swift sword.' In June 1862, Congress abolished slavery in the western territories, and in July, it passed the Second Confiscation Act, which explicitly freed slaves of all persons 'in rebellion,' excluding no parts of the slaveholding South. These measures provided a public and legal backdrop for President Lincoln's subsequent Emancipation Proclamation, issued in two parts and calculated to boost northern morale, prevent foreign intervention, and keep four slaveholding border states in the Union. In the preliminary procla-

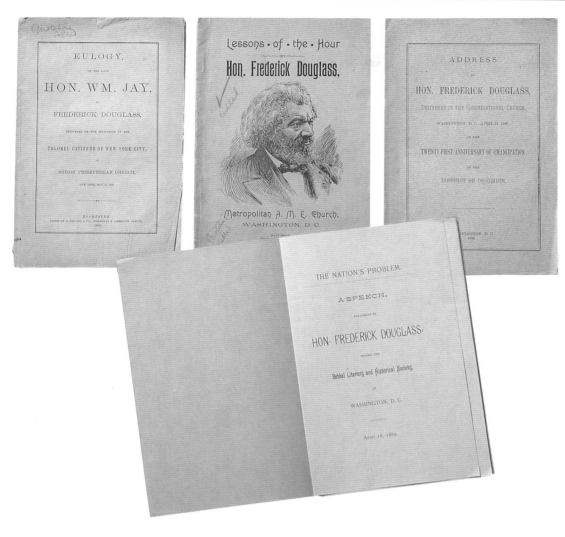

mation of 21 September 1862, issued in the aftermath of the Battle of Antietam, the President announced that if the South had not ceased the war by 1 January 1863, all slaves in the 'states in rebellion' would be 'forever free.' Lincoln had preferred the path of gradual, compensated emancipation as a means of ending the war and returning the South to the Union. But no such limited aim could realize what had already become a revolutionary struggle for ends much larger than most had imagined in 1861.

Lincoln had always considered slavery an evil. It was he who had committed the Republican Party in the late 1850s to putting slavery 'on a course of ultimate extinction.' At the outset of the war, he valued saving the Union above all else. But after he signed the Emancipation Proclamation and set off Jubilee celebrations across the North, Lincoln's historical reputation has forever been tied to his role in black freedom. Emancipation did, indeed, require presidential leadership to commit America to a war to free slaves in the eyes of the world; in Lincoln's remarkable command of moral meaning and politics, he understood that this war had become a crucible in which the entire nation could receive a 'new birth of freedom.' Emancipation was inherently a legal *and* a moral proposition, and like all great matters in American history, it had to be finalized in the Constitution (the 13th Amendment was passed in early 1865, with Lincoln's strong support). But black freedom was something both given and seized. Many factors made it possible for Lincoln to say, by February 1865, that 'the central act of my administration, and the greatest event of the nineteenth century' was emancipation.[9]

The actual process and timing of emancipation across the South depended on at least three circumstances: the character of slave society in a given region; the course of the war itself; and the policies of the Union and Confederate governments. These combined factors determined when, where, and how slaves became free. Octave Johnson was a slave on a plantation in St. James Parish, Louisiana, who ran away to the woods when the war came. He and a group of 30, 10 of whom were women, remained at large for a year and a half. Johnson's story, as he reported it in 1864, provides a remarkable example of the social-military revolution underway across the South. 'We were four miles in the rear of the plantation house,' said Johnson. His band stole food and borrowed matches and other goods from slaves still on the plantation. 'We slept on logs and burned cypress leaves to make a smoke and keep away mosquitoes.' When hunted by bloodhounds Johnson's group took to the deeper swamp.

> [We] killed eight of the bloodhounds; then we jumped into Bayou Faupron; the dogs followed us and the alligators caught six of them; the alligators preferred dog flesh to personal flesh; we escaped and came to Camp

Above: *Frederick Douglass was an active campaigner and writer for half a century. This selection of his pamphlets spans the period. A lifelong advocate of the need to struggle for reform, he declared that 'Power concedes nothing without a demand. It never did and it never will.'*

Below: *In 1877 Douglass, the former slave, and his wife Anna moved to this house called Cedar Hill in Anacostia, breaking a 'whites only' covenant. He died there in 1895 after a rally for women's rights. The house is now a National Park Service museum.*

Parapet, where I was first employed in the Commissary's office, then as a servant to Col. Hanks; then I joined his regiment.

From survival in the bayous, Octave Johnson found his freedom as a corporal, Company C, 15th Regiment, Corps d'Afrique.[10]

The Meaning of Freedom

Emancipation was a matter of overt celebration in some places, and a slow culmination in others. But what freedom meant in 1863, how livelihood would change, how the war would progress, how the masters would react, how freedpeople would find protection in the chaotic South, how they would meet potential rent payments, how agricultural laborers attached to the soil might now become owners of the land, and whether they would achieve citizenship rights were all unanswered ques-

Above: *A Freedmen's Village at Arlington, Virginia. Intended to house dislocated slaves beginning new lives, the villages were set up by the Freedmen's Bureau, the first federal welfare agency, which existed from 1865 to 1872 and protected and aided the former slaves.*

tions during the season of emancipation. Joy mixed with uncertainty, songs of deliverance with expressions of fear. The actual day on which masters gathered their slaves to announce that they were free was remembered by freedpeople with a wide range of feeling. Some remembered hilarity and dancing, others a sobering, even solemn time. A former South Carolina slave recalled that on his plantation, 'some were sorry, some hurt,' and some 'silent and glad.' James Lucas, a former slave of Jefferson Davis in Mississippi, probed the depths of human nature in his description of the day of liberation:

> Dey all had diffe'nt ways o' thinkin' 'bout it. Mos'ly though dey was jus' lak me, dey didn' know jus' zackly what it meant. It was jus' sompn dat de white folks an' slaves all de time talk 'bout. Dat's all. Folks dat ain' ever been free don' rightly know de *feel* of bein' free. Dey don' kno de meanin' of it.[11]

But quickly the feel of freedom took on vivid meaning. For ex-slaves who followed Union armies, freedom meant life in contraband camps, where black families struggled to survive in the face of great hardship and occasional starvation. In western Tennessee, northern Mississippi, southern Illinois, coastal Virginia, the District of Columbia, and many other places, the freedpeople forged a new life on government rations, and received a modicum of medical care, often provided by 'grannies,' black women who employed home remedies from plantation life. For thousands the contraband camps became the initial entry into free labor practices, and a slow but certain embrace of a new sense of dignity. Nearly all who witnessed or supervised these camps, or organized freedmen's aid societies and schools, were stunned by the determination of the freedpeople. In 1863 each superintendent of a contraband camp in the western theater of the war was asked to respond to a series of interrogatives about the freedmen streaming into their facilities. To the question of the 'motives' of the ex-slaves, the Corinth, Mississippi superintendent described the range of what he saw:

> Can't answer short of 100 pages. Bad treatment – hard times – lack of the comforts of life – prospect of being driven South; the

Left: *Former slaves gathered in contraband camps to await their fate, such as these seen here at Cumberland Landing, Virginia, in May 1862. Although determined, until a new order was established freedmen faced an uncertain future.*

Above: *The attack on Fort Wagner by the black 54th Massachusetts Regiment was a demonstration of bravery which earned the respect of white northerners. It was one of a number of gallant charges by black troops during 1863.*

Left: Forever Free *by Edmonia Lewis, the first black American to gain an international reputation as a sculptor, dates from 1869 and shows a slave couple hearing the news of emancipation; the kneeling woman might be deftly suggestive of the continued subjugation of women in domestic and public life. Lewis attended Oberlin College, Ohio, and was encouraged in her arts career by William Lloyd Garrison, among others. Her early pieces both concerned the 54th Massachusetts Regiment: a clay model of the African American William H. Carney holding aloft the flag at Fort Wagner, and a bust of Robert Gould Shaw, the regiment's white officer, which was such a big success with the public that it financed her move to Europe and a studio in Rome.*

more intelligent because they wished to be free. Generally speak kindly of their masters; none wish to return; many would die first. All delighted with the prospect of freedom, yet all have been kept constantly at some kind of work.[12]

The Civil War attracts the historical imagination because it is an event so full of drama, sacrifice, and change. This epic story was not only revealed on battlefields; valor of a less heralded kind had an equal place around the watchfires of contraband camps.

Inexorably, emancipation meant that black families would be both reunited and torn apart. In contraband camps, where women and children greatly outnumbered men, extended families cared for each other. But often, when thousands of black men entered the Union army, they left women and children behind in destitution, often under new labor arrangements that required rent payments. Louisiana freedwoman, Emily Waters, wrote to her husband who was still on duty in July 1865, begging him to get a furlough and 'come home and find a place for us to live in.' The joy

SUSIE KING

Susie King escaped from slavery in Georgia during the Civil War and worked as a laundress with a black regiment, the First South Carolina Volunteers.

'I learned to handle a musket very well and could shoot straight and often hit the target. I assisted in cleaning the guns and used to fire them off, to see if the cartridges were dry, before cleaning and reloading. I thought this great fun. I was also able to take a gun apart and put it together again.

Fort Wagner being only a mile [1.6km] from our camp, I went there two or three times a week and would go up on the ramparts to watch the gunners send their shells into Charleston. Outside of the fort were many skulls lying about. Some thought they were the skulls of our boys; others thought they were the enemies'. They were a gruesome sight, those fleshless heads and grinning jaws, but by this time I had become accustomed to worse things.

We landed on Morris Island between June and July 1864. Orders were received for the boys to prepare to take Fort Gregg. I helped to pack haversacks and cartridge boxes. About four o'clock, July 2, the charge was made. The firing could be plainly heard in camp. I hastened down to the landing when the wounded began to arrive, some with their legs off, arm gone, foot off and wounds of all kinds imaginable.

There are many people who do not know what colored women did during the war. Hundreds of them assisted Union soldiers by hiding them and helping them to escape. Many were punished for taking food to the prison stockades for the prisoners. When I went into Savannah in 1865 I was told of one of these stockades in the city. The colored women would take food there at night and pass it to them through the holes in the fence. The soldiers were starving and the women did all they could towards relieving those men, although they knew the penalty should they be caught.'[1]

Note

[1]Susie King Taylor, *Reminiscences of My Life in Camp*, Boston: 1902. Quoted in Dorothy Sterling (ed.), *Speak Out in Thunder Tones*, Garden City, New York: Doubleday & Company, Inc., 1973, pp. 354–6.

THE BUFFALO SOLDIERS

African-American soldiers had always fought in America's wars since colonial times, but after the Civil War they became regulars and thousands served in the US Army which was committed to the military campaigns in the West until the 1890s.

The Indians dubbed the black troopers 'Buffalo Soldiers' because their tightly curled hair resembled that of the buffalo. It was also meant as a compliment, since the buffalo was respected by the Indians as a proud, brave, and strong animal.

Organized into four regiments – the 9th and 10th Cavalry formed in 1866 and the 24th and 25th Infantry formed in 1868 – they performed so admirably on the frontier that they earned 18 Medals of Honor. As seasoned troops (they had the lowest desertion rate in the US Army), they fought valiantly in the Spanish-American War of 1898, with more honors.

Their distinguished record stands on its own account, but when one considers the discrimination and racial hostility they suffered then the Buffalo Soldiers are even more deserving of respect.

Clockwise, from left to right, the artifacts below are: a mug; a scaled bronze by Eddie Dixon of his statue which stands at Fort Leavenworth, Kansas, where the 10th Cavalry was organized; a horse brush; a belt and ammunition pouch; a regular troop manual; a curry comb; a field mess kit; a campaign hat; and a dress helmet of the 9th Cavalry dating from 1881.

of change mixed with terrible strain. 'My children are going to school,' she reported, 'but I find it very hard to feed them all, and if you cannot come I hope you will send me something to help me get along . . . Come home as soon as you can, and cherish me as ever.' The same Louisiana soldier received a subsequent letter from his sister, reporting that 'we are in deep trouble – your wife has left Trepagnia and gone to the city and we don't know where or how she is, we have not heard a word from her in four weeks.' The sources do not tell us whether Emily Waters ever saw her husband again. But such letters demonstrate the depth with which freedom was embraced, and the human pain through which it was achieved.[13]

Black Soldiers in Blue

Nothing so typified the eventual antislavery character of the Civil War as the black soldier in Union blue. The initial exclusion policy proved untenable; due to mounting white

Below: *Soldiers of the 10th Cavalry escort of General Wesley Merritt posted to Montana in 1894 after 20 years in the southwest where they participated in the campaign against Geronimo.*

casualties and an unpopular conscription law, by 1863, northern public opinion grew increasingly favorable to the employment of black troops. In July 1862, Congress enacted the Second Confiscation Act, empowering President Lincoln to 'employ . . . persons of African descent . . . for the suppression of the rebellion.' Under vague authority, black regiments had already been organized by zealous Union commanders in Louisiana and Kansas. But, by August 1862, the War Department authorized the recruitment of five regiments of black infantry in the sea islands of South Carolina and Georgia. In the wake of the Emancipation Proclamation in early 1863, the Lincoln administration authorized three northern states to raise black regiments. White abolitionist George L. Stearns was commissioned to supervise black recruiters, and by April a dozen or so black abolitionists were enlisting young free blacks from across the North in the 54th Massachusetts Regiment. That spring, as a recruiting document, Frederick Douglass published 'Men of Color to Arms!', a pamphlet that captured the revolutionary character of the war now imagined in black communities. 'I urge you to fly to

Above: *Unit insignia, from left to right, of 10th Cavalry, 25th Infantry, 9th Cavalry, and 24th Infantry, adopted in the 1920s reflect the regiments' backgrounds in the Indian Wars.*

arms and smite with death the power that would bury the government and your liberty in the same hopeless grave,' Douglass demanded of young recruits, including his own, the first two of which were his sons Lewis and Charles.[14]

The 54th Massachusetts became the famous test case of what the northern press still viewed as the experiment with black troops. Their valorous assault on Fort Wagner – on the sands around Charleston harbor in South Carolina, 18 July 1863, where the regiment suffered 259 dead, wounded, or missing – served as a tragic but immensely symbolic demonstration of black courage. Blacks joined this war for the simplest of causes: their own freedom and that of their families. They fought because events seemed to provide an opening to a new future, to the birthright of *citizenship* through military service. Because they lived in a world that so often defined 'manhood' as that recognition gained by the

Above and left: *Good combat performances bolstered black demands to be treated as equals. This Medal of Honor (far left) was awarded to Christian Fleetwood for a heroic act at Chapin's Farm in 1864. The other medal (left) was awarded for courage shown by colored troops in the 1864 Campaign Before Richmond. At war's end troops were mustered out, such as these being greeted by their families at Little Rock in April 1865.*

In May 1863, the War Department established the Bureau of Colored Troops, and from then until the end of the war quartermasters and recruiting agents labored competitively to maximize the number of black soldiers throughout the South. Black enlistment became the most direct way to undermine and destroy slavery. By the end of the war in April 1865, the 180,000 blacks in the Union forces included 33,000 from the free states. Wherever northern armies arrived first and stayed the longest, there the greatest numbers of black men became Yankee soldiers. They changed the aims of the war, its meaning, look, and even its sound. Their music was omnipresent, bringing whites unfamiliar with black music 'into the midst of a kindred world of unwritten songs . . . simple . . . indigenous . . . quaint and . . . poetic.'[16]

As the war dragged on, some black men eagerly enlisted but others were forced into service by impressment gangs – sometimes composed of black soldiers – as a means of filling the ranks. Black soldiers faced possible re-enslavement or execution if captured, and they encountered several overt forms of discrimination. Virtually all commissioned officers in black units were white, and though promises had been made to the contrary during the early recruiting period, the federal government capitulated to racism with an explicitly unequal pay system for black soldiers. White privates in the Union army received $13 per month (plus $3 for clothing), while black men received only $7. The unequal pay issue

angered black soldiers and recruiters more than any other form of injustice. During 1863 many black regiments resisted the policy, refusing to accept any pay until it was equalized. Open revolt resulted in some regiments, such as the 3rd South Carolina Volunteers, where black Sergeant William Walker was convicted of mutiny and executed for leading protests in 1864. Military law, mixed with racism, made war in this instance an unforgivingly ugly business.

Black women suffered not only the dislocations of war, but tremendous physical and financial hardship as well. Many, like Rachel Ann Wicker of Piqua, Ohio, wrote in protest to governors and President Lincoln. In September 1864, Wicker wrote to Governor John Andrew of Massachusetts (her husband was in the 55th Massachusetts) demanding to know, 'why it is that you Still insist upon them taking 7 dollars a month when you give the Poorest White Regiment that has went out 16 dollars.'[17] Under pressure from such women, as well as abolitionists and governors, Congress enacted equal pay for blacks and whites in June 1864.

Feeling a sense of dignity that perhaps only military life could offer, and politicized as never before, black soldiers participated in some 39 major battles during the last two years of the war. Critics were silenced when black units fought heroically and suffered terrible casualties in several decisive battles. Sometimes Confederate troops gave no quarter to their captured black opponents. At Fort Pillow, Tennessee, in April 1864, Confederates massacred at least 200 black soldiers after they had surrendered. In all, nearly 3,000 blacks died in battle during the Civil War, and a staggering 33,000 more died of disease. Many of the white officers who led black units testified to the courage and devotion of their men. Thomas Wentworth Higginson, commander of the First South Carolina Volunteers, declared that he never had to 'teach the

act of soldiering, they also fought for the right to fight. Like other soldiers, blacks wrote letters home full of pride and fear. On the morning of 18 July 1863, Sergeant Robert J. Simmons of the 54th Massachusetts, an immigrant from Bermuda, wrote to his wife describing fateful and imminent events. 'We are on the march to Fort Wagner, to storm it,' said Simmons. 'We have just completed our successful retreat from James Island; we fought a desperate battle there Thursday morning . . . the poor fellows were falling down around me, with pitiful groans . . . God has protected me through this my first fiery, leaden trial, and I do give Him the glory.'[15] Later that day, Simmons was wounded and captured in the assault on Fort Wagner; one month later, he died in a Charleston prison.

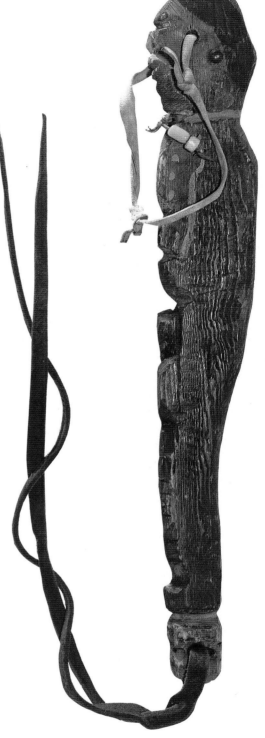

principles of courage' to his regiment of freed slaves. He especially admired one of his black sergeants, named Prince Rivers.

> There is not a white officer in this regiment who has more administrative ability, or more absolute authority over the men; they do not love him, but his mere presence has controlling power over them. He writes well enough . . . if his education reached a higher point, I see no reason why he should not command the Army of the Potomac.[18]

By the time Lincoln called emancipation the 'result so fundamental and astounding' in his Second Inaugural Address in March 1865, there was no better symbol of national regeneration than the sacrifices of black soldiers and their families in the crusade for their own freedom.

Reconstruction Begins

In its immediate context the meaning of the Civil War for African Americans had no more poignant illustration than the fall of Richmond, the capital of the Confederacy, in the first week of April 1865. Black troops were among the first Union forces to occupy the city, and the freed population welcomed them in what the black newspaper correspondent, T. Morris Chester, called 'a spectacle of jubilee.' Jubilant black folk welcomed President Lincoln when he visited Richmond on 4 April, only two days after Confederate evacuation. Chester reported that the freedpeople formed a 'great concourse of American citizens of African descent' as Lincoln strode through the streets of Richmond. Such revolutionary transformations were cause for explosions of hope and joy.[19]

For most blacks, Reconstruction began with emancipation. As the war lurched to its devastating conclusion across the South, black men and women began to defy old symbols of bondage and seek new identities. They were

Above and right: *The Indians respected the black soldiers that fought against them and these two depictions of buffalo soldiers are both the work of Indian warriors. This drawing (above) is rendered in typical Plains Indian style. The Sioux riding whip or quirt (right) carries a stylized carving which represents a black soldier and may have served as a talisman.*

helped immeasurably by a host of private, northern freedmen's aid societies which provided food, supplies, schooling, and assistance in the transition to free labor. By the last months of the war, the federal government established the Bureau of Refugees, Freedmen, and Abandoned Lands (the Freedmen's Bureau), the first such agency of public social uplift in American history. Many freedpeople embraced new names, and insisted on being addressed as 'Mrs.' or 'Mr.' Thousands of black women removed themselves from field labor, devoting themselves to the security and cohesion of their families. Nuclear families survived slavery, but not without a terrible legacy recorded in slave traders' profits, and stories of long-lost kin. Although the vast majority of the freedpeople would end up living in their old places in time, many moved about in demonstration of their freedom. In these revolutionary circumstances, extraordinary hopes could flourish. A whole black Virginia regiment spent the final winter of the war in a freedmen's school learning to read and write. One of its sergeants wrote home in March 1865: 'Surely this is a mighty and progressive age in which we live.'[20] The world of southern planters had been destroyed, an entire social order crushed by war. Southern whites understood their predicament. Some took out their frustration in random violence against the freedpeople, while others faced reality stoically and accepted a new order.

Radical Republicanism

No change was more apparent than the new relationship blacks now had with the American nation state, with *politics* itself. By right and by blood, African Americans now insisted that they were part of the polity. For the first several years of Reconstruction, the leaders of the Republican Party agreed, although, during the period known as 'Presidential Reconstruction' (1865–7), they were thwarted by Lincoln's successor, Andrew Johnson of Tennessee. Motivated by racist beliefs and the doctrine of states' rights, Johnson believed Reconstruction should preserve 'the Union as it was, the Constitution as it is.' He did not view emancipation as a victory, but as an unfortunate, if necessary, result of defeating the Confederacy. Johnson opposed black suffrage and the extension of citizenship rights to blacks; he especially

DISTINGUISHED COLORED MEN

ROBERT BROWN ELLIOTT.
EX-MEMBER OF CONGRESS.

BLANCHE K. BRUCE.
EX-SENATOR, U.S.

WM WELLS BROWN, M.D.
AUTHOR OF THE "RISING SON."

HENRY HIGHLAND GARNETT.
LATE MINISTER OF LIBERIA.

PROF. R. T. GREENER.
DEAN HOWARD UNIVERSITY.

P. B. S. PINCHBACK.
EX-GOVERNOR OF LOUISIANA.

FREDERICK DOUGLASS.
THE COLORED CHAMPION OF FREEDOM.

RT. REV. RICHARD ALLEN.
1ST BISHOP OF THE AFRICAN M. E. CHURCH.

JOHN MERCER LANGSTON.
MINISTER TO HAYTI.

E. D. BASSETT.
EX-MINISTER TO HAYTI.

J. H. RAINEY.
EX-MEMBER OF CONGRESS.

Left: *A wood engraving from* Harper's Weekly *of 25 July 1868 shows a scene of electioneering in the South, the first time blacks there had had an opportunity to participate in the process.*

and black leaders had little choice but to make the most of a halfway victory.

Perhaps the most remarkable revolution during Radical Reconstruction was the emergence of a group of black politicians at nearly every level of government. Consisting of many free-born, northern-educated ministers, former soldiers, and activists (although some ex-slaves as well) over 600 black men served in state legislatures and 16 served in Congress during Reconstruction (22 served in Congress between 1869 and 1901). At the state and local level these men helped to establish public school systems, more equitable taxation, bargaining mechanisms between laborers and planters, and economic development.

Political mobilization in southern black communities was a stunning achievement in 1867–8. The Union Leagues, originally founded as northern patriotic clubs during the Civil War, became the nexus of a remarkable political awakening. Blacks attended meetings and rallies where Republican newspapers were read aloud, and speeches were delivered by dozens of black itinerant lecturers. Sometimes work stoppages and strikes were born in Union League activities. Through this season of great hope, southern blacks, who had never witnessed an abolitionist meeting or read an antislavery newspaper like their northern cousins, now wrapped themselves in the heritage of the Declaration of Independence as well as recollections of slavery, enjoyed a freedom of expression they had only previously dreamed of, and claimed, as did an Alabama meeting, 'exactly the same rights, privileges and immunities as are enjoyed by white men – we ask nothing more and will be content with nothing less . . . The law no longer knows white nor black, but simply men.'[21] On such principles are democratic societies built. But the days of power and security for blacks in Reconstruction politics were all too short.

Southern Redemption

In 1868, black votes were crucial to the election of Republican Ulysses S. Grant to the Presidency. Across the South, radical state constitutions provided a legal basis for the new order. But Reconstruction policies, and all the new aspirations that blacks had hitched to them, depended directly upon federal enforcement. 'These constitutions and governments,' declared a Charleston, South Carolina opposition newspaper, 'will last just as long as the bayonets which ushered them into being . . .'[22] That year the Ku Klux Klan launched a campaign of political violence and terror directed at black and white Republicans. During Grant's first term in office, a legal and military campaign against the Klan was undertaken that was temporarily effective, but only after such groups had committed hundreds of

resisted the aim of some Radical Republicans to redistribute land to the freedpeople. Johnson attempted to *restore* the ex-Confederate states to the Union at the end of 1865, with very little of southern society *reconstructed*. The 'Johnson governments' included the notorious 'Black Codes,' laws written across the South in 1865 restricting the freedmen's economic options and mobility, and utterly denying them political or civil rights. Designed as labor controls and plantation discipline, such laws were clear evidence of white southerners' refusal to accept the deeper meanings of emancipation.

Whether the Civil War had truly fomented a Second American Revolution depended on the fateful debates over the place of black civil, political, and economic liberty in a restored Union. America's national history and the actual lives of black folks were never more interdependent. Outraged at the Black Codes, and led by Radicals Thaddeus Stevens of Pennsylvania and Charles Sumner of Massachusetts, northern Republicans in Congress seized control of Reconstruction policies during 1866–7. What ensued was an unprecedented Constitutional struggle between Congress and President over the function of the federal government and the meaning of the war. The Radical Republicans produced a blueprint for Reconstruction. Their ideology was grounded in the idea of an activist federal government, a redefinition of American citizenship that guaranteed equal political rights for black men, and a faith in free labor. The

Left: *This chromolithograph from 1883 pays homage to those black politicians and community leaders who had done so much to further the cause of emancipation, equal rights, and respect for the abilities of African Americans.*

Radicals greatly expanded federal authority, and they envisioned Reconstruction as a process of 're-making' a nation by remaking the defeated South. Their cardinal principle was *equality before the law*, which in 1866 they enshrined in the 14th Amendment, expanding citizenship to all those born in the US without regard to race. That same year Congress also renewed the Freedmen's Bureau, and passed the first civil rights act in American history.

The southern states' rejection of the 14th Amendment, Johnson's repeated vetoes of Reconstruction measures, as well as his repudiation at the polls in the Congressional elections of 1866, gave the Radicals increased control over federal policy. In 1867 Congress divided the ex-Confederate states into five military districts, and made black suffrage a condition of readmission to the Union. By 1870 all ex-Confederate states had rejoined the Union, and in most, the Republican Party, built as a coalition of 'carpetbaggers' (northerners who moved South during Reconstruction), 'scalawags' (native southerners who gave allegiance to the new order), and black voters held the reins of state governments. Indeed, black voters were the core constituency of southern Republicanism and the means to power. In February 1869, Congress passed the 15th Amendment, a limited guarantee of equal suffrage which forbade states from denying the right to vote on grounds of race or previous condition of servitude. But the amendment was silent on the 11 northern states that still denied the vote to blacks; it also ignored women's suffrage, and most importantly, did nothing to stop future enactment of inequitable qualifications tests. Despite these limitations, many northerners saw the 15th Amendment as a final act of Reconstruction,

murders in their effort to re-establish conservative white control of southern politics.

During the 1870s the power of the Radical Republicans waned dramatically. Driven by an ideology of laissez-faire government and economic expansion (especially in the wake of the depression of 1873), a postwar northern disinterest in social issues, and a desire to leave the South to its own devices, the federal government *retreated* from Reconstruction. In this context, aided by violence and terrorism, a white counterrevolution, known as 'southern redemption,' occurred through the resurgent Democratic Party. The final retreat, and the collapse of Reconstruction, came in the disputed Presidential election of 1876. Only

three states, South Carolina, Florida, and Louisiana, remained under tenuous Republican Party control. Due to corruption and intimidation, the election returns in those states were fiercely disputed, leading to a late-hour national political compromise giving the Republican Rutherford B. Hayes the Presidency in return for acquiescence in Democratic Party control ('home rule') of the remaining southern states. This sectional compromise, reached under threats of marching troops and a new disunion, brought an irrevocable end to Reconstruction in spring 1877.

These events had dire consequences for African Americans. Frederick Douglass had anticipated such results at least as early as

1875. In a speech in Washington, DC, he reflected upon the nation's impending celebration of the centennial of American independence. The nation, Douglass feared, would 'lift to the sky its million voices in one grand Centennial hosanna of peace and good will to all the white race . . . from gulf to lakes and from sea to sea.' Douglass looked back upon 15 years of unparalleled change for his people, worried about the hold of white supremacy on America's historical consciousness, and asked the core question in the nation's struggle over the memory of the Civil War and emancipation: 'If war among the whites brought peace and liberty to the blacks, what will peace among the whites bring?'[23] Answers to Douglass's poignant question would determine the character of American race relations in the late nineteenth century. The ultimate tragedy of the era was that, while the sections reconciled, the races divided.

The Birth of Sharecropping

Some of the deepest legacies of slavery were the beliefs among whites that without compulsion, blacks would not work, and that they had no essential need for education. From the Day of Jubilee into the 1890s, as the postfreedom generation came of age, southern blacks proved these notions wrong; and they did so in

Left: *African-American lawyer, Samuel Lowry, from Alabama, arguing his case before the Supreme Court in 1880. Just 15 years earlier John S. Rock, from Boston, had been the first black lawyer ever to be allowed to do so.*

the face of a pervasive popular culture that made the 'old time plantation Negro' the central figure of minstrelsy and popular literature. What freedpeople most wanted during Reconstruction was land; the lack of land redistribution became the most enduring failure of the era. The freedpeople faced diminishing economic choices, but not before they left ample testimony to their heroic quest for land and literacy. By 1869 the Freedmen's Bureau alone had created some 4,000 schools attended by 250,000 people. At a freedmen's meeting in the heady days of 1866 in Virginia, an ex-slave named Bayley Wyatt left this eloquent statement of the labor theory of value:

> We now as a people desires to be elevated, and we desires to do all we can to be educated . . . I may state to all our friends, and to all our enemies, that we has right to the land where we are located. For why? I tell you. Our wives, our children, our husbands, has been sold over and over again to purchase the land we now locate upon; for that reason we have a divine right to the land . . .[24]

Wyatt's understanding of the natural rights tradition notwithstanding, most blacks would lose the tug-of-war between the white planters' desire for labor control and the freedpeople's demands for mobility and land.

From early contracts working by 'task' and for wages, to renting arrangements that blacks came to resist because of the South's chronic cash scarcity, the sharecropping system was born as a compromise between landowners and farmers. Freedmen accepted, even sought, tenancy because it appeared to provide a degree of autonomy over their economic lives. Sharecroppers generally worked on 'halves,' giving half of their cotton crop to the landowner, keeping the rest for their own maintenance. But this system evolved into debt dependency for most sharecroppers. Gone were slavery and the huge plantations of the antebellum period; gang labor no longer existed except in some sugar-growing districts. But a new institution – the rural furnishing merchant – now stymied hopes for self-sufficiency. The merchant at the crossroads general store now monopolized credit, forcing the

Below: *A freedmen's schooolhouse in South Carolina. Education was one of the main needs of the black community and they raised a great deal of money to establish schools.*

sharecropper to pay in crops for his family's supplies. From season to season, most tenants found themselves deeper in debt to the man at the store. Such were the roots of the persistent post-Civil War poverty that engulfed black and white southerners. Although they were 50 percent of the southern population, by 1900 blacks owned just over 2 percent of farms.

Black Colleges

Across the South in the 1880s, blacks continued to build schools and found their own newspapers. With bricks, mortar, and sometimes curriculum provided or influenced by northern white philanthropy, colleges became the mainstays of black hopes. Institutions such as Howard (Washington, DC), Fisk (Nashville), and Atlanta Universities, as well as Hampton (Virginia) and Tuskegee Institutes (Alabama) were only the most famous among numerous centers for training black youth as teachers, farmers, and early industrial workers. Many of the most accomplished black musicians were trained at these schools. Starting in the fall of 1871, 11 singers and a 'skillful young Negro pianist [Ella Shepard]' electrified audiences in America and Europe as the Fisk Jubilee Singers, performing 'their own

music' and raising funds for their school.[25] Whether these colleges should offer industrial or liberal arts education would remain a fierce controversy among black leaders well into the twentieth century, crystallizing in the epic disputes between Booker T. Washington and W. E. B. DuBois. But the presence of these colleges as beacons in postemancipation black life cannot be overestimated. To this day DuBois's answer to how the sons and daughters of the freedpeople should be educated reverberates in curricular debates. 'Shall we teach them trades, or train them in liberal arts?' asked DuBois in 1903. 'Neither and both . . . ,' he answered. 'The final product of our training must be neither a psychologist nor a brickmason, but a man.'[26] Humanism and vocationalism would both be essential in the machine age.

During the 1880s, blacks continued to vote and hold office in southern and northern states. Perhaps as many as a million black farmers joined the Populist movement by forming locals of the segregated Colored Farmers' National Alliance. The farmers' revolt against the monopolistic power of the railroads, furnishing merchants, and banks accomplished much in radicalizing American politics. A cooperative spirit sometimes drew black and white farmers together and threatened landowners and traditional Democrats. A movement rooted in anger at the unrestrained capitalism of the New South, and in the universal pride of dirt farmers, nevertheless foundered on racism, especially when exploited by demagogic politicians bent on using racial fear to increase segregation in American life.

Black Migration

Driven by economic desperation, and sometimes by religious zeal, some blacks sought to migrate from the South. Large numbers from the lower Mississippi Valley (the 'Exodusters') moved to Kansas in 1879–80. In the 1880s and 1890s, Bishop Henry McNeal Turner of the African Methodist Episcopal Church advocated emigration to Liberia and other parts of Africa. Still others sought to establish colonies on the far western frontier, where many black men had already migrated as cowboys, soldiers, or adventurers. Meanwhile, many blacks engaged in migrations of the mind, dreaming of recovering their lost kin from slavery times. Until the end of the century black newspapers ran advertisements for information on lost relatives. In 1880, Patience Arnett searched for her mother:

> Information wanted of my mother. I was parted from her about the year 1852 and sold to a speculator by the name of Alex. Hopkins and was brought to Georgia. She only had two children at that time . . . My sister's name was Pilsey. My mother's name is Harriet, and at that time was owned by Wm. Harrison, of Nash County, North Carolina . . . Please help me to find her.[27]

THE EXODUSTERS: MOVING WEST

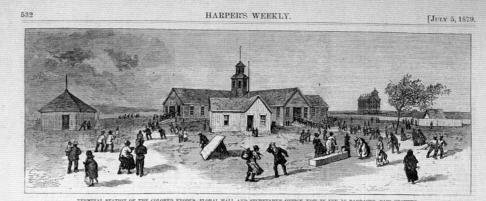

532   HARPER'S WEEKLY.   [July 5, 1879.

TERMINAL STATION OF THE COLORED EXODUS—FLORAL HALL AND SECRETARY'S OFFICE, NOW IN USE AS BARRACKS—FAIR GROUNDS.

RELIGIOUS SERVICES IN THE NORTH WING OF FLORAL HALL.

GROUP IN THE SOUTH WING OF FLORAL HALL.

THE COLORED EXODUS—SCENES AT TOPEKA, KANSAS—From Sketches by H. Worrall.—[See Page 532.]

By the 1870s the optimism that had characterized the emancipation celebrations of the previous decade had faded under the harsh white light of southern Democratic restoration of white supremacy. The 13th Amendment to the Constitution had officially abolished slavery and the 14th and 15th Amendments provided citizenship and voting rights without regard to race. Blacks served in the state and federal legislatures and in powerful local offices throughout the South. But the future was not encouraging. Most blacks remained dependent on those who had held them in bondage.

The Ku Klux Klan and other 'nightriders' terrorized blacks at the polls, in the fields, and

Above: *After Redemption, hostility to blacks was such that thousands migrated west to Kansas, a center of the antebellum antislavery struggle.* Harper's Weekly *of 5 July 1879 shows the Floral Hall, Topeka, serving as a kind of Ellis Island.*

in their homes. The few black sheriffs and a handful of black judges in the South could not protect them. 'We are in the hands of murderers,' wrote 300 alarmed black voters from Vicksburg, Mississippi.[1]

Their alarm was justified and their description accurate. Across the South, blacks were assaulted or even killed for being too prosperous, too self-confident, too smart, or too determined to make good on the promise of recent Constitutional guarantees. In Florida, Alabama, and other states in the South, the story was the same, so that blacks began arming themselves to protect their communities from such violence. But the cards were stacked in favor of white terrorists who were often allied with or part of the southern Democratic political authority. Before mid-decade, especially in the rural area of the deep South, the situation began to seem hopeless.

Blacks in Louisiana and Mississippi sent investigators into Kansas, Nebraska, Colorado, and westward, to determine the feasibility of a westward migration. At the same time, they petitioned Washington to support their emigration to Liberia, West Africa, or to help them acquire land in the far West. Receiving no positive response, many determined to move west on their own. By the late 1870s, thousands of poor, landless blacks moved out of the deep South headed in that direction. Some were led by Henry Adams, a former Georgia slave who had lived in Louisiana after the war. This 'Exodus of 1879,' or the 'Exoduster Movement' as it is sometimes called, brought 20,000–40,000 blacks out of Mississippi by riverboat or on foot, walking the Chisholm Trail toward Kansas.

In 1879 a black delegation was received by the Governor of Kansas who pledged assistance. A Freedman's Relief Association was established to provide temporary support in the form of housing, food, and medical supplies, and aid came from elsewhere in the North from as far away as Chicago and New England. Within a few years blacks had purchased over 20,000 acres (8,100 hectares) of land and built more than 300 homes in new Kansas communities. But life was not easy on the Kansas frontier. In Nicodemus, a community which continues to this day, the black settlers spent their first winters in dugout shelters unable to build during the harsh weather. Then their crops failed from lack of water, or storm or wind that blew seeds and even full-grown plants away.

The reception black migrants received from western whites was not always tolerant. One hundred black migrants were driven out of Lincoln, Nebraska in the early 1880s; but by mid-decade blacks were graduating from Nebraska's integrated high schools, and Tom Cunningham was serving as Lincoln's first black police officer. Davis Patrick carried the mail by pony express and in 1884 ex-slave M. O. Ricketts graduated from the University of Nebraska College of Medicine and, later, was twice elected to the state legislature. Five other blacks served in the Nebraska state house during this period. In Denver, black migrants initially found few who would rent them housing or land but some black Denverites teamed with progressive whites to build housing for them, and several of the

newcomers became landholders.

The West was not the promised land but it did provide greater opportunities than generally available in the South. In the small western communities, blacks might become landholders; they panned for gold in California and explored the wilderness as mountain men or Indian scouts. Some, like James Beckworth, lived with and even led Indian tribes and war parties against invading settlers, while others served as Buffalo Soldiers, keeping the peace in western settlements and defending settlers against Indian attack. Black workers built the railroad that linked east and west and manned the ships that sailed around the Horn of South

America bringing supplies to West-coast settlements before the Panama Canal. Starting with their entrance into the West with the Spanish explorers in the sixteenth century, black people contributed to western settlement and carved out a life on the American frontier. The 'Exodusters' increased their numbers but followed in the footsteps of those who had come west long before.

James Oliver Horton

Note
[1] William Loren Katz, *Eyewitness: The Negro in American History*, 3rd ed., Belmont, CA: Fearon Pitman Inc., 1974, p. 267.

Below: *The West was a harsh environment, and families struggled to eke out an existence there; black settlers also faced racial discrimination. This picture was taken in Oklahoma Territory.*

Above: *Just like the whites who settled the frontier, many blacks were cowboys (above, left), gunfighters, and lawmen. Baz N. Reeves (above) was one of a number of blacks who worked for 'hanging judge' Isaac Parker.*

Countless such advertisements – from Connecticut to Florida, and Texas to Iowa – record the pain and the hope of black families in an American diaspora shaped by slavery and emancipation.

African Americans also migrated internally to cities; by the turn of the century, two-thirds of northern blacks and about 20 percent of southerners lived in cities. As the urbanization of southern life increased, a *de facto* segregation occurred in public schools and transportation. Moderate whites gradually supported more rigid segregation laws in the 1880s, and by 1891, all but three southern states had Jim Crow railway statutes, justified by the fiction of a 'separate but equal' doctrine. After 1890, southern states, first in Mississippi, began to replace hostility and custom about black suffrage with explicit disfranchisement laws. Extreme racists, advancing theories of Negro inferiority, came to dominate school boards and legislatures.

Hopes and Fears

The postfreedom generation of young African Americans increasingly refused to acquiesce in old mores of racial etiquette. They resisted the Jim Crow practices and insisted on their own respectability. John Gray Lucas, a young black legislator in Arkansas and a recent graduate of Boston University, confronted his white colleagues: 'Is it true, as charged, that we use less soap and God's pure water than other people,' demanded Lucas. 'Or is it the constant growth of a more refined, intelligent, and I might say a more perfumed class, that grow more and more obnoxious as they more nearly approximate to our white friends' habits and place of life?'[28] Such ironic truths lay deep in the roots of the American apartheid that began to take hold by the 1890s.

Radical racists, such as Mississippi's Governor, J. K. Vardaman, stoked the flames of racial hatred, denounced black education, and advocated lynching black men accused of crimes. Indeed, lynchings as public rituals across the South reached a hideous peak of 235 in 1892, becoming for some white southerners an acceptable way to control the mobile, politicized, postfreedom generation of blacks. Such ritualized violence had white critics, but no American denounced lynching so effectively as Ida B. Wells, a young black woman raised in northern Mississippi during Reconstruction, who became a great journalist and civil rights activist. After three black men were lynched in Memphis, Tennessee, in 1892, she published *Southern Horrors*, exposing the 'thread bare lie' of white accusations about black rapists. Wells believed the facts about lynching would 'serve . . . as a defense for the Afro-American Samsons who suffer themselves to be betrayed by white Delilahs.'[29] Wells wrote voluminously about the twisted logic of southern miscegenation laws, especially their manipulation of gender and race to protect white men's sexual abuse of black women. Wells's Memphis newspaper was

Above: *The lynching figures tell an appalling story of white racist violence: between 1890 and 1900 some 1,700 blacks were brutally murdered. This 1899 petition pleaded for federal action.*

destroyed, but her voice was never silenced. She took her antilynching campaign to the North and abroad, combining it with women's rights activism as few others did.

The late nineteenth century was a time of anguished hopes and increasing self-reliance for African Americans. Black churches grew, especially the Baptist and the African Methodist Episcopal, and became centers of leadership and community power. Some urban churches in northern cities were bastions of the middle-class, while small country congregations served ordinary folk. 'Does I believe in 'ligion?' reflected an old South Carolina freedman. 'Dat is all us has in dis

world to live by and it's gwine to be de onliest thing to die wid. Belief in God and a 'umble spirit is how I's tryin' to live these days.'[30]

By the 1890s, African Americans looked to the future with a profound sense of generational change. Looking hard at the past was difficult; it meant facing legacies of slavery in the poverty of too many people's lives. The Fisk Jubilee Singers sang stylized versions of the Negro spirituals, taking the pathos - but not the pain – of slavery on their tours. Leaders like Frederick Douglass (born in 1818), who had lived with and conquered slavery, insisted on a vibrant use of memory. 'Well the nation may forget . . . it may shut its eyes to the past,' said Douglass in 1888, 'but the colored people of this country are bound to keep the past in lively memory till justice shall be done them.' Anna Julia Cooper, born in 1858, educated at Oberlin, and principal of Washington's M Street High School, spoke for the hopes of the postfreedom generation in *A Voice from the South* (1892):

> Everything is new and strange and inspiring. There is a quickening of the pulse, and a glowing of its self-consciousness. Aha, I can rival that! I can aspire to that . . . ! Something like this is the enthusiasm which stirs the genius of young Africa in America and the memory of past oppression and the fact of present attempted repression only serve to gather momentum for its irrepressible powers.[31]

That same year, W. C. Handy, an out-of-work cornet player, heard some 'shabby guitarists' singing about walking great distances with 'but one po' measly dime.' Handy, who became a great songwriter, called the song he heard the 'East St. Louis Blues.' From

Left: *Accused of a crime, this man was lynched by a crowd in Florida. A number of women were also hanged, burned and mutilated by such mobs.*

mysterious origins at 1,000 train stations, country stores, and on prison gangs, the 'Blues' soon became an infinitely adaptable music that allowed black people to 'look up at down.' Blues guitars were not always welcome within earshot of where the Gospel was preached; but both became essential to imagining the future, to exploring the sacred and secular meanings of the 'trouble in mind.'[32]

The postfreedom generation picked cotton, wrote history and novels, built colleges, edited newspapers, believed in America and was betrayed by it. They tried to fill in missing pages of their family albums, went to Congress, migrated to the West, and shipped out to sea. They helped America remember Fort Wagner as well as Gettysburg, the 14th Amendment as well as southern 'redemption,' lynch ropes alongside the internal combustion engine. Born at the end of Reconstruction, an old sharecropper named Nate Shaw observed:

> Time passes and the generations die. But the condition of the people that's livin today aint now like it's goin to be for the people that comes after us. I can't say exactly what the future way of life will be, but I has a idea. My color, the colored race of people on earth, goin to shed theirselves of these slavery ways. But it takes many a trip to the river to get clean.[33]

Shaw peered into the human condition and into the challenge of African-American life in the second half of the nineteenth century.

Above: *Howard University, Washington, DC, was founded in 1867 during the Reconstruction period. It was named after General Oliver O. Howard, a founder and head of the Freedmen's Bureau which had played an important part in the establishment of institutions such as Howard which were vital to the creation of a black professional class. This turn of the century photograph shows a Native American posing for the benefit of the student class.*

Notes

[1] George Hatton, quoted in Leon F. Litwack, *Been in the Storm So Long: The Aftermath of Slavery*, New York: 1979, pp. 64–5.

[2] Frederick Douglass, *Douglass Monthly*, March 1861.

[3] James M. McPherson, *The Negro's Civil War: How American Negroes Felt and Acted During the War for the Union*, New York: 1965, pp. 19, 20, 22.

[4] *Ibid.*, pp. 31, 34; *Christian Recorder*, 20, 27 April 1861; *Anglo-African Magazine*, 24 August 1861; and *Douglass Monthly*, September 1861.

[5] Eileen Southern, *The Music of Black Americans: A History*, New York: 1971, p. 234.

[6] *Ibid.*, p. 233.

[7] Williams, quoted in Benjamin Quarles, *The Negro in the Civil War*, New York: Da Capo Press, 1953, p. 95.

[8] Frederick Douglass, 'The War and How to End It,' speech at Corinthian Hall, Rochester, 25 March 1862, *Douglass Monthly*, April 1862.

[9] Lincoln, quoted in Quarles, *Negro in the Civil War*, p. 82.

[10] Testimony of Octave Johnson, before the American Freedmen's Inquiry Commission, February 1864, in Ira Berlin *et al.* (eds), *Freedom: A Documentary History of Emancipation, 1861–1867*, ser. 1, vol. I, *The Destruction of Slavery*, New York: 1985, p. 217.

[11] Quoted in Litwack, *Been in the Storm So Long*, pp. 212–13.

[12] Ira Berlin *et al.* (eds), *Freedom*, ser. 1, vol. III, *The Wartime Genesis of Free Labor: The Lower South*, New York: 1990, p. 692.

[13] Letters by Emily Waters, Roseland Plantation, Louisiana, 16 July 1865; and Alsie Thomas, 30 July 1865, in Ira Berlin *et al.* (eds), *Freedom*, ser. 2, *The Black Military Experience*, New York: 1982, pp. 698–9.

[14] Frederick Douglass, 'Men of Color to Arms!' a broadside, Rochester, 21 March 1863, in Philip S. Foner (ed.), *The Life and Writings of Frederick Douglass*, vol. III, New York: 1952, pp. 318–19.

[15] Letter by R. J. Simmons, 18 July 1863, from *New York Tribune*, 23 December 1863, in Edwin S. Redkey (ed.), *A Grand Army of Black Men*, New York: 1992, pp. 33–4.

[16] Southern, *The Music of Black Americans*, p. 230.

[17] Letter by Rachel Ann Wicker, Piqua, Ohio, 12 September 1864, in Berlin, *et al.* (eds), *Freedom*, ser. 2, *The Black Military Experience*, p. 402.

[18] Thomas Wentworth Higginson, *Army Life in a Black Regiment*, New York: 1962, pp. 235, 73.

[19] Dispatches, 6, 10 April 1865, in R. J. M. Blackett (ed.), *Thomas Morris Chester: Black Civil War Correspondent: His Dispatches from the Virginia Front*, Baton Rouge: 1989, p. 296.

[20] *Christian Recorder*, 18 March 1865.

[21] *Alabama State Sentinel*, 21 May 1867, in Eric Foner, *Reconstruction: America's Unfinished Revolution, 1863–1877*, New York: Harper and Row, 1988, p. 288.

[22] *Charleston Mercury*, 5 February 1868, in Foner, *Reconstruction*, p. 333.

[23] Frederick Douglass, 'The Color Question,' speech at Hillsdale, Washington, DC, 5 July 1875, Frederick Douglass Papers, Library of Congress, reel 15.

[24] Bayley Wyatt, quoted in Eric Foner, *Nothing But Freedom: Emancipation and its Legacy*, Baton Rouge: 1983, p. 56.

[25] Southern, *The Music of Black Americans*, p. 249.

[26] W. E. B. DuBois, *The Souls of Black Folk*, 1903, reprint New York: 1969, p. 119.

[27] *Christian Recorder*, 1 January 1880.

[28] John Gray Lucas, quoted in Edward L. Ayers, *The Promise of the New South: Life After Reconstruction*, New York: 1992, p. 140.

[29] Ida B. Wells, *Southern Horrors: Lynch Law in All Its Phases*, in Trudier Harris (comp.), *Selected Works of Ida B. Wells-Barnett*, New York: 1991, pp. 17, 19.

[30] George P. Rawick (ed.), *The American Slave: A Composite Autobiography*, South Carolina Narratives, vol. II, part 1, Westport, CT: 1972, p. 69.

[31] Frederick Douglass, 'Address Delivered on the Twenty-Sixth Anniversary of Abolition in the District of Columbia,' 16 April 1888, Frederick Douglass Papers, Library of Congress, reel 16; Anna Julia Cooper, in Dorothy Sterling (ed.), *We Are Your Sisters: Black Women in the Nineteenth Century*, New York: 1984, p. 450.

[32] Handy, quoted in Robert Palmer, *Deep Blues: A Musical and Cultural History of the Mississippi Delta*, New York: 1981, p. 42. The lyric and song, 'Trouble in Mind,' is explained in Lawrence W. Levine, *Black Culture and Black Consciousness: Afro-American Folk Thought from Slavery to Freedom*, New York: 1977, p. 230.

[33] Theodore Rosengarten, *All God's Dangers: The Life of Nate Shaw*, New York: Knopf, 1974, p. 577.

Chapter 6

A CERTAIN KIND OF SOUL

Historian Rayford Logan dubbed the last decade of the nineteenth century 'the Nadir' in American race relations. The rise of the Jim Crow South, increasing racial terrorism, the withdrawal of federal protection, and the sanctioning of racial discrimination by the Supreme Court made these bleak days for fairness and equal opportunity in America. In the early twentieth century, African Americans moved from the rural South to the urban North, from sharecropping to factory work and northern black ghettos. They continued to serve the nation's needs as agricultural workers, supplying the demands of the northern textile industry for raw cotton, as soldiers in the Spanish-American War and World War I, and as factory employees supplying equipment for the Allied cause. Pain and disillusionment, the heartache of leaving home, the excitement of city life and hopes for equality and prosperity all infused the literature and music which emerged from black life to help shape the evolving American culture.

Pictured prior to World War I, this group of immaculately dressed female students are gathered together outside a building on the original site of the National Training School for Women and Girls founded by Nannie Helen Burroughs. By 1900 there were more than 21,000 black teachers and by the time war broke out the literacy rate had increased to over 70 percent, from just 7 percent half a century before.

'AMONG THIS PEOPLE there is no leisure class.' Traveling through Dougherty County, Georgia, around the turn of the century, W. E. B. DuBois was struck not only by how hard people worked in this rural county in the cotton belt, but also by 'the monotony of toil with a glimpse at the great town-world on Saturday.'[1] Not all African Americans during the closing years of the nineteenth century spent most of their waking hours either tending a cotton crop or housekeeping in a ramshackle cabin and helping out in the fields. Black people lived in all regions of the United States in all kinds of places, filling a variety of occupations. DuBois himself had grown up in a small Massachusetts town. His mother had worked as a domestic and kept boarders; his father had tried his hand at barbering, selling, and preaching. DuBois was a sociologist with a Harvard Ph.D., in the early years of a career that would establish him as one of the preeminent American intellectuals of the twentieth century. But in 1890 most black Americans had some connection to the world he encountered in Dougherty County; more than three-quarters lived in the rural South. Thirty years later, slightly less than half remained, as migration – first largely to southern cities but increasingly to the urban North – transformed the American urban landscape. The story of black America during this period begins in the southern countryside and travels to the city. A minuscule and vulnerable upper class, if not a leisure class, did emerge; most people remained poor or working class. And rural life, less monotonous than the urbane DuBois presumed, provided the basis for a vibrant urban culture.

Agricultural Working Conditions

Among African Americans who had reached their 10th birthday in 1890, half of the males and nearly one-sixth of the females were engaged in some form of agricultural employment, nearly all in the South. Most grew cotton, along with some corn. In Virginia, North Carolina, and Kentucky, tobacco barns dotted the landscape; in Louisiana black workers continued to harvest and process sugar cane. Most black southerners organized their lives around the seasonal grind of preparing ground, planting, cultivating, and harvesting. As novelist Richard Wright, who grew up in Tennessee and Mississippi later put it,

> When time comes to break the sod, the sod must be broken; when the time comes to plant the seeds, the seeds must be planted, and when the time comes to loosen the red clay from about the bright green stalks of the cotton plants, that, too must be done . . . The seasons of the year form the mold that shapes our lives, and who can change the seasons.[2]

Below: *Cotton remained king in the South and images like this suggest that slavery had given way to other forms of exploitation.*

Like other farmers black southerners watched the weather: 'Dry weather can cut the growth of that cotton,' recalled a former sharecropper.

> Too much rain can cause it to overgrow itself. Cotton's a sun weed, cotton's a sun weed. Too much water and it'll grow too fast, sap runs too heavy in the stalk and it'll make more stalk than cotton . . . You just runnin a risk farmin; you don't know whether you goin to win or lose.[3]

Such was – and remains – the lot of all farmers. But for southern black farmers, the game was rigged; it was almost impossible to win. The vast majority rented their land, whether as cash renters who paid a fixed sum of money in exchange for the use of a farm, or sharecroppers who split the crop with the landlord. Rental agreements encompassed seemingly endless permutations, depending on what crops were being grown and who provided the work animals, tools, and fertilizer. Sharecroppers did not own their crop; technically they were wage laborers paid in kind. Even cash tenants, seemingly (and sometimes actually) more independent, often had to use their crop as collateral for loans necessary to purchase not only seeds and fertilizer but usually food and clothing as well. In most cases this mortgage meant that they also did not own the crop. This technicality mattered, because it determined who controlled the marketing of the crop, who could claim their share first

Left: *A late nineteenth-century tobacco label presents an almost idyllic representation of the life of a satisfied sharecropper, taking a pleasant smoking break outside his cabin watched by his faithful dog. The reality was very different.*

before other loans were paid off, and who controlled the labor process. A landlord who owned his tenant's crop could even influence black family life, determining what household goods could be purchased with loans secured by the crop, how the crop would be worked, and how much labor was needed at any time.

The landowner – or in the case of some cash tenants and even some black farm-owners, the 'furnishing merchant' – also controlled the end-of-year 'settlement.' Even in years of good weather and high commodity prices, the tenant's share seldom amounted to what he owed

Below: *Two women from Charleston, South Carolina, carrying their produce-filled baskets – which they probably made themselves – on their heads in traditional fashion.* .

for that year's 'furnish.' A 'popular couplet' heard across the rural South stated the relationship clearly:

Naught's a naught, figger's a figger,
All for the white man, and none
for the nigger.[4]

Most black farmers carried their debts over to the following year, even if they tried their luck with a new landlord. In some cases, the debt tied them to a particular creditor, even to the point of coercion. It was not unusual for a landlord to inform a tenant that he could not move until he had worked off a debt.

Even more vicious than debt peonage was the convict-lease system which benefited taxpayers, politicians, planters, mine operators,

sawmill owners, and railroads. Instead of serving a term in the penitentiary, black criminals (whose offenses ranged from vagrancy or petty theft to homicide) were leased by the state to private employers; in some places police seemed especially conscientious in their search for black vagrants during periods of peak labor demand. By the end of the century some states operated penitentiaries mainly for women and white men; black men served their time at no cost to taxpayers. Indeed, the system generated public revenues despite the low fees paid by politically connected contractors who mercilessly worked their captive labor force. When, in the early twentieth century, reformers denounced the system's corruption, southern states simply replaced coercion in the private sector with coercion in the public sector. Black criminals were relegated to chain gangs and prison farms, the most famous of which was Parchman, Mississippi, which spawned more than its share of blues musicians.

All of these approaches to recruiting and managing black workers shared a set of assumptions about the place of blacks in the southern economy, the nature of race, and the prerogatives attached to employing African Americans. By the late nineteenth century the South was committed to a low-wage economy, heavily weighted toward harvesting what grew on the land and extracting what lay underneath it. White southerners who were not dependent on black labor – workers, small farmers, businessmen operating outside of areas with large black populations – generally would have been happy to send the region's black population packing. But the major political and economic players in the South recognized, as the editor of the *Atlanta Constitution* put it, that it was 'impossible for the people of the south, either now or hereafter, to get along without the negro.'[5]

In a region where most white families earning at least a craftsman's wage employed a black domestic worker, this observation could easily have referred to a perennial complaint about the difficulty of finding 'good help': African-American women who did not express dissatisfaction by exercising their prerogative to change jobs. But the reference was to black *men*, whom southern gentlemen assumed were peculiarly suited to their place in the southern economy. Indeed, white planters and industrial managers unabashedly pointed to the advantages of hiring black workers: they supposedly were naturally dependent, docile, and suited to heavy work. Assumed to be incapable of all but the most menial employment, they had few options and therefore could be paid less than whites, and they could be denied even the most basic rights

that white workers might invoke to protect themselves against certain types of coercion.

Blacks in the Urban North

Notions of African Americans as inherently passive and naturally fitted for subordinate roles and specific tasks were hardly the exclusive property of white southerners. Most white Americans understood culture and society in racial terms in the years surrounding the turn of the century. Slavs, Italians, Negroes, Jews, Gypsies: the list of supposedly distinct 'races' was endless for some social scientists. Others lumped immigrants into such broader entities as 'Eastern Europeans' or 'Semites.' In any case, the conventional wisdom attributed specific characteristics to specific races. Blacks generally ended up at the bottom, except on

Above: A slice of African-American life in the South as a celebratory parade is held at the so-called Negro Fair in Bonham, Texas, in the years immediately prior to World War I.

the West Coast where the Chinese seemed to pose a greater threat than the relatively small black population. In the northern states, African Americans were a more visible presence than in the more heterogeneous West, but they still constituted a small minority. Excluded from most industrial employment because northern employers considered them less efficient, less dexterous, less mechanical, and less intelligent than other races, blacks tended to cluster in service occupations.

Black urbanites, North and South, also tended to cluster in certain neighborhoods. In

some cities recognizable ghettos were emerging by the turn of the century; elsewhere African Americans lived in enclaves that would consolidate into ghettos within two decades. Few black people, other than servants, lived on blocks inhabited mainly by whites. Especially in the North, whites increasingly moved away from areas populated by blacks and made it difficult for blacks to move into 'white' neighborhoods. In Cleveland, where some African Americans lived outside the three main black enclaves, and many whites lived in or near those enclaves, a black clerk's boast that 'we have no "LITTLE AFRICA"' suggests the more restrictive pattern elsewhere.[6]

To some extent the increasing residential segregation of African Americans was part of a broader urban trend towards segregation by class. As improved transportation enabled the urban middle and upper classes to move away from the central city, workers remained closer to jobs near the core. But the African-American middle class was excluded – usually by threat of (or by actual) violence – from joining the exodus to new neighborhoods. Unlike the white working class, with its access to a variety of neighborhoods, often characterized by proximity to particular workplaces, black workers were restricted to the emerging ghetto. For black urbanites this meant higher rents or purchase prices for equivalent housing because the isolated market for 'Negro housing' invariably expanded less quickly than the city's broader market. With fewer choices,

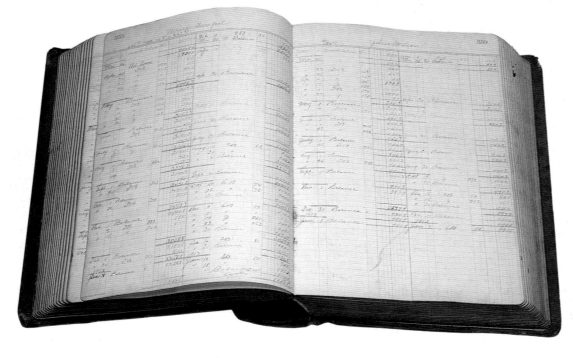

Left: A planter's ledger book from the 1912–13 period which was used to record the transactions with his sharecroppers: crop amounts, credit advanced, tools lent, and so on. The system left most southern blacks in perpetual debt.

African Americans had to take what was available: what black nurse Jane Edna Hunter described in 1905 Cleveland as 'the least disreputable room we encountered.'[7]

Indeed, it was this premium, along with the lack of choice and basic services, that most blacks considered objectionable. There is little evidence that black urbanites sought integration because they valued living alongside white people. What mattered was access to the kinds of amenities and resources one expected to find in a city. Ellen Tarry's middle-class black neighborhood in Birmingham, Alabama, had no playgrounds. But 'only two blocks away there was a beautiful city park . . . We were not permitted to sit on any of the benches, or lie on the grass or drink water from the fountains on scorching hot days. We could not even get close enough to the flowers to get a good smell.'[8] Other aromas, however, were plentiful. Water and sewer lines, like garbage collection routes, usually ended where southern black neighborhoods began.

In the North, where blacks generally lived in changing neighborhoods previously occupied by whites, such basic services were taken for granted. But many other amenities of urban life could be more problematic. Despite state civil rights acts enacted in the two decades preceding the epidemic of racism in the 1890s, such public places as hotels and restaurants informally communicated a disinclination to

Above: *Typically rural everyday items from the black South at the turn of the century. The large wooden bowl is from Mississippi and was shown in the 1905 New Orleans Exposition. The stone-bladed finishing tool is West Virginian.*

Below: *Domestic service remained a mainstay of black female employment in the early twentieth century. This nanny has two white children in her charge and was photographed in 1910 in a middle-class district of Washington, DC.*

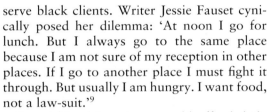

serve black clients. Writer Jessie Fauset cynically posed her dilemma: 'At noon I go for lunch. But I always go to the same place because I am not sure of my reception in other places. If I go to another place I must fight it through. But usually I am hungry. I want food, not a law-suit.'[9]

Few African Americans could afford daily lunch at a restaurant, but the color line circumscribed their access to other basic services and to jobs. Generally settlement houses, even when located in neighborhoods with significant black populations, were more interested in Americanizing immigrants than providing services to African Americans. Across the United States, the YMCA, Salvation Army, and scores of other institutions dedicated to sheltering the homeless, feeding the hungry, or caring for the sick, turned African Americans from their doors.

Racism circumscribed black opportunities in the North and kept African Americans at arm's length socially, but it was not as central to social order in general as it was in the South. There was less at stake. The economy churned ahead on the backs of working-class immigrants rather than African Americans. Most whites could live their lives insulated from racial issues. This was small comfort to blacks who did not have this luxury, but it did mean that race and social order were not as tied together in the minds of northern whites.

A Sense of 'Place'

In the South, however, most whites were obsessed with 'the Negro question.' A joke that made the rounds of southern black communities around the turn of the century centered on a young boy who found a job as a servant for an affluent white family in Georgia. His relatives, curious about what such people thought about, and ever attuned to the need for black people to keep up with what white folks were doing, questioned the boy about mealtime conversation. 'Mostly they discusses us culled folks.'[10]

Discussion, however, was the most benign form of white concern with 'their Negroes.'

Above: *African Americans' creative musical output was a strong influence on mainstream white society. Syncopated forms such as the black musicals or cakewalks were popular, as were the vibrant piano compositions of ragtime which introduced African-inspired rhythms into popular music. Thomas Turpin's 'Harlem Rag' was the first to be published, while Joplin's 'Maple Leaf Rag' was the more popular.*

The dependence of so many white men and women in the South on black labor coexisted with two important beliefs. First, black labor needed to be coerced to be reliable, a notion rooted in a combination of the heritage of two centuries of slave production and ideas about 'negro character.' 'That the negro will not work unless he is forced to work' stood as conventional wisdom according to a South Carolina judge.[11] Second, few whites doubted that black people were dangerous, not quite as civilized as white people, and certainly not as orderly. Firm mechanisms of control, therefore, seemed essential to maintain both civic stability and continued production.

The ideological underpinnings of this control lay in the concept of 'place,' a term ubiquitous in southern conversation regarding African Americans. Whites who believed that black people had a place in the South defined that place as subordinate, dependent, and permanent. In the North, black and white workers were told that ambition, hard work, orderly lives, and good citizenship established the potential to rise, or to provide better

Below: *Using three people to sweep the yard gives an indication of how cheap black female labor was to employ, whether in the South or the North. The faces of the women tell their own story.*

opportunities for one's children. Some believed the nostrums; others did not. And the extent of actual mobility is less relevant here than the ideological function of mobility in maintaining social order. Elites assumed that convincing workers of these principles of American life enhanced civic order and productive work. An ambitious worker was a diligent worker; an independent homeowner had a stake in the defense of property. Workers, black or white, who became managers, entrepreneurs, or merely homeowners were held up as examples of what lay in store for the virtu-

Below: *Jack Johnson defeated the 'Great White Hope', Jim Jeffries, for the world heavyweight title in 1910. Johnson was the embodiment of the black man who did not know his 'place,' and his win increased black pride.*

ous and ambitious. In the South, however, blacks were told that their subordinate and dependent place was permanent, natural, and just. Ambition implied dissatisfaction, a rejection of the ideology of place. Prosperity, unless accompanied by extreme humility, could be dangerous to black southerners; even a provocation for lynching. In Tennessee, a black newspaper observed that 'signs of prosperity' on the part of a black farmer aroused white 'nightriders,' ready to perform their civic duty of driving him from his land, to remind blacks of their proper place.[12] A black farmer in Georgia reflected bitterly on why the famed American success ethic meant something different in the South: 'Better not accumulate much, no matter how hard and honest you work for it, as they – well you can't enjoy it.'[13]

The reminders were constant, ranging from

SOUTHERN SHARECROPPING

All over the face of the land is the one-room cabin, – now standing in the shadow of the Big House, now staring at the dusty road, now rising dark and somber amid the green of the cotton fields. It is nearly always bare, built of rough boards, and neither plastered nor ceiled. Light and ventilation are supplied by the single door and by the square hole in the wall with its wooden shutter. There is no glass, porch, or ornamentation without. Within is a fireplace, black and smoky, and usually unsteady with age. A bed or two, a table, a wooden chest, and a few chairs compose the furniture; while a stray show-bill or a newspaper makes up the decorations for the walls . . . In such homes, then, these Negro peasants live. The families are both small and large; there are many single tenants, – widows and bachelors, and remnants of broken groups. The system of labor and the size of the houses both tend to the breaking up of family groups: the grown children go away as contract hands or migrate to town, the sister goes into service; and so one finds many families with hosts of babies, and many newly married couples, but comparatively few families with half-grown and grown sons and daughters.[1]

Note
[1] W. E. B. DuBois, *The Souls of Black Folk* [1903], in John Hope Franklin (ed.), *Three Negro Classics*, New York: Avon Books, 1965, pp. 304–5.

the imperative that black pedestrians step from the sidewalk into the street as whites approached, to titles of address (for a white southerner to address an African American as 'Mr.' or 'Mrs.' was taboo; for a black person to address a white as anything else was dangerous), to the protocol that required black men to look down when they addressed whites, especially women. The intricate rules of racial etiquette were mechanisms by which blacks were first taught and then reminded that they lacked civic dignity, that they were something less than second-class citizens.

By the 1890s, however, white southerners were increasingly concerned that young blacks were less likely to accept these roles. These fears had something to do with a peculiar version of southern history that graced the pages of newspapers, amateur local histories, and academic treatises: paternalistic antebellum planters had supposedly guided grateful slaves in building the region, but their material and cultural accomplishments had been reversed during a Reconstruction which had mistakenly placed the 'bottom rail on top.' This new generation of black southerners was the first born during the Reconstruction years when blacks had been permitted to occupy an 'inappropriate place' in southern society.

There was, in fact, something to this notion

Above: *Because black troops were believed to be more resistant to tropical diseases, they were used a great deal in the campaigns in Cuba and the Philippines. This attack by the 9th and 10th Cavalry occurred during the Battle of Quasimas.*

of a new and problematic generation. Young black men and women during the 1890s had experienced the violence of 'Redemption,' the end of Reconstruction, only as children; a bitter memory but not the crushing of hope their parents had experienced. Moreover they were coming of age during a period of unstable economic growth, with the men working in inherently transient rural industries like lumbering and turpentine. Many moved into cities, where black women were welcomed as domestics but black men had few places in the economy. The emergence of popular and occasionally interracial political movements like the Knights of Labor in the 1880s and the Populists in the 1890s suggested the unthinkable: a coalition of black and white farmers or workers.

Community Activism, Social Marginalization

The heroic exploits of black troops in the West, where they were known as the 'Buffalo Soldiers,' encouraged the kind of pride that most whites saw as dangerous. Even more

threatening was their role in the Spanish-American War, participating in the successful assault of Teddy Roosevelt's Rough Riders on Cuba's San Juan Hill. Attempts to suppress these stories in the South were not entirely successful, and their telling added to the self-awareness of younger blacks. Perhaps this generation *was* more 'uppity' than their parents, more likely to walk into a country store and slyly ask for a can of *Mr.* Prince Albert tobacco in mock deference to the white man on the can. To many white southerners it seemed that protocol, etiquette, and custom no longer regulated behavior. Perhaps, however, black southerners of all ages simply had never accepted the 'rules of the game' that whites thought were part and parcel of the overthrow of Reconstruction. James Weldon Johnson's description of an incident in Jacksonville, Florida, suggests both the implications of a minor transgression and the mood of the black community:

A Negro walking along the street eating a banana throws the peel on the sidewalk. A white policeman orders him to pick it up. He refuses. The policemen draws his club, and a struggle ensues. The Negro is down and is being severely clubbed by the policeman. He somehow gets hold of the policeman's pistol

COLONEL CHARLES YOUNG

In 1889, after becoming only the third black American to graduate from West Point, Charles Young served in the West then began his rise through the army structure, seeing action in the Spanish-American War and Mexico, serving in Haiti as America's first black military attache, and helping to organize a force in Liberia. In 1916 the National Association for the Advancement of Colored People (NAACP) awarded him their Spingarn Medal. By 1917 he was the highest ranking black officer but was forced to retire on medical grounds. He fought to be reinstated but was recalled with less than a week of World War I left. On a second tour of duty in Liberia in 1922 he became ill and died. He was buried at Arlington in 1923.

The objects below all belonged to Charles Young. Clockwise, they are: the (nonstandard) cadet lap desk which he used at West Point; his portrait from 1899; the flag used at his burial at Arlington; gold bullion epaulettes from his colonel's dress uniform; a copy of sheet music for which he wrote the lyrics and music; a cover of *Puck* magazine (21 April 1880) with a cartoon criticizing the treatment meted out to black Americans at West Point; *Crisis* magazine of February 1912 with the then Captain Young on its cover; two service medals: Spanish War Veteran's medal (left) and the Mexican Republic medal (right) from 1915; his captain's insignia; the sword presented to him by his friends in Wilberforce when he became a major; a note of support from a friend following his 'retirement'; and his razor.

and shoots him through the heart. The Negro is rushed to the Duval County jail . . . Lynching is in the air.

Here the script takes a seemingly unexpected turn. Black men with weapons surround the jail.

Women supply them with food and hot coffee. Some of the more daring of the women parade cans of kerosene, vowing that if the prisoner is lynched, they will lay the town in ashes . . . The prisoner is not lynched.[14]

Heroism and community activism aside, however, the power equation remains. Alonzo Jones, the affluent African American who bought most of the rifles is then arrested and charged with conspiracy to incite a riot. Other prominent black residents are arrested as well. Jones takes most of the heat, eventually jumps bail, flees to a small black community in a New York suburb, and dies in poverty.

This was one way to enforce white supremacy. But it was disorderly, unpredictable, and potentially destructive of property, as in Oxford, North Carolina, in 1887 where a similarly explosive situation ended with a fire. Communities dependent on a tractable black labor force were better off enforcing racial hierarchy through legislation. But first, black southerners had to be removed from the process of creating those laws.

Disfranchisement
Black voting had already been curtailed after the defeat of the Reconstruction experiments. But there was no 'solid South' yet. Although the Republican Party was barely a factor in most southern states, white Democrats split often enough to permit blacks to occasionally exercise a balance of power. In some cases powerful landowners bought the votes of black laborers, whose disdain for both factions left them prepared to squeeze whatever they could out of the political process. At other times, especially during the Populist campaigns of the 1890s, alliances between black and white farmers produced election victories – some won in the balloting but lost in the counting. Often couched in terms of 'reforming' the system by cleansing it of the corruption allegedly inherent in the participation of a dependent black electorate, disfranchisement of African Americans was also sold to white workers and farmers as necessary for the maintenance of white supremacy. Following the lead of Mississippi in 1890, southern states erected barriers and then cut loopholes through which whites could squeeze. A voter had to be able to read the state constitution, unless the registrar (invariably a white Democrat) certified his ability 'to understand the same when read to him, or give a reasonable interpretation thereof.'[15] A property or literacy requirement, or a poll tax, might be waived for men descended from 1867 voters. Known as the 'grandfather

Above: *Bessie Smith had a pedigree blues background, having been raised in southern poverty in Chattanooga, Tennessee. She was a pioneer of this sad yet triumphant musical form and became a national star during the 1920s.*

Early in the twentieth century, even before the Great Migration, traveling African-American minstrel productions, musicals, and tent shows featuring blues singers brought African-American music to northern audiences. Carnivals, circuses, and Wild West shows included African-American bands performing the latest popular songs, blues, and jazz. The migration brought spirituals and gospel songs as well as jazz and blues to Chicago, Detroit, Cleveland, and New York; various kinds of black music reached West Coast cities and points in between.

The jazz age reflected the influence of this form of African-American music not only on nightclubs, cabaret life, and musicals, but also on popular dances, such as the Charleston and the Lindy Hop. And the first sound motion picture was entitled *The Jazz Singer*, even though it was not about jazz music. Jazz expressed the rebellious spirit and general mood of abandon that seemed to dominate life in American cities during Prohibition.

Initially, many so-called blues and jazz songs were not that at all; often the genuine articles were found in the repertoires of southern black guitarists and pianists – Blind Lemon Jefferson, Sammy Price, Robert Johnson, and John Lee Hooker – rather than in the more famous white dance bands. These (at the time) lesser-known African-American musicians migrated to southern cities, Dallas and Memphis, before moving onto the black enclaves of Chicago and Los Angeles in the 1930s and 1940s.

Blues flourished in jazz bands and blues combos, and became known as rhythm and blues in the 1940s, then was adopted by whites under the designation 'rock and roll' in the 1950s. Band leaders Count Basie and Louis Jordan, tenor saxophonist Lester Young and vocalist Billie Holiday, guitarist-composer-singer Chuck Berry, and singers such as Dinah Washington all popularized blues as well as popular songs in the mid-twentieth century. White singer Elvis Presley gained fame from material sung and played in accordance with black aesthetic and musical principles, which led to wider acceptance of rock and roll. In the 1950s, blues musicians' overseas tours inspired European rock bands, particularly the Beatles and the Rolling Stones.

Black music and dance innovations revolutionized American culture. Louis Armstrong transformed trumpet (and brass), playing as well as singing; Robert Johnson and Jimi Hendrix were perhaps the only others to profoundly affect both playing and singing styles. Vocal combos of the 1930s, the Ink Spots and Mills Brothers, recast ideas about group singing. Before the rappers, bluesmen recited 'talking blues,' which were spoken more than they were sung. Lindy dancers introduced 'air steps,' catapulting their partners upward and also moving low down on the floor, like the breakdancers of the 1980s.

Despite their innovations, black musicians were not very successful in controlling the sale of their product. White businessmen dominated the music industry despite the efforts of black firms such as H. H. Pace and W. C. Handy in the 1920s. With the possible exception of band leaders Fletcher Henderson and Edward 'Duke' Ellington, or the rare soloist like Louis Armstrong, Ethel Waters, or Nat 'King' Cole, few African Americans reaped financial benefits to match their talents. Blues women Ma Rainey and Bessie Smith were typical of those whose careers did not survive the Great Depression. Only the fortunate few played the popular white nightspots – the Cotton Clubs in New York City and Los Angeles; most black showpeople performed in small 'juke' joints down South and in black dance halls and cabarets – the Savoy Ballroom, Hotcha, and Downbeat.

In Detroit in the late 1950s, black entrepreneur Berry Gordy signed composers, jazz musicians, and young singers and organized the Motown record company, and publishing and booking firms. His singular business enterprise launched singing groups – the Temptations, the Supremes, and the Jackson Five, and solo artists Stevie Wonder, Diana Ross, and Michael Jackson. Motown recordings used jazz and rock-and-roll rhythms, blues-inflected lyrics and harmonies, gospel shouts, and tambourines fused with electronic and stringed instruments to mirror the complexity of black American music culture. Like their blues, jazz, and rock-and-roll forebears, Motown singers became examples of black success as well as talent; their recordings

and performances shaped popular music, dance, language, and cultural styles throughout the world. The influence of African-American music has been profound and enduring. Blues, jazz, rock and roll, and rap became dominant music forms in the world during this century.

Douglas Henry Daniels

Above: *Louis Armstrong was one of the great jazz musicians. He changed it from an ensemble form to one with solo virtuosos, and he developed swing jazz and 'scat' vocals. 'Yellow Dog Blues' was written by W.C. Handy.*

Below: *Billie Holiday was nicknamed 'Lady Day' because of her style and charisma. From Baltimore she moved to New York and learnt her trade in the Harlem clubs. She seemed to embody the loneliness of much of blues music.*

clause,' this was occasionally supplemented by a 'fighting grandfather clause,' which enfranchised otherwise ineligible descendants of Civil War veterans, Confederate or Union. By 1910 black southerners had been virtually eliminated from the American electorate. The few who were left on the voter rolls could participate only in general elections, generally after a 'white primary' had determined the Democratic candidate. The Supreme Court would overturn these measures only gradually during the following half-century: only after the Voting Rights Act of 1965, and the bloodshed it entailed, would black southerners obtain meaningful access to the ballot box.

With political disfranchisement came social marginalization. Between 1890 and 1910, every state south of the Mason-Dixon line, from the Atlantic Coast to Texas and Oklahoma, established legislation that defined the place of African Americans in southern society. The first laws generally pertained to transportation facilities. Railroad stations had segregated waiting rooms (or blacks would wait outside); trains had separate cars. On streetcars, whites were seated from the front, blacks from the rear. Segregation touched virtually all aspects of life, especially urban life where the uncertainty of place seemed greatest. Southern segregation ordinances – Jim Crow laws – sometimes even specified the size and shape of the signs marking off 'white' and 'colored' restrooms, drinking fountains, doorways, and stairways. Public facilities routinely either segregated blacks or excluded them. In North Carolina and Florida, school textbooks had to be stored separately; journalist Ray Stannard Baker found Jim Crow Bibles in Georgia courtrooms. When the Supreme Court ruled in 1896 that the provision of separate facilities was consistent with the Constitution's guarantees to all citizens so long as the facilities were 'equal,' it legitimated separation without providing any means of guaranteeing equality. The place that Jim Crow laws defined for black southerners was invariably separate and unequal and remained so through much of the twentieth century.

In the South, African Americans exercised 'no rights that a white man need respect'; in the North they were relegated to marginal roles in politics and the industrializing economy. In neither region, however, could white racism fragment black communities or stifle their cultural vigor. Black Americans mobilized what resources they had to build institutions and maintain the struggle for unlimited access to the perquisites of citizenship.

Above: *This Jim Crow bus sign dates from the post-World War II era and is designed to be reversible; it can be flipped over whereupon it displays the message: For Colored Passengers.*

Churches

In the rural South, families, schools, and churches constituted the main building blocks of black life. In towns and cities, fraternal organizations played an equally important role. Like their white neighbors, black southerners were fundamentalists; Methodist or Baptist, they read their Bibles literally and energetically. Women, according to one historian, found a

> 'psychological center' in religious belief, and the church provided strength for those overcome by the day-to-day business of living. For many weary sharecroppers' wives and others, worship services allowed for physical and spiritual release.[16]

Although women tended to be more active participants than men, the church provided a weekly respite for all rural black southerners, a place separate from both the toil of field and cabin and the anxieties of dealing with whites in town on Saturday. Especially in the rural South and in working-class urban churches, worship remained emotional; a minister's ability to arouse enthusiasm among the congregation was a mark of his leadership and his spirituality.

Yet the church was not an escape from secular despair. Across black America, North and South, the church was very much of this world, providing an anchor for black communities. One of the few institutions that African Americans could completely control, the church provided an arena for mobilization, education, and collective expression. Few could match the ambitious program initiated by the Reverend Reverdy Ransom at Chicago's Institutional Church and Social Settlement, which included child-care, an employment bureau, classes in sewing and cooking, concerts, lectures, and a gymnasium. A black social worker's recollection of Atlanta in 1910 describes a more typical pattern:

Below: *This applique quilt was produced in Georgia in 1880 by one of the great practitioners of the art, Harriet Powers. Its panels are inspired by biblical stories which were read literally by fundamentalist southerners, both black and white.*

most of the churches had what they called a Social Service Department . . . Each Sunday the pastor would take up an 'after collection,' and during his pastoral visits the following week he would divide the amount among the shut-ins or those on the sick list.[17]

Paying in when times were good, and accepting assistance when down on their luck,

church members could give without condescension and receive without shame.

In rural areas, small cities, and even some of the largest urban communities churches stood at the center of black public life. In the South such urban public places as libraries and parks were generally unavailable, leaving the church as the universal gathering place. Other centers of conversation, such as the barbershop or

poolroom were important, but these were male spaces. The church provided women with an opening into public life, often leading them into the women's club movement and, in the North by the second decade of the twentieth century, the political arena. Men generally occupied the pulpits and controlled the finances, but women were the activists, representing two-thirds of the membership of the National Baptist Convention, the largest organization of black Americans. For men and women, the church provided openings into a broader black community through national conventions and newspapers. The African Methodist Episcopal Church's *Christian Recorder* is perhaps the best known, but in 1900 black Baptists published 43 newspapers, mostly in the South.

Fraternal Organizations

Like churches, fraternal organizations provided a focus for community activity and leadership and an opportunity to participate in a regional or national institution. Fraternals had grown slowly after the formation of the Prince Hall Masons in Boston in 1787, but by the time of the Civil War were important sites of male community life in northern cities. Encompassing men and women (usually, though not always, separately), they grew rapidly in the South after emancipation. By the early twentieth century, many combined insurance functions with social and political activities. Some operated small businesses and even banks. The Saint Luke Penny Savings Bank in Richmond founded by Maggie Lena Walker drew the small depositors suggested by its name, with an especially strong base of support among washerwomen. Its parent body, the Independent Order of Saint Luke, also operated an educational loan fund, a department store, and a weekly newspaper. For men, membership in such organizations as the Elks, Knights of Pythias, Masons, Oddfellows, or scores of other organizations, could be a badge of respectable manhood. Especially in small towns and modest cities, members who traveled to national conventions in such places as Chicago and New York had rare opportunities to glimpse urban sophistication and patterns of race relations in other places. The lodges also provided a political base; R. R. Jackson, elected to the Illinois legislature in 1912, belonged to approximately 25 fraternal orders, a guarantee of high community visibility in an era when visibility had to be built rather than purchased.

For women, with access to fewer public arenas than either African-American men or white women, voluntary associations were an especially important vehicle of leadership. Women joined traditional benevolent associa-

Left: *The well dressed congregation of the Abysinnian Baptist Church assembled outside their church hall in 1910. The church stood at the center of African-American life and provided public roles for both men and women.*

tions such as the Sisters of Charity, Daughters of Bethlehem, or Sisters of Colanthe, and by the turn of the century were also active in the women's service club movement. The formation in 1896 of the National Association of Colored Women's Clubs provided a network for women dedicated to 'lifting as we climb' and a forum for national leadership.

School Provision

The third central institution in black communities, especially in rural areas, was likely to be the school. In northern and western cities, black children frequently attended schools that were at least minimally integrated, as the process of ghettoization was still sufficiently incomplete as to yield few all-black neighborhood schools. These schools were highly valued for what they could provide children, but were *for* the black community, rather than *of* it. Whites staffed the bureaucracies that encompassed them, administered them as principals, and sat at the front of most classrooms. More often than not, these teachers accepted contemporary scientific notions about differential aptitudes according to race, or at best believed that black children were crippled by the cultural heritage of Africa and the slave South.

In the South, the first question was whether there was a school at all; then, how many months it was open, and how many children it could serve. Only half of all southern black children between 10 and 14 attended school in 1900. Among 5–9-year-olds, the proportion was one in five. Among those who did attend school, 86 percent attended for less than six months each year. In some rural areas the school 'year' was often as brief as two months. Instead, children worked in the fields. Where school was available, children went, which suggests that black parents chose school over child labor whenever possible. Planters recognized this preference and tried to keep schools unavailable, especially when the crops demanded attention. Alabama sharecropper Ned Cobb remembered 'white folks' schools was right on till May,' long after the doors had closed where he, and later his children, went to school.

> We little colored children had to jump in the white man's field and work for what we could get, go choppin cotton, go to hoein; white folks' schools runnin right on and the white man's children goin to school while we workin in his field.[18]

Rural schools were tragically inadequate when they were open. Booker T. Washington found most of them 'wretched little hovels with no light or warmth or comfort of any kind.'[19] Low teachers' salaries, a fraction of what white instructors earned, rendered it almost impossible for most communities to hire teachers with much more education than the pupils; in Tennessee, for example, 42 percent of all rural, black elementary-school

Above: *Another great institution of black life is the fraternal organization. The various lodges helped focus the community's economic strength and give people confidence. Regalia was issued to members, such as the sorority cape, cap, and sword seen here. Grand Lodge No 2 was pictured in 1897 in Greenville, Illinois.*

teachers had not completed high school.

Conditions in southern cities were somewhat better, with attendance generally ranging from 64 to 75 percent of black children between 6 and 14, slightly lower than the rate among their white peers. Considering the facilities and the financial pressures on black families, these statistics again suggest the inclination among black families to keep their children in school as long as possible. In Atlanta, black children had to endure double sessions in overcrowded buildings described by one federal official as 'dangerous and unsanitary.'[20] As late as 1915, Atlanta had no public high school for black children, nor was there one anywhere else in the state, or in Mississippi, South Carolina, North Carolina, or Louisiana. Florida, Delaware, and Maryland provided one in each state. The revolution in American secondary education, transforming a private privilege into a public right, bypassed southern black teenagers.

Left: *A classroom of black female students in Virginia in 1914. Most southern black students had to attend private schools due to the limited resources offered by public ones. Note the portrait of Lincoln, the emancipator.*

high school. But it did permit a broadened perspective. Unlike most of their parents, these men and women could read their Bibles and peruse black newspapers; judging from the mail received by their leaders and institutions, even the barely literate considered themselves correspondents, capable of writing and receiving letters.

For further schooling black southerners generally had to rely on private schools. Some of these were small institutions supported by the financial contributions and labor of local residents who bore a burden of dual taxation. They supported both a public system that provided only meager resources at the elementary level to black children, and a private school that was a community institution in the most expansive sense. At the turn of the century, three-quarters of black secondary-school students in the South attended private schools. These were the leaders of the next generation, the young men and women who learned responsibility to the community while they read history and philosophy, practiced domestic science or agriculture, and studied chemistry. There was no strict dichotomy between 'industrial' schools like Tuskegee and Hampton Institute on the one hand, and liberal arts colleges like Atlanta University. Most of the private black colleges included 'preparatory' divisions; most combined 'practical' and 'academic' subjects with an emphasis on forming character. 'Industry' was as likely to refer to a character trait as it was to a sector of the economy.

Booker T. Washington and W. E. B. DuBois

But there was a difference in philosophy, a difference that seemed more pronounced because it symbolized a division among African-American elites as to the most effective response to the rising tide of racism at the end of the nineteenth century. Tuskegee, Hampton, and their numerous offshoots were less concerned with preparing black students to compete with whites or to challenge directly the ideological underpinnings of racism than to earn a living in the South and raise the moral and material standards of southern black communities. Booker T. Washington's speech at the 1895 Atlanta Exposition advised black southerners to 'cast down your bucket where you are,' and reassured white southerners that his mission to improve the living conditions of his people implied no ambition to social or political equality.[22] This reassurance explains the willingness of whites, North and South, to recognize Washington as the preeminent spokesman of black America at the turn of the century. Indeed, Washington's biographer has argued that, had he not been so conciliatory and nonthreatening,

Above: *Booker Taliaferro Washington was born into a slave family in 1856 but benefited from emancipation. A leading advocate of vocational education, he established the Tuskegee Institute and became a leading black conservative figure.*

Their exclusion stemmed not only from a reluctance to allocate funds for the benefit of African Americans. Although many white southerners believed that 'Negro education' was useful if it taught diligence and patient subordination, many others increasingly opposed all education for blacks. 'Whites should cease to support free schools for the blacks,' declared the chair of the University of Virginia faculty at the 1900 meeting of the Southern Educational Association. 'The schools tended to make some negroes idle and vicious . . . and others able to compete with whites.'[21] The argument had come full circle. Education for African Americans was a waste of time since they couldn't learn anything; and it was dangerous because they might learn enough to compete with whites.

Most did learn, although seldom beyond the basics. Black literacy rates in the South rose from 7 percent at emancipation, to 44 percent in 1890 and 77 percent in 1920. This education seldom translated into better jobs; few were available even for those who completed

'another Washington would be created.'[23]

Washington was not, however, purely a creature of his white patrons, most of whom were northern philanthropists. Despite his insistence that the quest for political rights and power during Reconstruction had been a mistake – in part because it had raised the specter of 'social equality' and in part because a solid agricultural base should have been established first – he was a brilliant politician and organizer. Using funds provided by his philanthropic patrons, he subsidized black newspapers in cities across the country, which complemented the network of Tuskegee offshoots dotting the southern countryside. The Tuskegee machine commanded enough influence by 1900 to win control over the Afro-American Council, transforming the 10-year-old organization from a militant protest organization into a rather mild annual gathering. That same year, Washington established the National Negro Business League, which grew to 320 branches within eight years. Although the organization did little to promote black business, it created a nationwide network emanating from Tuskegee and at least rhetorically underscored his celebration of business values. Although Washington apparently worked behind the scenes in the fight against disfranchisement and segregation, he and Tuskegee emerged as icons of accommodation both to the racial order of the South and to the shibboleths of industrial capitalism.

Above: *Tuskegee Institute opened originally in 1881, but nationwide fund raising success allowed new buildings to be built subsequently, and the marching band seen assembled here in 1913 is preparing for a commencement day parade.*

Below: *Popular prejudice categorized African Americans as lacking mechanical aptitude, but these miniature tools – tongs and hammers – were made for the Colored Peoples Industrial Exhibition held in September 1886.*

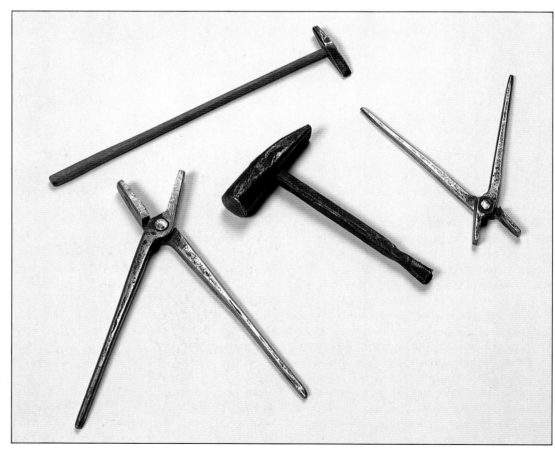

Washington's stature among black Americans derived as much from pride in what he had accomplished as from agreement with his educational or political philosophy. The intelligentsia of the race, especially, were quick to reject what became known as the 'Atlanta Compromise.' John Hope, a young black educator and future college president, heard the speech and declared five months later that it was 'cowardly and dishonest for any of our colored men to tell white people or colored people that we are not struggling for equality.'[24] An even stronger rebuff came from Boston, where newspaper editor William Monroe Trotter denounced 'Pope Washington, the Black Boss, the Benedict Arnold of the Negro race, the Exploiter of Exploiters, the Great Traitor, and the Great Divider.'[25]

The most significant voice in opposition to Washington belonged to W. E. B. DuBois, already prominent at the turn of the century as a sociologist and educator. Like Washington, DuBois believed in self-help, racial solidarity, and thrift. The Tuskegee agenda of industrial education for the masses and the encouragement of black business enterprise was equally amenable. But he shared neither Washington's faith in the potential of the South nor his willingness to work within the framework of white supremacy. In 1902 DuBois explained his sense of dislocation: 'a certain sort of soul, a certain kind of spirit finds the narrow repression, the provincialism of the South almost unbearable.'[26] Nor could he stomach the abandonment, or even the postponement, of the quest for full citizenship. The rhetorical choice of vocational education over the kind of liberal education that was assumed appropriate for white college students was a closely related issue; leading citizens needed a first-class education. Moreover, argued DuBois, it was not the shallow materialism of Gilded Age commerce that provided a potential basis for a national consensus across racial lines. Rather it was the values taught in a liberal arts curriculum and was related to citizenship in a modern state: justice, truth, and the aesthetic and moral bases of civic culture.

Citizenship remained the key issue. In 1905, a group of young African Americans, led by DuBois, met at Niagara Falls to form an organization to confront white racism and demand all rights of American citizenship and the abolition of racial distinctions. Although it commanded little attention from whites, and never became a political force, the militant Niagara Movement represented a turning point in African-American politics. When a group of white and black reformers met in response to the 1909 race riot in Springfield, Illinois, the Niagara Movement was folded into their new organization dedicated to the battle for full citizenship: the National Association for the Advancement of Colored People (NAACP). To those uncertain about the large role whites played in the new organization, Ida B. Wells reiterated a statement she had made at an Afro-American League meet-

Above: *William Edward Burghardt Du Bois was of a school of black thought very different from that of Washington. He was a militant advocate of self-pride, agitation to obtain equality, and argued for an elite, black leadership class.*

Below: *George Washington Carver was Tuskegee's most famous agricultural scientist. He developed more than 300 products from the peanut and over 100 from the sweet potato, helping the South out of a dependence on cotton.*

African-American life in the rural South was hard. The forces of law and order were discriminatory, political life was stifled, and economic life was incredibly tough and unrewarding. The promise of new opportunities in the North – or even limited ones in the cities of the South – acted as a beacon of hope for many, but new challenges existed there too. Many found the new life did not suit them and returned to the South

Above: *Four black convicts in a chain gang. The Jim Crow system made chain gangs an essential part of the system of control and suppression. African Americans were arrested for supposed misdemeanours, convicted, and then leased out – effectively put into servitude – to businesses that profited from their enforced labor.*

ing in 1898: the American race problem was more a 'white problem' than a 'Negro problem.' Progress required white investment in the process of change.

The Great Migration North

While educated African Americans in leadership positions organized and joined with white allies in the struggle against the 'color line,' black southerners began to look to migration as a route to new opportunity. Until 1916 this quest had generally remained oriented toward landownership. Exodusters had headed toward Kansas thinking about homesteads. Families working worn-out lands in Georgia and North Carolina had been receptive in the 1880s and 1890s to rumors of rich land and generous rental arrangements in the Missis-

sippi Delta. But the agrarian hopes of the freedmen, embodied in Booker T. Washington's vision of a race of sturdy yeomen, remained unfulfilled by their grandchildren. Then in 1916, a combination of circumstances occasioned by World War I opened a new set of possibilities, a new future for African Americans. Producing for European combatants and a domestic market stimulated by the preparedness program of Woodrow Wilson's administration, northern industrialists needed labor. But the war had cut off European immigration, eliminating the usual source of additional labor. Casting about for possibilities, employers opened their gates to white women and African Americans. The mobilization of the American forces in 1917, which included 260,000 black troops, exacerbated the labor shortage, opening more opportunities.

These jobs, in railroad yards, steel mills, packinghouses, and other industries, paid wages far beyond what was available in the rural or urban South. Northern cities also offered schools, voting booths, legal rights, and simple human dignity. In essence they seemed to promise black southerners life with

that they were at least familiar with.

The rural, southern homes that blacks left behind were, all too often, not their own; they belonged to the landowners for whom they worked and sharecropped. Not surprisingly, most homes were therefore small and poorly constructed because of the quality of materials available.

Typically, homes were one- or two-room wooden-framed houses or cabins, many built in the 'dogtrot' or 'shotgun' styles so common in the South. Dogtrot houses got their name from

an open breezeway or 'trot' between two enclosed rooms, each of them having a fireplace and deriving originally from an English design.

The shotgun house is believed to have originated in the early 1800s from an old African design brought to the New Orleans area by free blacks from the West Indies. The name may be derived from the West African word 'to-gan,' meaning a place of assembly. The shotgun was one story high with a gable end and the front door facing the street, other rooms (if any) running behind in a line.

The occupants did, of course, try to brighten up their surroundings and lend homely touches to create a warmer, more comfortable atmosphere but, very often, this could not disguise the fact that in these very cramped quarters families usually cooked, ate, lived, and slept together in the same room. This particular cabin has one room downstairs and one room upstairs. It was built by the family that lived in it and is preserved in the National Museum of American History, Smithsonian Institution, in Washington, DC.

all the 'priveleg that the whites have' as one New Orleans woman declared before heading for Chicago.[27]

So they moved, some 500,000 black southerners between 1916 and 1919, and twice that many in the following decade. This movement, often referred to as the 'Great Migration,' ebbed and flowed until the 1970s, shifting the center of gravity for African-American culture from the rural South to the urban North. Southern cities also attracted considerable numbers of black men and women from the nearby countryside, but the best opportunities lay in the North where wages were higher. Southern cities offered no respite from Jim Crow, poor schools, and a continuation of second-class citizenship. Northward migration, by contrast, affected one's state of mind. Some migrants stopped their watches when they crossed the Ohio River; others placed triumphant banners on the sides of their trains, or walked proudly (if sometimes nervously) out of the Jim Crow car.[28]

The Great Migration, like the movement of immigrants from abroad, was anything but a random relocation of people fleeing from oppression. Nor was it structured purely by the vicissitudes of the labor market, distributing workers across the North according to where the jobs were and how much they were paid. The folklore of the Great Migration scripts a major role for labor agents –

Below: *Helen Burroughs was an admirer of Booker T. Washington. She trained her students to work hard and proposed the three Bs as well as the three Rs – Bible, bath, and broom – for a clean life, a clean body, and a clean home.*

ALBERT CREW

Above: *Rufus Crew, father of Albert and grandfather of Spencer, sat on the porch of his modest home. The family history encapsulates the black experience of the Great Migration.*

Albert Crew's journey from the South to Cleveland, Ohio, did not follow a direct or a predetermined path. His was, however, a resettlement pattern followed by many African Americans during the Great Migration. Born in 1906, Albert lived in Norris, South Carolina, for the first seven years of his life. He was the third child in a young, growing family. His father, Rufus Crew, worked as a stationary engineer operating machinery at a nearby sawmill. He did not earn high wages, but the work was steady and provided a regular income for his family. Madie, Rufus's wife, supplemented his earnings and provided food for the family by planting a small plot of land. Combined, the truck garden and Rufus's salary allowed the family a stable, though modest existence.

The nearby presence of the parents and siblings of both Rufus and Madie added to the

contentment of living in Norris. Madie, in particular, was very close to her family and regularly visited with her sisters. Albert had many cousins to play with and was able to explore the surrounding areas. It was an enjoyable existence for a young African American growing up in the South at the turn of the century.

In 1913 the family left Norris and moved to Atlanta, Georgia. At the time Albert was not sure why they relocated. Later he learned they left because his father had a violent falling-out with his supervisor at the sawmill. Fearful about the safety of his family, Rufus decided to leave the area. In addition, Madie's sisters had left Norris to resettle in Atlanta, and, with her mother's death, she was anxious to join them. With these incentives, the family packed their belongings and took the Southern Railroad from South Carolina to Atlanta. Albert vividly remembered the train ride with his family and their arrival in the city. He recalled his uncle's meeting them at the station and transporting them in his wagon to his home. As they traveled through the city, Albert found it very hard to obey his mother's instructions not to stare and point at all the new sights.

The family stayed with Madie's sister until they moved into a place of their own. Albert remembers moving several times while they lived in Atlanta. Rufus found a job working as a stationary fireman, and Madie held several jobs until the family opened a small neighborhood grocery store that she operated. Albert attended school and performed odd jobs to supplement the family income. As they had in Norris, the family established a stable existence.

Life in segregated Atlanta did have its shortcomings. Nearly everywhere African Americans traveled they faced restrictions that limited their choices. Albert learned to take these restrictions in stride, but he saw the roadblocks they placed in his way. His father recognized them, too, and encouraged his children to get out of the South and escape the problems he had faced all of his life.

With the start of World War I, new opportunities opened for African Americans in northern cities suffering from a shortage of workers. Gene, Albert's older brother, left Atlanta, joining his mother's sister, Margaret, in Cleveland, Ohio. After Gene's departure, Albert's two older sisters followed. Albert's turn came in May 1923 when he headed North by train, using a free pass his uncle, a porter, obtained for him. The overnight ride on the Southern Railroad carried him to Cleveland by way of Cincinnati.

His cousin Josh met Albert at Union Station and took him to stay with his brother, Gene.

Below: *A poor, rural black family in the American South; in 1890 three-quarters of African Americans lived in the South in situations similar to this, but just three decades later only half remained.*

Albert had heard the stories about the high wages available to northern workers. He expected to find a job quickly and to make his fortune in a couple of years. The work world Albert found in Cleveland differed from his expectations. His first job was cleaning cars at the Pullman Company, but within the first month the company cut his hours and reduced his earnings. Hoping to make more money, he quit that job, but found his options severely limited. After more than a year of intermittent work at a variety of places, he eventually found steady employment at the Damascus Great Beam Company. He stayed at the Damascus Company until the Depression hit when he and many other workers lost their jobs. Albert eventually found work in the Cleveland public school system.

Even with these difficulties, Albert found Cleveland better than Atlanta. It offered many more choices and greater opportunities. Cleveland was not the promised land, but Albert felt it offered a much better general existence than he could have had in the South. He never regretted making the choice to resettle.

Spencer R. Crew

recruiters who went South to entice uninformed and provincial African Americans to work for northern employers. At the beginning of the process, northern railroads did hire such agents, as did industries in small northern cities. How else could steel plants in Beloit, Wisconsin, or Lorain, Ohio, attract black workers? But generally people moved to where they already knew someone, usually a relative, possibly a former neighbor, lodge brother, or member of the same church. Whole congregations relocated. Drawing on these networks, women and men wrote before leaving, seeking information about housing, jobs, and the weather. 'What do they pay per day in those plants now?' wrote J. W. Mitchell to Pittsburgh. 'Can wommen find work to do up there at a living wag? What does house rent and fuel cost per month?'[29] Letters, newspapers, visits among family members, fraternal and church conventions, black railroad men, musicians: taken together these constituted a communications network that permitted prospective migrants to plan their move.

The Urban League and World War I

Those who did not write letters could glean information from the many black newspapers with significant circulation in the South. Read aloud in pulpits, barbershops, poolrooms, and other gathering places, newspapers like the *Chicago Defender*, *New York Age*, and *Pittsburgh Courier* shaped black southerners' images of what they would find. They also informed prospective migrants about services available upon arrival, most notably the Urban League. Founded in 1911 to seek out and pry open new job opportunities for blacks, and to assist migrants, the League's local branches mushroomed in 1916. Known in parts of the South as an organization 'that cares for colored emigrants,' the Urban League provided assistance and tried to shape newcomers' behavior so that they would not embarrass the community by acting excessively southern or rural.[30] This included working with employers (many of whom were major donors) to inculcate proper work habits among laborers generally new to factory routines. In many cities, this activity spilled over into advising workers whether to join unions or participate in strikes. Although at the national level the League supported unionization whenever a union admitted black workers on an equal basis, few unions satisfied this requirement. Most local branch officials, with the notable exception of T. Arnold Hill of Chicago, regarded union-organizing drives as opportunities for black workers to demonstrate their reliability.

Indeed it was this notion of the race 'proving itself' to whites that seems to have united a variety of otherwise disparate perspectives. Like Washington, many Urban Leaguers and other community leaders believed barriers to equal employment opportunity would fall in the face of massive evidence of black competence and loyalty. Nannie Helen Burroughs,

Above: *Despite the Charles Young affair, hundreds of thousands of African Americans served in the armed forces during World War I, and the first two Americans to be cited for valor were both African Americans.*

founding president of the National Training School for Women and Girls (established in 1909), was confident that professionalizing domestic service would transform it into a respected profession. DuBois and most of his allies in the NAACP encouraged African Americans to 'join ranks' behind the war effort, assuming service and citizenship were related; by proving their valor and loyalty on the battlefield, black men would win respect at home. Thousands of black church women envisioned group advancement emanating from a 'politics of respectability that equated public behavior with individual self-respect.'[31] Hence their eagerness to join with the Urban League and black newspapers in teaching newcomers how to dress and act.

It was impossible, however, to shield

northern black urban culture from the world the migrants brought with them. The emotionalism of the storefront church, the transformation of rural work songs into a hard-edged urban blues, southern cooking – southern culture imprinted itself indelibly on the northern urban cultural landscape.

But that landscape would not become the 'promised land' described on banners hanging from northbound trains. At the end of the war, layoffs struck black workers first. Black women would wait another generation before finding many alternatives to cleaning other people's houses. Newcomers lived in housing that was vastly superior to sharecropper's cabins, but rapidly deteriorating due to overcrowding and landlord neglect. By 1920 New York's Harlem had become a slum, a condition already common in urban black America. Most ghettos had by then grown sufficiently large that school boards could gerrymander districts to segregate black children. Migration had brought access to workplaces, schools, and ballot boxes; but access was clearly not

Right: The cover of Collier's Weekly *of 26 November 1898 distorted events in Wilmington, North Carolina. A white mob had murdered 11 blacks to intimidate them out of politics. It summed up the turn of the century South.*

enough without sufficient material and political resources.

In 1917 racial violence struck East St. Louis, a prelude to the 'red summer' of 1919, when approximately 25 riots victimized black Americans during the last seven months of the year. Most of these took place in the North, sparked by tensions over jobs or neighborhood turf. In the South, riots often reflected white concern over the return of black World War I veterans, men whose guns and uniforms implicitly threatened assumptions about the relationship between place, citizenship, and black self-assertion.

That riots were a national phenomenon confirmed the persistence of racism in American culture. But the regional comparison is important. To most black men and women who had taken the initiative to 'better their condition' by moving from South to North, there had indeed been a 'second emancipation.'[32] 'I havent heard a white man call a colored a nigger you no now – since I been in the state of Pa.,' wrote one migrant to a doctor in his home town in 1917. 'I can ride in the electric street and steam cars any where I get a seat . . . I am not crazy about being with white folks, but if I have to pay the same fare I have learn to want the same acomidation.'[33]

Notes

[1]W. E. B. DuBois, *The Souls of Black Folk* [1903], in John Hope Franklin (ed.), *Three Negro Classics*, New York: Avon Books, 1965, p. 307.

[2]Richard Wright, *Twelve Million Black Voices: A Folk History of the Negro in the United States*, New York: Viking, 1941, p. 64.

[3]Theodore Rosengarten, *All God's Dangers: The Life of Nate Shaw*, New York: Knopf, 1974, p. 181–2.

[4]E. Franklin Frazier, 'King Cotton,' *Opportunity*, 4, 38 (February 1926): 51.

[5]Henry Grady [1883], quoted in Paul M. Gaston, *The New South Creed: A Study in Southern Mythmaking*, Baton Rouge: Louisiana State University Press, 1975, p. 125.

[6]Robert Drake, quoted in Kenneth L. Kusmer, *A Ghetto Takes Shape: Black Cleveland, 1870–1930*, Urbana: University of Illinois Press, 1976, p. 42.

[7]Quoted in Kusmer, *A Ghetto Takes Shape*, p. 42.

[8]Ellen Tarry, *The Third Door: The Autobiography of an American Negro*, New York: Guild Press, expanded edition, 1966; original publication, 1955, p. 14.

[9]Jessie Fauset, 'Some Notes on Color,' *World Tomorrow*, 5 (March 1922): 76. Quoted in David M. Katzman, *Before the Ghetto: Black Detroit in the Nineteenth Century*, Urbana: University of Illinois Press, 1973, p. 94.

[10]Lawrence W. Levine, *Black Culture and Black Consciousness: Afro-American Folk Thought from Slavery to Freedom*, New York: Oxford University Press, 1977, p. 315.

[11]William Cohen, *At Freedom's Edge: Black Mobility and the Southern White Quest for Racial Control 1861–1915*, Baton Rouge: Louisiana State University Press, 1991, p. 282.

[12]*Nashville Globe*, 23 July 1909. Quoted in Lester Lamon, *Black Tennesseans, 1900–1930*, Knoxville: University of Tennessee Press, 1977, pp. 117–18.

[13]Letter to *Chicago Defender* (name withheld by request), 28 April 1917.

[14]James Weldon Johnson, *Along This Way: The Autobiography of James Weldon Johnson*, New York: Viking, 1933, pp. 131–2.

[15]Mississippi *Constitution*, 1890, article 12, sections 240–3. Quoted in Neil McMillen, *Dark Journey: Black Mississippians in the Age of Jim Crow*, Urbana: University of Illinois Press, 1989, p. 42.

[16]Jacqueline Jones, *Labor of Love, Labor of Sorrow: Black Women, Work, and the Family from Slavery to the Present*, New York: Basic Books, 1985, p. 102.

[17]Jesse O. Thomas, *My Story in Black and White: The Autobiography of Jesse O. Thomas*, New York: Exposition Press, 1967.

[18]Rosengarten, *All God's Dangers*, p. 25.

[19]Booker T. Washington, 'Rural Negro and the South,' *Proceedings of the National Conference of Charities and Correction*, 41 (1914): 125.

[20]Thomas Jesse Jones, *Schools for Colored People*, pamphlet, Washington, DC: Government Printing Office, 1915, p. 8.

[21]Paul B. Barringer, quoted in James D. Anderson, *The Education of Blacks in the South, 1860–1935*, Chapel Hill: University of North Carolina Press, 1988, p. 96.

[22]Booker T. Washington, *Up From Slavery*, reprinted in Franklin, *Three Negro Classics*, pp. 146–7.

[23]Louis Harlan, 'Booker T. Washington and the Politics of Accommodation,' in John Hope Franklin and Leon F. Litwack (eds), *Black Leaders of the Twentieth Century*, Urbana: University of Illinois Press, 1982, p. 9.

[24]John Hope, quoted in Anderson, *The Education of Blacks in the South*, p. 104.

[25]Trotter quoted in Harlan, 'Booker T. Washington,' p. 6.

[26]Quoted in *Savannah Tribune*, 8 March 1902, in John Dittmer, *Black Georgia in the Progressive Era, 1900–1920*, Urbana: University of Illinois Press, 1977, p. 174.

[27]Emmett J. Scott (comp.), 'Additional Letters of Negro Migrants of 1916–1918,' *Journal of Negro History*, 4 (October 1919): 426.

[28]Emmett J. Scott (comp.), 'Letters of Negro Migrants of 1916–1918,' *Journal of Negro History*, 4 (July 1919): 315.

[29]J. W. Mitchell to John T. Clark, 12 December 1922, quoted in Peter Gottlieb, *Making Their Own Way: Southern Blacks' Migration to Pittsburgh, 1916–1930*, Urbana: University of Illinois Press, 1987, p. 52.

[30]Scott, 'Letters': 291.

[31]Evelyn Brooks Higginbotham, *Righteous Discontent: The Women's Movement in the Black Baptist Church, 1880–1920*, Cambridge: Harvard University Press, 1993, p. 14.

[32]James R. Grossman, *Land of Hope: Chicago, Black Southerners, and the Great Migration*, Chicago: University of Chicago Press, 1989, p. 35.

[33]Scott, 'Additional Letters': 461.

Chapter 7

FROM HARD TIMES TO HOPE

World War I catapulted the nation into the position of world military and economic power. At home it helped change the color and culture of major American cities and ultimately the nature of American race relations. Economic hardships continued in overcrowded, newly formed, northern urban ghettos, but the concentration of African-American culture meant a flourishing literature, music, art and theater – in New York's Harlem, in Chicago, in Philadelphia, Washington, DC, and other cities – and constituted a black cultural renaissance. Adversity and opportunity mingled as the millions of African Americans who came North formed a political force that brought black politicians into office for the first time since the end of Reconstruction. Despite their increased economic misery, the Great Depression created a shift in politics toward a new deal even for black people, while wartime opportunities and the national mobilization against Nazi racism in Europe promised new hope for racial equity in America.

Migrating north by car was the exception rather than the rule, and the vast majority of southern African-American migrants used the railway system to seek new lives and better opportunities in northern cities such as Chicago, Detroit, New York, and Philadelphia. Despite the massive transfer of population which these changes entailed, the majority of African Americans continued to live in the South.

Nearly a million blacks left the South for northern and western cities between 1920 and 1930, bringing the proportion of blacks living in cities up from 27 to over 43 percent. Under the impact of rapid industrial expansion, new immigration restriction legislation, and the persistence of abusive conditions in southern agriculture, African Americans continued to gain jobs in the mass-production industries of iron, steel, automobile, rubber, and meatpacking. In heavy manufacturing cities like Detroit, Cleveland, Pittsburgh, and Milwaukee, the percentage of black men employed in the industrial sector increased from little more than 10–20 percent in 1910 to over 60–70 percent in 1920 and 1930.

Wages in northern industries averaged $3–5 per eight-hour day compared to little more than 75¢ in southern agriculture. Even in southern cities, blacks made $2.50 per 12-hour day, much higher than income in the agricultural South. Few black women gained jobs in the industrial sector, but female domestic and personal servants also earned more in cities than their counterparts in the rural South.

Above: Crisis, *the publication of the National Association for the Advancement of Colored People, presented stories of black achievement and cause for pride. This June 1916 edition honored African Americans in military service.*

The New Negro, 1921–9

Although these 'New Negroes' slowly improved their position in the urban-industrial environment of the nation, they soon faced new patterns of inequality. Employers, labor unions, and urban institutions confined blacks to the so-called 'Negro jobs.' As one northern black worker recalled, African-American men 'were limited, they only did the dirty work . . . jobs that even Poles didn't want.'[1] White workers also described black workers as a 'scab race' and excluded them from unions and higher-paying skilled positions. Even more so than black men, black women faced the impact of discriminatory employer and labor-union policies. As black men gained increasing access to factory jobs and as white women moved into clerical and professional positions in growing numbers, few black women managed to move out of domestic and personal-service work. Moreover, black men and women were invariably the 'Last Hired and the First Fired.'

Below: *This picture was taken in Newark, New Jersey, in 1918, and shows African-American veterans of World War I relaxing in a club opened specially for black servicemen by these patriotic women in order to welcome them home.*

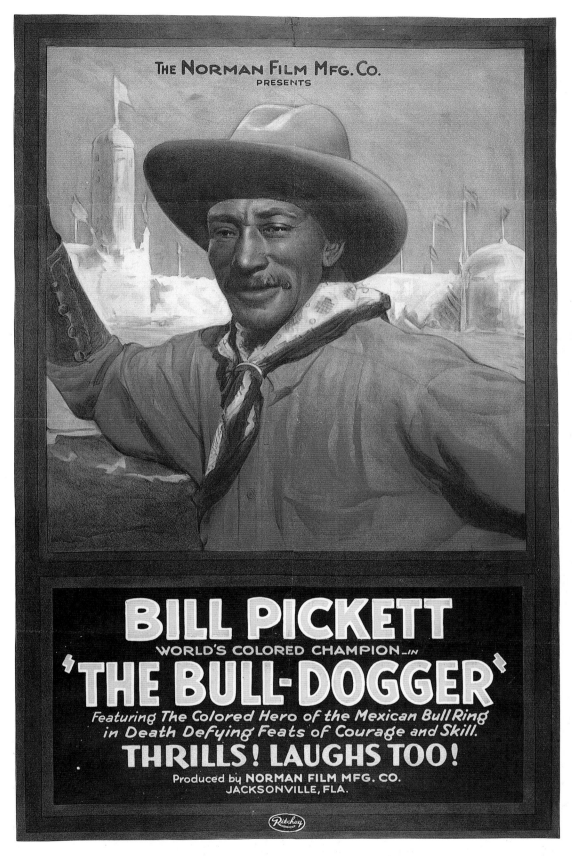

Above: *A poster from* The Bull-Dogger, *a movie about black rodeo cowboy Bill Pickett. The 1918 period onward saw the creation of a genre of all-black cast films which broke from the stereotypical roles of mainstream productions.*

Above: *Two early examples of African-American grooming and beauty products. The market for such items was large and Madame C.J. Walker and Mrs A.E. Malone both became millionairesses from sales of products they created.*

African Americans also confronted restrictions on where they could live. White property-owners' associations, realtors, and municipal authorities resisted black occupancy of previously all-white neighborhoods. City governments approved the use of restrictive covenants barring the sale of property to African Americans, Jews, and other despised minorities, and residential segregation increased. In various cities, African Americans were relegated to the vice districts, and 'ordinary conveniences were often non-existent: toilets were broken or leaked; electricity was rare; heating and hot water facilities failed to function.'[2] By the late 1920s, racial restrictions in housing intensified the problems of crowding, crime, sanitation, and health care for urban blacks.

African Americans devised a variety of strategies for dealing with urban discrimination. The increasing numbers of urban black workers, their access to higher wages, and their segregation within the city established the foundations for the growth of black business and professional enterprises. 'New Negroes' developed new services in law, medicine, dentistry, journalism, and music, to serve an increasingly segregated predominantly working-class black clientele. Black businesspeople created new insurance, real-estate, restaurant, cosmetic, boarding, recreational, and sports establishments, including professional baseball teams like the Homestead Grays, the Pittsburgh Crawfords, and the Kansas City Monarchs. The cosmetics industry, established by Madame C. J. Walker, the first black woman millionaire and pioneer in beauty products for black women, attracted increasing numbers of black patrons during the 1920s. As the newspaper columnist George Schuyler wrote:

The psychological effect of Madame Walker's great activity has been of great importance and can hardly be over-estimated. Besides giving dignified employment to thousands of women who would otherwise have had to make their living in domestic service, she stimulated a great deal of interest generally in the care of their hair.[3]

'New Negroes' also launched a rigorous

THE BARBERSHOP

African-American men valued barbershops as places where they could discuss courtship and marriages, health and family matters, and politics. Fathers brought young boys to barbershops to enjoy an all-male environment and to become socialized in its ways. Women used beauty parlors in a similar way; they were a single-sex environment where women discussed community issues, health problems, family, parenthood, and men.

new era of institution-building activities and raised new demands for full inclusion in American society, as citizens. Churches, fraternal orders, and social-welfare organizations, together with labor unions, civil rights, and political organizations, all rapidly expanded. These institutions enabled African Americans to forge bonds across class, gender, generational, and regional lines. Religious and churchgoing activities retained their hold on many blacks as they made the transition from rural to industrial America. As one migrant put it, 'I was born in Church.' Another said, 'The church was the only thing we had.'[4] Black urbanites not only continued to join established Baptist and Methodist bodies, but opened new 'storefront' holiness churches, which gave them greater freedom to pursue their southern rural forms of worship, including 'shouting' and 'speaking in tongues.' Even as African Americans built upon their southern rural traditions, they transformed them to meet the new demands of urban life. Although blacks carried their rural spirituals to the city, for example, they soon created 'a more expressive' gospel music. Alongside the transformation of spirituals into gospel, African Americans also elaborated upon the blues form. They soon fused the older rural blues traditions with 'the new learning' and produced the urban blues. Beginning in 1920, when the Okeh Record Company released its first commercial blues recordings, urban blues flourished as a popular form on 'race record' labels.

The Struggle Revived

During World War I, African Americans had 'closed ranks,' supported the war, and post-

Above: *Large and ornate, this busy barbershop in late 1920s Harlem exemplifies the importance of the black hairdressing business as well as the single-sex meeting-place atmosphere.*

poned their grievances in the interest of national defense, but in the war's aftermath they revived and extended their struggle against racial and class inequality. W. E. B. DuBois, editor of the National Assocation for the Advancement of Colored People's (NAACP's) *Crisis* magazine captured the spirit of their fight. 'We Soldiers of Democracy,' he wrote, 'return . . . We return from fighting. We return fighting. Make way for Democracy. We saved it in France, and by the Great Jehovah, we will save it in the United States of America, or know the reason why.'[5] W. E. B. DuBois, James Weldon Johnson, and the NAACP waged a relentless fight against racial barriers and demanded full citizenship rights for 'all Americans.' In 1920, James Weldon Johnson became the first black to occupy the top executive secretary's post of the NAACP. Under his leadership and that of assistant secretary Walter White, African Americans gradually controlled the organization and set its agenda. Although unsuccessful, during the 1920s the organization launched a vigorous antilynching campaign. At the same time, it continued to attack the legal foundations of Jim Crow, disfranchisement, and mob violence. When a black dentist, Dr. Ossian Sweet, shot and killed a member of a white mob who attacked his home in a previously all-white neighborhood in Detroit, the NAACP defended the rights of blacks to use violence in self-defense.

Mary Talbert, Ida B. Wells-Barnett, and the militant antilynching activists reinforced the

The barber, or beautician, often shared customers' secrets and offered advice on a range of topics – unsurprisingly, their shops became community centers where people dropped by to talk or just to watch television.

Black Americans had dominated the trade of barber since the earliest days. In the mid-nineteenth century Frederick Douglass had noticed that immigrants were beginning to make inroads into the black dominance of the trade and in 1853 he wrote a piece entitled 'Learn Trades or Starve' in which he observed that: 'a few years ago, and a white barber would have been a curiosity – now their poles stand on every street.' With strong roots in his own community the black barber survived.

At the turn of the century, two African-American barbers, John Merrick and Alonzo F. Herndon, demonstrated the importance of that role in the community, and that of the emerging black business class, by being the prime movers behind the establishment of black-run insurance companies: the North Carolina Mutual in 1898 and the Atlanta Life Insurance Company in 1905, respectively.

Barbershops, and beauty parlors, were independent businesses with a steady clientele and, as such, were important expressions of black entrepreneurial activity. Their owners were commonly among the wealthiest and most prominent people in black communities, and such was their role in the social life of the community that some became important organizational centers during the civil rights period. This particular preserved interior dates from the 1940s.

THE KU KLUX KLAN

Founded in Tennessee in 1866 the secretive, white supremacist organization known as the Ku Klux Klan (from the Greek for circle and the English for clan) was the largest of many groups intent on reversing the tentative progress made in establishing and protecting the rights of African Americans. They aimed to restore a system of white political domination and black subservience, and their methods were those of nightime terror, intimidation, and murder. Poor whites feared that political equality and social equality would leave them at the bottom alongside black Americans, bereft of what privilege their white skin afforded.

The Klan was suppressed by the government in the 1870s, but whenever the white community of the South found themselves under pressure to concede political rights to African Americans, the Klan grew.

Its heyday was in the 1920s when, following the changes wrought by World War I, it gained a membership of nearly nine million. The bizarre rituals and clothing were very much part of its self-perceived sense of power and drama; the distinctive white hood and robe seen here date from the 1920s.

Again, during the late 1950s and the onset of the civil rights era, the Klan was among those elements of southern white society most committed to opposing integration and retaining the status quo. Although much reduced in size, power, and influence, it continues to this day.

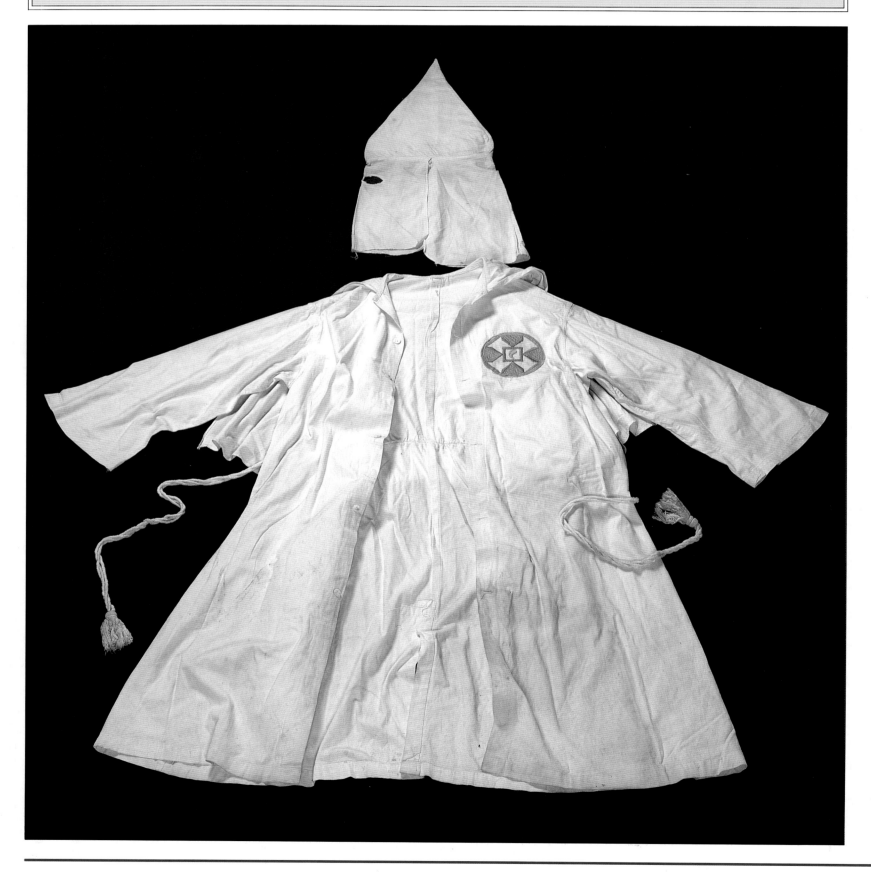

Below: *In the 1920s and 1930s the Klan spread beyond the South; this midnight gathering near Chicago is of 30,000 members, many of them perhaps reacting against the newly-arrived black migrants from the South. The brochure and form (left and above) base some of their appeal on mysticism.*

NAACP's campaign for full citizenship and equal protection under the law. Under the leadership of Mary Talbert, president of the National Association of Colored Women, in 1922 black women launched the Anti-lynching Crusaders and supported the NAACP's campaign to achieve a federal antilynching law. Ida B. Wells-Barnett, a turn-of-the-century pioneer in the fight against lynching, also continued to advocate strong policies designed to halt mob violence. Although African Americans often fought their battles for social justice very much alone, interracial civil rights and social welfare organizations played important roles in the fight against racial injustice. Organized in 1919, the Commission on Interracial Cooperation (CIC) worked mainly in the South and supplemented the work of the National Urban League and the NAACP. Although it did not attack segregation directly, the CIC advocated equal treatment before the law, including the ballot, due process of law, and equal access to government-financed educational and social welfare programs.

The Harlem Renaissance

The spread of the Harlem Renaissance as a national movement gave literary and powerful cultural expression to the African-American quest for citizenship. The Great Migration transformed Harlem into the 'race capital of the world.' The city's black population increased from nearly 152,500 in 1920 to over 327,700 in 1930. Most of the increase came from southern black migration, but immigrants from Africa as well as the West Indies made up nearly a quarter of the city's black population. Plays, musical compositions, poems, and other artistic productions emerged from the creative interactions of African peoples from diverse regional and national backgrounds. In his classic poem, 'If We Must Die,' the poet Claude McKay expressed the growing militancy of the 'New Negroes': 'If we must die, let it not be like hogs. Hunted and penned in an inglorious spot. If we must die, o let us nobly die . . . Pressed to the wall, dying, but fighting back.'[6]

In his *New Negro* (1925), a collection of essays on the Harlem Renaissance, Alain Locke articulated the contrast between the old and new generation of African Americans:

> In the last decade something beyond the watch and guard of statistics has happened in the life of the American Negro . . . For the younger generation is vibrant with a new psychology; the new spirit is awake in the masses, and under the very eyes of the professional observers – is transforming what has been a perennial problem into the progressive phases of contemporary Negro life.[7]

The social movements of the 1920s also signaled the dawn of a new day in black politics. Despite the continuing disfranchisement of southern blacks, African Americans slowly reentered mainstream electoral politics on the basis of their growing concentration in northern cities where they could vote. In Chicago, African Americans elected Oscar DePriest to Congress in 1928 and foreshadowed the resurgence of black political power at the local, state, and national levels.

While the 'New Negroes' developed an amazing degree of unity in their demands for social justice, they were by no means fully unified. Some of their activities appealed to the specific needs, desires, and aspirations of the black poor and revealed important cleavages along class lines. A. Philip Randolph, Milton P. Webster, and others in the Brotherhood of Sleeping Car Porters and Maids (BSCP) insisted on the necessity of black and white working-class unity. They demanded full inclusion within the organized 'house of labor,' as part of a larger multiracial working class. Although the union failed to gain American Federation of Labor (AFL) or employer recognition before the 1930s, it symbolized a growing connection between blacks and organized labor. Marcus Garvey, the Universal Negro Improvement Association (UNIA) and the 'Back to Africa' movement also appealed to the predominantly working-class black masses. Unlike the BSCP, however, the UNIA appealed to black workers as a 'race' with distinct interests from whites regardless of class background.

Race Pride

Marcus M. Garvey founded the UNIA in Jamaica in 1914. During World War I he migrated to the United States and established a Harlem branch of the UNIA in 1916. By 1923, although scholars estimate a membership of 500,000, the organization reported a membership of 6 million, with branches throughout the United States and West Indies. The Garvey movement advocated a separate and independent existence for blacks, emphasizing 'race pride' and pan-African unity. In 'unity,' Garvey repeatedly told blacks, 'there is strength.' Moreover, more than any other leader, Garvey urged African Americans to purge the 'white gods' and standards of beauty from their minds and confirm the beauty of blackness. Despite its broad appeal among the black masses, however, the Garvey movement declined by the mid-1920s, partly under the combined assault of civil rights and labor organizations as well as the state. Garvey was imprisoned in 1923 for mail fraud, and by 1927 he was deported from the United States.

Closely intertwined with class and political differences within the black community were gender, generational, and regional conflicts deeply rooted in the southern rural experiences of African Americans. As one historian of black women notes, for example, 'Many black women quit the South out of a desire to achieve personal autonomy and to escape . . . from sexual abuse at the hands of southern white as well as black men.'[8] Young black men from landowning southern families often

THE WORLD FAMOUS
COTTON CLUB

BROADWAY AT 48TH STREET

After World War I, the section of New York City called Harlem became the center of black cultural achievement. The war had created new job opportunities for African Americans in northern industries, sparking an upsurge in migration from the South. At the war's end, black men who had fought for their country returned to civilian life with a heightened sense of the disparities between America's promises and the reality of their lives. Black poets and writers, emboldened by the relative freedom of the North, gave voice to their discontent. Political leftists among New York's white intellectuals were heartened by the Russian Revolution and saw it as the beginning of a worldwide struggle for equality. They focused attention on the oppressed in America, giving new respect to the lives of those at the bottom of the economic ladder and expressing a particular appreciation for the cultural heritage of African Americans.

Above: *This is the menu and program from the mid-1930s for the Cotton Club. The painting by Julian Harrison, featuring nude African Americans, emphasizes the exotic and erotic in entertainment for the white clientele.*

In this charged atmosphere, the intellectual and cultural life of the black community flourished. Amid poverty and injustice, new freedoms and new opportunities stimulated the artistic, literary, and musical achievements that became known as the Harlem Renaissance. At its peak in the 1920s, this cultural expansion reintroduced Europe and white America to black music through jazz performances such as those by W. C. Handy and concerts of spirituals and songs by such artists as Paul Robeson and Roland Hayes. The most popular musical show in New York City in 1921 and 1922 was the long-running musical extravaganza *Shuffle Along*, written, produced,

and performed by African Americans and featuring the immensely popular songs 'I'm Just Wild About Harry' and 'Love Will Find a Way.'[1]

African-American writers introduced a new kind of cosmopolitanism into the literary salons of New York and Paris. Many journals and magazines in New York encouraged publications by black writers, and stages both in Harlem's black community and in other areas of the city presented plays about black life. Claude McKay's poetry in *Harlem Shadows* and his novels, *Home to Harlem* and *Banjo*, Jean Toomer's poems and novel, *Cane*, Zora Neale Hurston's short stories and her novels, *Jonah's Gourd Vine* and *Their Eyes Were Watching God*, Countee Cullen's books of poetry, including *Color*, *The Ballad of the Brown Girl*, and *Copper Sun*, and Langston Hughes's successes in many literary forms are only a sampling of the writing which established Harlem as an important cultural center.[2]

While African-American art, the black literary movement, and stage performances all introduced white Americans to black culture, probably the most widespread participation in black life was through the popular music of the time. By 1929, *Variety* magazine contended that Harlem's dance halls and nightclubs were even more popular than Broadway.[3] Some clubs, such as Connie's Inn on Seventh Avenue at 132nd Street and the Cotton Club on Lenox

Left: *The sheet music for 'Mood Indigo,' with words and music by Duke Ellington, Irving Mills and Albany Bigard, and 'Underneath The Harlem Moon' with lyrics by Mack Gordon and music by Harry Revel.*

Below: *Duke Ellington was a prolific musician who produced some 1,500 original works during a career which took off after he first appeared at the Cotton Club in 1927.*

Avenue at 142nd Street, both white-owned and operated, catered mainly to whites, including celebrities and the well-to-do seeking the excitement of black entertainment and 'slumming.' These clubs barred racially mixed parties and admitted few blacks, except as employees and performers. At the popular black-owned Small's Paradise, African-American musicians entertained an interracial clientele with style. Customers ranged around the large circular bar or were served at their tables by waitresses on roller skates and waiters who danced while balancing their loaded trays. According to the *New York Daily News* in 1929, the price of entertainment by a big band and a floor show at Small's averaged an expensive $4 per person for an evening, still only a fraction of the approximately $12–15 it cost at Connie's Inn.[4]

The Savoy Ballroom, an enormous dance hall, provided the quintessential Harlem experience. Opening in early 1926 on Lenox Avenue between 140th and 141st Streets, the Savoy's owner Moe Gale, a white man, hired a black man named Charles Buchanon to manage this elegant, thoroughly integrated establishment. The Savoy Bearcats and Fess Williams's 12-piece Royal Flush Orchestra played for the opening. European royalty, Hollywood celebrities, black professionals, and domestic servants all entered through the lobby with its marble staircase and cut-glass chandelier into the orange and blue hall to dance on its 10,000ft^2 (930m^2) dance floor or to sit at tables and couches watching dancers display their creative talents. Unlike many other clubs, the Savoy hired both black and white musicians to play on its two bandstands. At the height of its popularity over 4,000 people danced nightly under the colored spotlights and the watchful eyes of tuxedo-clad bouncers to the music of bands led by such famous musicians as Benny Goodman, Tommy Dorsey, Louis Armstrong, Chick Webb, Count Basie and Cab Calloway. Along with her orchestra, singer Ella Fitzgerald, billed as the 'First Lady of Swing,' was among the popular artists regularly featured. The Savoy Ballroom entertained its interracial clientele during the Great Depression, World War II, and through most of the 1950s, finally closing its doors in 1958 to make way for an urban renewal housing project in Harlem.[5]

Lois E. Horton

Notes
[1] John Hope Franklin, *From Slavery to Freedom*, 5th edition, New York: Alfred A. Knopf, 1980, p. 369.
[2] *Ibid.*, p. 366.
[3] David Levering Lewis, *When Harlem Was in Vogue*, New York: Alfred A. Knopf, 1981, p. 208.
[4] Lewis, *When Harlem Was in Vogue*; Jervis A. Anderson, *This Was Harlem*, New York: Farrar Straus Giroux, 1982; Allon Schoener (ed.), *Harlem on My Mind*, New York: Random House, 1968, p. 83.
[5] Anderson, *This Was Harlem*, p. 310.

defied the will of their fathers who sought to keep them on the land. On one southern farm, two sons requested a car in exchange for staying on the land. When their father refused, they made good on their threat and moved away. Upon arrival in northern cities, southern blacks often faced an entrenched and hostile black population that feared their impact on the prevailing racial status quo. 'Instead of Colored Northern citizens trying to help lift up your Colored neighbor,' wrote one black female newcomer, 'you run him down.'[9] The woman then exclaimed that 'We shall prove to you that we are good worthy law-abiding citizens.'[10] Such conflicts also influenced the residential and institutional development of the black community. In Harlem, black elites lived on the borders of the expanding black community, while the poor and working class clustered in the center. In Chicago, the better-educated business and professional people

Below: *A middle-class, African-American clientele in a bar in South Side Chicago in 1941. More than 160,000 African Americans moved there in the 1940s alone, and the city's black population doubled from 1930 to 1950.*

lived on the extreme South Side, while the poor and working-class blacks occupied the northernmost sections of the community.

A Raw Deal, 1929–34

The Great Depression was a national calamity. It brought mass suffering to all regions of the country. National income dropped from $81 billion in 1929 to $40 billion in 1932. At the same time, unemployment rose to an estimated 25 percent of the total labor force. In the wake of plant closings, bank failures, and rising unemployment, nearly 20 million Americans turned to public and private relief agencies for assistance. Being the 'Last Hired and the First Fired,' African Americans entered the Depression earlier and stayed there longer than other Americans. As sociologists St. Clair Drake and Horace R. Cayton noted in their detailed study of Chicago during the period, African Americans represented a 'barometer sensitive to the approaching storm.'[11]

Long before the stock-market crash in 1929, African Americans sensed that the 'fat years' were about to give way to the 'lean years.' Street begging, drunkenness, and idle

men loafing in local poolhalls and on street corners became common sights. In February 1931, the Milwaukee Urban League reported that,

> The slogan of the Urban League movement; 'Not alms but opportunity' . . . becomes more significant each day as many individuals who at one time called at the Urban League in search of a job now seem to give work but little thought. They now come to be referred for the second, third, or fourth time to some relief agency.[12]

By 1933, African Americans found it all but impossible to find 'jobs of any kind' in agriculture or industry. As cotton prices dropped from 18¢ per pound (0.454kg) on the eve of the Depression to less than 6¢ for the same amount in 1933, some 12,000 black sharecroppers soon lost their precarious footing in southern agriculture. Moreover, mechanical devices had already slowly reduced the number of workers required for plowing, hoeing, and weeding, but now planters also experimented with mechanical cotton-pickers as well. One black woman complained that

many jobs had 'gone to machines, gone to white people or gone out of style.'[13] Despite declining opportunities in cities, destitution in the countryside continued to thrust rural blacks toward southern, northern, and western cities.

Faced with a rising number of rural blacks seeking jobs in the contracting urban economy, urban black workers also experienced increasing difficulties. Black urban unemployment reached well over 50 percent, more than twice the rate of whites. In the steel industry of Pittsburgh, African-American workers complained of 'kickbacks' to foremen, in order to keep their jobs. According to one steelworker, 'I was just laid off . . . Why? Because I wouldn't pay off the foreman.'[14] Another steelworker stated that, 'I just got tired of that way of doin' and wouldn't pay him; now I'm out of a job.'[15] In southern cities, white workers rallied around such slogans as, 'No jobs for niggers until every white man has a job' and 'Niggers, back to the cotton fields – city jobs are for white folks.'[16] The most violent episodes took place on southern railroads, as unionized white workers and the railroad brotherhoods intimidated, attacked, and

Above: *An aspect of street life from 1930's Harlem: young children playing leap frog. For adults, this was a time of great cultural creativity and relative prosperity for Harlem's African-American inhabitants.*

Below: *A clapboard house in a Chicago slum neighborhood in 1941 on the northern side of the city. Chicago differed from New York in having mostly two or three story housing rather than tall tenement blocks.*

When the migrant African Americans arrived at their new destinations in the cities of the North, they altered the shape of the existing black communities there. Prior to the Great Migration, northern African Americans lived in multiracial neighborhoods, but the massive influx during the Great Migration led to the creation of predominantly black enclaves, such as Harlem in New York.

Migrants sought affordable areas but racism

murdered black firemen in order to take their jobs. Nearly a dozen black firemen lost their jobs in various parts of the South. As one contemporary observer succinctly stated, 'The shotgun, the whip, the noose, and Ku Klux Klan practices were being resumed in the certainty that dead men not only tell no tales, but create vacancies.'[17]

Reinforcing hard times within the black urban community was the declining economic position of black women. Under the impact of the Depression, large numbers of white women entered the labor force and competed with black women for jobs as maids, cooks, and housekeepers. Consequently, black women were forced into the notorious Depression era 'slave market,' where even working-class white women employed black women at starvation wages – as little as $5.00 per week for full-time laborers. In their studies of the market in Bronx, New York, two black women compared the practice to the treatment of slaves in the novel *Uncle Tom's Cabin*:

She who is fortunate (?) enough to please Mrs. Simon Legree's scrutinizing eye . . . is

Above: *An interior view of one of Chicago's overcrowded living quarters where many of the incoming migrant families lived. Discriminatory rental policies exacerbated the situation for African Americans.*

permitted to scrub floors on her bended knees, to hang precariously from window sills, cleaning window after window or to strain and sweat over steaming tubs of heavy blankets, spreads and furniture corners.[18]

Despite mass suffering the Republican administration of Herbert Hoover did little to aid the poor and destitute. On the contrary, the federal government established the Reconstruction Finance Corporation, which relieved the credit problems of large banking, insurance, and industrial firms. Despite Hoover's conviction that such policies would create new jobs, stimulate production, and increase consumer spending, benefits did not 'trickle down' to the rest of the economy and end the Depression. Still, African Americans rallied to the slogan 'Who but Hoover' in the Presidential contest of 1932. The Republican

greatly limited their choices, contributing to the growth of ghettos; in fact, rents were often higher in Harlem than in many white working class areas. Housing in these black neighborhoods was often of poor quality and lacking in sanitation. This created health problems and deaths due to diseases such as tuberculosis. Overcrowding made the health problems worse, but the low wages and lack of housing meant the housing was often shared out of economic necessity.

The migrants did, of course, add their own finishing touches to their homes, often things to remind them of their former homes and way of life. Some changes were for the better; the cities offered running water and electricity, a liberating experience for poor, rural people. Also, city life offered broader opportunities and people became much better informed about the events and people that affected their lives.

This room is representative of a boarder's in a Philadelphia row house. Boarders would stay until they had found places of their own, but until then they performed useful functions: if they were working they brought in money; if they were not they could perform the household duties which enabled other residents to go to work.

Row houses such as this had porches or steps, known as 'the stoop,' and these were adapted by the southern newcomers to perform the same social function as their yards had. People sat out during warm weather and talked to their neighbors, passed on or received news, and so on. It helped create a new sense of community.

> Being denied of work so long I was forced to apply for direct relief and the woman Parish director of [F.]E.R.A. told me . . . because I had written several letters to Washington reporting this office she said you will not get any direct relief here.[19]

When the AAA paid farmers to withdraw cotton lands from production, county officials barred African Americans from representation and deprived them of government checks. For their part, by exempting domestic service and unskilled labor from minimum-wage and participatory provisions, the NRA and the social security programs eliminated nearly 60 percent of African Americans from benefits. When the jobs of African Americans were brought under the provisions of the NRA in southern textile firms, employers reclassified such jobs and removed them from coverage of the higher wage code. Black youth who enrolled in CCC camps also faced unequal and discriminatory policies and practices. According to one black New York City recruit:

> When the busloads were made up at Whitehall Street an officer reported as follows: '35, 8 colored' . . . before we left the bus [at Camp Dix, New Jersey], the officer shouted emphatically: 'Colored boys fall out in the rear.' The colored from several buses were herded together, and stood in line until after the white boys had been registered and taken to tents . . . This separation of the colored from the whites was complete and rigidly maintained at this camp.[20]

African Americans could only conclude that the so-called New Deal was indeed a 'raw deal.' Although all Americans benefited from the massive federal effort to aid the unemployed and destitute, racial discrimination

Party retained its aura as the party of emancipation, as blacks delivered about 66 percent of their votes to Hoover.

Democratic candidate Franklin Delano Roosevelt looked little better than Hoover in the eyes of African Americans. FDR had not only adopted the segregationist Warm Springs, Georgia, as his home, but accepted the state's system of racial proscription. As assistant secretary of the Navy, he had also supported the expansion of Jim Crow policies in the armed forces. Moreover, unlike the Republican Party, the Democratic Party rejected a National Association for the Advancement of Colored People (NAACP) proposal for a civil rights plank, urging an end to racial discrimination in American public institutions.

Following his inauguration, Roosevelt's attitude toward African Americans changed little. He not only opposed vital federal civil rights legislation like the antilynching bill, but refused to meet with civil rights leaders at the White House. Although Roosevelt claimed that his segregationist white party members tied his hands on civil rights matters, he showed little interest in challenging even the

most blatant manifestations of racial injustice in the proliferation of New Deal agencies that soon followed his inauguration. The National Recovery Administration (NRA), Agricultural Adjustment Administration (AAA), the Works Progress Administration (WPA), the Tennessee Valley Authority (TVA), the Civilian Conservation Corps (CCC), and the Federal Emergency Relief Administration (FERA), to name only a few, all failed to protect blacks against discriminatory employers, agency officials, and local whites.

Southern state and local officials were most callous in their administration of relief programs. Officials set up differential benefit scales for blacks and whites. In Atlanta, Georgia, for example, blacks received over $13 less per month than the average white recipient. In Jacksonville, Florida, the city allotted 5,000 needy whites 45 percent of all relief funds, while 15,000 destitute African Americans received only 55 percent. When African Americans complained of inequalities, they faced even greater difficulties securing relief. One Louisiana man explained his case to the NAACP:

ensured that such benefits would reach African Americans on slow freight. Only during the mid-1930s would African Americans gain broader access to the New Deal social programs.

Emergence of a New Deal
By the mid-1930s, a variety of forces helped transform the 'raw deal' into a 'new deal' for African Americans. Shifting attitudes about race and class in American society, the development of new interracial coalitions, and the increasing participation of blacks in electoral politics combined to encourage a more helpful focus on the needs of African Americans. By 1939, income from New Deal work and relief programs nearly matched African-American

Below and right: *The cities seemed to offer opportunity and care while the countryside perpetuated poverty and neglect. This clinic is in New York's Tuberculosis and Health Association, Inc., and the farm kitchen is in Missouri in 1938; the contrast could hardly be starker.*

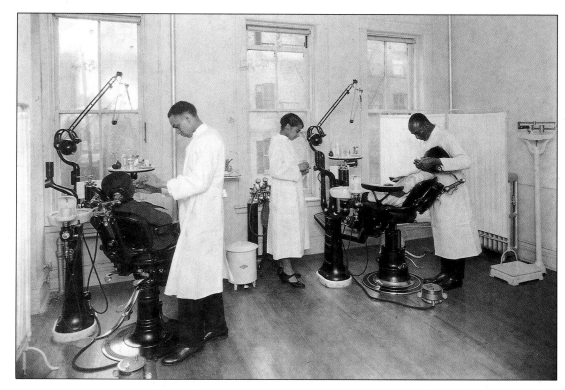

income from private employment. African Americans occupied about one-third of all federal low-income housing projects, gained a growing share of CCC jobs, Federal Farm Security loans, and benefits from WPA educational and cultural programs. African Americans now frequently hailed the New Deal as 'a Godsend.'[21] When some blacks sug-gested that God 'will lead me' and relief 'will feed me,' they articulated their belief that a 'new deal' was indeed in the making. African Americans were hopeful enough to shift their political allegiance from the Republican to the Democratic Party.

The transformation of the 'raw deal' into a 'new deal' was closely intertwined with the

growth of the Communist Party, the resurgence of organized labor, and the increasing efforts of these groups to attract African Americans to their ranks. Although few blacks joined the Communist Party, when the party helped save nine black youth, the Scottsboro Boys, from execution and secured the release of their own black comrade, Angelo Herndon, from a Georgia chain gang, the African-American community took notice. When the party helped to initiate hunger marches, unemployed councils, farm labor unions, rent strikes, and mass demonstrations to prevent the eviction of black families from their homes, their work gained even greater recognition within the African-American community. As one black newspaper editor, William Kelley of the *Amsterdam News* reported, 'The fight that they are putting up . . . strike[s] forcefully at the fundamental wrongs suffered by the Negro today.'[22]

The emergence of a new and more egalitarian labor movement reflected as well as stimulated changes in the relationship between blacks and the New Deal. Buoyed by New Deal labor legislation, the labor movement dramatically expanded. In 1935 under the

leadership of John L. Lewis, head of the United Mine Workers of America, the Committee for Industrial Organization (CIO) broke from the old, all-white American Federation of Labor (AFL). Renamed the Congress of Industrial Organizations in 1938, the CIO made a firm commitment to organize black and white workers. The organization soon launched the Packing-house Organizing Committee (POC), the United Automobile Workers (UAW), and the Steel Workers Organizing Committee (SWOC). The new unions appealed to civil rights organizations like the NAACP and Urban League, recruited black organizers, and advocated an end to unequal pay scales for black and white workers. Although the AFL unions continued to exclude black workers, the national leadership gradually supported a more equitable stance toward black workers. The union finally approved an international charter for the Brotherhood of Sleeping Car Porters and Maids (BSCP) in 1935 and endorsed efforts to free the convicted Scottsboro Boys and Angelo Herndon.

Following the lead of anthropologist Franz Boas and his associates, social scientists, as early as the 1920s, challenged the biological

Above: *By the 1940s, sophistication and beauty were deemed by advertisers to be appropriate portrayals for black models.*

Below: *The Scottsboro Boys' case was the most charged racial case of the decade, with nine boys convicted of rape on very dubious evidence. This protest against the convictions was held in Harlem in 1932.*

determinists' belief in hereditary racial inferiority. Legal change lagged significantly, yet, even here, African Americans witnessed the slow transition to a new deal. In 1935, the Maryland Court of Appeals ordered the University of Maryland to admit blacks to the state's law school or set up a new separate and equal facility for blacks. Rather than face the expense of establishing a new all-black law school, university officials lowered racial barriers and admitted black students.

By the onset of World War II, African Americans had come to view the New Deal more favorably. Yet, even the most egalitarian programs exhibited huge gaps between policy and practice. Although blacks gained increasing access to low-income public housing, for example, the government rejected mortgage applications for houses in white neighborhoods. Similarly, blacks gained a rising proportion of Farm Security Administration (FSA) loans, but the agency established stiff credit requirements which disqualified most black tenant farmers and sharecroppers.

Despite new regulations mandating an end to racial discrimination in Works Progress Administration (WPA) projects, southern public-works officials instituted discriminatory

Above: *A. Philip Randolph, the great African-American labor leader in November 1942. During the war the protests he organized against discriminatory employment practices helped convince Roosevelt to outlaw them.*

gender, as well as racial, practices against black women. According to a white physician in a South Carolina town, black women were placed on projects otherwise designated for men: 'Women are worked in "gangs" in connection with the City's dump pile, incinerator and ditch piles.'[23] Black women worked under the supervision of armed guards in Jackson, Mississippi, while in Oklahoma they were removed from government projects in order to coerce them into picking 'an abundant cotton crop.'

Despite the transition from a raw deal to a new deal between 1935 and 1939, the persistence of racial discrimination within and outside governmental agencies limited its achievements. As whites returned to full-time employment during the late 1930s, African Americans remained dependent on public-service and relief programs. While the CIO aided blacks who were fortunate enough to maintain or regain their jobs during the Depression years, it did little to enhance the equitable reemployment of black and white workers as the country slowly pulled itself out of the Depression. The Communist Party helped to change attitudes toward racial unity, but the benefits of such changes were largely symbolic, as racial injustice continued to undermine the material position of African Americans. Social changes of the 1930s bequeathed to African Americans an ambiguous legacy. They would have to take charge of their own lives, unite, and wage an even stronger battle against the barriers of racial and class inequality.

Below: *The contralto Marian Anderson was barred from singing in Constitution Hall in 1939 by the Daughters of the American Revolution. She did so instead before a crowd of 75,000 on the Lincoln Memorial's steps.*

Responding to Hard Times

African Americans developed a complex and creative set of responses to hard times. They strengthened their connections with family, friends, and the African-American community; moved toward the organized labor movement; and expanded their participation in the political process. As the Depression took its toll on black families, women played a primary role as 'kin-keepers' and helped families remain intact. As novelist Richard Wright put it, 'We reckon kin not as others do, but down to the ninth and tenth cousin.'[24] Black women cared for each other's children, offered emotional support, and creatively manipulated their family's resources. As one Georgia relief official noted,

> These people are catching and selling fish, reselling vegetables, sewing in exchange for old clothes, letting out sleeping space, and doing odd jobs . . . Stoves are used in common, wash boilers go their rounds, and garden crops are exchanged and shared.[25]

Some urban blacks maintained small vegetable gardens to help make ends meet, but larger numbers used the 'rent party.' Sponsors provided 'down home' food, music, and a place to dance for a small admission fee. Rent parties became even more profitable when sponsors added gambling and liquor to food, music, and dance. The 'policy' or numbers game was so important to Chicago's South Side that one contemporary observer believed that: '7,000 people would be unemployed and business in general would be crippled' if the numbers game collapsed.[26]

Alongside the 'rent party,' policy, and mutual assistance among kin and friends, the church helped people cope with the Depression. Sometimes their activities took on the characteristics of the 'rent party.' In Milwaukee, for example, a Holiness minister and his wife often held services in their home. As later revealed by their daughter,

> My mother's home was always open to all strangers . . . when my father would come home, she would have a house full, we would go from home to home, and sing and pray and administer the Word of God. We'd wash dirty clothes. We'd take food and feed them, and every day every evening, we'd bring like 6, 7, 8 souls to God.[27]

New religious movements also expanded their efforts to feed the poor. Started during the 1920s, for example, Father Divine's Peace Mission moved its headquarters from New Jersey to Harlem in 1932 and gained credit for feeding the masses and offering relief from widespread destitution. At about the same time, Bishop Charles Emmanuel Grace, known as 'Daddy Grace,' founded the United House of Prayer of All People, opened offices in 20 cities, and offered thousands of people food, clothing, and a respite from suffering.

Organized Action

African-American workers also organized in their own interests. Perhaps more than any other single figure, A. Philip Randolph epitomized their persistent struggle. Born in Crescent City, Florida, in 1889, Randolph had migrated to New York City in 1911 and spearheaded the formation of the Brotherhood of Sleeping Car Porters and Maids in 1925. When New Deal federal legislation (the Railway Labor Act of 1934) legitimized the rights of workers to organize, Randolph and the Brotherhood of Sleeping Car Porters and Maids (BSCP) intensified its organizing drive among black porters. By 1933, the union represented some 35,000 porters. Two years later, the union defeated a company union and won the right to represent porters at the bargaining table with management, which signed its first contract with the union in 1937. The BSCP victory not only helped to make African Americans more union-conscious, it increased their impact on national labor policy.

The NAACP, Urban League, and other civil organizations also increased their focus on the economic plight of African Americans. In 1933, these organizations formed the Joint Committee on National Recovery (JCNR) and helped publicize the racial inequities in New Deal programs. African Americans also launched the 'Don't Buy Where You Can't

Above: *The African-American churches and education were often very closely associated with one another. This school lesson is being conducted in a church building at Gee's Bend, Alabama, in April 1937.*

Below: *Charismatic religious leaders emerged during the Depression years: one was Daddy Grace and another was George Baker, otherwise known as Father Divine. Here his enthusiastic followers parade in Harlem.*

GOSPEL

The twentieth century saw the development of a specific form of religious song in African-American society that became known as gospel. This music derived from a combination of church worship services and spiritual and blues singing.

The impetus for gospel's development was probably the rise of the Pentecostal churches in the late nineteenth century. Their form of fundamentalist Christianity emphasized the activity of the Holy Spirit, stressed the holiness of living ('Let everything that breathes praise the Lord' – Psalms, 150), and encouraged followers to express their religious feelings uninhibitedly – often by speaking in tongues. Gospel's growth was assisted by the development of recordings and radio broadcasts, which brought it to a white audience as well.

Recordings of sermons by Pentecostal preachers accompanied by instruments, choirs, and participating congregations became very popular during the 1920s, and the growth continued during the Depression of the 1930s, fuelled by song publishing, concerts, and television.

Gospel music was filled with improvised recitative passages executed in an extravagantly expressive manner. Choirs, where used, chanted or sang the prayer responses in the preacher's sermon. Gospel could also be performed individually, as well as by harmonizing, choreographed male quartets (an influence on later black musical styles).

138

A prominent early practicioner was Thomas A. Dorsey whose most notable work was 'Precious Lord.' Other early gospel songs were produced by the Reverend Charles Albert Tindley and published in his book *New Songs of Paradise* in 1916. One of Tindley's compositions was 'I'll Overcome' which was changed into the civil rights anthem 'We Shall Overcome.' In 1921 the National Baptist Convention Sunday School Board issued *Gospel Pearls*. During the 1930s gospel was taken into the nightclubs and concert halls by

Sister Rosetta Tharpe, a formidable performer.

One of the greatest solo exponents of gospel was Mahalia Jackson. She began recording in 1945 and her 'Move On Up a Little Higher' was the first gospel record to sell a million copies. Her singing career is interesting because it shows clearly the links between the religious and secular roots of jazz, and the unmistakable influences of secular blues singers such as Bessie Smith. The gospel route is now a well trodden path for many now mainstream African-American singers.

The gospel artifacts here, clockwise from left to right, consist of: a selection of fans used by congregations in the South to cool themselves during services; an advertising banner from the Martin & Morris Music Studio, a Chicago company which produced and sold sheet music and gospel supplies through its chain of stores; a gown and hat belonging to a Church Mother, an important figure in the congregation; and a copy of *The Service Hymnal* from Mount Helm Church, Jackson, Mississippi.

offered the most appropriate response to the deepening crisis of African Americans. Some African Americans joined the Socialist Southern Tenant Farmers Union (STFU) and resolved to defend their rights in the hostile rural environment of the South. In rural Alabama blacks formed the Communist Alabama Sharecroppers Union. Nate Shaw (Ned Cobb) recalled that he had joined the sharecroppers union to fight the system that oppressed him. As he put it, he had to act because he had labored 'under many rulins, just like the other Negro, that I knowed was injurious to man and displeasin to God and still I had to fall back.'[28] One morning in December 1932, when deputy sheriffs came to take away his neighbor's livestock, Shaw refused to 'fall back,' and he took part in a shootout with local law officers. As he described it:

> . . . run my hand in my pocket, snatched out my .32 Smith and Wesson and I commenced a shooting . . . before I could reload my gun . . . every one of them officers [4 in all] out-run the devil away from there . . . that .32 Smith and Wesson was barking too much for em to stand.[29]

Although Nate Shaw was later arrested and spent several years in a penitentiary, his actions underscored the increasing militance of rural blacks. In Birmingham, Alabama, the party's League of Struggle for Negro Rights (LSNR) and its energetic fight on behalf of the Scottsboro Boys attracted unemployed workers, like Al Murphy and Hosea Hudson. As Hosea Hudson put it, 'I always did resent injustice and the way they used to treat Negroes . . . My grandmother used to talk about these things. She was very militant herself, you know.'[30]

Although some blacks joined radical social movements and parties, most worked hard to broaden their participation in the New Deal coalition. Although Republicans continued to take black votes for granted, blacks increasingly turned toward the northern wing of the Democratic Party. As early as 1932, the editor of the black weekly *Pittsburgh Courier* had urged African Americans to change their political affiliation: 'My friends, go turn Lincoln's picture to the wall . . . that debt has been paid in full.'[31] By the mid-1930s, nearly 45 blacks had received appointments to New Deal agencies. Referred to as the 'Black Cabinet,' these black advisors included Robert L. Vann, editor of the *Pittsburgh Courier*, Robert C. Weaver, an economist, and Mary McCleod Bethune, founder of Bethune-Cookman College in Florida. In 1936, African

Work' campaign in New York, Chicago, Washington, DC, and other cities. They boycotted white merchants who served the African-American community but refused to employ blacks except in domestic and common laborer positions. When Harlem store owners refused to negotiate, New York blacks formed the Citizens League for Fair Play and set up pickets around Blumstein's Department Store. In 1938, their actions produced concrete results, when the New York Uptown Chamber of Commerce and the Greater New York Coordinating Committee for Employment agreed to give African Americans one-third of all new retail executive, clerical, and sales jobs.

African Americans usually expressed their grievances through organized and peaceful action, but sometimes their despair led to violence. Racial violence erupted in Harlem in 1935, when a rumor spread that a black youth had been brutally attacked and killed by police. Although the rumor proved false, African-American crowds soon gathered and smashed windows and looted stores in a night of violence that left one person dead, over 50 injured, and thousands of dollars in property damage. Some blacks believed that radicalism

Americans formed the National Negro Congress (NNC), aiming to unite all existing political, fraternal, and religious organizations to gain policies designed to bring about the full socioeconomic recovery of the black community. Spearheaded by Ralph Bunche, professor of political science at Howard University, and John Davis, executive secretary of the JCNR, the founding meeting of the NNC brought together some 600 organizations and selected A. Philip Randolph as its first president. The NNC symbolized, as well as promoted, the growing political mobilization of the African-American community. In the Presidential election of 1936, African Americans voted for the Democratic Party in record numbers: Roosevelt received 76 percent of northern black votes.

After the election of 1936, African Americans intensified demands on the New Deal administration of FDR, placing a high priority on justice before the law. As early as 1933, the NAACP organized a Writers League Against Lynching and intensified its national movement for a federal antilynching law. The Costigan-Wagner antilynching bill gained little support from FDR and failed when southern Senators filibustered the measure in

Below: *The NAACP campaigned strongly against lynching and flew this flag from their New York offices every time there was one. They had to stop in 1938 when threatened with loss of their lease.*

1934, 1935, 1937, 1938, and 1940. Nevertheless, partly because of the campaign, the number of recorded lynchings dropped from 18 in 1935 to 2 in 1939.

Black attorneys like Charles Hamilton Houston and William Hastie assaulted the legal supports of Jim Crow, while black historians, social scientists, and writers challenged its intellectual underpinnings. Under the leadership of historian Carter G. Woodson, the Association for the Study of Negro Life and History (founded in 1915) continued to promote the study of African-American history, emphasizing the role of blacks in the development of the nation. To its scholarly *Journal of Negro History*, the organization added the *Negro History Bulletin*, designed for broader circulation. African-American intellectuals like E. Franklin Frazier, W. E. B. DuBois, Charles S. Johnson, Langston Hughes, and Richard Wright reinforced Woodson's work and the *Journal of Negro History*. In 1938 Richard Wright won a WPA writing prize for his book *Uncle Tom's Children*. Two years later, he published his famous novel, *Native Son*, which emphasized the destructive impact of racism on African-American life. According to one observer, 'The day *Native Son* appeared, American culture was changed forever.'[32] Born on a plantation near Natchez, Mississippi, Wright later wrote that his head was 'full of a hazy notion that life could be lived with dignity, that the personal-

LANGSTON HUGHES

Above: *Langston Hughes, pictured in April 1942. He was one of the great writers of a self-confident, black cultural renaissance which began during the 1920s.*

I TOO

I, too, sing America.

I am the darker brother.
They send me to eat in the kitchen
When company comes.
But I laugh,
And eat well,
And grow Strong.

To-morrow
I'll sit at the table
When company comes
Nobody 'll dare
Say to me,
'Eat in the kitchen'
Then.

Besides, they'll see how beautiful I am
And be ashamed, –
I, too, am America.

Langston Hughes

DREAM VARIATION

To fling my arms wide
In some place of the sun,
To whirl and to dance
Till the bright day is done.
Then rest at cool evening
Beneath a tall tree
While night comes gently
Dark like me.
That is my dream.
To fling my arms wide
In the face of the sun.
Dance! Whirl! Whirl!
Till the quick day is done.
Rest at pale evening,
A tall, slim tree,
Night coming tenderly
Black like me.

Langston Hughes

ities of others should not be violated.'[33]

African-American responses to poverty varied. Women manipulated household resources, while black men predominated in the organized labor and civil rights movements. Elite males dominated the leadership positions of organizations like the NAACP and the Urban League. Yet, African Americans during the period were closely linked to each other through a common history, color, and culture. The emergence of Joe Louis as a folk hero is perhaps the most potent evidence of African Americans' sense of common plight, kinship, and future. His exploits helped to unify African-American peoples and gave them hope that they could demolish the segregationist system. When Joe Louis lost, as he did in his first fight with the German, Max Schmeling (who symbolized Adolf Hitler's doctrine of Aryan supremacy), African Americans lamented. And when Louis knocked out Schmeling in the first round of their rematch, black people celebrated. Singer Lena Horne offered one of the most powerful statements on Joe Louis as a folk hero:

Joe was the one invincible Negro, the one who stood up to the white man and beat him down with his fists. He in a sense carried so many of our hopes, maybe even dreams of vengeance.[34]

World War II and Its Early Aftermath

As the nation moved toward World War II and protested against the racism and atrocities of Nazi Germany, racial inequality persisted in America. African Americans confronted racial

THE AFRICAN AMERICAN IN PROFESSIONAL SPORTS

Above: *The success of Jessie Owens during the 1936 Olympic Games, held in Nazi Germany, was a boost to black morale and a blow against white supremacists.*

Throughout much of the twentieth century, African Americans have participated in, and often dominated, professional sports. The exploits of Jackie Robinson, Hank Aaron, Willie Mays, and Reggie Jackson in baseball; Wilt Chamberlain, Earvin 'Magic' Johnson, and Michael Jordan in basketball; Fritz Pollard, Jim Brown and Jerry Rice in football; and Jack Johnson, Joe Louis, 'Sugar' Ray Robinson, and Muhammad Ali in boxing, have done much to shape and popularize professional sport in America. Yet for African-American athletes the challenge was not just to hit, shoot, box, and run, but also to have the opportunity to compete. Professional sport became more than a game – it was a way that black Americans could combat racism by proving through athletic achievement that they were equals.

Until the late nineteenth century, though their presence was limited by racial discrimination, African Americans participated in an array of professional sports such as baseball, horse racing (three black jockeys won the Kentucky Derby during the 1880s), and boxing. By 1900 a series of informal 'gentleman's agreements' effectively eliminated African Americans from all professional sports, save for boxing. These agreements grew out of two parallel actions: the codification of institutionalized racism and the cult of professionalism. During the nineteenth century, many middle-class Americans embraced the culture of professionalism that institutionalized standards of behavior, expertise, and training in law, medicine, and sport. While this process

compete with whites in the newly emerging professional baseball leagues. Yet by 1900, professional baseball decided that it was 'a white man's game.' Not until Jackie Robinson broke the color line when he joined the Brooklyn Dodgers in 1947, did African Americans reenter major league baseball. But that does not mean that there were no black professional baseball players. From 1905 until the 1950s a series of 'Negro Professional Leagues' allowed the best black athletes an opportunity to play professional baseball. These leagues, originally the creation of Andrew 'Rube' Foster, who was one of the first great black baseball stars, showcased the talents of Leroy 'Satchel' Paige, James 'Cool Poppa' Bell, Josh Gibson and Buck Leonard. Teams like the Kansas City Monarchs, Homestead Grays, and Birmingham Black Barons provided the training for the generation of black ball players that reintegrated professional baseball after 1947 like Jackie Robinson, Roy Campanella, and Larry Doby.

In part, baseball integrated because of the great, untapped talent that was in the Negro leagues, talent that came to dominate professional baseball in the 1950s and 1960s. Baseball also changed because the composition of America's cities had changed. By the end of World War II, thousands of blacks had settled in northern and western cities. This was a potential market that many owners felt could keep baseball profitable for decades.

The patterns in other professional sports such as football and basketball, though the development and evolution of each was unique, were similar to professional baseball. These sports went from a time when there was a modest African-American presence to a period of overt restriction and discrimination, to an era where black players are crucial to the appeal and financial success of the sport.

In the 1990s, professional sport without African-American players is almost inconceivable. After all, blacks now hold many of the most coveted records in professional sport from the most career home runs (Henry Aaron) to the most points scored (Kareem Abdul Jabbar); and the naming of an African American as the most valuable player is now commonplace. Clearly black professional athletes have gained parity on the field. The real question is whether the ability to hit, run, and shoot will translate to meaningful jobs as managers, coaches, vice-presidents, and owners. That is the continuing challenge of the African American in professional sport.

Lonnie Bunch

brought order, and uniforms to differentiate professionals from amateurs, to professional sport, it also formalized the exclusion of those whose class, educational status, or race did not fit the American ideal of sport and masculinity. These actions kept most African Americans out of professional sport until World War II.

Two sports that illuminate the limits and possibility of professional sport for African Americans in this era were boxing and baseball. As early as 1805, freed slaves Bill Richmond and Tom Molineaux fought as professional boxers. Throughout the nineteenth and early twentieth centuries, African-American boxers like Joe Gans, Sam Langford and Joe Jeannette gained prominence but were denied the opportunity to fight for world championships. Not until Jack Johnson defeated Tommy Burns in 1908 did an African American become heavyweight champion of the world. Due to the

response to Johnson's victory and his refusal to accept the limits of racial discrimination, boxing promoters ensured that no African American fought for the heavyweight crown for more than two decades, until Joe Louis defeated James J. Braddock in 1937. After Joe Louis's 12-year reign, numerous African Americans have come to dominate all weight groups, from the highly skilled Henry Armstrong to the 'Sugar' Rays, Robinson and Leonard, to Muhammad Ali and 'Iron' Mike Tyson. Even though African Americans were able to box throughout the nineteenth and twentieth centuries, it was not until the 1930s that blacks won the opportunity to compete equally with whites for championships.

Until 1887, nearly 30 African Americans performed in professional baseball. Players like Moses Fleetwood Walker, Bud Fowler, and George Stovey had proved that blacks could

BASEBALL

The separate black baseball leagues came into existence because of the exclusion of blacks by the white-controlled professional major leagues after 1900. The formation of the Negro leagues in the 1920s came at a time when black racial pride and self-awareness was growing. It gave the black community a popular sport – a business – with black stars and management. It bolstered those who advocated autonomous action and control.

The Negro National League (NNL) was founded in February 1920 with eight teams, one of which was the Kansas City Monarchs. In 1923 the Eastern Colored League was founded, resulting in a Black World Series which ran from 1924 until 1928. The first winner was the Kansas City Monarchs. In 1937 the Negro American League (NAL) was formed, and from 1942 until 1948 the NNL and NAL competed in a World Series. By then the segregated leagues did not have much longer to survive.

All the items seen here date from the 1940s and 1950s. The jersey and pants are from the Kansas City Monarchs team, winners of the Negro World Series in 1942; the Mexican League contract is from 1952 and was signed by Walter 'Buck' Leonard, awarding him $550 per month; the 1946 yearbook cost 25 cents, and features Jackie Robinson on the cover; the 1946 NAL contract is between Jimmie Crutchfield and Chicago American Giants; and the ticket and report relate to a NNL game at Yankee Stadium.

Above: *The Indianapolis ABCs were one of the eight founding teams in Rube Foster's Negro National League. Foster explained that he intended to create a profession with good earning potential and 'do something concrete for the loyalty of the race.'*

Below: *There was no shortage of recruits on the first day that the U.S. Army Air Corps opened enlistment to African Americans. This picture was taken at the recruiting office at Mitchell Field, the men to be assigned to 99th Pursuit Squadron, which became the famous 99th Fighter Squadron.*

injustice in defense industries and the armed services. In 1940, blacks made up less than 2 percent of employees in the nation's aircraft industry, and management vowed to keep them down or out. As the head of the huge North American Aviation firm put it, 'Negroes will be considered only as janitors and in other similar capacities.'[35] When black women applied for defense-industry jobs, managers sometimes told them that 'my wife needs a maid.' In Detroit, a personnel manager in a bomber plant remarked that, 'When a department is nice and peaceful [we] don't go around looking for trouble by putting colored people in the department.'[36]

AFL craft unions, vocational education programs, and the U.S. Armed Forces reinforced racial barriers in defense work. White plumbers, bricklayers, carpenters, electricians, cement finishers, and painters excluded blacks from their unions by either constitutional provision or by 'ritual.' According to labor leader A. Philip Randolph, the International Association of Machinists was the chief offender. It barred blacks from the metal trades and the aircraft industry, including the Boeing Aircraft Corporation in Seattle as well as North American Aviation. For its part, the U.S. Office of Education financed the Vocational Education National Defense (VEND) Training Program, but failed to train blacks for skilled jobs. More importantly, at

the outset of World War II, the air and signal corps as well as the marine corps and coast guard barred African Americans; the army accepted them primarily for labor battalions; and the navy accepted them as 'messmen only.' According to Rear Admiral Chester Nimitz, the use of blacks as messmen only represented 'the best interests of general ship efficiency.'[37] Nonetheless, by war's end nearly 1 million black men and women had served in the armed forces, nearly three-quarters in the U.S. Army, followed in smaller numbers by the navy (and coast guard) and marine corps. Nearly 500,000 of these African Americans saw service overseas in the European, Mediterranean, and Pacific theaters of war. Many of these units received the Presidential Citation for their contributions to winning the war. The air corps awarded the Distinguished Flying Cross to 82 African-American pilots, and several blacks received the Navy Cross.

African Americans served and achieved

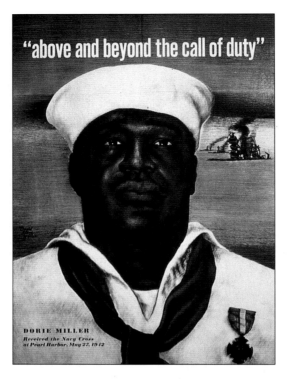

"above and beyond the call of duty"

DORIE MILLER
Received the Navy Cross
at Pearl Harbor, May 27, 1942

against great odds at home and abroad. With World War II another 1.6 million blacks moved into the nation's cities, bringing the proportion of urban dwellers among blacks up from less than 40 percent to nearly 60 percent by the war's end. Western cities like Los Angeles, San Francisco, and Seattle experienced sharp population increases, joining established northern and southern cities as major centers of black urban population growth. As the black urban population increased, it placed growing pressure on available housing and public facilities, and violence broke out in several cities. Some contemporary observers described wartime race relations as 'a growing subterranean race war.' Part of the violence took focus in the so-called 'Zoot Suit Riots,' in which white sailors and civilians attacked African Americans and Latino residents. Marked by their color as well as their dress – broad felt hats, pegged trousers, and pocket knives on gold chains – African-American and Latino youth were

Above: *Messman Dorie Miller had manned an anti-aircraft gun (a position not open to blacks) on the USS* Arizona *during the attack on Pearl Harbor and, although untrained, managed to down some Japanese aircraft. Even so, only after a*

press campaign was he awarded the Navy Cross in May 1942. He remained a mess attendant, however, and was one of the 600-plus crew of the USS Liscombe Bay *that died when she was torpedoed in November 1943.*

Below: *Sergeant Rance Richardson, veteran of two wars, taking a moment's rest during the American advance in April 1944 along the Numa-Numa Trail on Bougainville in the South Pacific theater of operations.*

Right: *African-American pilots pictured during service in the Italian theater of operations where, in July 1943, the all-black 99th Fighter Squadron claimed its first kill of the war over Sicily.*

assaulted in Los Angeles, San Diego, Chicago, Detroit, and Philadelphia, but the most serious outbreaks of racial violence occurred in Harlem and Detroit. In 1943, when a policeman shot a black soldier, Harlem exploded. The riot resulted in at least five deaths, 500 injuries, hundreds of arrests, and $5 million in property damage. The actor Sidney Poitier later recalled the scene:

> After work I came up out of the subway; and there was chaos everywhere – cops, guns, debris, and broken glass all over the street. Many stores had been set on fire, and the commercial district on 125th Street looked as if it had been bombed.[38]

The Detroit riot left even more deaths, injuries, and arrests in its wake. On 20 June 1943, violence started on the city's Belle Isle and soon spread to the black Paradise Valley area. Only the arrival of federal troops put down the violence, which resulted in 34 deaths, 675 injuries, nearly 1,900 arrests, and about $2 million in property damage. In both cases, blacks made up the bulk of deaths, arrests, and injuries, while damaged property belonged almost exclusively to whites. Similar to the Depression years, federal housing policies insisted on racial separation in wartime and low-income housing, and helped to fuel the underlying forces leading to race riots. In Detroit, for example, the city's race relations had deteriorated as early as 1941, when the federal government approved an all-black housing project in a predominantly white area. To offset white dissatisfaction over the black Sojourner Truth Housing Project, the government soon opened an all-white project at the Ford Motor Company's new Willow Run facility. Despite efforts on the part of blacks and their CIO allies to open the facility to all workers regardless of race, the government insisted on racial separation and helped to heighten racial tensions in wartime Detroit.

Unlike World War I, when African Americans 'closed ranks' and supported the war effort, they now waged a militant 'Double V' campaign for social justice at home and abroad. When FDR delivered his radio address urging all Americans to put aside differences 'until victory is won,' African Americans heightened rather than curtailed their demands. In an editorial, the *Chicago Defender* exclaimed,

> Why die for democracy for some foreign country when we don't even have it here? . . .

Right: *This early flying helmet and goggles were worn by Tuskegee airmen. Among the signatories are Chief Charles A. Anderson and Doctor Lewis A. Jackson, both important instructors at Tuskegee.*

What Democracy have we enjoyed since the last World War? Are our people segregated? Are they not Jim-Crowed and lynched? Are their civil and constitutional rights respected?[39]

According to a writer for the *Courier*, 'Our war is not against Hitler in Europe, but against Hitler in America. Our war is not to defend democracy, but to get a democracy we have never had.'[40] Popularized by the *Pittsburgh Courier*, the 'Double V' campaign enabled African Americans to criticize government and industry policies, while simultaneously declaring their patriotic support for the United States' war effort.

From the outset of wartime preparations, the NAACP attacked the navy's policy of recruiting African Americans as messmen only. The organization decried the use of black tax dollars to benefit whites only:

> Our taxes help to keep up the Naval Academy at Annapolis where our boys may not attend. They help to maintain the numerous naval bases, navy yards, and naval air bases, from which we are excluded . . . This is the price we pay for being classified as a race, as mess attendants only.[41]

Under the leadership of Mabel K. Staupers, executive director of the National Association of Colored Graduate Nurses, African Americans also fought to integrate the army and navy nurse corps. The navy barred black women nurses altogether, while the army set discriminatory quotas on the number of black women permitted to enlist. Only in 1945, with a growing shortage of white nurses and the government's threat to draft white women, did the army end its racial quota system and the navy permit black women to serve.

The rise of the March on Washington Movement (MOWM) symbolized the growing militance of the 'Double V' campaign. Spearheaded by A. Philip Randolph of the Brotherhood of Sleeping Car Porters and Maids, the MOWM emerged following a meeting of civil rights groups in Chicago. An African-American woman helped to give rise to the movement when she angrily addressed the chair:

> Mr. Chairman . . . we ought to throw 50,000 Negroes around the White House, bring them from all over the country, in jalopies, in trains and any way they can get there, and . . . keep them there until we can get some action from the White House.[42]

TUSKEGEE AIRMEN

Hundreds of thousands of African Americans served in the armed forces during World War II, of whom some 1,000 were trained as pilots by the United States Army Air Force (USAAF). This was a great advance from the situation which existed during World War I (African American pilot Eugene Bullard had had to fly with the French), and more so still when one considers that just over 100 black civilians, men and women, held pilot's licenses before the war.

The black military pilot training unit was set up at the Tuskegee Institute in Alabama in 1941. This was the first time that the United States had opened its doors to black involvement in the military aeronautical community. Even so, not until April 1943 did the trained pilots – now the 99th Fighter Squadron (FS) – get transferred to an operational theater in North Africa. In 1944, they were joined in Italy by the 100th, 301st, and 302nd fighter squadrons and merged to become the all-black 332nd Fighter Group (FG)

which saw action flying bomber escort missions against enemy targets. Incredibly, they never lost a bomber to an enemy fighter, a unique record for a unit flying over 1,500 missions.

Also activated in 1943 was the all-black 477th Bombardment Group (BG) composed of the 616th, 617th, 618th, and 619th bombardment squadrons (BS); the war ended, however, before the 477th could reach a war zone. All the items shown here date from 1941-1949 and were owned and used by Tuskegee airmen and technicians.

1 12th Air Force (AF) shoulder patch, 1944.
2 332nd FG patch.
3 AAF shoulder patch.
4 1st AF shoulder patch.
5 15th AF shoulder patch.
6 Air cadet insignia.
7 Pilot wings.
8 Charm bracelet given to Lieutenant James Knighten of 100th FS by his girlfriend.
9 Air Corps' 'Wing and Prop' color insignia.
10 Overseas summer cap for cadet with Wing and Prop.
11 Winter overseas cap.
12 Color insignia part for uniform.
13 Razor and lighter.
14 Polaroid sun goggles.
15 Survival fishing kit.
16 Sergeant Eugene Booker, a radio operator assigned to 477th Bomb Wing (BW).
17 M40 flying suit worn by First Lieutenant Walter Palmer assigned to 100th FS.
18 'Mae West' lifejacket signed by Lieutenant Palmer.
19 A-10A oxygen mask.
20 A-11 flying cap with earphones.
21 U.S. Army first-aid kit.
22 A-11 summer flying cap.
23 Standard goggles, 1944.
24 B3 flying jacket.
25 Pistol belt.
26 Water canteen.
27 A-9 oxygen mask.
28 AN-B-H-1 headphones.
29 Officer's cap and tunic from 15th AAF.
30 Winter tunic belonging to gunner/radio operator Alvin Miller of 477th BW.
31 Pilot wings.
32 Communications patch.
33 Bomb technician's patch.
34-38: chevrons:
34 Technical Sergeant
35 Staff Sergeant
36 First Sergeant
37 Buck Sergeant
38 Corporal

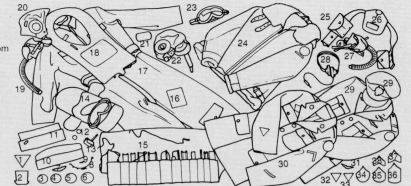

Above: *Charles White's mural, 'The Contribution of the Negro to Democracy in America,' was painted in 1943 to provide a record of African-American accomplishments for ordinary people. On the left half of the mural, working approximately clockwise from the bottom, can be seen: a bill to outlaw slavery being destroyed in 1775, Crispus Attucks dying at the Boston Massacre, American Revolutionary soldier Peter Salem, Nat Turner, Denmark Vesey (on horseback) inspired by a winged angel with a sword, Frederick Douglass, and (at center) black soldiers in the Civil War. On the* *right half of the mural, working clockwise from the center top, can be seen: Sojourner Truth beckoning slaves to the Underground Railroad (the arch), runaway Peter Still, Harriet Tubman, Booker T. Washington, George Washington Carver, Marian Anderson, Ferdinand Smith, Paul Robeson, Leadbelly, a contemporary African-American family with a blueprint for a planned society free from social wrongs (bottom), and a figure clutching the machinery of industrial society, a symbol of opposition confronting black efforts to gain equality (top).*

Randolph endorsed the proposal and the MOWM soon established offices in Harlem, Brooklyn, Washington, DC, Pittsburgh, Detroit, Chicago, and San Francisco. The movement gained the support of local NAACP and Urban League chapters, churches, and fraternal orders. The official organ of the BSCP, *The Black Worker*, became the official newspaper of the MOWM. In its May 1941 issue, the paper printed its official call to march:

We call upon you to fight for jobs in National Defense. We call upon you to struggle for the integration of Negroes in the armed forces . . . of the Nation . . . We call upon you to demonstrate for the abolition of Jim Crowism in all Government departments and defense employment . . . The federal Government cannot with clear conscience call upon private industry and labor unions to abolish discrimination based upon race and color so long as it practices discrimination itself against Negro Americans.[43]

Finally, on 18 June 1941, FDR invited A. Philip Randolph and Walter White of the NAACP to the White House. A week later, FDR issued Executive Order 8802, banning racial discrimination in government employment, defense industries, and training programs. The order also set up the Fair Employment Practices Committee (FEPC) to receive, investigate, and address complaints of discrimination in the defense program. Randolph later recalled the details of his meeting. The turning point came when FDR turned to White and asked, 'How many people will really march?' 'White's eyes did not blink. He said, "one hundred thousand, Mr. President."'[44]

Executive Order 8802 was a turning point. It linked the African-American struggle even more closely to the New Deal coalition and made the federal government a significant ally. Although resistance to the order abounded, particularly in the South, African Americans gradually increased their footing in defense-industry jobs. The FEPC enabled African Americans to break the 'job ceiling' at the level of semiskilled and skilled jobs. The percentage of blacks in war production increased from less than 3 percent in March 1942 to over 8 percent by 1944. Blacks gained increasing access to skilled jobs in the electrical and light manufacturing industries as well as new airplane-engine factories. African Americans also slowly gained access to lower-level managerial and clerical positions. While AFL unions and the railroad brotherhoods continued to resist the advancement of black workers, the CIO unions often supported the FEPC claims of black workers and helped them to penetrate the job ceiling. Although they continued to face stiff racial barriers in the industrial sector, by war's end, African Americans claimed the CIO, the Democratic Party, and the federal government as significant allies in their fight against racial inequality.

In the immediate postwar years, the wartime alliance between black workers, the federal government, and organized labor deteriorated. The federal government enacted the repressive Taft-Hartly Act (1947). The new Labor Relations Act curtailed the ability of unions to organize, facilitated the rise of right-to-work laws in the southern states, and pushed Communists out of civil rights and labor organizations.

Although some black workers gradually improved their position under new seniority clauses in northern and western industries, postwar federal labor policy undermined the position of black workers even more so than

Below: *Joyous enlisted men aboard the warship* USS Ticonderoga *celebrate the news of Japan's surrender in August 1945 and the end of World War II.*

whites. The federal government refused to renew the FEPC and left blacks vulnerable to the resurgence of racial discrimination in industrial jobs. Although President Harry S. Truman soon issued an executive order banning discrimination in federal employment, this limited measure did little to lift blacks upward in the postwar economy. Similarly, the U.S. Supreme Court outlawed restrictive covenants in 1948, but federal housing policies, exclusionary local zoning laws, and discriminatory real-estate and lending agencies continued to fuel the rise of new and more segregated black urban communities.

A Stake in the System

Despite the persistence of class and racial inequality in American life, by the end of World War II African Americans had gained a foothold in the New Deal coalition. Their increasing participation in the larger political system was intertwined with the transformation of southern rural blacks into a new urban-industrial people, with roots in the South and branches throughout the nation. African Americans gained the indispensable support of white allies, but only their persistent organizational and political activities in their own behalf enabled them to move gradually from oppressive conditions in a racist society to hope in a democratic one. The militant MOWM not only enabled blacks to merge their struggle for justice at home with the fight against tyranny abroad, but helped to lay the ideological and political foundation for the growth of the modern civil rights movement.

Notes

[1] Joe William Trotter, Jr., *Black Milwaukee: The Making of an Industrial Proletariat, 1915–45*, Urbana: University of Illinois Press, 1985, p. 47.

[2] Alan H. Spear, *Black Chicago: The Making of a Negro Ghetto*, Chicago: University of Chicago Press, 1967, p. 148.

[3] Quoted in Paul A. Giddings, *When and Where I Enter: The Impact of Black Women on Race and Sex in America*, New York: Bantam Books, 1984, p. 189.

[4] Joe William Trotter, Jr., *Coal, Class, and Color: Blacks in Southern West Virginia, 1915–32*, Urbana: University of Illinois Press, 1990, p. 178.

[5] Quoted in Elliott Rudwick, *W. E. B. DuBois: Voice of the Black Protest Movement*, 1960, reprint Urbana: University of Illinois Press, 1982, p. 238.

[6] See James Weldon Johnson, *Black Manhattan*, 1930, reprint New York: Athenaeum, 1968, p. 264.

[7] Alain Locke (ed.), *The New Negro* [1925], New York: Athenaeum, 1992, p. 3.

[8] Darlene Clark Hine, 'Black Migration to the Urban Midwest: The Gender Dimension, 1915–1945,' in Joe W. Trotter, Jr. (ed.), *The Great Migration in Historical Perspective*, Bloomington: Indiana University Press, 1991, p. 130.

[9] Trotter, *Black Milwaukee*, p. 129.

[10] *Ibid*, p.129.

[11] St. Clair Drake and Horace R. Cayton, *Black Metropolis*, revised edition New York: Harcourt, Brace, and World, 1962, vol. I, p. 83.

[12] Trotter, *Black Milwaukee*, p. 60.

[13] Jacqueline Jones, *Labor of Love, Labor of Sorrow*, New York: Basic Books, 1985, p. 197.

[14] Milton Meltzer (ed.), *In Their Own Words: A History of the American Negro*, New York: Thomas L. Crowell Company, 1967, p. 93.

[15] *Ibid*, p.93.

[16] Harvard Sitkoff, *A New Deal for Blacks: The Emergence of Civil Rights as a National Issue, the Depression Decade*, Oxford: Oxford University Press, 1978, p. 36.

[17] *Ibid*, p.36.

[18] Thomas R. Frazier, *Afro-American History: Primary Sources*, Chicago: Dorsey Press, 1988, p. 266.

[19] William Loren Katz, *Eyewitness: The Negro in American History*, New York: Putnam Publishing Company, 1967, p. 435.

[20] Katz, *Eyewitness*, pp. 442–3.

[21] Sitkoff, *New Deal for Blacks*, p. 70.

[22] Mark Naison, *Communists in Harlem during the Depression*, Urbana: University of Illinois Press, 1983, p. 75.

[23] Jones, *Labor of Love, Labor of Sorrow*, p. 219.

[24] Richard Wright and Edwin Rosskam, *Twelve Million Black Voices*, New York: Thunder's Mouth Press, 1941, p. 61.

[25] Jones, *Labor of Love, Labor of Sorrow*, p. 228.

[26] Drake and Cayton, *Black Metropolis*, vol. 2, p. 494.

[27] Trotter, *Black Milwaukee*, p. 132.

[28] Theodore Rosengarten, *All God's Dangers: The Life of Nate Shaw*, New York: Alfred A. Knopf, 1974, p. xiii.

[29] *Ibid.*, p. 312.

[30] Robin D. G. Kelley, *Hammer and Hoe: Alabama Communists during the Great Depression*, Chapel Hill: University of North Carolina Press, 1990, p. 25.

[31] Leslie H. Fishel, Jr. and Benjamin Quarles, *The Negro American: A Documentary History*, Glenview, IL: Scott, Foresman and Company, 1967, p. 447.

[32] Quoted in Wright and Rosskam, *Twelve Million Black Voices*, p. xiii.

[33] Wright and Rosskam, *ibid.*, p. xiv.

[34] Lawrence Levine, *Black Culture and Black Consciousness: Afro-American Folk Thought from Slavery to Freedom*, New York: Oxford University Press, 1977, p. 434.

[35] Philip Foner, *Organized Labor and the Black Worker, 1619–1973*, New York: International Publishers, 1974, p. 238.

[36] Jones, *Labor of Love, Labor of Sorrow*, p. 238.

[37] Jack D. Foner, *Blacks and the Military in American History*, New York: Praeger Publishers, 1974, p. 135.

[38] Herbert Shapiro, *White Violence and Black Response: From Reconstruction to Montgomery*, Amherst: University of Massachusetts Press, 1988, p. 331.

[39] Quoted in Sitkoff, *New Deal for Blacks*, p. 301.

[40] Sitkoff, *New Deal for Blacks*, p.301.

[41] Foner, *Blacks and the Military*, p. 135.

[42] Jones, *Labor of Love, Labor of Sorrow*, p. 233.

[43] Frazier, *Afro-American History*, pp. 291–2.

[44] Jervis Anderson, *A. Philip Randolph*, Berkeley: University of California Press, 1972, p. 257.

Chapter 8

A SEASON OF STRUGGLE

During the 1950s and 1960s, black people struggled to establish a firm hold on citizenship, and thousands acquired education under the GI bill. The voice of the urban ghetto, rhythm and blues, became rock and roll, the music of young America which provided material and style for Elvis Presley and many other white stars. Black artists such as the Supremes, the Four Tops, Stevie Wonder, and Smokey Robinson and the Miracles, became teen idols packaged and produced by Motown Records. Johnny Mathis sang love songs that crossed racial boundaries, and Chubby Checker's 'Twist' had blacks and whites dancing the same dance to the same song.

In his novels and in his essays, James Baldwin dared whites to face the hypocrisy of racial inequality in a nation billing itself as leader of the free world. The expanding war in Vietnam spawned conflict at home as disproportionate numbers of black men were killed in Southeast Asia.

The modern civil rights movement typified this period of ferment and change, bringing a new generation into the struggle for racial justice.

Martin Luther King, Jr. photographed during one of the great orations of modern times, the 'I Have a Dream' speech delivered on the steps of the Lincoln Memorial following the March on Washington in August 1963. The march was attended by over 200,000 people, up to one-quarter of them white supporters, but there were still many battles left to fight in the season of

THE DECADE AFTER the end of World War II was both a time of hope and a time of discouragement for African Americans. Rapid social changes of the war years fed optimism about black advancement, but postwar racial reform came only piecemeal. Wartime labor demands gave black workers new employment opportunities that often disappeared when white soldiers returned. During the 1940s and early 1950s, more than 1.5 million African Americans migrated from Jim Crow conditions in the South to somewhat more subtle forms of racial discrimination and segregation outside the region. When the Supreme Court announced its 1954 *Brown v. Board of Education* decision outlawing school desegregation, Roy Wilkins, a leader of the National Association for the Advancement of Colored People (NAACP), remembered the ruling as 'one of life's sweetest days. We had won a second Emancipation Proclamation.' But the ruling only promised change – 'another fifteen years of tribulation was just beginning.'[1]

Although the *Brown* decision repudiated the doctrine of 'separate but equal,' the nation was still far from the ideal of racial equality. Indeed, the ruling reinforced the notion that the 'Negro problem' was to be resolved by whites in positions of power. African Americans remained an insignificant political force. Ten percent of the nation's population was black, but there were no black governors or senators and only two black congressmen among the 435 members of the House of Representatives. Black southerners wishing to participate in electoral politics faced daunting obstacles: poll taxes, literacy tests, intimidation, and sometimes violent retaliation. On Christmas Eve 1951, Florida NAACP leader Harry T. Moore, founder of the Progressive Voters League, was killed along with his wife by a bomb at their home. In 1953, Mississippi voter-registration activist, George Lee, was shot. In neither case were the killers tried.

Throughout American history, black people had used their limited resources to struggle for advancement. Adeptly working within the dominant political system and improvising unconventional tactics outside it, they had resisted racial subordination and sometimes forced concessions from white political leaders. During the 1950s, however, the NAACP's strategy of working within the system through litigation and lobbying faced little competition from once-vibrant traditions of black political radicalism.

Black nationalist militancy had declined after the heyday of Marcus Garvey in the early 1920s, and street corner orators, isolated urban intellectuals, and a few small organizations represented what remained of the nationalist tradition. Malcolm X, the era's most effective black nationalist advocate, recalled that his own organization, the Nation of Islam, was almost unknown in 1954: 'Even

Above: *In the nation's capital, Washington, DC., African-Americans had long constituted a majority, yet the situation of discrimination, poverty, and disadvantage in their community remained overlooked by the country's lawmakers.*

among our own black people in the Harlem ghetto, you could have said "Muslim" to a thousand, and maybe one would not have asked you "What's that?"'[2]

African-American leftist politics had also declined since its high point in the 1930s. Cold War repression of political dissent led to the persecution of leftist black leaders such as W. E. B. DuBois, Paul Robeson, and Benjamin Davis. In 1950, the NAACP's board of directors voted to expel all communists in the organization. Only leftists who had broken or hidden their ties to the Communist Party could play significant roles in the major civil rights groups. Moreover, the effects of McCarthyism extended beyond the few black members of the Communist Party, inhibiting discussion of Marxian and socialist ideas that had long influenced African-American political thought.

Participants in the black protest movements increasingly drew their inspiration from con-

temporary movements rather than older radical traditions. Some saw anticolonial movements in Africa, Asia, and Latin America as models for the mass movement they hoped to build in the United States. The success of the Indian independence movement in 1947 strengthened the longstanding African-American interest in Mohandas Gandhi's strategy of nonviolent protest. Besides elements of leftist, nationalist, and Gandhian thought, the most significant influence on black activism of the 1950s was social-gospel Christianity, a tradition deeply rooted in African-American culture. These existing traditions would themselves be transformed as new radical ideas emerged from the series of sustained protest movements that spread throughout the South during the 1950s and 1960s.

The Montgomery Bus Boycott Movement
The initiators of the modern freedom struggle were typically not national civil rights organizations and leaders but rather black activists of southern communities who launched grassroots campaigns against segregation and other forms of racial discrimination. There were many individual protests against the Jim Crow

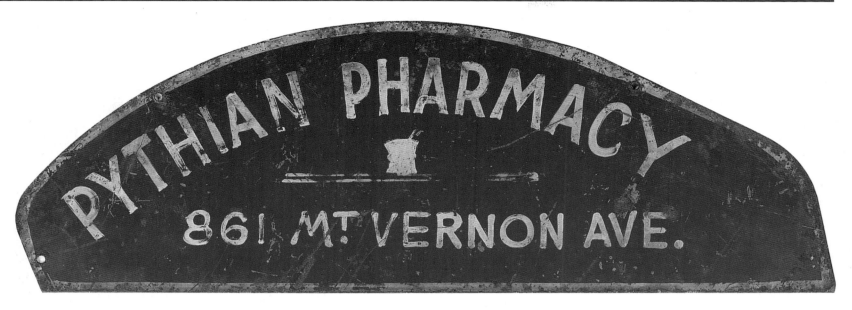

system, but a spontaneous act of rebellion by a woman became the catalyst for a major movement – the Montgomery bus boycott.

News accounts later described Rosa Parks as a seamstress to emphasize the fact that an ordinary black woman had taken the first step, but she was also a civil rights activist, prepared for the role she played. Since the 1940s, Parks had been an active NAACP member, working closely with the head of Montgomery's chapter, E. D. Nixon. During the summer of 1955, she attended workshops at Tennessee's Highlander Folk School, a training center for labor and civil rights organizers.

Boarding a Montgomery city bus on the afternoon of 1 December 1955, Rosa Parks did not plan to launch a protest movement, but she had long resented the humiliation of being forced to sit at the back of the bus behind all the white passengers. Several times before, after she had paid her fare, white bus

Above: *A 1950's sign for an African-American owned pharmacy in Columbus, Ohio. The name was almost certainly influenced by a black fraternal order to which the owner belonged.*

drivers had forced her to reenter the bus through the rear door, sometimes driving away before she could reboard. After many years of enduring such treatment, she finally reached breaking point. When white passengers came aboard the full bus, the bus driver asked her to stand in order that a white man might sit. Parks, who was seated behind the last row of 'white' seats, refused to move. The bus driver threatened to have her arrested; Parks still refused to move. Police arrived, took her to the police station, and charged her with violating Alabama segregation laws.

Black residents of Montgomery mobilized quickly. Members of the Women's Political Council proposed that black people refuse to ride the buses for one day as a protest against discriminatory treatment. The boycott, which began on 5 December, was an overwhelming success, with almost no blacks riding the buses, and black residents decided it should continue. They formed the Montgomery Improvement Association and selected the Reverend Martin Luther King, Jr. as president.

King, only 26 years old, had served little more than a year as the pastor of Montgomery's Dexter Avenue Baptist Church. 'I did not start this boycott,' he later told protest participants. 'I was asked by you to serve as your spokesman.'[3] King's oratorical abilities and dedication were apparent to those who knew him. The son and grandson of ministers who were also civil rights advocates, King's

strong commitment to social justice was evident even before he enrolled at Morehouse College at age 15. He and other students listened to inspirational lectures by Morehouse President, Benjamin E. Mays, a social-gospel proponent. While at Morehouse, King responded to his 'inescapable urge to serve society' by deciding to study for the ministry. Attending Crozer Theological Seminary, he traced his 'anticapitalistic feelings' to memories of Depression-era poverty.[4] After receiving his doctorate in systematic theology from Boston University, King felt a responsibility to return to his native South, and became pastor of Montgomery's Dexter Avenue Baptist Church.

King's address to the first mass meeting of the boycott movement combined militancy with moderation. He aroused the overflow audience at Holt Street Baptist Church by proclaiming the larger meaning of the boycott.

Left: *Sidney Poitier and Ruby Dee acting in a 1959 production of Lorraine Hansberry's A* Raisin in the Sun. *Both were pioneers of black theater in the post-World War II period.*

Right: *James Baldwin took the literary explosion which had begun during the Harlem Renaissance to new heights. He infused his many works, such as* Notes of A Native Son *and* Another Country, *with political metaphor and social commentary.*

Above: *These sorority and fraternity items from chapters at Central State University, Wilberforce, Ohio, include two paddles: (top) an Omega Psi Phi Fraternity one made by Phillip Wright in 1952, and (middle) a Delta Sigma Theta Sorority one owned by co-ed Jane Lee.*

'And you know, my friends, there comes a time when people get tired of being trampled over by the iron feet of oppression,' he told listeners. Urging Montgomery blacks to remain nonviolent and true to their Christian values, he identified their cause with the traditional values of the nation. 'If we are wrong, the Supreme Court of this nation is wrong! If we are wrong, God Almighty is wrong!'[5]

Black residents of Montgomery understood that their movement symbolized more than simply a desire for desegregation; it represented a new direction in African-American politics. Boycott leaders refused to back down even in the face of violent white retaliation. King's home was bombed, and Montgomery officials indicted him and other leaders on charges of violating a state law against boycotts.

Despite such intimidation, the protest movement continued for one year, until December 1956 when the Supreme Court ruled against the bus segregation policy. African Americans had shown that nonviolence could succeed if blacks remained united and their leaders refused to be intimidated. King and other politically active black ministers formed the Southern Christian Leadership Council (SCLC) to build upon the success in Montgomery. As president of the new organization, King strengthened his commitment to the use of Gandhian tactics, believing 'that the Christian doctrine of love operating through the Gandhian method of nonviolence was one of the most potent weapons available to the Negro in his struggle for freedom.'[6] He was

BAYARD RUSTIN AND THE 'MIRACLE IN MONTGOMERY'

The Montgomery bus boycott of 1955-6, an unexpected mass protest in the deep South, eventually brought nonviolent direct action to the foreground of the civil rights struggle and forced civil rights leaders to reconsider their assumptions. The successful year-long boycott made their reliance on northern-directed legal challenges to segregation seem unnecessarily restrictive by demonstrating that southern blacks could be enlisted in their own liberation. What civil rights leaders observed in Montgomery – the economic and moral vulnerability of segregation, the inability of even moderate white segregationists to compromise, the resolute courage of many southern blacks, the emotional power of African-American religious belief, and the viability of nonviolent direct action in the deep South – helped reshape the philosophical and

organizational contours of the movement.

Initially, the only national leader who seemed to grasp the boycott's significance was Bayard Rustin, the executive director of the War Resisters' League, and even he did not comprehend its full meaning until he visited the city in February 1956. Rustin was a free-wheeling black intellectual who put little stock in organizational discipline or orthodoxy – Nat Hentoff once called him 'the Socrates of the Civil Rights movement.'[1] A native of West Chester, Pennsylvania, where his family, enthusiastic Quakers, eked out a living cooking and catering for local Quaker gentry, Bayard early on encountered the pacifist doctrines that anchored his lifelong commitment to nonviolence. A brilliant student, he studied at Cheyney State Teachers College and Wilberforce University before the Great

Depression forced him to drop out. In 1931, at age 21, he moved to Harlem, embarking on an odyssey of survival and discovery that took him down the backroads of radical politics and bohemian culture. For a time, he recruited for the Young Communist League, but in 1941, disillusioned with the Communist Party, he shifted his allegiance to A. Philip Randolph, the black labor leader and socialist. Randolph appointed Rustin youth organizer for his planned mass march on Washington and later helped him secure a field secretary position with the pacifist Fellowship of Reconciliation (FOR), where he became acquainted with the writings and teachings of Gandhi. In 1942, after helping found the Congress of Racial Equality (CORE), he became a friend and disciple of Krishnaial Shridharani, author of *War Without Violence*. Rustin's commitment to nonviolent resistance and noncooperation with evil deepened, and in 1943 he rejected the traditional Quaker compromise of alternative service in an army hospital. Convicted of draft evasion, he spent the remainder of the war in a federal penitentiary.

Following his release, as race relations secretary of FOR, he organized a Free India Committee, directed Randolph's Committee Against Discrimination in the Armed Forces, and masterminded CORE's 1947 Journey of Reconciliation, precursor to the 1960s Freedom Rides. Rustin's integrated bus ride earned him a savage beating by North Carolina police and 22 days on a chain gang, but this only reinforced his belief in Gandhian activism. Virtually unknown to the general public, by the mid-1950s he was revered in the international subculture of Gandhian intellectuals.

Left: *Bayard Rustin was one of the central organizational figures of the civil rights period and an architect of nonviolent protest.*

Below: *Black religious and community leaders in Montgomery, pictured following their release after having been arrested in February 1956.*

Rustin had never been to Alabama, but early news reports about the bus boycott convinced him to seek a sponsor; 'fly to Montgomery with the idea of getting the bus boycott temporarily called off'; then organize 'a workshop or school for non-violence with a goal of 100 young Negro men who will then promote it not only in Montgomery but elsewhere in the South.'[2] Eventually his friend and mentor Randolph agreed to fund the trip.

Rustin arrived in Montgomery on 21 February – the day local white authorities indicted the leaders of the Montgomery Improvement Association (MIA) for violating a state antiboycott statute. The MIA office was in chaos, and the Reverend Martin Luther King, Jr. was away preaching at Fisk University in Nashville, but Rustin gained an audience with the Reverend Ralph Abernathy who warned him Montgomery was a dangerous place for an unarmed black activist. Later, he talked with local black labor leader and former NAACP official E. D. Nixon, legendary in black Montgomery for his courage, who became an instant ally when Rustin produced Randolph's letter of introduction. 'They can bomb us out and they can kill us,' Nixon vowed, 'but we are not going to give in.'[3] When Nixon confessed he was not sure how the boycotters should respond to the mass indictments, Rustin promptly suggested the Gandhian option of voluntarily filling the jails. As Rustin laid out the rationale for nonviolent martyrdom, Nixon became intrigued, and the next morning he became the first boycott leader to turn himself in. As news of Nixon's arrest spread, there was a virtual stampede at the county courthouse, as scores of black leaders joined in the ritual of self-sacrifice.

When King returned from Nashville two days later, he wholeheartedly embraced the new strategy and, at Nixon's urging, invited Rustin to attend an MIA executive committee meeting. King's forthright leadership impressed Rustin, and when the committee voted to organize future mass meetings around five

prayers, including 'a prayer for those who oppose us,' he knew they had begun to master the art of moral warfare.[4] Realizing he had underestimated his southern hosts, he quietly abandoned his plan for a suspension of the boycott.

What he saw that evening at the First Baptist Church confirmed his growing optimism and deepened his appreciation for black evangelicalism's capacity to blend emotional fervor with a spirit of forgiveness. When the 90 indicted leaders gathered around the pulpit to open this first mass meeting since the indictments, the sanctuary exploded with emotion. As Rustin related:

> Overnight these leaders had become symbols of courage. Women held their babies to touch them, the people stood in ovation . . . [King] began: 'We are not struggling merely for the rights of Negroes, but for all the people of Montgomery black and white. We are determined to make America a better place for all people. Ours is a non-violent protest. We pray God that no man shall use arms.'[5]

Rustin spent the following Sunday with King, beginning with morning services at Dexter Avenue Baptist Church where the young minister preached a moving sermon on the philosophy of nonviolence. 'We are concerned not merely to win justice in the buses,' King insisted, 'but rather to behave in a new and different way – to be non-violent so that we may remove injustice itself, both from society and from ourselves.'[6] Later, the two men spent several hours discussing nonviolence, the struggle for civil rights, and other moral imperatives, and by the end of the evening their personal and philosophical bond was sealed. In the following years, they became close friends and collaborators, merging Gandhianism and African-American evangelism, and the protest traditions of North and South, into a coherent vision of the 'beloved community.' In August 1963, when King delivered his eloquent and influential speech on the steps of the Lincoln Memorial – informing the world of his dream of simple justice and true equality – the primary architect of this remarkable event was Bayard Rustin, the strange visitor to Montgomery on a fateful day in 1956.

Raymond Arsenault

Notes
[1]Charles Moritz (ed.), *Current Biography Yearbook 1967*, New York: H.W. Wilson Company, p. 360.
[2]John M. Swomley, Jr., to Wilson Riles, 21 February 1956, FOR Papers, Swarthmore College Peace Collection, Swarthmore, Pennsylvania.
[3]Bayard Rustin, 'Montgomery Diary,' *Liberation* 1 (April 1956): 7.
[4]*Ibid.*, p. 8.
[5]*Ibid.*
[6]*Ibid.*, p. 10.

This period room from the late-1940s or early-1950s recreates the living room of a home owned by a middle-class black family in the South; actually it is not dissimilar to a home in almost any part of the country which might also have contained furniture like this.

In this period racial restrictions limited the residential and social choices of African Americans, further complicating lives already circumscribed by poverty. But black people also

still reluctant to publicly challenge the more cautious litigation strategy of the NAACP, but in 1960 students at predominantly black colleges initiated their own militant challenges to the southern Jim Crow system.

Rise of the Student Movement in the 1960s

When the Supreme Court announced in 1955 that its earlier *Brown* decision would be enforced 'with all deliberate speed,' instead of immediately, southern white officials sought to postpone school integration. Southern blacks soon realized that they would have to prod the federal government into action, and black students were more willing to assume this role than were the established civil rights leaders. Even before the 1960s, black students had played crucial roles in the school desegregation efforts. The NAACP had succeeded in the courtroom, but implementing the *Brown* decision required courageous youngsters willing to endure hostility when they entered previously white schools. The nine black students who in 1958 had braved white mobs to attend Little Rock's Central High School became heroes to other young blacks. The students' determination forced a reluctant President Dwight D. Eisenhower to respond to Arkansas Governor Orvil Faubus's public challenge to federal authority by nationalizing the Arkansas National Guard and sending soldiers to protect the black students. The 'Little Rock Nine' joined Parks and King as heroic figures for future black activists. 'When they spoke, they said what I was thinking,' recalled Cleveland Sellers, then a teenager in Denmark, South Carolina. 'When they suffered, I suffered with them. And on those rare occasions when they managed to eke out a meager victory, I rejoiced too.'[7]

Above: A group of African-American professionals at a family dinner in 1957. The Washingtons are evidence of a comfortable, black middle-class, but economic success, which still eluded most, did not compensate for political exclusion.

Sellers was still in high school on 1 February 1960 when he learned that four first-year students at North Carolina Agricultural and Technical College had initiated a new wave of protests. After debating what could be done about segregation at the lunch counter of Greensboro's Woolworth variety store, David Richmond, Franklin McCain, Joseph McNeil, and Ezell Blair, Jr., decided to 'sit-in,' that is, remain seated at the lunch counter until they were served or arrested. When the surprised store manager decided not to arrest them, they returned to their campus to recruit more students. After several days of increasingly large protests, students at nearby colleges decided to try the sit-in tactic.

During the following weeks, thousands of black college and high-school students in many southern communities launched sit-ins. Many went to jail singing 'freedom songs,' adding their own words to church songs and popular rock-and-roll tunes. SCLC, the Congress of Racial Equality (CORE), and the NAACP attempted to provide guidance for student protesters after the initial sit-in in Greensboro, but student activists insisted on forming their own local groups under student leadership.

Student Nonviolent Coordinating Committee

Although sit-in protesters admired and respected leaders of the established civil rights groups, most wanted to maintain their independence from the existing civil rights organi-

chose to live together; many preferred the security of going to local churches, shopping at local businesses, and participating in black community life.

In terms of educational levels, incomes, aspirations and social status, black communities were diverse. Unemployment was low and many black people lived in extended households, often with grandparents, aunts, and uncles as well as parents and children.

The kind of family who could have afforded a comfortable room like this probably would have been a married couple that had earned a steady income for years. Perhaps the wife taught at the nearby black college, or maybe the man was a minister, the woman worked as a nurse, or the family owned a funeral home.

In black communities, status was somewhat more complex than among other Americans. Most Americans viewed income as the most important factor in determining class. Black people defined class with less emphasis on income and more on education, church attendance, family background, and manners.

Owners of businesses, such as morticians, and professionals, such as doctors and dentists, were often among the elite. The teachers were poorly paid, but were among the most respected members of the community. A taxicab driver who was a deacon in a large church may have enjoyed higher status than a postal worker of similar income who did not attend church.

Note the copies of *Sphinx*, magazine of the top African-American fraternity, and the *Journal of Negro History*.

Above: *Three African-American lawyers celebrate their success on 17 May 1954 in having public school segregation declared unconstitutional. From left to right, they are George E.C. Hayes, Thurgood Marshall, and James M. Nabrit.*

Below: *The Supreme Court's destruction of the legal foundations of segregation caused a white backlash in the South. White Citizens Councils were formed and Klan-inspired violence was once again an actuality rather than a possibility.*

Above: *NAACP official Daisy Bates (center) poses with eight of the nine students who had become the first black students to be admitted to Little Rock's Central High School in 1957. All 10 were awarded the Spingarn Medal.*

zations. James Lawson, expelled from Vanderbilt Divinity School because of his involvement in the sit-ins, expressed the militant student mood when he questioned the cautious tactics of older leaders. He called upon Christians to overcome 'social evil' and warned against too much patience – 'All of Africa will be free before the American Negro attains first class citizenship.' Lawson had lived in India for several years, and for him Gandhian nonviolence was a philosophy of life. He wrote the Student Nonviolent Coordinating Committee's (SNCC) idealistic statement of purpose:

> Nonviolence as it grows from Judaic-Christian traditions seeks a social order of justice permeated by love . . . [Love] matches the capacity of evil to inflict suffering with an even more enduring capacity to absorb evil, all the while persisting in love.[8]

Not all the student activists accepted Lawson's Gandhian precepts, but most agreed with his view that the sit-ins were the start of a 'nonviolent revolution.' Ella Baker was one of the few older civil rights leaders who sym-

HELP FIGHT COMMUNISM AND INTEGRATION JOIN THE KKK

pathized with the students' militancy and desire for independence. Baker had a long career in the NAACP and was administrator of SCLC's Atlanta headquarters, but she questioned whether southern blacks could depend on a few charismatic leaders like King. As a woman working within male-dominated civil rights organizations, she met 'the frustrations and the disillusionment that come when the prophetic leaders turn out to have heavy feet of clay.' Baker invited activists in the sit-ins to attend an Easter-weekend gathering at Shaw University in North Carolina and encouraged them to form their own independent organization. She also urged students to practice 'group-centered' leadership.[9] What the movement needed, she said, were 'people who are interested not in being leaders as much as in developing leadership among other people.' After the students voted to establish the Student Nonviolent Coordinating Committee, she left SCLC and became one of SNCC's adult advisors. 'She was much older in terms of age,' Nashville student John Lewis explained, 'but in terms of ideas and philosophy and commitment she was one of the youngest persons in the movement.'[10]

Above: *Black students engaged in the lunch counter sit-in demonstration at F.W. Woolworth's segregated facilities in Greensboro, North Carolina, in February 1960. The protest was started by four students on 1 February and soon spread throughout the South, initiating an era of student protest and activism. Thousands took part, and the success of the sit-ins encouraged the freedom rides which followed. The counter (below) is now preserved at the Smithsonian.*

Student Activists and Kennedy

In October 1960, when Atlanta student protesters deftly maneuvered Martin Luther King, Jr. to join their demonstration at a downtown store, young activists unexpectedly became aware of their ability to create a crisis which compelled more powerful forces to respond. John F. Kennedy's sympathy call to King's wife, Coretta Scott King, together with his brother Robert Kennedy's intervention to gain King's release from jail, strengthened the Democratic candidate's black support. A heavy turnout of black voters in key states produced a close victory over Richard Nixon, but, fearing the loss of southern white support, Kennedy, as president, refused to give priority to civil rights. Black student activists, particularly those in SNCC, continued to seek new ways of pushing his administration to act on civil rights. As in the Atlanta sit-in during the presidential campaign, students could not always predict the consequences of their actions, but their spontaneous militancy often caught Kennedy and older civil rights leaders off guard.

Thus, during the spring and summer of 1961, student activists unexpectedly gained an

opportunity to force federal action when CORE sent a small group of 'freedom riders' to expose segregated transportation facilities in the southern states. After white mobs in Alabama forced the interracial CORE contingent to end their campaign, Nashville student activist Diane Nash immediately mobilized other students to continue the ride. Nash and other student freedom riders took buses into Jackson, Mississippi, where they were quickly arrested and charged with violating the state's segregation laws. After the first group went to jail, dozens of others followed, spending their summer vacations in Mississippi prisons. In prison they kept their spirits high, singing freedom songs and discussing how to continue their movement. Many decided to leave college to become full-time participants. Such activists took pride in their identity as militant freedom riders. Diane Nash saw herself as part of 'a group of people suddenly proud to be called "black".'[11]

Demanding federal protection, the brash freedom riders forced Kennedy to balance his desire to support civil rights against his fear of upsetting southern whites. He and Attorney General Robert Kennedy made behind-the-scenes efforts to stop the rides. Kennedy administration representatives tried to convince the students to engage in voter-registration efforts instead of desegregation protests. Although some student activists recognized the need for such efforts, they were disap-

pointed by Kennedy's unwillingness to take political risks. As they continued protesting for 'Freedom Now,' their disillusionment with liberal leaders increased.

The Albany Movement

The freedom rides into Mississippi were part of a larger campaign that brought the protest movement from the upper South to the regions of the deep South. Unlike the small-scale sit-ins of 1960, the protests after the summer of 1961 were increasingly massive, involving large segments of the black populace and sometimes disrupting entire communities. These expanding demonstrations focused on economic as well as civil rights issues.

In Albany, Georgia SNCC field secretary, Charles Sherrod, attempted to mobilize local students for sustained protest. As the Albany Movement intensified during December 1961, King and other SCLC officials arrived, bringing national publicity. Continuing in 1962, the Albany protests exposed the contrasting approaches of SCLC (orchestrating demonstrations in order to achieve national civil rights reform) and SNCC (insisting on local autonomy). Sherrod reflected the growing militancy of the students when he asserted that his generation wanted 'to go ahead in a new way – maybe not the way the whites have shown . . . We are *not* the puppets of the white man.'[12]

When King announced that he would remain in jail through Christmas after his arrest on 16 December, the Albany Movement seemed unified, but white officials quickly arranged to have him released on bail. SNCC workers suspected that King's presence undermined local residents' confidence in their own grassroots leaders. Though his presence brought press coverage and the possibility of federal intervention, once he left, SNCC organizers claimed, local blacks could not gain concessions from white officials.

When King and Ralph Abernathy returned to Albany for sentencing the following July,

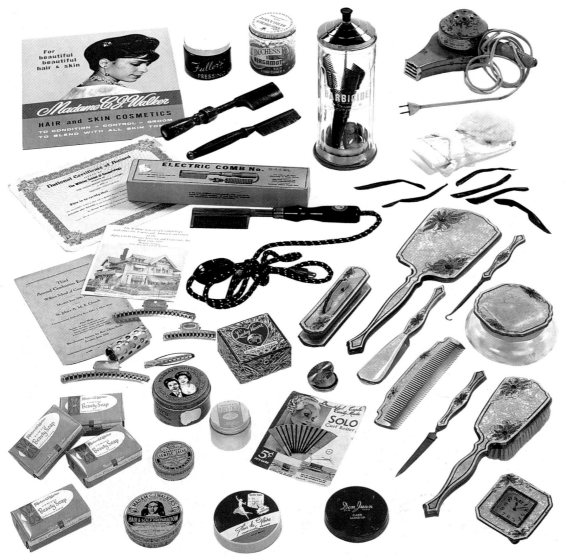

Left: *Attractiveness was especially highly regarded in the 1950s and most women needed help from beauticians and beauty products to approximate the ideal. Most women wore their hair 'straightened' (permed with a hot comb), but in the early 1960s, new brands of 'permanent' were developed which used chemicals rather than heat. Skin color was also important, and black women who had lighter skin, straighter hair, and thinner features were often considered the most attractive. (Many black movie stars and singers fit this pattern.) In the 1950s, black men often married women with skin lighter than their own; thus in the 1960s the phrase 'Black is Beautiful' was popularized as a reaction to this.*

Above: *The late 1950s was an era of changing fashions, new music (be-bop, rock and roll), and growing prosperity. Black people dressed similarly to other Americans, using dress and style as critical signs of higher aspiration. A lady, black or white, wore a dress, gloves and a hat – not pants – to a public occasion. A gentleman wore a hat, a suit and a white or light print shirt as well. A bohemian world was also emerging which conflicted with middle-class values; transistor radios meant that everyone could hear, and be influenced by, new musical styles. In the big cities 'beat' subculture developed, heavily influenced by black music and style and critical of mainstream society's materialism and racial hypocrisy.*

there were renewed massive demonstrations, particularly after he announced that they would serve their sentences rather than pay fines. As in December, however, the escalating protests lost momentum when white officials arranged for a black man to pay the SCLC leaders' fines. After his release King remained in Albany attempting to revive the movement, but he encountered criticism from young activists, especially SNCC workers, who questioned his militancy. The Albany Movement convinced them that their emphasis on group leadership rather than a single leader was correct, but also showed that mass protests could be stopped by efficient use of police and mass arrests of demonstrators. As one SNCC activist put it, 'We ran out of people before [Albany Police Chief] Pritchett ran out of jails.'[13]

Birmingham Campaign of 1963

By 1963, the Reverend Fred Shuttlesworth had decided that the Birmingham, Alabama, movement needed outside help and invited King into the city. Shuttlesworth had been fighting for civil rights many years before the Birmingham campaign of 1963. A founder of the Alabama Christian Movement for Human Rights, Shuttlesworth's church had been

Right: *Washington, DC's first jazz festival was staged in 1962 and the Eureka Brass Band from New Orleans marked the occasion by playing in front of the White House. In the foreground here are Alcide 'Slow Drag' Parageau, Duke Ellington, and Matthew 'Fats' Houston.*

bombed, and he had been arrested while helping freedom riders.

King and other SCLC leaders were determined to build a more effective movement in Birmingham than in Albany and, since SNCC was not active there, realized they would have a freer hand. Under a plan called 'Project C' (for 'Confrontation'), King's strategy was to provoke confrontations with local white officials, especially the openly antiblack police commissioner, Eugene T. 'Bull' Conner. King believed that televised confrontations between nonviolent protesters and brutal police with clubs and police dogs would attract the sympathy of northern whites and would lead to federal intervention.

During April, SCLC officials, along with local black leaders, organized a series of sit-ins, marches, and rallies. Denounced by a group of Birmingham's white ministers, King defended his protest strategy in one of his most famous statements, the 'Letter from Birmingham City Jail.' He argued that white resistance to black equality had forced blacks to move outside legal channels to express their discontent. It was necessary, he said, for

blacks to create a crisis rather than wait forever for change.

> When you have seen vicious mobs lynch your mothers and fathers at will . . . when you see the vast majority of your twenty million Negro brothers smothering in the airtight cage of poverty . . . when you are forever fighting a degenerating sense of 'nobodiness'; then you will understand why we find it difficult to wait.

He also warned that whites who refused to negotiate with nonviolent black leaders would soon have to deal with more militant leaders. Frustrated blacks, he argued, might turn to nationalism, 'a development that will lead inevitably to a frightening racial nightmare.'[14]

The Birmingham protests grew during the spring of 1963. By early May, more than 3,000 blacks had been jailed. On 7 May, after thousands of school children marched into Birmingham's business district, Governor

Above: *Civil rights protestors being hosed from the streets of Birmingham, Alabama, during the violent confrontations of 1963. The city, with its segregationist police commissioner, was widely seen as a stronghold of bigotry.*

Below: *President Kennedy opened the doors of the White House for a meeting with the leaders of the March on Washington. In a message to Congress on the Emancipation Centennial Kennedy had noted blacks' continuing disadvantage.*

George Wallace sent state patrolmen to reinforce Conner's police forces, who used water hoses to disperse the children. A few days later, when bombs exploded at the home of King's brother and at SCLC's local office, angry demonstrators threw rocks at police. Finally, white officials indicated their readiness to make concessions, and the Birmingham protests subsided.

By this time, the Birmingham protests had sparked many other local protest movements. An estimated 930 public protest demonstrations in more than 100 cities would take place during the year. Unlike the lunch-counter protests, some of the larger protests during the spring and summer of 1963 involved poor blacks who had little sympathy for nonviolence. Each of the national civil rights organizations tried to offer guidance for the mass marches and demonstrations, culminating in the Birmingham protests of 1963, but none of them could completely control these protests. King and other nonviolent leaders feared that they might lose control of the black struggle to black nationalist leaders, such as Malcolm X.

March on Washington

That summer, veteran civil rights leader A. Philip Randolph proposed a march on Washington to give blacks an opportunity to express their discontent in a nonviolent way. When President Kennedy initially objected to the idea of a march, Randolph told the President that 'Negroes were already in the streets. It is very likely impossible to get them off.' He asked Kennedy:

If they are bound to be in the streets in any case, is it not better that they be led by organizations dedicated to civil rights and disciplined by struggle rather than to leave them

to other leaders who care neither about civil rights nor about nonviolence?[15]

The March on Washington for Jobs and Freedom, held on 28 August 1963, was the largest single demonstration of the Civil Rights Movement. Over 200,000 people gathered at the Lincoln Memorial to hear singers, such as Mahalia Jackson, and leaders of the major civil rights groups. In his speech, SNCC Chairperson John Lewis charged that American politics was 'dominated by politicians who build their careers on immoral compromises and ally themselves with open forms of political, economic, and social exploitation.'[16] Lewis's speech was the most controversial delivered, but King's address was the one most remembered. Calling upon America to live up to its ideals, King recounted the difficulties the black freedom struggle had faced. But he added, 'I still have a dream . . . that one day this nation will rise up and live out the true meaning of its creed – we hold these truths to be self-evident, that all men are created equal.'[17]

The black-white coalition that supported

Below: *The artifacts here symbolize the confrontational but non-violent direct action campaign undertaken by the Freedom Movement against the forces of segregation, a campaign which reached its symbolic peak with the March on Washington on 28 August 1963. The items range from pins, posters and pamphlets, placards and leaflets, magazines and segregation signs, to the official album with speeches by the 10 civil rights leaders heard at the Lincoln Memorial, a commemorative publication called* The Day They Marched, *and most poignant of all, the 28 June 1963* Life *magazine cover showing Medgar Evers' widow consoling her son at Evers' funeral.*

civil rights reform came apart during the years after the March on Washington. Civil rights leaders recognized that they were caught in the middle between increasingly angry blacks, frustrated by the slow pace of change, and white political leaders resisting rapid social change. SNCC workers bitterly criticized the Kennedy administration for failing to protect southern blacks from racist violence. Even moderate leaders reacted angrily a few weeks after the march when a bomb planted in a Birmingham church killed four black children. An angry group of black spokespersons confronted President Kennedy at the White House, and King warned that 'the Negro community is about to reach a breaking point.' He cautioned, 'If something isn't done to give the Negro a new sense of hope and a sense of protection, there is a danger we will face the worst race riot we have ever seen in this country.' Taken aback, Kennedy urged the delegation to forestall violence while he sought passage of a major new civil rights bill. 'Tell the Negro communities that this is a very hard price which they have to pay to get this job done.'[18]

Kennedy's assassination a few months later reflected the nation's violent mood. Timid federal responses to racist violence had created a climate in which political violence could flourish. King noted that, 'in the life of Negro civil-rights leaders, the whine of the bullet from ambush, the roar of the bomb have all too often broken the night's silence.'[19] Malcolm X called the assassination a case of the 'chickens coming home to roost.'

To the surprise of some activists, the new president, Lyndon Baines Johnson, not known as a strong advocate of civil rights, pushed through Congress one of the most important reforms of the period, the historic Civil Rights Act of 1964. The most dramatic result of the

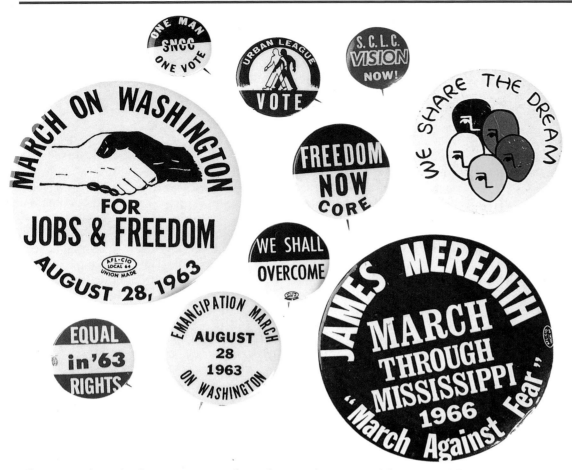

Act was the elimination of 'whites only' public facilities, but it also brought about major changes in American life, both in the South and the North. Title VII of the Act was originally designed to deal with discrimination against African Americans, but women and nonblack minorities were affected by provisions outlawing racial bias in employment and education.

Mississippi Voting Rights Movement

Despite passage of the Civil Rights Act of 1964, substantial racial barriers remained in the South, particularly in the rural areas of Mississippi and Alabama where blacks made up most of the population. In such areas, widespread poverty among blacks made desegregation of public facilities less important as a racial goal than political and economic gains. Because racial control was at stake, white resistance to civil rights reforms was particularly intense in these states. The black belt region of the South had a notorious history of lynchings and other acts of racial violence, and Mississippi was known as the stronghold of southern segregation. In 1963 the United States Commission on Civil Rights reported there was 'danger of a complete breakdown of law and order' in the state. 'Citizens of the United States have been shot, set upon by vicious dogs, beaten and otherwise terrorized because they sought to vote,' the Commission observed.[20]

Above: *Pins from the demonstrations and marches of the 1963-66 period. 'We Share the Dream' refers to the races and religions – Christians, Jews, and Moslems – which united for the cause.*

Below: *Tens of thousands of demonstrators, black and white, assemble behind the multiracial leadership for the march from the Washington Monument to the Lincoln Memorial.*

Robert Moses, a SNCC worker who directed the voting rights effort of Mississippi's Council of Federal Organizations (COFO), implemented Ella Baker's strategy of developing leadership at the 'grassroots' level. Convincing black Mississippians to become active in voting rights efforts was often difficult, given the imminent threat of violence. In September 1961, a white state representative had killed Herbert Lee, a black resident who supported voter registration, and an all-white jury quickly absolved the assailant. The following fall, federal troops had to be sent to the University of Mississippi when a large mob of whites rioted in violent protest against the admission of a black student, James Meredith. In June 1963 a white supremacist murdered NAACP leader Medgar Evers at his home in Jackson, Mississippi.

Civil rights workers responded by showing black residents that it was possible to resist white domination. When the sheriff of Greenwood, Mississippi, asked SNCC worker Sam Block to pack his clothes and leave town, Block replied, 'Well, sheriff, if you don't want to see me here, I think the best thing for you to do is pack your clothes and leave, get out of town, cause I'm here to stay, I came here to do a job and this is my intention, I'm going to do this job.'[21] Block and other civil rights organizers sought to reverse the effects of generations of racial oppression. For blacks who had become accustomed to their status as second-

Above: *World War II veteran and NAACP campaigner Medgar Evers was shot dead in 1963 by Byron DeLa Beckwith, who was eventually convicted of the murder in 1994. Evers' widow, Myrlie, was elected to the NAACP's chair in 1995.*

class citizens, joining the freedom struggle involved a dramatic transformation in their lives.

Fannie Lou Hamer, for example, had spent her life on a cotton plantation before she heard about the voting rights movement. Her parents, like many blacks in the state, had been sharecroppers. 'All of us worked in the fields, of course, but we never did get anything out of sharecropping,' she remembered. Having dropped out of elementary school to work, Hamer was 44 years old when she attended a voting rights meeting and listened to Moses and other SNCC workers. When the civil rights workers asked who would go to the voter-registration office, Hamer raised her hand. 'I guess if I'd had any sense I'd a-been a little scared, but what was the point of being scared,' she explained. 'The only thing they could do to me was kill me, and it seemed like they'd been trying to do that a little bit at a time ever since I could remember.'[22]

Soon afterwards, Hamer and 17 other blacks were arrested for trying to register. When she was released on bail, the plantation owner told her to withdraw her registration application. She left the plantation instead,

Below: *This poster of a Mississippi policeman was issued by the Student Nonviolent Coordinating Committee. The governor's attempt to prevent James H. Meredith's enrollment at the University of Mississippi led to two deaths in campus riots.*

IS HE PROTECTING YOU?

STUDENT NONVIOLENT COORDINATING COMMITTEE
8½ RAYMOND STREET, N.W. ATLANTA 14, GEORGIA

and, during the next year, she could not find employment. In June 1963 she was beaten in the Winona, Mississippi, jail. Rather than turning back, however, she joined SNCC and became one of its oldest organizers.

Mississippi Summer Project of 1964
By the end of 1963, Moses, Hamer, and other Mississippi civil rights workers had concluded that blacks in the state were unlikely to make gains without federal protection. Hoping that the presence of whites would bring national attention to restrain racist violence, they developed a plan to recruit a large number of white volunteers to work in Mississippi. Although some black COFO organizers believed this would hamper their long-term effort to develop self-reliant local black leadership, most recognized the need for outside support.

The 1964 Mississippi Summer Project attracted the attention of the nation. In June, even as the volunteers were preparing to go to the state, they learned that three civil rights workers had not returned from a trip to investigate the burning of a black church near Philadelphia, Mississippi. The disappearance of the two white and one black civil rights workers led to a massive investigation by the Federal Bureau of Investigation (FBI), which had been reluctant to offer protection to civil rights workers. In August, following a massive search involving military personnel, the bodies of James Chaney, Mickey Schwerner, and Andrew Goodman were found buried in an earthen dam. The killers were never tried on state murder charges, but several were later convicted on federal charges of interfering with the civil rights of the victims.

Despite the killings, the Summer Project continued. It had a profound impact on the lives of many participants who worked closely with local black residents. For many white volunteers, the summer provided their first opportunity to work on an equal basis with blacks. Among the most successful aspects of the project were 'freedom schools,' which developed new techniques to improve the academic and political skills of black children and some adults. For the first time, many students learned African-American history.

The Summer Project ended with an attempt to challenge the seating of the all-white Mississippi delegation to the Democratic National Convention held that August in Atlantic City, New Jersey. Civil rights workers organized the Mississippi Freedom Democratic Party (MFDP), open to all races and generally conforming to the national Party's regulations. 'We decided to form our own party because the whites wouldn't even let us register,' explained Fannie Lou Hamer. The MFDP delegates made clear their support for President Lyndon Johnson, while many in the regular delegation hinted that they would support Republican Barry Goldwater because of Johnson's civil rights policies. The MFDP presented evidence that black voters suffered discrimination and racist violence. Speaking on

MOTOWN

Above: *This picture was taken in 1966 after the name change of Motown's dominant all-female group to Diana Ross and the Supremes. Florence Ballard left and Cindy Birdsong (right) joined Mary Wilson (center) and Diana Ross.*

Music based in the African-American musical tradition has often captured an interracial audience in American history. In fact, African music provided part of the foundation of many identifiable American music forms: planters had gathered to listen to their slaves make music in the yard between the slave quarters and plantation house, Harlem 'slumming' was popular with whites during the 1920s and 1930s, and black musicians informed American musical tastes in the jazz era of the World War II years. Yet, the emergence of rock and roll signaled the dawn of a new musical era. A black male rhythm and blues group called the Chords recorded 'Sh-Boom' in 1954, and within a few weeks of its release the song moved into the Top 10 on the pop chart, the first rhythm and blues song to do so. Its success among whites as well as blacks inspired a recording phenomenon characteristic of the period – the 'white cover.' A white group from Canada named the Crew-Cuts brought out the cover, and their version of 'Sh-Boom' quickly

outsold the original and rose to number five on the Top 10 chart. Record companies reaped large financial rewards for cover records, and many white singers made their reputations approximating the music of black artists. The hit 'Shake Rattle and Roll' by Bill Haley and the Comets had been recorded earlier by Joe Turner; Gale Storm covered Smiley Lewis's 'I Hear You Knocking'; Elvis Presley, a young country music singer strongly influenced by black gospel music, covered Big Mama Thornton's 'Hound Dog'; and Pat Boone's singing, television, and motion picture career began with covers of such popular hits as Little Richard's 'Tutti Frutti' and Fats Domino's 'Ain't That a Shame.' The financial returns for most of these white singers far outstripped the profits of the arguably more talented original black artists. Even successful black singers found most of their profits controlled by white agents and white-owned record companies.

'My mama told me, you better shop around': in 1960 these words and the falsetto voice of William (Smokey) Robinson backed by the Miracles were familiar to young people all over America. 'Shop Around' was the first major hit produced by Motown Records, a company created the previous year by Detroit record-shop owner Berry Gordy. The distinctive sound of Motown's recordings captured the American market and changed much of the world's musical tastes. Part rhythm and blues, part gospel, part big band jazz and part pop, the combination was all Detroit, and its driving beat made it difficult for listeners to remain passive. It was crossover music, bridging the gap between the pop music of the white middle class in the 1950s and the rhythm and blues which animated black Americans. It was just the right music for a nation in the midst of the modern civil rights movement which aimed to integrate American society. In the early 1960s converging musical tastes brought blacks and whites together in common, or at least similar, dance movements, and Motown provided the background music for the emerging youth culture.

In 1961 the Marvelettes, one of the earliest of the 1960s girl groups, marked the increasing popularity of female vocalists with their recording of 'Please Mr. Postman.' As soloists and in groups, female song-stylists topped the pop charts. The next year, Mary Wells reflected the assertive female social style with 'You Beat Me to the Punch.' Martha Reeves and the Vandellas warmed the crowd with 'Heat Wave,' and in 1964 Diana Ross and the Supremes, the most popular female group of the era, brought on the main event with 'Where Did Our Love Go' and 'Baby Love.'

Smokey Robinson and the Miracles continued to excite their fans with hit after hit. They were quickly joined by the Contours who, in 1962, musically screamed out the age's burning teenage question, 'Do You Love Me, Now That I Can Dance?' Little Stevie Wonder sang and played his harmonica on his recording of 'Fingertips,' and by mid-decade the Four Tops, the Temptations, and a talented group of young brothers called the Jackson Five, featuring their remarkable youngest member Michael, filled the upper ranks of Motown.

The advent of Motown Records marked a significant change in this aspect of the American music business. For the first time in history, blacks controlled the profits of some of the world's most famous, highest-grossing black music stars. Motown carried the American listening public from the cover imitations and 'Crew-Cut' sounds of the 1950s to commercialized black music and symbolized a new age in race relations. African Americans demanded more freedom, autonomy, and

Above: *Marvin Gaye was one of the triumvirate of Motown's great male solo artists, with Smokey Robinson and Stevie Wonder. The Temptations' lilting balladry was a contrast in style and made them one of the label's headline groups.*

Below: *Diana Ross with the precocious teenage talents, the Jackson Five, whom she brought to Motown after seeing them in a show in their hometown of Gary, Indiana.*

control. Motown helped give voice to growing racial tensions in American society and bespoke a new confidence among African Americans. Singer James Brown, the 'Godfather of Soul' and 'Soul Brother Number One,' shouted the message in 1968, 'Say It Loud: I'm Black and I'm Proud.' Aretha Franklin, 'The Queen of Soul,' made the signification plain – black people in America were demanding a long-denied 'Respect.'

James Oliver Horton and Lois E. Horton

Above: *Martin Luther King, Jr. and Ralph Bunche join crowds of marchers in Selma, Alabama, en route to the state capital of Montgomery in 1965. The violence of local police shocked the nation and spurred President Johnson into action.*

Below: *President Lyndon B. Johnson, the first southern-based president since Andrew Johnson, presents one of the pens used to sign the Voting Rights Act of 1965 to James Farmer, Director of the Congress of Racial Equality.*

behalf of the MFDP before the Democratic Party's Credentials Committee, Hamer attracted national television coverage when she gave an emotional account of being fired from her job and later being beaten in jail. 'All of this is on account we want to register, to become first-class citizens, and if the Freedom Democratic Party is not seated now, I question America,' she testified.[23]

President Johnson feared losing southern white support and refused to support the MFDP. The new party's support weakened as liberal leaders such as Hubert Humphrey, many black politicians, and even Martin Luther King himself, felt pressures from Johnson. Many former supporters urged MFDP delegates to accept a compromise that would give them two 'at-large' seats along with a promise to ban discrimination at the next convention in 1968. Most of the MFDP delegates opposed such a compromise, insisting that they had risked their lives, and that politicians should therefore be willing to take political risks. Hamer scoffed, 'We didn't come all this way for no two seats.'[24] The delegation voted to reject the compromise.

The MFDP challenge in 1964 marked the beginning of a major transformation of African-American politics. Disappointment with the failure of Democratic leaders to back the MFDP challenge created a sense of disillusionment among civil rights activists. Many agreed with Fannie Lou Hamer's conclusion that 'we learned the hard way that even though we had all the law and all the righteousness on our side – that white man is not going to give up his power to us.'[25] Black organizers involved in the Summer Project were disturbed that the presence of college-educated white volunteers had sometimes undermined the confidence of less-educated black leaders. After the tumultuous summer, some civil rights workers even began to question whether the ideal of racial integration was achievable.

Alabama Voting Rights Movement in 1965

While SNCC workers were moving in new directions, Martin Luther King's SCLC also began a new voting rights campaign in Selma, Alabama. As in other places, King hoped that mass rallies would focus national attention on the issue. Early in March, SNCC and SCLC organizers planned a march from Selma to the state capital in Montgomery. Because of a previous commitment, however, King was not present when several protesters left Selma on the afternoon of Sunday 7 March. At Pettus Bridge on the outskirts of Selma, police on horseback, using tear gas and clubs, attacked the marchers when they refused to turn back. Television and newspaper pictures of policemen attacking nonviolent protesters shocked the nation and angered black activists. SNCC chairperson, John Lewis, who suffered a fractured skull during the melee, afterwards remarked, 'I don't see how President Johnson can send troops to Vietnam . . . and can't send troops to Selma, Alabama.'[26]

News of the attack at Pettus Bridge – activists referred to it as 'Bloody Sunday' – brought hundreds of civil rights sympathizers to Selma. White officials obtained a court order against further marches and young SNCC activists challenged King to defy the court order, but SCLC leaders were reluctant to do anything that would lessen public support for the voting rights cause. On 10 March, King turned back a second march to Pettus Bridge when marchers reached a police barricade. That evening a group of Selma whites killed James Reeb, a northern white minister who had joined the demonstrations. In contrast to the killing a few weeks before of a black demonstrator, Jimmy Lee Jackson, Reeb's death led to a national outcry against racial violence in Selma. President Johnson sent flowers to his widow.

After several postponements, civil rights advocates finally gained court permission to proceed with the march. The Selma to Montgomery march was the culmination of the stage of the African-American freedom struggle that led to the passage of the landmark Voting Rights Act of 1965, but it was also the last major racial protest movement to receive substantial white support. When the marchers arrived at the capital in

Below: *The scene in Peachtree, Alabama, in 1966 as African Americans voted in large numbers for the first time in 100 years. Edward Brooke of Massachusetts became the first black elected to the U.S. Senate since Reconstruction.*

Montgomery, King delivered one of his most memorable speeches. 'Our aim must never be to defeat or humiliate the white man but to win his friendship and understanding.'

> We must come to see that the end we seek is a society at peace with itself, a society that can live with its conscience. That will be the day not of the white man, not of the black man. That will be the day of man as man.

Despite setbacks, King insisted that the struggle would succeed, because 'however difficult the moment, however frustrating the hour, it will not be long, because truth pressed to earth will rise again.'[27]

'We *shall* overcome,' President Johnson announced in a televised address presenting new voting rights proposals that subsequently became law; but change was still piecemeal. Antiblack violence continued in the South, and the material conditions of life for most blacks throughout the nation remained unchanged. Blacks could enter restaurants, but many lacked the money to pay for a meal. Blacks could vote, but they still had not gained the power to improve their lives through the political system.

Rise of Militant Group Consciousness

As civil rights activists began to question their own long-term goals, many began to respond to influences from outside their own movement. As a member of the Nation of Islam, Malcolm X had been a harsh critic of King's nonviolent approach and integrationist goals,

but by 1964 he began to question Elijah Muhammad's racial-separatist doctrine and lack of involvement in the protest movement. Although remaining critical of King's approach, he sought ties with 'grassroots' leaders, such as Fannie Lou Hamer. Malcolm decided to leave the Nation of Islam to form his own group, the Organization of Afro-American Unity.

During the last year of his life, Malcolm's ideas converged with those of many civil rights veterans. Despite their differences over tactics, Malcolm increasingly recognized that he and King were part of the same struggle. Malcolm's assassination in February 1965 cut short his efforts to reach out to militant activists in the civil rights movement.

Malcolm's ideas expressed the anger of northern blacks who had not benefited from civil rights reforms. This anger burst into public awareness in August 1965, when the arrest of a black man in Los Angeles led to several days of violence. More than 30 blacks were killed by police as they suppressed the black rebellion. Many other large cities later experienced similar outbreaks of violence. During the summer of 1967, for example, 23 people were killed in a rebellion in Newark, New Jersey, and 43 were killed in Detroit.

SNCC reflected this growing racial militancy when it selected Stokely Carmichael as the new chair to replace John Lewis, a veteran of the sit-ins and freedom rides, and who was now considered insufficiently militant. After helping black residents of Lowndes County, Alabama, establish the all-black Lowndes

Right: A collection of radical pins from the late 1960s supporting Black Power, the Black Panthers, and Malcolm X.

County Freedom Organization, better known as the Black Panther Party, Carmichael popularized a phrase that symbolized SNCC's disillusionment with white liberal allies. First used during a voting rights march through Mississippi, 'Black Power' quickly became popular in black communities. The 'Black Power' slogan symbolized a broader cultural transformation. African Americans began to express their enhanced sense of pride through art and literature as well as through political action. Playwright Leroi Jones, who changed his name to Amiri Baraka, became a leader of the Black Arts movement which sought to create positive images for blacks. Popular black singers such as James Brown and Aretha Franklin expressed the spirit of 'Soul.' Sports figures such as Muhammad Ali also identified with Black Power sentiments. During the playing of the national anthem at the 1968 Olympics, two African-American athletes raised clenched fists in a 'Black Power salute' on the victory stand after their event. At numerous colleges and universities, black students demanded Black Studies programs emphasizing the contributions of African and African-American people.

Although Martin Luther King believed the Black Power movement would decrease white support for the black struggle, he acknowledged that black people needed a positive sense of identity in order to advance. 'Psychological freedom, a firm sense of self-esteem, is the most powerful weapon against the long night of physical slavery,' he said. 'No Lincolnian emancipation proclamation or Johnsonian civil rights bill can totally bring this kind of freedom.' King urged blacks to say to themselves and the world, 'I am somebody. I am a person. I am a man with dignity and honor. I have a rich and noble history.'[28]

To encourage northern urban blacks to recognize the potential effectiveness of militant nonviolent tactics, King launched a campaign in Chicago. Like many other veterans of the civil rights movement, however, King discovered that the problems of northern blacks were even more difficult to solve than the problem of southern segregation. Eliminating segregation did not require the large expenditures that were required to eliminate poverty. Northern liberals who supported the southern civil rights movement often were less willing to support black advancement efforts in their own cities.

By the end of 1967, King had decided that a Poor People's Campaign was needed to prod the nation into action. His plan was to bring to

Left: Malcolm X was a seminal figure in the 1960s, who came to represent the voice of the underclass. A militant separatist in the Nation of Islam, by 1965 he had moved away from them, although remaining a symbol of black anger.

Above: *Boxer Cassius Clay was a role model for many blacks and his actions had significance. He converted to Islam in 1964, changing his name to Muhammad Ali, and was stripped of his title in 1967 for refusing to be drafted for Vietnam.*

Above: *American medal-winning athletes Tommie Smith and John Carlos made this defiant black-gloved, Black Power salute on the podium at the 1968 Olympic Games in order to protest against racism in the United States.*

Washington thousands of poor people – blacks, poor whites, Native Americans, Mexican Americans and other Hispanics – to engage in protests designed to pressure President Johnson into increasing funding for his 'War on Poverty.' After King criticized Johnson for diverting funds from antipoverty efforts to the war in Vietnam, he was caught between Black Power advocates who thought he was too cautious and Johnson supporters who saw him as too militant. King lost much of his popularity as he pushed ahead with plans for the Poor People's Campaign.

In early April 1968, King came to Memphis, Tennessee, to offer his support for garbage workers who were striking for higher wages and better working conditions. He was depressed about the opposition he faced from

Remember...

**UNCLE TOM SAYS-
"ONLY YOU CAN
PREVENT GHETTO FIRES"**

FREE BOBBY

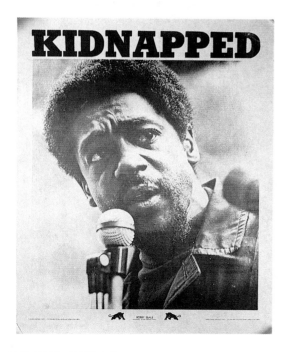

KIDNAPPED

Left: *Feelings ran high in the black urban areas during the late 1960s. Moderates were accused of being Uncle Toms and the militant Black Panther movement came under attack from the FBI. Panther leader Bobby Seale was imprisoned for inciting riots at the 1968 Democratic convention.*

former allies and disturbed that some young blacks in Memphis had turned to violence to express their grievances. Although many newspapers urged an end to the campaign, King met with young gang leaders in order to convince them to return to nonviolent tactics. On 3 April, he addressed a mass meeting in Memphis and confessed that he was uncertain about what lay ahead. 'We've got some difficult days ahead,' he told the audience. 'But it really doesn't matter with me now, because I've been to the mountaintop.' King hinted that he might not be there, but that black people would 'get to the promised land.'[29]

The following evening, an assassin shot King as he stood on the balcony of his Memphis hotel room. King's death led to a new wave of urban racial violence. Thousands of blacks took to the streets to protest the loss of the most well-known advocate of nonviolence. Even after King's death, the Poor People's Campaign continued for several months under the leadership of Ralph Abernathy, but the campaign had little success in changing national policies. Eliminating poverty would remain one of the unachieved goals of the black freedom struggle.

The late 1960s were a period of black militancy and white repression. White politicians, such as Alabama Governor George Wallace, encouraged a 'white backlash' against black protests and civil rights gains. The African-American freedom struggle had become a national rather than a southern movement, and white opposition was as strong in some northern cities as it had been in the South. Many northern whites strongly opposed efforts to end de facto segregation in northern cities.

Black frustrations continued to grow because civil rights reforms had increased the expectations of many blacks that their lives would change for the better. Indeed, antidiscrimination legislation made new economic and educational opportunities available to some segments of the black community. For the first time, a few large cities elected black mayors. But for poor blacks conditions remained the same, or even got worse.

The Black Panther Party

The Black Panther Party was one of the new organizations that reflected the increased militancy and frustration of urban blacks. Inspired by the example of SNCC in the South, Huey Newton and Bobby Seale formed the Oakland-based party in 1966. Attracting mainly young people, the Panthers quickly became the most widely known black militant political organization of the late 1960s. The Panthers urged blacks to 'pick up the gun' to

defend themselves. Wearing the group's distinctive black leather jackets, Panthers openly carried weapons and stood their ground when police questioned their right to bear arms. The party's ideas were drawn from a variety of sources, including Malcolm X, Stokely Carmichael, and the examples of revolutionary movements in Asia and Africa. The political goals of the Panthers were summarized in the last item of their 10-point Platform and Program: 'We want land, bread, housing, education, clothing, justice and peace.'[30]

The Black Panther Party attracted considerable support from young blacks, but police repression severely weakened the group. In August 1967, the FBI identified the Panthers as a major target of its counter-intelligence program (COINTELPRO). COINTELPRO was designed to prevent 'a coalition of militant Black nationalist groups' and the emergence of a 'Black messiah' 'who might unify and electrify these violence-prone elements.'[31] When Black Panther leaders recruited Carmichael to join their ranks, the FBI used anonymous letters and phone calls to disrupt plans for an alliance between the Panthers and SNCC.

Assaults by local police also contributed to the decline of black militancy. On 28 October 1967, Oakland police arrested Huey Newton on murder charges, after a clash with Oakland police that resulted in the death of one policeman and the wounding of another. In September 1968, Newton was convicted of voluntary manslaughter and sentenced to 2–15 years in prison. The following

Below: *Declared a national day of mourning, the funeral of Martin Luther King, Jr. was attended by more than 200,000 people. His coffin was drawn through the streets of Atlanta, Georgia, on a farm wagon pulled by two mules.*

Above: *News of King's assassination led to outbreaks of sporadic violence in black urban areas. Here, passersby in Harlem stroll through the debris left after looting had subsided.*

December, two Chicago leaders of the party, Fred Hampton and Mark Clark, were killed in a police raid. By the end of the decade, more than 20 Panthers had been killed and many other Panthers were facing long prison terms. By the early 1970s, the Black Panther Party was no longer an effective organization at the national level.

The Legacy of the Modern Black Struggle

The repression of the Panthers signaled the end of an era of mass protest and militancy. Many of the institutions created during the era remained in existence after the 1970s, but they functioned mainly to consolidate and protect earlier gains rather than to bring about a major social transformation such as that which King envisioned at the end of his life. The number of blacks elected to political office increased dramatically during the 1970s and 1980s, but, without the leverage of a mass

Below: *Boatswain's Mate Bobby J. McGrath from St. Louis, Missouri, was serving his country in Vietnam while trouble of a different nature raged at home in 1969. McGrath is manning a machine gun during a U.S. Navy river patrol.*

BLACK VIETNAM WAR VETERANS

Although evenly represented overall during the Vietnam War, African Americans were present in higher proportions in front line units, and their rate of reenlistment was higher too. For black soldiers, the civil rights struggle at home and movements for independence in Africa complicated the racial aspects of the war in Vietnam.

STAFF SERGEANT DON F. BROWNE, WASHINGTON, DC:

'When I heard that Martin Luther King was assassinated, my first inclination was to run out and punch the first white guy I saw. I was very hurt. All I wanted to do was go home. I even wrote Lyndon Johnson a letter. I said that I didn't understand how I could be trying to protect foreigners in their country with the possibility of losing my life where in in my own country people who are my hero, like Martin Luther King, can't even walk the streets in a safe manner. I didn't get an answer from the President, but I got an answer from the White House. It was a wonderful letter, wonderful in terms of the way it looked. It wanted to assure me that the President was doing everything in his power to bring about racial equality, especially in the armed forces. A typical bureaucratic answer.'[1]

PRIVATE FIRST CLASS REGINALD 'MALIK' EDWARDS, PHOENIX, LOUISIANA:

'There was only two black guys in my platoon in boot camp. So I hung with the Mexicans, too, because in them days we never hang with white people. You didn't have white friends. White people was the aliens to me. This is '63. You don't have integration in the South. You expected them to treat you bad. But somehow in the Marine Corps you hoping all that's gonna change. Of course, I found out this was not true, because the Marine Corps was the last service to integrate . . . I remember a survey they did in the mess hall where we had to say how we felt about the war. The thing was, get out of Vietnam or fight. What we were hearing was Vietnamese was killing Americans. I felt that if people were killing Americans, we should fight them. As a black person, there wasn't no problem fightin' the enemy. I knew Americans were prejudiced, were racist and all that, but, basically, I believed in America 'cause I was an American.'[2]

Notes

[1]Quoted in Wallace Terry, *Bloods: An Oral History of the Vietnam War by Black Veterans*, New York: Random House, 1984, p. 172.
[2]Quoted in Terry, *Bloods*, pp. 6–8.

Above: *An African-American sergeant in Vietnam in 1967 can see only a small, refugee child needing help; back home in the United States there were still many of his fellow citizens prepared to treat with contempt anybody with a skin color different to their own.*

Below: *A perfect symbol of token integration: African-American student Vivian Malone graduating from Tuscaloosa, Alabama, in 1965, a black face in a sea of white faces. Black graduates of the 1960s owed much to the student activists of the late 1950s, although much remained to be done.*

protest movement, they could not resist the overall trend toward conservatism. The black middle class also increased considerably in size, as black college students took advantage of new employment opportunities, but conditions of life for many urban blacks deteriorated as a result of declining public school systems and urban infrastructures.

The militant racial consciousness of the 1960s did not thrive in the conservative political climate that followed, but significant aspects of the black power consciousness endured. The vigorous political debates about African-American identity and destiny led to an explosion of cultural activity during the late 1960s and early 1970s. In the struggle between self-described revolutionary nationalists and cultural nationalists, the latter were generally less vulnerable to repression. Cultural transformation of black communities was difficult given the influence of American mass culture but was far more feasible than transforming the nation as a whole. The cultural flowering was evident in newly organized or revived drama and dance companies, informal poetry workshops, Black Studies departments at colleges and universities, increased awareness of African culture, and in a generalized pride among blacks in their racial heritage. Los-Angeles-based cultural nationalist, Maulana Karenga, initiated an annual black celebration called Kwanzaa that grew in popularity after the 1960s.

The racial consciousness movement left a complex and ambiguous legacy, however, because concern with racial identity divided blacks as well as unified them. Leadership competition often led to intense unresolvable arguments about the nature of blackness and about the ultimate destiny of African Americans. At a birthday celebration for Ella Baker held in 1978, Bob Moses remarked that SNCC and the black struggle as a whole became stymied by the question King had addressed in his last book, *Where Do We Go from Here?* 'The problem with that question is "We," who we are,' he explained. 'Because, if you really stop to think about it, that's where we left off.'[32] Debates over racial identity and destiny were important, but they also reflected the growing divisions within black communities, between those seeking better treatment as American citizens and those attempting to build black-controlled cultural, social, political, and economic institutions. These two directions in African-American politics were each outgrowths of the modern black freedom struggle and were not necessarily in conflict with one another. Nevertheless, many advocates of narrowly conceived integrationist or separationist strategies acted as if the two positions represented total rather than partial insights.

The modern African-American freedom struggle had revived dormant leftist and black nationalist traditions, and their revival during the late 1960s initially seemed to presage a more radical thrust. But the sectarianism that

Right: *In 1968, Lou Smith and Robert Hall founded Shindana Toys ('shindana' being Swahili for competitor) in order to create realistic dolls for the black community. From left to right, the dolls are: 'Tamu' ('sweet'), a talking doll with 18 sayings; 'Kim Jeans 'n Things' (center) who came with three assorted tie-dye denim outfits; and 'Malaika' ('angel'), a doll with an 'Afro' hairstyle.*

Right, below: *Black Power salutes being given by a classroom of children at a Black Panther-run 'Liberation School'.*

characterized these traditions had a destructive impact on black movements that had been ideologically eclectic. Some constructive elements of the black nationalist tradition – particularly its emphasis on building black-controlled institutions and maintaining African-American culture – were reflected in the emergent ideas of the modern struggle, but so too were a predominance of authoritarian male leaders and a pessimistic outlook for racial advancement within the United States. The machismo, apocalyptic rhetoric, and ideological competition of the Black Power campaign blinded many subsequent black activists to the importance of nonviolent tactics in any sustained mass struggle, to the reality of worldwide interracial interdependence, and to the necessity of deriving political ideas from shared experience.

The modern African-American freedom struggle resulted in major changes in American life. Many groups gained new opportunities as a result of civil rights reforms. The United States also became more democratic as previously excluded groups were included in the mainstream of society. Although, at the end of the 1960s, the United States remained divided by various kinds of social conflicts, the struggles forced Americans to confront the fundamental question of whether it was possible to create a multicultural democratic nation.

Notes

[1] Roy Wilkins, with Tom Mathews, *Standing Fast: The Autobiography of Roy Wilkins*, New York: Da Capo Press, 1982, 1994, p. 216.

[2] Malcolm X, with the assistance of Alex Haley, *The Autobiography of Malcolm X*, New York: Ballantine Books, 1965, p. 217.

[3] Quoted in *Montgomery Advertiser*, 31 January 1956.

[4] King quotations from Clayborne Carson *et al.* (eds), *The Papers of Martin Luther King, Jr.*, vol. I, *Called to Serve, January, 1929–June, 1951*, Berkeley: University of California Press, 1992, pp. 144, 363.

[5] Clayborne Carson *et al.* (eds), *The Eyes on the Prize Civil Rights Reader*, New York: Penguin Books, 1991, pp. 49–50.

[6] Martin Luther King, Jr., *Stride Toward Freedom: The Montgomery Story*, San Francisco: Harper & Row, 1958, p. 85.

[7] Cleveland Sellers with Robert Terrell, *The River of No Return*, New York: William Morrow & Company, 1973, p. 17.

[8] Clayborne Carson, *In Struggle*, Cambridge: Harvard University Press, 1981, pp. 23–4.

[9] Carson *et al.*, *Eyes on the Prize Civil Rights Reader*, p. 121.

[10] Carson, *In Struggle*, pp. 20, 24.

[11] *Ibid.*, p. 17.

[12] *Ibid.*, p. 57.

[13] *Ibid.*, p. 61.

[14] James Melvin Washington, *A Testament of Hope: The Essential Writings of Martin Luther King, Jr.*, San Francisco: Harper & Row, 1986, pp. 292–3, 297.

[15] Quoted in Arthur M. Schlesinger, Jr., *A Thousand Days: John F. Kennedy in the White House*, Boston: Houghton Mifflin Company, 1965, pp. 884–5.

[16] Carson *et al.*, *Eyes on the Prize Civil Rights Reader*, pp. 163–4.

[17] Washington, *Testament of Hope*, p. 219.

[18] Transcript of tape of 19 September 1963, meeting from The John F. Kennedy Library, Item No: 111.7, Title: 'Civil Rights Birmingham.'

[19] Statement re. Assassination of John F. Kennedy, 22 November 1963.

[20] Carson *et al.*, *Eyes on the Prize Civil Rights Reader*, p. 179.

[21] Quoted in James Forman, *The Making of Black Revolutionaries*, New York: Macmillan, 1972, p. 283.

[22] Fannie Lou Hamer, 'To Praise Our Bridges,' reprinted in Carson *et al.*, *Eyes on the Prize Civil Rights Reader*, p. 177.

[23] Quoted in Carson, *In Struggle*, p. 125.

[24] *Ibid.*, p. 126.

[25] Carson *et al.*, *Eyes on the Prize Civil Rights Reader*, p. 179.

[26] Carson, *In Struggle*, p. 159.

[27] Washington, *Testament of Hope*, p. 230.

[28] King, *Where Do We Go from Here: Chaos or Community?*, Boston: Beacon Press, 1967, pp. 43–4.

[29] Washington, *Testament of Hope*, p. 286.

[30] The full document is in Philip S. Foner (ed.), *The Black Panthers Speak*, New York: Da Capo Press, 1995.

[31] See relevant documents in Ward Churchill and Jim Vander Wall, *The COINTELPRO Papers: Documents from the FBI's Secret Wars Against Domestic Dissent*, Boston: South End Press, 1990, pp. 92–3, 108–11.

[32] Address at 75th Birthday Celebration for Ella Baker, 9 December 1978, New York City.

Chapter 9

RACE, CULTURE, AND CONSERVATISM

America stood at a crossroads as the post-World War II period closed with the turbulent 1960s. Blacks were energized by the rise of black power, a growing awareness of Africa, and the popularity of African cultural styles even as they mourned the assassination of their greatest leader of the mid-twentieth century. The Motown sound continued to move blacks and whites to a similar beat, but a new conservatism invigorated by 'white backlash' strained the liberal alliances forged in the 1960s. Alex Haley's *Roots* riveted millions to their television sets for many nights and stimulated interracial discussions in classrooms and workplaces. Alice Walker's novel, *The Color Purple*, expanded the conversation to race and gender. Black stars achieved greater recognition in new arenas and were developing a new image for African Americans. Children of all races wanted to 'be like Mike' (Michael Jordan). Hopeful signs of a more expansive culture were often overshadowed, however, by a constricting conception of social responsibility. The absence of victory in the Vietnam War, and challenges by women and people of color to traditional white male privilege and power, left many Americans searching for a strong, manly political leader. The culture of the 1980s was more consciously diverse but also more politically and socially conservative.

General Colin Luther Powell became the highest ranking military officer in the United States with his appointment in 1989 to the chair of the Joint Chiefs of Staff, the first African American ever to hold the office. He saw combat in Vietnam, was a chief aide to Caspar Weinberger, and then served as national security advisor under President Reagan. He played a key role in the American deployments in Panama and the Persian Gulf, where he is seen here greeting American soldiers.

BY THE MID-1970s, even the most optimistic advocates of the rights of blacks had begun to be persuaded by the mounting evidence that America was fed up with black claims on the national consciousness. There had been some who had hoped that Richard Nixon's election in 1968 had been an aberrational response to the urban riots and the Vietnam War. And, despite a good deal of coded antiblack rhetoric, the Nixon administration had not called a halt to all social-justice efforts. Nevertheless, the rhetorical and political attacks on government civil rights efforts – developed in the 1968 and 1972 Presidential campaigns of Alabama Governor George C. Wallace – had become staples of Republican politics. Former President Lyndon B. Johnson's Great Society anti-poverty programs were regularly denounced as expensive failures and Nixon administrators were successful in pruning many of them out of the federal budget. From May 1954 when the Supreme Court decided *Brown v. Board of Education*, through the summer of 1968, racial issues had dominated the domestic headlines. By 1975, with Gerald Ford, the post-Watergate president, occupying the White House and the last Americans being driven out of Vietnam, the attention of the media and its consumers had moved on.

Some blacks had benefited enormously from the civil rights movement. Affirmative action programs had begun to open up working-class jobs for bank tellers, telephone operators, policemen, firefighters, and low- and mid-level employees in all layers of government across the country. Blacks had become far more active in political life since the enactment of the Voting Rights Act of 1965.

Moreover, the black presence in ordinary American life was becoming more visible and more accepted by the white American public. William T. Coleman, a distinguished black corporate lawyer, who had made massive contributions to the legal success of the National Association for the Advancement of Colored People (NAACP) Legal Defense Fund, was secretary of transportation in President Ford's cabinet. Redd Foxx – a brilliant comedian who had made his career on a segregated vaudeville circuit, delighting black audiences with hilarious X-rated material – was starring in *Sanford & Son*, a family television sitcom. Athletes like football's Joe Greene, baseball's Reggie Jackson and basketball's Julius Erving of the Philadelphia 76ers were loved by sports fans of all colors. Well-educated blacks had made breakthroughs in the professions, in journalism, and even in Hollywood, where a succession of offerings – dubbed in some quarters as 'blacksploitation' films – on black subjects starring black actors had been much noticed. Most big-market local television stations had felt obligated to hire at least one black reporter and some were even beginning

to hire black anchors. While these shifts affected a relatively small percentage of the black population, virtually the entire white population had to make psychic space for blacks, whether it was in the workplace, on professional playing fields or on their television screens.

Economic Change in the Early 1970s

While blacks were casting about for the strategies to attack the monumental problems that remained, white people's attitudes toward what appeared to them to be a massive new American racial reality were beginning to gel. The new white view of black America first fell on the thin screen of fortunate blacks who were now located in good places where they hadn't been at all just a decade earlier. Some whites saw that real change had occurred, and

Below: *Justice Clarence Thomas taking the oath before the Senate Judiciary Committee hearing his nomination to the Supreme Court in 1991. He pledged to remember his southern black heritage.*

Above: *Justice Thurgood Marshall, famed civil rights activist and leader, whose retirement from the Supreme Court after 24 years' service created the vacancy that Justice Thomas filled.*

many of them were pleased at the great measure of justice the nation had achieved. Others felt threatened and crowded by the new physical or psychic proximity of blacks.

Blacks, themselves, had a different view. They saw a deeper reality of widespread poverty and deprivation in the cities and in the hidden rural places in the South. The poverty and squalor that had spawned the urban riots had not diminished and the southern rural places that had been the original home to many of the poorest urban dwellers remained as poor as ever and were out of mind as people argued about 'urban problems,' which had become the euphemism for black issues on the national agenda. Moreover, even successful blacks continued to encounter racism in virtually every aspect of their lives.

By now, civil rights thinkers were trying on and discarding a variety of strategies as if they were garments in a clothing store. There were, in rapid succession: community control; from protest to politics; black entrepreneurship and economic empowerment; and finally, self-help. It was as if as opposition thickened, the movement had begun a frantic search for the one magic solution that put progress back on the road again.

Culture, politics, economics, and inertia were throwing such a thick blanket around what little energy was left in the movement after two decades of intense struggle that no single strategy was sufficient to the task. Moreover, there remained a substantial residue of America's fundamental racism. Some politicians were becoming adept at delivering shrewdly sculpted slogans, which carefully preserved the white feeling of moral accomplishment, but which activated the racist resentment remaining in the culture.

Nixon and others had played to the 'silent majority' with a 'law and order' theme as opposed to noisy protesters of all stripes who

Above: *Sport could provide a political platform. Here, heavyweight boxing champion Joe Frazier addresses the South Carolina legislature in April 1971. Just a month earlier he had beaten Muhammad Ali in a title fight.*

Below: *Redd Foxx, television star of* Sandford and Son *which lasted from 1972 until 1977. It was set in a family-run junk dealership in Los Angeles and introduced self-conscious racial humor set in an Afrocentric context.*

had tried to change America. Anger about school integration was made respectable by targeting the busing of children of tender age to distant schools. Somehow, this concern hadn't surfaced when very young black children had been bused to accomplish segregation.

Finally, a phrase used in a memorandum by the then White House aide, Daniel Patrick Moynihan, came to characterize what blacks and their allies viewed as the Nixon-Ford social policy. Moynihan's words were 'benign neglect.' Where Moynihan, in explaining himself, emphasized the word 'benign' – as in calling for a constructive and healing cooling period – social activists tended to hear a call for willful and unpardonable neglect of urgent human and social problems.

Economic developments were rendering obsolete the single-strand strategies being tried on by the social justice theorists, while simultaneously adding fire and glue to the growing and rapidly closing ranks of those resisting more social progress. Long-term economic trends which had begun in 1973 were taking their toll on American wages. A variety of economic factors – the oil price increase caused by the OPEC oil embargo, a decline in the fortunes in the American auto industry and changing manufacturing patterns – had begun to cause middle-class wages to stagnate in 1973. Economists and journalists alike would soon begin to notice that two incomes were now necessary to maintain middle-class status for a large portion of that segment of the population.

The impact on lower-income families and individuals was even more dramatic. Low-skilled jobs began to disappear altogether or to move from inner cities to suburban settings, where urban residents found it hard to find and maintain employment. As a result, wages for low-skilled individuals, particularly for

black men, fell precipitously and many such low-skilled men dropped out of the labor market altogether.

While real weekly earning for all American men fell from $488 (in constant 1984 dollars) in 1969 to $414 in 1984, the impact on low-skilled men in general and on low-skilled *black* men, in particular, was devastating. White, male high-school dropouts between the ages of 25 and 34 experienced a mean weekly earnings drop from $447 to $381. For blacks of the same age and with the same education the weekly figures were in 1969, $334 and 1986, $268. The *highest* figure for blacks (1969) was only 87 percent of the *lowest* figure for whites (1986). Moreover, the income loss for whites was serious at 14 percent, but that for blacks was almost 10 percentage points higher than that.

Unemployment Rates and Economic Distress
Unemployment rates tell another part of the same story. Economically, the end of the 1960s was a very good time for blacks. The combination of the atmosphere created by the civil rights movement and the policies it generated, together with the tight labor market produced by the Vietnam War, resulted in the lowest black unemployment rates recorded in the 30 years between 1960 and 1990. In 1968 the rate was 6.7 percent and in 1969, it dropped to 6.4. Those were the only two years in the entire 30-year period when the rate was below 7 percent. It hovered just below double digits in the early 1970s, but then the pattern that was to hold for the next 20 years kicked in. The rate shot from 9.5 percent in 1974 to 14.8 in 1975. The unemployment rate for

Above: Modern commercial skyscrapers loom on the skyline of this backyard in a downtown slum area of Atlanta, Georgia, in 1971.

African Americans has not dipped below double digits since.

There are several ways to underscore the severity of the economic distress that has afflicted black America between the mid-1970s and the mid-1990s. Few are more pointed than comparisons to what was happening to white Americans at that time. The economy was deemed to be in a mild recession in 1975 and 1976 when the white unemployment rate was 7.5 and 7.0 percent. The recession of 1982 was deemed to be more severe. In those years, when dire economic news domi-

Below: The Julia lunch box dates from 1969 and refers to a television series in which Diahann Carroll became the first black woman to have her own series in a nonstereotypical role.

nated our domestic discourse, the white unemployment rate was 8.6 and 8.4 percent. The lowest black unemployment rate in those decades was 11.3 percent, achieved in 1979 and 1980, two years in which the economy was not in recession. The white rates for those years were 5.1 and 4.1 percent. The *lowest* black rate over those decades was two and a half points higher than the highest white rate. And the highest black rate, 19.5 percent in 1983 (this figure does not include people who are so discouraged that they have given up looking for work or those who want a full-time job but can obtain only part-time work), is of full-blown depression dimensions.

The detachment of large numbers of black men from the labor force was one of the most dramatic results of the unraveling of the low-skilled end of the economy during the last 20 years. In examining the characteristics of inner-city neighborhoods where large portions of those affected by these economic forces are to be found, William Julius Wilson, the distinguished University of Chicago sociologist, found an alarming 40-year trend.

In 1940, a typical black man would be employed for 37.8 years, unemployed for 4.0 years, and out of the labor force for 3.2 years from age 20 to 65. This was almost identical with the employment experiences of the average white man in 1940. By 1985, as he ages from 20 to 65, the average black man will be employed for 29.4 years, unemployed for 5 years, and out of the labor force for 11 years. His white counterpart will experience 35.6 years of employment, 2 years of unemployment, and 7 years of non labor-force participation. The greatest declines of employment for both black and white men have occurred since 1970. The expected years of employment for the typical white man decreased from 39 to 36 from 1970 to 1985. For the typical black man, it declined even more sharply from 36 to 29 years (Jaynes and Williams 1989). The joblessness of black men is severest in the inner city. For example, whereas urban black fathers aged 18 to 44 nationally had worked approximately 7 out of every 8 years since age 18, inner-city Chicago black fathers had worked an average of only 2 out of every 3 years. Those aged 18 to 24 in the inner city had only worked 39 percent of the time (Tienda and Steir 1991).[1]

Chicago was not unique in its levels of black inner-city unemployment. In an interview, Dr. William Spriggs, an economist with the Economic Policy Institute, estimated that the United States had lost 2 million production jobs in the manufacturing sector between 1979 and 1990. I was a government official sent by President Lyndon B. Johnson to work in Watts during the 1965 riot and returned to the area as a journalist in 1988. During the late summer and fall of 1965, there was enormous media focus on Watts and South Central Los Angeles. All levels of government – city, county, state, and federal – engaged in planning and pledging about improvements in the lives of people in the area. By 1988, by every visible measure, South Central Los Angeles was worse than it had been in 1965. By the accounts of local governmental and social welfare officials, rates of unemployment, crime, homelessness, and single-parent families were all higher than the rates had been in 1965.

The Underclass

From the mid-1970s through the next two decades, the nature and behavior of the 'black underclass' became a subject for intense examination and debate. This same group had been the focus of intense policy discussions and initiatives during the 1960s. Those efforts had been designed to find ways to alleviate the suffering and to widen the opportunities of the black poor; it was an inclusive impulse. The studies and policy initiatives of the 1980s and 1990s, by contrast, appeared to emphasize the differences of the urban black poor and, as time passed, their aberrant behavior and the dangers it posed to society.

The prevailing view in the national debate proceeded from a general popular consensus that the Great Society had been a wasteful and enormously costly failure. That spawned a powerful antitax and antispending tide which started in California and quickly spread. It animated the profound tax-cutting policies of the Reagan administration, which had enormous consequences for the lives of poor citizens across the country.

As a result of the civil rights movement, most of the public discourse on race had been cleansed of overtly racist language. Direct

Above: *The Wings Over Jordan Choir pictured at the Wilshire Ebell Theatre in Los Angeles on Mother's Day on 10 May 1970. The conductor was Frank C. Everett who designed the gospel singers' robes which were worn for the first time at that concert, a production called 'The Third Generation.' The group had became known nationally in 1937 and performed their spirituals nationwide during World War II. They undertook a successful tour of Asia during 1953-54, including Japan where they were very popular.*

public assertions of black inferiority had virtually disappeared. But the clear implications of the public debate about domestic social spending were that expenditures designed to improve employment and educational opportunities for poor blacks were hopelessly wasteful. The terrible economic problems being encountered by this group were more and more often being attributed to defects in their own character or to misguided attempts to aid them.

This analysis conflicted with journalistic accounts of the problems encountered by white Americans during recessions. During those periods, when white rates of unemployment did not approach even the rates normal for blacks, newspapers would publish stories which detailed the results of the terrible stress being encountered by white workers who had been separated from the economy. Such articles reported increased rates of self-destructive behavior across the spectrum: alcohol and drug abuse, spouse and child abuse, divorce, and suicide. The clear thrust of these articles was that even short-term economic stress could cause widespread human disintegration. This insight was rarely encountered in journalistic or public policy analyses of the condition and behavior of the *black* poor.

Social and Behavioral 'Explanations'

The substantial increase in out-of-wedlock births to black women has been one of the behavior developments in the poorest black communities that has had a profound impact on American public opinion. The combination of sex and race has been an explosive force in American culture since the colonial period.

The percentage of black out-of-wedlock births has increased steadily since 1950 (as has the white rate, which started in 1950 on a much lower base). In 1950 the black rate was 16.8 percent; in 1960, 21.6; in 1970, 37.6; in 1980, 56.4; and in 1988, 63.7. The white rate increased during those 38 years from 1.7 percent in 1950 to 14.9 percent in 1988. The black rate was 9.9 times the white rate in 1950, and, after the multiple fell steadily over the 38-year period, the black rate was only 4.3 times the white rate by 1988. It should be noted that the out-of-wedlock birth rate rose significantly during this period in every industrialized nation in the world, with the exception of Japan.

Powerful forces were clearly abroad in the world, to which American blacks were intensely sensitive. There are several points of significance here. The first is that the 1950–70 period included the peak of the black migration from South to North and the period of deep northern urban black disillusionment as the civil rights movement wrought significant changes in people's lives in the South, while making hardly a dent in the North.

Secondly, the sharp 19 percent jump in out-of-wedlock births during the 1970s occurred during the years of the powerful economic blows to the low-skilled, low-income segment of the black community. While social and cultural changes were occurring throughout society in the post-birth-control-pill era, something special was exaggerating their effects in black America. A number of theories would soon gain traction in the public policy debates. One theory with ancient roots in American culture was simply that blacks were, by nature, more promiscuous than other people. A second theory that found wide popular acceptance was that overly generous welfare policies were

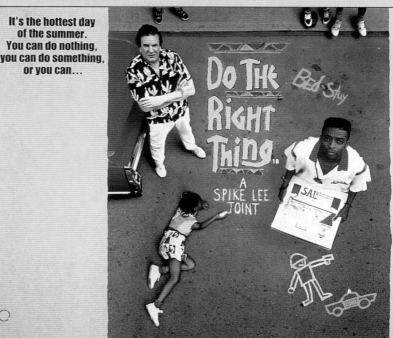

BLACK HOLLYWOOD

The success of Spike Lee's first commercial feature film, *She's Gotta Have It*, in 1986, drew attention to young African-American directorial talent. Made on a shoestring budget of $175,000, this movie about an independent, sexually adventurous black woman won the Prix Jeunesse at the Cannes Film Festival and generated enormous controversy and impressive box office sales. Hollywood funding immediately became available for *School Daze* (1988), which parodied color and class tensions among students, and *Do the Right Thing* (1989), which explored Brooklyn's racial tensions and future choices. Lee's next two movies were *Mo' Better Blues* in 1990 and *Jungle Fever* in 1991, the latter catalyzing yet more controversy by focusing on interracial sex. The climax of Spike Lee's career to date has been his film *Malcolm X*. Released in 1992, the movie paid homage to the message and style of the charismatic black nationalist. Lee allowed himself the license of writing in a part for himself – keeping up the tradition he had established of playing a leading character in all his movies.

This is also a characteristic of Robert Townsend, another young black film maker who made his directorial debut only a few months after Spike Lee. Townsend, however, had far more acting experience when he made *Hollywood Shuffle* in 1987. Produced on a budget of mere $100,000, the movie was a semi-autobiographical satire on the stereotyping and misuse of ability faced by African-American actors in Hollywood. Townsend's subsequent movies, *The Five Heartbeats* (1991) and *Meteor Man* (1993), skillfully combined humor and music to provide insight into black life. The movies commanded large Hollywood budgets and top-quality black casts and technicians.

Other low-budget directors, such as Julie Dash, have won critical acclaim but have not yet been able to obtain the large-scale distribution deals that ensure huge audiences and thus commercial success. Dash has been making movies for 17 years, seeking to use the screen as a medium for telling 'the stories we want to tell.' Her poetic *Daughters of the Dust* (1991) focused on women at the beginning of the century, describing how they guarded and handed on African cultural traditions. Southern, African-based, folktales told to her by her grandmother were also the foundation for another powerful; albeit low-circulation movie, *To Sleep with Anger*, directed by Charles Burnett in 1990. Although already an experienced writer-director by the time the movie was released, Burnett has so far won more in the way of accolades than profits.

Other directors not in the first flush of youth have made their debuts with movies for television. Bill Duke's artistically and historically impressive film about organizing interracial unions in the Chicago stockyards, *The Killing Floor*, was made for PBS in 1984. He has since made the commercially successful *Rage in Harlem* (1991) and *Deep Cover* (1992). Reginald Hudlin made the runaway teen success *House Party* in 1990 on a low budget before being very well funded for Eddie Murphy's *Boomerang* in 1992.

Far more immediate Hollywood, as well as critical, acceptance has recently greeted the directorial debuts of some very young African-American film makers. Matty Rich was only 19 when he made the tough and uncompromising *Straight out of Brooklyn* (1991), and John Singleton was just 22 when he was given a three-year contract with a major Hollywood studio while he was directing *Boyz n the Hood* 1991). Singleton had based this powerful

Left: *The poster for Spike Lee's 1989 movie* Do the Right Thing, *a controversial examination of racial tensions in Brooklyn. The commercial and artistic success of the film enabled Lee to demand larger budgets for subsequent movies.*

drama about growing up in South Central Los Angeles on his own experiences. He chose the South Central rap artist, Ice Cube, as one of his leading actors and touched a chord of recognition with the black youth of America. When the movie was first screened, riots broke out in several cities, but the movie itself condemned rather than condoned violence. Singleton feels it important to portray the truth about black youth on the screen, and expects to go on being funded because 'there's money to be made telling black stories.'

Above: *Richard Roundtree (left) had been one of the star figures created in an earlier genre of black movies labeled 'blacksploitation' – the* Shaft *movies (above) and* Superfly *were just two examples of many from the early 1970s.*

Almost as successful as Singleton's was the directorial debut in 1991 of Mario Van Peebles' *New Jack City*, which was set in a drug-ridden Harlem, and which also starred a South Central LA rapper known as Ice T. Van Peebles did, of course, have the advantage of

Below: *Spike Lee (left) on the set of* Do the Right Thing, *and a poster from the film which followed it,* Mo' Better Blues. Vanity Fair *credited Lee with the creation of the black film industry during the 1980s.*

being the son of one of the most famous of the earlier African-American directors, Melvin Van Peebles. On the cusp of the 1960s and 1970s, Melvin Van Peebles had shown just how effective and popular both Hollywood-funded and independently produced black-directed films could be with the studio-backed *Watermelon Man* (1970) and the self-financed *Sweet Sweetback's Baadasssss Song.*

Together with Gordon Parks' *Learning Tree* and *Shaft* (1971), these were the movies that had been the models for the latest wave of black directorial talent. Twenty years ago control slipped all too quickly out of black hands; this is something that African-American film makers of the 1990s are determined will not be repeated.

Lois E. Horton

Left and above: *Sport is an area in which African Americans have often excelled. Arthur Ashe (above) was the first African American to win the men's titles at the US Open and at Wimbledon. He also wrote a definitive history of African-American athletes. His aluminum, graphite, and fiberglass racket dates from 1975. The basketball is that used by Bill Russell of the Boston Celtics when scoring the 10,000th rebound in late 1962. The Pittsburgh Pirates baseball cap was worn in the 1979 World Series by Willie Stargell.*

encouraging women to have children without getting married. This theory flourished and became the basis for serious public policy initiatives despite numerous scholarly studies which demonstrated that the value of welfare benefits actually fell during the 1970s, 1980s, and early 1990s. Only a small band of black and white intellectuals made the argument consistently that the increase in single-parent families was magnified by the massive changes and the hideous economic and social conditions being experienced by the black poor.

By the 1990s, these conditions had matured. According to the 1990 census, 27 percent of adult black males age 25 to 54 were either unemployed or out of the labor force altogether. The Urban Institute reported that in 1993, 53 percent of black males aged 25–34 – the prime career-starting and family-formation years – were either unemployed or earned

too little to support a family of four above the poverty level.

It is beyond dispute that these factors influenced both the rate of black poverty and the decline in black family formation. From an astronomical level of about 93 percent at the end of the Depression, the black poverty rate dropped steadily through the early 1970s. The drop was precipitous between 1959 and 1973 when the poverty rate fell from 55 to 31 percent. Then, despite increasing affluence at the upper end of the black income spectrum, the rate basically leveled off in the low 30s.

The breakdown within the black community is dramatic. The preliminary 1990 census showed an overall black poverty rate of 31.9 percent. The rate for all black families was 29.3 percent, but for female-headed households, 56.1 percent. The poverty rate for black children was a staggering 44.8 percent. According to Harry Smith at the Children's Defense Fund, that figure, when broken down, was also even more troubling. For children under six the poverty rate stood at 50 percent and for those under three it was 53 percent.

Crime

The other behavioral characteristic of blacks that was deeply embedded in national consciousness and in the national public policy debates at the end of the two-decade period was crime. A 1990 report by the Sentencing

Above: Poverty is greatest among female-headed households such as that seen here in Chicago. A lucrative career in sport is often the dream of deprived children with limited alternative careers. This pin (below) commemorates Muhammad Ali's 1978 feat in becoming the first boxer to win the heavyweight title three times.

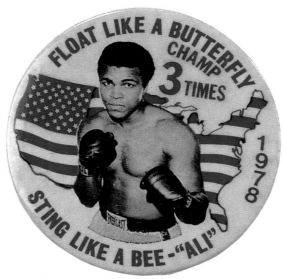

Project calculated that 23 percent of black men in the United States were subject to some form of criminal judicial supervision on any given day. That year, the black share of arrests for robbery was 61.2 percent; for murder and manslaughter, 54.7 percent; for rape, 43.2

percent; and for drug violations, 40.7 percent. Violent crime became such a staple of local television news across the country that electronic journalists invented the maxim: 'If it bleeds, it leads.' Much of what 'bleeds and leads' involves black crime. By the summer of 1994 public opinion polls showed that crime was the top concern of the American people.

Even allowing for exculpatory arguments put forth by advocates for blacks: that blacks are often arrested indiscriminately; that arrest does not equal conviction; that crimes perpetrated by the poor are often more visible and usually prosecuted more often than crimes perpetrated by the rich; that America's criminal justice systems are often operated in a biased manner, it is still clear that blacks are involved in criminal activities in numbers that are far greater than their presence in the population. It is also true that while whites – often living far away from high-crime neighborhoods – report great concern about crime, most crimes committed by blacks are committed against other blacks. Finally, it should be noted that by the end of the 1980s and the beginning of the 1990s, the polls showed that crime was also one of the largest concerns in the black community.

As drugs swept through poor black neighborhoods, and with 200 million guns in private hands, murder became the leading cause of death for black men aged 16 to 24. Death became so commonplace that newspapers began to report that some youngsters in poor communities were known to spend time planning their own funerals.

The dead were not the only ones to suffer. Thousands of victims across the country survived their shootings and were disabled for life. Young men in wheelchairs or walking with canes became a fairly common sight in ghetto areas. Not all the victims were involved in criminal activity. In New York a popular school principal was killed; in Washington it was a pretty young girl, and in Chicago, a 4-year-old boy.

Anticrime Legislation

Around the country, black mothers and others began to organize to combat violence. By 1994, there was enough of this type of activity for the Black Community Crusade for Children to put together an extensive nationwide network of black grassroots organizations that had been formed to combat violence.

The perception of poor blacks as promiscuous and criminally violent had an enormous impact on the political culture by the middle of the 1990s. Throughout the 1980s, the Republicans had been successful in painting the Democrats as 'soft on crime.' In the 1992 election, the Clinton-Gore team had adopted a tough-on-crime posture designed to counter that particular Republican thrust. In addition, Governor Clinton promised a program to 'end welfare as we know it' in response to the concerns about the high rates of out-of-wedlock black births.

By the summer of 1994 a crime bill which had been wending its way through Congress for six years was on the cusp of passage. It contained measures for building more prisons and putting more police on the streets. It imposed the death penalty in 60 situations where it had not previously been deemed necessary. It contained one popular provision popularly labeled 'three strikes and you're out,' which provided a mandatory life sentence for an offender convicted of a third violent offense.

Liberal members of Congress managed to include education, training, and recreation programs for inner-city residents as crime prevention measures. At the last moment, conservatives in the House of Representatives attached the prevention measures and forced the administration to trim them by $3 billion in order to secure passage of the overall measure. An effort by Senate Republicans to trim even more, accompanied by derisive descriptions of the prevention programs as 'pork,' barely failed when four of their number defected. When Republicans won majorities in both houses of Congress in the fall elections, they announced that one of their top priorities would be to repeal the preventive program portion of the crime bill.

This legislative maneuvering is notable because tucking preventive measures into anti-

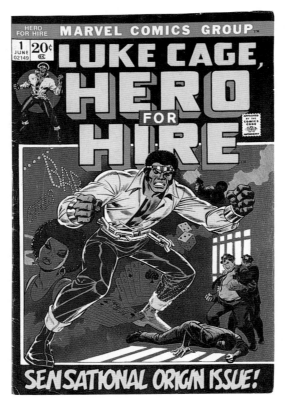

Above: Luke Cage, *published by Marvel in June 1972 and relaunched as* Cage *in April 1992, was the first black superhero with his own comic book.* Black Panther *(also Marvel) was an African king who fought evil and injustice wherever it existed.* Purge, *from ANIA in 1993, had an anti drug-dealing 'purification agenda.'*

crime legislation was the only way blacks and their allies were able to pass any social legislation in the 103rd Congress.

The welfare issue did not come to the floor of the Congress in 1994, but the administration prepared a bill and Republicans began preparing alternatives. The general outline of the administration bill was to attempt to provide training and child-care support as inducements for poor women to get off welfare and get into the world of work, begetting another catchy phrase: 'Two years and you're off.' Even before the administration put its finishing touches on the bill, conservatives in both parties were preparing harsher and more punitive measures. There were some who simply believed that welfare women should be given two years to obtain private sector employment and then simply be dropped from the welfare rolls no matter what the consequences.

Desegregation/Resegregation

Despite all of those erosions in the fortunes of the black poor, even by 1994, most Americans believed that the nation had progressed in race relations since the middle of the century. The measure for black progress that most people in civil rights would have accepted in 1954 at the time of the *Brown* decision would have been the degree to which the country had been desegregated. By 1974, many blacks, probably a minority, but a substantial one, were less attached to that goal than people had been in earlier years. It was still a real goal for most blacks, but in 1974, the Supreme Court crippled the prospects for integrated education in the North. In *Milliken v. Bradley*, the court denied the possibility of needing to combine suburban and inner-city school districts in order to desegregate central-city systems.

The result was white flight, followed by some measurable black middle-class flight, from the cities and concentrated segregation in the big cities of the North. Professor Gary Orfield of Harvard found, for example, in a study for the National School Boards Association, that by 1993, 50.1 percent of the black students in the Northeast attended schools that were at least 90 percent black. Orfield found that even black students living in the suburbs were attending predominantly black schools.

From the election of Ronald Reagan in 1980

through the end of the presidency of George Bush in January 1993, the efforts of the federal government to press desegregation in housing and in schools either stopped or were actively reversed. The Civil Rights Division of the Reagan Justice Department even initiated an effort to remove school districts from court-supervised desegregation efforts. Scholars who study these issues have concluded that a good deal of school resegregation ensued in the late 1980s and early 1990s.

Although a modicum of housing desegregation has taken place in the years since the civil rights laws were passed, inner-city blacks still suffer a concentration and isolation in center cities that is different from that affecting all other groups. Researchers call it 'hypersegregation.' Only blacks live in such neighborhoods.

Roderick J. Harrison, chief of the Census Bureau's racial statistics branch told Rochelle L. Stanfield of the *National Journal*:

> If you thought that segregation of blacks was a problem in 1960, the numbers you're seeing today would indicate that it's still a problem.

Above: *Gang violence has become a major problem in cities like Los Angeles. Dress very often distinguishes gang members, hence the identification and arrest of this 'Rolling 60's' member on an outstanding warrant.*

Below: *There is a disproportionately high rate of African-American involvement in the criminal justice system, the explanations for which are complex. This plainclothes' arrest in the Bronx occurred after an attempted street robbery.*

If you were hoping that civil rights, fair-housing laws, the growth of the black middle class would over a 20–30 year period, really change the picture, I think everybody would agree that they haven't.[2]

Harrison concluded that the current rate of integration might require 100 years just for black segregation to fall to the level of Hispanic segregation.

Black Middle Class

Yet, in the case of both education and housing, integration was available to those blacks who could afford it and desired it. Affluent blacks were to be found in many suburban settings around the country and in upscale neighborhoods inside the cities. Their children could be found in the public schools that had the best reputations (and were often the whitest in the cities where they were located) or in the best private schools in the community. The presence of these people – in their new neighborhoods and their new jobs in professional or other upper-income occupations in integrated settings that had been closed to blacks prior to the 1960s – gave America the impression that much had changed in race relations.

Above and below: *A man's* dashiki *and a woman's* caftan, *both are patterned with African-inspired abstract designs and were worn as graduation robes in 1971 by Spencer R. Crew and Sandra P. Crew respectively. The brightly patterned and multicolored clothing captured many blacks'*

identification with African cultures during this period. The dashiki *(above) is seen here with a variety of African-style necklaces for men and women which incorporate beads, leather, animal fur, and metal to create an attractive collection of jewelry.*

And there was progress which was real and tangible. The first measure was the growth of a black middle class. From 1970 to 1990, the proportion of black households with incomes over $50,000 increased by 46 percent. Though there is a factual basis to the widespread reports of the growth over the last two decades of a black middle class, the picture is not one of unalloyed success. The gap between the incomes of middle-class whites and blacks is still significant, largely because black middle-class status is much more likely to have been achieved by sending a second earner into the workplace.

According to an exhaustive report published by *Money* magazine in its December 1989 issue, the black two-earner family achieves a median income of $36,709 (in 1988 dollars), only $8,751 more than that achieved by a white family with a lone male earner. With the additional costs incurred by putting

Left: *Students being instructed in ballet by director Arthur Mitchell of the Dance Theater of Harlem School founded by him in 1969 to shatter the myth that blacks could not dance the classics.*

of March 1989, black professionals and managers were twice as likely to be unemployed as whites (3.9 percent compared to 1.8).

Black women consistently do better in income comparisons to their white counterparts than do black men. For example, a census study examined the earnings of attorneys between the ages of 35 and 45. While black men averaged only $790 for every $1,000 earned by their white counterparts, the figure for black women lawyers was $930. Stripped of all obfuscation, these disparities bespeak a continuing intense antipathy for, and fear of, black males in American society.

The income and wealth lags that plague blacks can also be attributed to the great difficulty blacks still have in getting really well-paying jobs. As *Money* magazine reports,

the second earner into the job market, such as added transportation and clothing costs and child care, it is doubtful that the black two-earner family gets to keep as much of its income as does the white one-earner family.

Moreover, income figures tell only a part of the story. *Money* pegs middle-class income at $24,000–48,000. Its research reveals that, as of 1989, white households in that income range had accumulated three times the net worth of blacks in the same income category – $54,644 compared to $17,627. Moreover, *Money* reports, at income levels above $48,000, whites have accumulated wealth at twice the rate of blacks.

A number of factors account for these differences. Chief among them are that past discrimination prevented talented blacks from accumulating wealth and thus intergenerational transfers of wealth within families were very unequal. This, in turn, led to much more limited business formation by blacks because of a severe shortage of start-up equity.

Even in these relatively elevated circumstances, blacks encounter other disparities that only racism can explain. In 1987, for example, black male college graduates earned 26 percent less than similarly educated white men. At the graduate-school level, black men still lagged behind white men by 15 percent, and as

Despite widely held claims that affirmative action and equal employment opportunity initiatives have allowed underqualified black applicants to squeeze out better qualified whites, the truth is that such programs have not loosened whites' hold on most upper level job categories.[3]

Though blacks make up 10.1 percent of the employed population, they hold only 6.1 percent of the professional and managerial jobs. They were, for example, only 1 percent of the partners in major law firms, 4 percent of newspaper and magazine journalists, and 0.25 percent of the partners in major CPA (Certified Public Accountant) firms.

However small these advances appear to be, they did represent progress beyond the absolutely negligible numbers that characterized these activities in the early 1970s. More measurable progress was being registered in the areas of business enterprise and politics.

Headway in Business

The 'Black Capitalism' initiative launched by the Nixon administration fanned a muted, but sturdy flame of entrepreneurial spirit in black America. The Nixon initiative came at a propitious time because even the limited amount of integration that had occurred since the mid-1960s had dealt devastating blows to much of black business. The central cities where black enterprises had been located were suddenly left populated primarily by poor people. Moreover, black restaurants, clubs, and theaters that had provided the only sources of relaxation and entertainment for blacks now had to compete for middle-class business with downtown restaurants and clubs and theaters.

Left: *African-American executive Leroy Callendar (second from the left, at the front) was the head of this structural engineering firm in New York City employing a multiracial staff in the 1970s.*

Above and right: *African forms of identity grew during the 1970s. This dress and headwrap were typical; the 'Afro Rake' or Pik features powerful symbols of the era: a clenched black fist representing pride, strength, and self-determination, and the anti-war symbol.*

The Nixon administration's direct efforts to shore up black businesses with special help from the Commerce Department and the Small Business Administration were complemented by Congressional and local governmental efforts to set aside portions of contracting business for minority enterprises.

As a result of these factors and the strong initiatives of scores of black businesspeople around the country, minority enterprises grew substantially during the period from 1974 to 1993. *Black Enterprise* magazine provides a good measure of that growth. Each year it publishes a list of the 100 leading black businesses. For the year 1974, the top five black businesses employed 1,675 people and had gross sales of $144.8 million. For 1993, the last year for which figures are available, the second- through sixth-largest black businesses employed 5,842 people and had gross sales of $969 million.

The 1993 figure changes dramatically when the sixth company is dropped and TLC Beatrice, the top company, is added to the calculation. Assessing 1993 that way yields a total employment figure of 10,262 and gross sales of $2.554 billion. While neither measure begins to take the black-owned and -operated companies anywhere near the Fortune Five Hundred stratosphere, either measure demonstrates that, in those two decades, blacks had begun to make entrepreneurial headway.

One measure of this aspect of black progress was that during the 1992 Presidential campaign, blacks held a fundraiser for Bill Clinton, the Democratic Party nominee, at which each attendee was required to contribute $10,000. The event, a pathbreaker for blacks in terms of individual donations and of total money raised, produced $700,000 for Clinton's campaign.

Politics and the Congressional Caucus
The black presence in the political arena grew in other ways as well. The Voting Rights Act of 1965 had added millions of black voters to the rolls by 1974, and southern politicians had begun to change their behavior. Most startling was the fact that Strom Thurmond of South Carolina, the old Dixiecrat from 1948, was

the first southern member of the Senate to hire a black staffer and, in 1973, he nominated a black lawyer to the federal bench.

American cities had also undergone a political transformation. In 1967, as the urban riots had just about run their course, Carl Stokes in Cleveland, Ohio, and Richard Hatcher in Gary, Indiana, became the first African Americans to be elected mayors of major northern cities. By 1994, blacks had served as mayors of all of the four biggest American cities: New York, Los Angeles, Chicago, and Philadelphia, and many of the second-tier cities as well: Detroit, Baltimore, Washington, Atlanta, Cleveland, and Seattle.

Overall, the number of black mayors increased: from 108 in office in 1974, to 356 in office in 1994. The total number of black officeholders overall increased from 2,991 in 1974 to 8,015 in 1993.

The Congressional Black Caucus underwent a significant transformation. It had 17 members in 1974. That number included one African-American member of the Senate, Edward W. Brooke of Massachusetts. By

Above: *Three African-American mayors from three major American cities talking to Housing and Urban Development Secretary Robert Weaver in 1967. From the left, the three are Carl Stokes of Cleveland, Ohio; Walter Washington of Washington, DC; and Richard Hatcher of Gary, Indiana.*

1994, Caucus members had increased to 40 and included the first African-American woman member of the Senate, Carol Mosley Braun of Illinois. During the 103rd Congress, the first two years of the Clinton presidency, the Congressional Black Caucus played a more significant role than any blacks had ever played in the legislative history of the nation. The membership of the caucus had jumped from its 102nd Congressional level of 26, mainly by virtue of redistricting that had

Right: *David Dinkins (center) being sworn in as the first black mayor of New York in a ceremony conducted by Judge Fritz Alexander on the steps of City Hall. Dinkins's wife Joyce is holding the Bible, while Governor Mario Cuomo looks on.*

Above: *Whoopi Goldberg has emerged in recent years as one of the best-known African-American entertainers. A comedienne and actress, she is seen here accepting a Grammy Award in Los Angeles in 1986 for Best Comedy Recording.*

occurred in the South after the 1990 census. The new numbers in the House gave the caucus a legislative bulk it had never previously enjoyed.

The two most significant examples of legislative muscle-flexing by the caucus involved the Violent Crime Control and Law Enforcement Act of 1994 and the administration's policy toward Haiti. The maneuvering on the crime legislation has been discussed earlier.

The Clinton presidential campaign had put Haiti policy on the front burner when it criticized the Bush policy of intercepting Haitian refugees on the high seas and returning them for immigration processing in Haiti. When he became president, Clinton reversed himself and embraced the Bush policy. A majority of the caucus attacked this action as both racist and craven and sought a diplomatic reversal of the coup that ousted democratically elected Jean Bertrand Aristide. In the fall of 1994, the administration achieved a negotiated settlement only after the first wave of American paratroopers were in planes on their way to Haiti. Opponents of this policy sought to discredit it by alleging that foreign policy was being 'dictated' by the caucus. While an overstatement, the charge was a tribute to the enlarged influence of the black members of the national legislature.

Jesse Jackson
The other significant political developments

Above: *Grandmaster Flash, together with his group the Furious Five, was a pioneer of rap that carried messages of social criticism.*

In the early 1970s, groups of African-American, West Indian, and Puerto Rican youth in the South Bronx, New York City, launched one of the most important cultural movements of the late twentieth century. Known to the world at large as 'Hip Hop,' this predominantly black and Latino youth culture incorporated rap music, graffiti art, and break dancing, as well as the language and dress styles that have come to be associated with the Hip Hop generation.

Rap music is the most enduring and profitable aspect of Hip Hop culture. Rap has a long prehistory in African-American culture and can be traced back to preaching, singing the blues, and toasting (oral stories performed in rhyme that are usually humorous but often filled with explicit sex and violence).

Another part of rap's roots can be traced to the rhyming styles of pioneering black radio DJs such as Dr. Jocko and Dr. Jive. But what made Hip Hop music unique was the technology: DJs and producers transformed these oral traditions with electronic drum machines, turntables, mixers, and, later, digital samplers. They 'sampled' music from old recordings, whether it was a taped voice or an old record, to create new sounds. Boundaries between different kinds of music were disregarded.

The South Bronx DJs began mixing together different kinds of dance music at local parties, clubs, and outdoor events. Perhaps the most famous was Clive 'Kool D.J. Herc,' an émigré from Kingston, Jamaica, whence he brought a rich knowledge of the Jamaican dance-hall

By the late 1970s, Harlem and the Bronx claimed several major rap groups: Double Trouble, the Treacherous Three, the Funky Four Plus One, Grandmaster Flash and the Furious Five, and Afrika Bambaataa and his various groups – the Jazzy Five, the Cosmic Force, and the Soulsonic Force. Ironically, the genre went national when the obscure New Jersey group called the Sugar Hill Gang had a commercial success with 'Rapper's Delight,' with many of the lyrics taken from Bronx MC Grand Master Caz.

As the technology advanced and artists honed their verbal skills, some remarkable groups emerged on the scene. Eric B and Rakim, who released their first album in 1986, had a rhyme style unlike anything that came before – slow, smooth, with rhymes flowing into the next stanza. De La Soul brought Hip Hop into what they called the 'Daisy Age,' challenging listeners with way-out metaphors and almost mystical use of language. Their innovative lyrical style shaped later groups like A Tribe Called Quest, and Urban Dance Squad.

Picking up the Grandmaster Flash critique tradition there emerged dozens of rap groups devoted to radical political themes, including Public Enemy, Intelligent Hoodlum, X-Clan, and KRS-1. Some advocated black nationalist or Afrocentric themes; others, like the 'gangsta rappers' dominant on the West Coast, produced chilling stories of modern 'baaad men,' tales of street life, crime, and domination over women.

While not all rappers were driven by political themes, the use of profanity and sexually explicit lyrics pushed several rap groups into the center of controversy. In 1990, obscenity laws were vigorously enforced in several states to ban sales of recordings and live performances. When Body Count, produced by Ice-T, recorded 'Cop Killer' in 1992 citizens' and police groups called on Ice-T's record label, Time-Warner, to take the record off the market. In 1993 black community groups and African-American women's organizations denounced 'gangsta rap' for its offensive, violent and misogynist lyrics. The blacklash, in fact, spurred congressional hearings to investigate the matter.

Despite these attacks, Hip Hop was clearly a dominant force in American, and even international, popular culture by 1994. It had grown up in several different directions and developed its own subgenres, incorporating elements of reggae, jazz, punk, rock, and heavy metal. Although many artists and fans still see it as the voice of dispossessed inner-city youth, it has also become a multibillion dollar industry. What was once thought to be a passing fad has clearly secured a place in American cultural history.

Robin D.G. Kelley

Note

[1]David Toop, The Rap Attack, Boston: South End Press, 1984, p.60.

scene. What made his deejaying so compelling was his brilliant use of 'break beats' – fragments of a song that dancers enjoyed most. Herc would isolate these breaks and play them over and over by using two turntables, or mixing break beats from different songs. According to another South Bronx pioneer, Afrika Bambaataa (who became master of 'techno pop,' laying the foundation for later 'house' music): 'He just kept that beat going. It might be that certain part of the record that everybody waits for – they just let their inner self go and get wild.'[1]

Soon the parks, school yards and underground clubs in Manhattan and Brooklyn, as well as the Bronx, were overrun with DJs. One important figure was Grandmaster Flash, who is credited with inventing 'scratching' or back-cueing records on the turntable to create a new percussive sound over break beats. He also departed from the normal humorous or boasting lyrics to record songs like 'White Lines' and 'The Message' that critiqued racism, poverty, police brutality, and drug use.

Above: Afrika Bambaataa pictured in concert. A native of the Bronx, Bambaataa was an early master of 'techno pop.'

Pioneer rappers included Melle Mel and Cowboy, Eddie Cheeba, DJ Hollywood, and Kurtis Blow. There were also women, including Lady B, Sweet T, Lisa Lee, Sha Rock, the Mercedes Ladies, Sula, and Sequence. The women had to contend with sexism – especially when it came to getting recording contracts – and were often treated as novelty groups, despite the fact that they displayed skills equal to the best of their male counterparts. Not until the appearance of Salt-N-Pepa, and later MC Lyte and Queen Latifah, did women rappers gain legitimacy and respect, successfully challenging the notion that boasting and profanity were distinctly 'men's talk.'

Below: All-female group Salt-N-Pepa are seen here accepting their Grammy Award in Los Angeles in 1995 for Best Rap Performance by a Duo or Group, given for their hit 'None of Your Business.'

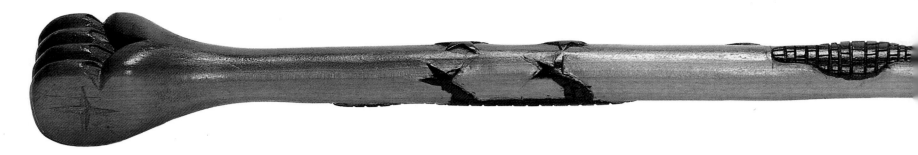

Above: *This cane carved from wood was made in Savannah, Georgia, and carries African-inspired motifs such as the clenched fist – a prominent, well-known symbol – and the carved alligators which wrap round the shaft.*

during the two decades were the campaigns mounted by the Reverend Jesse L. Jackson for the Democratic nomination for president in 1984 and 1988. In November 1983, Jackson announced his candidacy to a bewildered national political press corps. Nothing in Jackson's history as a civil rights leader had prepared the political press to deal with his candidacy.

While the political establishment was puzzled by Jackson's effort, he moved through the primaries earnestly and garnered enough votes

Below and left: *Marchers cross the Edmund Pettus Bridge in 1985 on the 20th anniversary of the Selma-Montgomery march. Between John Lewis and Rev. Joseph Lowery is Jesse Jackson who in 1988 ran a campaign for the presidency (left) during which he won several of the Democratic primaries.*

Left: *Heru, Son of Ausar (No.7, April 1993) is a notable publication because of its references to ancient Egypt, there being an Afrocentric school of thought which argues that many of the great civilizations of the past were black.*

Below: *Many black pride items can be bought at African-American street festivals. The 'Muntu' T-Shirt was bought at the 4 July festival held in Brooklyn's Bedford-Styvesant section. The Parliament T-Shirt has a slogan on its back: 'God Bless Chocolate City and its Vanilla Suburbs,' a reference to Washington, DC. The 'Happy I'm Nappy' items are statements of pride.*

to warrant continued attention. His major campaign theme was fairness to those left out of the process and inclusion of the humblest supporters of the Democratic Party in its major decision-making councils. Then one of Jackson's supporters, Minister Louis Farrakhan, leader of the Nation of Islam, called Judaism a 'gutter religion' and embroiled the Jackson campaign in deep problems with Jewish Americans and others who were offended by Farrakhan's remarks. The problem got worse when the *Washington Post* quoted Jackson using the word 'Hymie' and calling New York 'Hymietown.'

Though Jackson finally severed his connection with Farrakhan and apologized for his comments, his campaign never fully recovered from those problems. Nevertheless, when it was over, Jackson had garnered more than 3.25 million votes in the Democratic primaries and was credited with having motivated the registration of close to 1 million new black voters.

Jackson ran again in 1988. His campaign was considerably more professional than it had been in 1984, and for a brief period in March, after he had won the Michigan primary, Jackson appeared to be the Democratic front-runner. Though that early success

faded, Jackson more than doubled his 1984 achievement and gathered more than 6.75 million votes in the primaries.

Many political observers believed that, even in losing, Jackson had served the nation well. His campaigns had been something of a national civics lesson, spreading the idea that the presidency was not simply the preserve of white males, but was an office to which any American could realistically aspire.

It also proved productive for other black politicians. Douglas Wilder of Virginia capitalized on the new Jackson registrants in that state in his successful and historic 1989 quest to become the first African American to be elected governor in American history. In New York City in the same year, David Dinkins used the campaign machinery that Jackson had put into place in 1988 in his successful quest to become the first elected black mayor of New York.

Looking Backward/Looking Forward

By the 1990s the thin level of high-achieving blacks had made truly remarkable progress. General Colin Powell had served two terms as chairman of the joint chiefs of staff, Oprah Winfrey and Bill Cosby had become immensely rich and popular as television personalities, and Michael Jordan had achieved legendary status and wealth as a professional basketball player while leading the Chicago Bulls to three successive league championships. Toni Morrison won the Nobel Prize for literature in 1993, having previously won the Pulitzer Prize for her novel, *Beloved*. Alvin Ailey and Arthur Mitchell developed famous dance troupes while Alfrey Woodard, Cicely Tyson and Morgan Freeman became full-fledged movie stars.

Blacks trickled into the top ranks of academia, on-air broadcasting, and print journalism. More and more of them were to be seen in corporate boardrooms and in the top ranks of nonprofit institutions. Some became opera stars and many remained headline musicians and entertainers. It became commonplace for presidents to place some blacks in their cabinets. President Clinton appointed five: Mike Espy, Ron Brown, Hazel O'Leary, and Jesse Brown as secretaries of agriculture, commerce, energy, and veterans affairs, respectively, and Jocelyn Elders as surgeon-general.

Beneath the glitter, grimmer realities continued to unfold. In addition to the economic devastation at the bottom of the black income spectrum, there were bad organizational and political developments. A few new organiza-

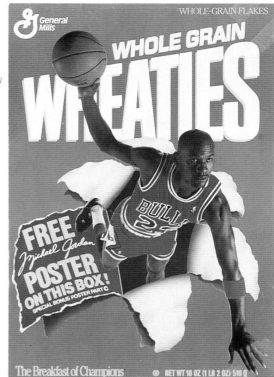

Below: *Five of the biggest names in the music business, all African Americans: Dionne Warwick, Stevie Wonder, Quincy Jones, Michael Jackson, and Lionel Ritchie with a collective Grammy awarded in 1986 for 'We Are the World.'*

Above: *A Harlem Globetrotters pennant and a 'Junior Trotter' jersey given to selected children at their skillful and humorous exhibitions. When founded in 1927 it was the only professional team open to black players.*

Above and below: *Basketball is the most popular sport in the black community and many young men yearn to become professionals, a hope captured so powerfully in the documentary* Hoop Dreams. *Some of the game's biggest recent stars have been black; men such as Michael Jordan (above, in a Wheaties' poster offer), and Earvin 'Magic' Johnson of the Barcelona Olympics' 'Dream Team.'*

Above: *Mike Tyson celebrating his first-round defense of the heavyweight crown against Carl Williams in Atlantic City in 1989. Three years earlier Tyson had become the youngest man ever to hold the title and many considered him invincible, but his activities outside the ring were to distract from his abilities within it.*

tional strengths developed. The Children's Defense Fund, which served effectively as an advocate for poor children, and the Joint Center for Political and Economic Affairs, a highly respected black think tank, were chief among these.

But during the 1970s and 1980s, the organizations which had formed the core of the civil rights movement either disappeared or became demonstrably weaker or quieter. The Student Nonviolent Coordinating Committee disappeared. The Southern Christian Leadership Conference almost discontinued all activity and, for all practical purposes, lost its voice in national affairs. The Congress of Racial Equality dissolved into a tiny band of New Yorkers.

Even the two great organizations, the National Association for the Advancement of Colored People (NAACP) and the National Urban League, had become less effective. While both retained their nationwide network of local units, the Urban League lost its national voice after 1981, when Vernon Jordan stepped down. The NAACP became quieter and quieter over the two decades and, in 1994, it began to unravel at the top when its executive director, Benjamin Chavis, was forced out because of scandals involving sex and money. By the end of 1994, its board leadership was under heavy fire because of an accumulated debt of $3.5 million. It was furloughing staff and contemplating massive layoffs.

Meanwhile, the 1994 congressional and gubernatorial elections swept away the Democratic leadership of the Congress and the statehouses. Republicans had campaigned on themes of smaller government, lower taxes, welfare reform, and strong anticrime measures. The South was solid once more, only this time it was solidly Republican, fulfilling

Lyndon Johnson's prediction, after the Democrat-led passage of the Voting Rights Act in 1965, that the Democrats would lose the South for a generation.

The new Republican majorities were aiming to slash welfare costs, getting tougher with criminals, and weeding out social programs in their drive to 'downsize' government. All of this was fueled by what political journalists had termed the angry votes of white men who had cast more than 60 percent of their votes for the Republicans. Although black men had been injured more severely than white men by the economic developments of the two decades, white men at middle-income, and especially lower-income and -skill levels had suffered real and measurable injury as well. There was much evidence to indicate that many of them laid their ills at the doorstep of programs to aid blacks, especially affirmative-action hiring plans.

So, as the period ended, blacks faced a difficult future with a number of their most valuable organizational assets either gone or crippled. It was understandable, then, that despite all the progress, the great black historian, John Hope Franklin, should survey the scene and declare that blacks in the mid-1990s faced their worst crisis since slavery.

Notes
[1]*Michigan Quarterly Review* 33 (Spring 1994): 255.
[2]*National Journal*, 2 April 1994: 18.
[3]*Money*, December 1989, p. 159.

STILL I RISE

You may write me down in history
With your bitter, twisted lies,
You may trod me in the very dirt
But still, like dust, I'll rise.

Does my sassiness upset you?
Why are you beset with gloom?
'Cause I walk like I've got oil wells
Pumping in my living room.

Just like moons and like suns,
With the certainty of tides,
Just like hopes springing high,
Still I'll rise.

Did you want to see me broken?
Bowed head and lowered eyes?
Shoulders falling down like teardrops,
Weakened by my soulful cries.

Does my haughtiness offend you?
Don't you take it awful hard
'Cause I laugh like I've got gold mines
Diggin' in my own back yard.

You may shoot me with your words,
You may cut me with your eyes,
You may kill me with your hatefulness,
But still, like air, I'll rise.

Does my sexiness upset you?
Does it come as a surprise
That I dance like I've got diamonds
At the meeting of my thighs?

Out of the huts of history's shame
I rise
Up from a past that's rooted in pain
I rise
I'm a black ocean, leaping and wide,
Welling and swelling I bear in the tide.

Leaving behind nights of terror and fear
I rise
Into a daybreak that's wondrously clear
I rise
Bringing the gifts that my ancestors gave,
I am the dream and the hope of the slave.
I rise
I rise
I rise.

Maya Angelou

TIMELINE

1513
Thirty Africans march with Balboa's expeditionary party to the Pacific Ocean.

1519
Three hundred Africans transport Spanish artillery used by Hernando Cortez to invade Mexico and defeat the Aztecs.

1526
Africans enslaved by the Spanish construct forts in the Carolinas. Many slaves escape to inland Indian communities.

1538
The African Estevanico becomes the first person who is not Native American to explore the Southwest.

1565
African craftsmen and farmers help the Spanish build and settle St. Augustine, Florida.

1619
In August the first Africans are brought to British North American colonies when a Dutch ship lands black laborers in Jamestown, Virginia.

1624
African labor is imported into the Dutch colony of New Netherlands. The first black child is born in British North America in Jamestown and is christened William in the Church of England.

1638
Native Americans transported from Salem, Massachusetts, to the West Indies and exchanged for African laborers, opening the New England slave trade.

1651
Anthony Johnson, probably one of the original 20 Africans imported into Jamestown, is freed and receives a land grant of 250 acres. He establishes an African-American community in Northhampton County, Virginia.

1676
Slaves and white indentured servants participate in Bacon's Rebellion in Virginia, raising fears of interracial action against the colonial authority.

1700
Slave population in British North America is 27,817 – 22,600 of whom are held in the South.

1712
New York City slave revolt. Nine whites are killed and 21 slaves are executed.

1739
In September a slave revolt in Stono, South Carolina, results in the death of 30 whites and the execution of 30 slaves.

1741
In March a series of fires in New York City leads to reports of slave revolt and a general panic in the city. A trial of suspected rebels is held, and the rebellion conspiracy is said to involve blacks and whites. Thirty-one slaves and five whites are executed.

1760
In December Jupiter Hammon, a New York slave, publishes his poem, 'An Evening Thought: Salvation by Christ, with Penetential Cries.' He is probably the first published slave poet.

1770
On March 5 black seaman and escaped slave Crispus Attucks is the first of five killed in the Boston Massacre, a pre-Revolution American mob action against the British. Attucks is recognized as the leader of the action.

1775
In April black men, including Lemuel Haynes, Pomp Blackman, Samuel Craft, Caesar and John Ferrit, and Peter Salem, are among the Minutemen who fight against the British at the battles of Lexington and Concord. About 5,000 African Americans served in the regular Centennial Army in integrated units and in a few all-black regiments. Another 3,000 or 4,000 blacks served in the American Navy or as guerrilla fighters and spies. Several hundred blacks also fought with the British.

In July black Masons in Boston led by Prince Hall organize African Lodge No. 1, the first black masonic lodge in America.

1783
As an eventual consequence of slaves' petition for freedom on the basis of Revolutionary principles, the state Supreme Court abolishes slavery in Massachusetts.

1787
Richard Allen and Absalom Jones organize the Free African Society in Philadelphia, Pennsylvania.

In July the United States Constitution is adopted with no direct mention of slavery but indirectly recognizing the existence of 'free persons' and 'other persons.'

1790
Free blacks organize the Brown Fellowship Society, a social, educational and mutual aid society for people of mixed racial heritage, in Charleston, South Carolina.

1794
Richard Allen founds the first African Methodist Episcopal church, Bethel Church in Philadelphia, Pennsylvania.

1800
A slave conspiracy to attack Richmond, Virginia, led by Gabriel Prosser and involving about 1,000 slaves is betrayed. Sixteen blacks, including Prosser, are hanged.

1808
In accordance with the provisions of the Constitution, Congress outlaws the African slave trade. The slave trade continues illegally, with greatly reduced numbers of Africans being smuggled into the United States thereafter.

1812
Blacks make up approximately 18 percent of the U.S. Navy during the War of 1812 against the British.

1815
Six hundred blacks stand with General Andrew Jackson

at the successful defense against the British at the Battle of New Orleans.

1816
The African Methodist Episcopal (AME) Church is organized in Philadelphia as the first black religious denomination in America with Richard Allen as bishop.

1821
Thomas L. Jennings awarded a patent for dry-cleaning. The first known patent given to a black inventor.

1822
In May a slave conspiracy in Charleston, S.C., led by former slave Demark Vesey is foiled when a slave informed authorities of the plan. Thirty five blacks, including Vessey are executed.

1827
Freedom's Journal, the first black newspaper in America, is published in New York City in March.

1829
In September, David Walker, a free black man from North Carolina living in Boston, publishes his militant antislavery tract *An Appeal to the Colored Citizens of the World*. Its publication gives rise to panic in the South and efforts to restrict its circulation.

1830
The first national convention of African Americans is held in Philadelphia. National conventions continue to meet periodically until 1864.

1831
In August slave Nat Turner leads the most successful slave rebellion in American history. Some 50 whites are killed and untold numbers of slaves are killed, some on the strength of rumor of their involvement. Turner is eventually captured and executed

1839
In July a slave rebellion aboard the slave ship *Amistad* leads eventually to a Supreme Court case which, in 1841, sets the slaves free and allows some 35 survivors to return to Africa.

1845
In May Macon B. Allen becomes the first black lawyer admitted to the bar when he passes his examinations in Worcester, MA.

1847
Liberia becomes an independent nation with Joseph Jenkins Roberts, of Virginia, as its president.

1848
In February, Benjamin Roberts brings suit against Boston seeking to gain admission for his daughter, Sarah, to the white school near their home. This first school integration suit was rejected by the Massachusetts Supreme Court in a "separate but equal" decision in 1850.

Right: *Early female factory labor pictured in April 1919, the fact they are black making it more interesting still. The couple weigh the wire coils and it is recorded in order to establish wage rates.*

1850

In September Congress passes the Fugitive Slave Law as part of the Compromise of 1850. This is the most harsh fugitive slave law ever passes by the federal government restricting the rights of accused fugitives to legal defense.

1853

Former slave Williams Wells Brown publishes *Clotel*, the first novel published by an African American.

1854

In June James Augustine Healy becomes the first black American Roman Catholic priest. He is ordained at Notre Dame Cathedral in Paris.

1857

In March the Supreme Court of the United States renders the Dred Scott decision declaring that black people are not and can not be citizens of the United States, that Dred Scot remained a slave even though he had lived for a long period outside the jurisdiction of slavery, and that Congress has no right to bar slavery from the western territories.

1859

In October white abolitionist John Brown leads a band of 12 whites and five blacks in a raid on the federal arsenal at Harpers Ferry in a failed attempt to foment slave revolt in Virginia.

1861

In September the Secretary of the U.S. Navy authorizes the enlistment of blacks into the navy. By the end of the war blacks are 25 percent of Union sailors.

1862

In July Congress authorizes the enlistment of blacks into the United States Army. More than 186,000 blacks serve in the army during the war.

1863

On 1 January President Abraham Lincoln issues the Emancipation Proclamation freeing slaves in areas then in rebellion against the United States. The proclamation did not free slaves in areas under the control of the United States.

1865

In February John S. Rock, Boston attorney, becomes the first African American admitted to practice before the U.S. Supreme Court.

In March Jefferson Davis signs a bill authorizing the use of slaves as soldiers in the Confederate Army.

In December the 13th Amendment to the Constitution outlawing slavery in the United States is ratified.

1868

In July the 14th Amendment providing citizenship rights for all those born or naturalized in the U.S. regardless of color is ratified.

In November John W. Menard from Louisiana is the first African American elected to Congress. During Reconstruction from 1869 to 1877, 14 African Americans serve in the U.S. House of Representatives and two serve in the U.S. Senate.

Edmonia Lewis's sculpture *Forever Free* celebrates the Emancipation Proclamation.

1870

Hiram Rhodes Revels is elected to fill the unexpired seat of former Confederate president Jefferson Davis, to become U.S. Senator from Mississippi, the first African American to sit in the U.S. Senate.

In March the 15th Amendment to the Constitution guaranteeing all male citizens the right to vote is ratified.

1871

In October the Fisk Jubilee Singers begin their first national tour.

1875

Congress enacts legislation banning discrimination in public accommodations.

1876

Edward M. Bannister's painting 'Under the Oaks' wins the bronze medal in Philadelphia at the Centennial Exposition.

1880

Jockey Barrett Lewis wins the Kentucky Derby.

1896

The Supreme Court establishes the constitutionality of 'separate but equal' public facilities in its decision in the case of Plessy v. Ferguson.

1905

W.E.B. DuBois, William Monroe Trotter and other blacks establish the Niagara Movement, forerunner of the integrated National Association for the Advancement of Colored People founded in 1909.

1908

Boxer Jack Johnson defeats Tommy Burns to become heavyweight champion of the world.

1911

In October the National Urban League is established.

1912

W.C. Handy's 'Memphis Blues,' the first published blues composition, goes on sale.

1916

Black nationalist Marcus Garvey migrates from Jamaica to the United States and establishes the Universal Negro Improvement Association to promote racial pride and emigration to Africa.

1917

American enters World War I. By the end of the war in November, 1918, 370,000 black soldiers and 1,400 commissioned officers have served.

1921

A renaissance of music, art, theater and literature in several northern black urban communities begins.

1925

In May A. Philip Randolph organizes the Brotherhood of Sleeping Car Porters.

1933

Paul Robeson stars in United Artists' movie *Emperor Jones*, the first Hollywood movie with an African-American star and white supporting actors.

1934

The first live show is staged at the Apollo Theater in Harlem.

1935

Mary McLeod Bethune establishes the National Council of Negro Women.

The Congress of Industrial Organizations is organized and creates integrated unions, including the United Mine Workers.

1936

Count Basie appears at the Roseland Ballroom in New York City.

Jesse Owens wins four gold medals at the Olympics in Berlin.

1937

Zora Neale Hurston publishes the novel *Their Eyes Were Watching God*.

Boxer Joe Louis becomes heavyweight champion of the world by defeating James J. Braddock.

1939

After being denied access to Constitution Hall, Marian Anderson performs before an integrated audience of 75,000 at the Lincoln Memorial.

1940

In February Richard Wright publishes *Native Son*.

Hattie McDaniel, who played 'Mammy' in *Gone with the Wind*, is the first African American to win an Academy Award.

In October Benjamin Oliver Davis, Sr. becomes the first black general in the regular army.

1942

Students at the University of Chicago led by James Farmer form the nonviolent Congress of Racial Equality.

1943

In October Paul Robeson opens at Shubert Theater in the title role of Othello and gives 296 performances, a record for a Shakespearean play on Broadway.

1945

By the end of World War II, over one million African Americans had enlisted or had been drafted into the armed forces. Almost 8,000 served as commissioned officers, and nearly 4,000 black women served in the army and navy auxiliaries.

1946

In the case of Morgan v. Commonwealth of Virginia the Supreme Court rules that segregation in interstate bus travel is unconstitutional.

1947

The first CORE Freedom Riders tests the ban on segregation with a bus trip through the South.

John Hope Franklin publishes his comprehensive black history *From Slavery to Freedom*.

Jackie Robinson is signed by the Brooklyn Dodgers, breaking the color line in major league baseball.

The NAACP presents a petition on racism, 'An Appeal to the World,' to the United Nations.

1948

President Harry Truman's Executive Order 9981 ends segregation in the U.S. Armed Forces.

1950

Ralph Bunche is awarded the Nobel Peace Prize for successful mediation between the Arabs and Israelis in Palestine.

Poet Gwendolyn Brooks wins the Pulitzer Prize for her book *Annie Allen*.

1952

Ralph Ellison wins the National Book Award for his novel *Invisible Man*.

1954

In the case of Brown v. Board of Education of Topeka, the Supreme Court rules that segregation in public education is unconstitutional, declaring that separate is 'inherently unequal.'

1955

In December Rosa Parks refuses to give up her seat to a white man on a bus in Montgomery, Alabama. She is arrested, the Montgomery Improvement Association is formed, a boycott is organized, and Martin Luther King, Jr. is elected president of the association.

Marian Anderson performs in Verdi's *A Masked Ball* at New York's Metropolitan Opera House, becoming the first African American to sing there.

1957

Congress passes the first important civil rights legislation since 1875, the Civil Rights Act of 1957, protecting the right to vote.

President Eisenhower sends troops to protect 18 black students attempting to integrate Central High School in Little Rock, Arkansas.

Althea Gibson becomes the first African-American tennis champion at Wimbledon, winning the women's singles and doubles. She had won the French Open and the U.S. National Championships in 1956.

1960

Students sit-in at a lunch counter in F.W. Woolworth's in Greensboro, North Carolina, to protest segregation.

The Student Nonviolent Coordinating Committee is organized in Raleigh, North Carolina.

1962

Twelve thousand federal soldiers are sent to quell riots and ensure James Merideth's enrollment at the University of Mississippi.

1963

Martin Luther King, Jr. delivers his 'I Have a Dream Speech' at the Lincoln Memorial during the March on Washington.

In June NAACP field secretary for Mississippi Medgar Evers is assassinated by a segregationist.

In November President John F. Kennedy is assassinated in Dallas, Texas.

1964

Martin Luther King, Jr. is awarded the Nobel Peace Prize.

Three civil rights workers are murdered in Philadelphia, Mississippi.

Congress passes and President Lyndon B. Johnson signs the Civil Rights Bill banning discrimination in education, employment and public accommodations.

1965

In February Malcolm X is assassinated at the Audubon Ballroom in Harlem.

Congress passes the Voting Rights Act providing for federal registrars where state officials refuse to register black voters.

1966

The Black Panther Party is founded in Oakland, California.

Martin Luther King, Jr. publicly denounces the Vietnam War.

1967

More than 40 riots make this the worst summer of racial disturbances in American history. The largest riots are in Newark, New Jersey, and Detroit, Michigan.

President Lyndon Johnson appoints Thurgood Marshall to the Supreme Court.

1968

In April Martin Luther King, Jr. is assassinated in Memphis, Tennessee.

John Carlos and Tommie Smith give the Black Power salute at the awards ceremony for their wins in track during the Olympics in Mexico City and are suspended from the team for their action.

1970

Toni Morrison publishes her first novel *The Bluest Eye*.

1971

The Congressional Black Caucus is created.

Jesse Jackson organizes People United to Save Humanity in Chicago.

1973

Marian Wright Edelman organizes the Children's Defense Fund.

1974

Hank Aaron of the Atlanta Braves breaks Babe Ruth's record in the major leagues when he hits his 715th home run.

1976

President-elect Jimmie Carter appoints Georgia Representative Andrew Young U.S. Ambassador to the United Nations.

1977

In January Alex Haley's novel *Roots* is televised and viewed by more than 130 million Americans.

1979

Five people are killed in Greensboro, North Carolina, when members of the Ku Klux Klan fire on an anti-Klan demonstration.

Congress honors the memory of Martin Luther King, Jr. by voting to make him the first African American with his likeness in the Capitol rotunda.

1981

Solidarity Day draws over 300,000 people from labor and civil rights organizations to protest the policies of President Ronald Reagan's administration.

1983

President Reagan signs a bill into law making the third Monday in January a federal holiday honoring Martin Luther King, Jr.

Jesse Jackson declares his candidacy for president of the United States.

Alice Walker's *The Color Purple* wins the Pulitzer Prize.

Michael Jackson's 'Thriller' becomes the best selling pop music album in history.

Artist Jacob Lawrence is elected to the American Academy of Arts and Letters.

Vanessa Williams, winner of the New York State beauty contest, becomes the first black woman to be crowned Miss America.

1987

Toni Morrison publishes her Pulitzer Prize winning novel *Beloved*.

1988

Doug Williams becomes the first black quarterback to play in the Super Bowl, ties the bowl record with four touchdown passes and is voted the game's most valuable player.

1989

Barbara Harris is confirmed as the first female bishop of the Episcopal Church.

General Colin Powell is named chair of the U.S. Joint Chiefs of Staff, the highest military position ever held by an African American.

L. Douglas Wilder is elected Governor of Virginia in November, becoming the first African American elected to the office of governor in any state.

1991

Clarence Thomas is confirmed in the closest Senate confirmation vote in history to occupy the Supreme Court seat vacated by retiring Justice Thurgood Marshall.

1992

Carol Moseley Braun becomes the first African-American woman to be elected to the U.S. Senate.

1993

President Bill Clinton appoints five African Americans to his cabinet: Michael Espy becomes secretary of agriculture, Ronald Brown becomes secretary of commerce, Hazel O'Leary becomes secretary of energy, Jesse Brown becomes secretary of veterans affairs, and Joycelyn Elders becomes surgeon-general.

Toni Morrison becomes the first African American to win the Nobel Prize in literature.

1994

Byron DeLa Beckwith is convicted of murdering Mississippi NAACP field secretary and civil rights activist Medgar Evers 31 years before and is sentenced to life in prison.

George Foreman, age 45, regains the heavyweight boxing title.

Beverly J. Harvard becomes the chief of police in Atlanta, Georgia, the first black woman to lead a major metropolitan police department.

1995

O.J. Simpson, television personality and former professional football star, goes on trial in Los Angeles, accused of murdering his ex-wife and her companion. The extended trial becomes a major national and international media event.

The NAACP board of directors elects Myrlie Evers-Williams, the widow of Medgar Evers, to be its chair in the wake of scandals which threaten the organization's reputation.

BIBLIOGRAPHY

Chapter 1

Breen, Timothy S. and Innes, Stephen, 'Myne Owne Ground' Race and Freedom on Virginia's Eastern Shore, 1640–1676, New York: Oxford University Press, 1980.

d'Azevedo, Warren L. (ed.), The Traditional Artist in African Societies, Bloomington: Indiana University Press, 1973.

Littlefield, Daniel, C., Rice and Slaves: Ethnicity and the Slave Trade in Colonial South Carolina, Urbana: University of Illinois Press, 1991.

Morgan, Edmund, American Slavery, American Freedom: The Ordeal of Colonial Virginia, New York: W. W. Norton, 1975.

Thomas J. Davis, A Rumor of Revolt: The 'Great Negro Plot' in Colonial New York, Amherst: University of Massachusetts Press, 1990.

Wood, Peter, Black Majority: Negroes in Colonial South Carolina from 1670 Through the Stono Rebellion, New York: Alfred A. Knopf, 1972.

Chapter 2

Berlin, Ira and Hoffman, Ronald, Slavery and Freedom in the Age of the American Revolution, Charlottesville: University of Virginia Press, 1983.

Frey, Sylvia, Water from the Rock: Black Resistance in a Revolutionary Age, Princeton: Princeton University Press, 1991.

Horton, James Oliver and Horton, Lois E., Black Bostonians: Family Life and Community Struggle in the Antebellum North, New York: Holmes & Meier, 1979.

Nash, Gary B., Forging Freedom: The Formation of Philadelphia's Black Community, 1720–1800, Cambridge, MA: Harvard University Press, 1988.

Nash, Gary B., Race and Revolution, Madison, WI: Madison House, 1990

White, Shane, Somewhat More Independent: The End of Slavery in New York City, 1770–1810, Athens: University of Georgia Press, 1991.

Chapter 3

Gutman, Herbert G., The Black Family in Slavery and Freedom, 1750–1925, New York: Pantheon, 1976.

Jacobs, Harriet, Incidents in the Life of a Slave Girl, 1861, introduction by Valerie Smith, New York: Oxford University Press, 1988.

Kolchin, Peter, American Slavery, 1619–1877, New York: Hill and Wang, 1993.

Levine, Lawrence, Black Culture and Black Consciousness: Afro-American Folk Thought from Slavery to Freedom, New York: Oxford University Press, 1977.

Tyler-McGraw, Marie and Kimball, Gregg D., In Bondage and Freedom: Antebellum Black Life in Richmond, Virginia, Richmond: Valentine Museum, 1988.

Vlach, John Michael, Back of the Big House: The Architecture of Plantation Slavery, Chapel Hill: University of North Carolina Press, 1993.

White, Deborah Gray, Ar'n't I a Woman? Female Slaves in the Plantation South, New York: W. W. Norton, 1985.

Chapter 4

Alexander, Adele Logan, Ambiguous Lives: Free Women of Color in Rural Georgia, 1789–1879, Fayetteville: University of Arkansas Press, 1991.

Berlin, Ira, Slaves Without Masters: The Free Negro in the Antebellum South, New York: Pantheon Books, 1974.

Douglass, Frederick, My Bondage and My Freedom, [1855], ed. William L. Andrews, Urbana: University of Illinois, 1987.

Horton, James Oliver, Free People of Color: Inside the African American Community, Washington, DC: Smithsonian Institution Press, 1993.

Jacobs, Donald M. (ed.), Courage and Conscience: Black and White Abolitionists in Boston, Bloomington: Indiana University Press, 1993.

Litwack, Leon, North of Slavery: The Negro in the Free States, 1790–1860, Chicago: University of Chicago Press, 1961.

Quarles, Benjamin, Black Abolitionists, New York: Oxford University Press, 1969.

Sterling, Dorothy (ed.), We Are Your Sisters: Black Women in the Nineteenth Century, New York: W. W. Norton, 1984.

Richardson, Marilyn, Maria W. Stewart, America's First Black Woman Political Writer: Essays and Speeches, Bloomington: Indiana University Press, 1987.

Chapter 5

Berlin, Ira, et. al. (eds), Free at Last: A Documentary History of Slavery, Freedom, and the Civil War, New York: The New Press, 1992.

Blight, David W., Frederick Douglass' Civil War: Keeping Faith in Jubilee, Baton Rouge: Louisiana State University Press, 1989.

Foner, Eric, Reconstruction: America's Unfinished Revolution, 1863–1877, New York: Harper and Row, 1988.

Jaynes, Gerald E., Branches Without Roots: Genesis of the Black Working Class in the American South, 1862–1882, New York: Oxford University Press, 1986.

Litwack, Leon F., Been in the Storm so Long: The Aftermath of Slavery, New York: Knopf, 1979.

Painter, Nell Irvin, The Exodusters: Black Migration to Kansas after Reconstruction, New York: Knopf, 1977.

Quarles, Benjamin, The Negro in the Civil War, [1953], New York: Da Capo Press, 1989.

Chapter 6

Crew, Spencer R., Field to Factory: Afro-American Migration, 1915–1940, Washington, DC: National Museum of American History, Smithsonian Institution, 1987.

Daniels, Douglas Henry, Pioneer Urbanites: A Social and Cultural History of Black San Francisco, Philadelphia: Temple University Press, 1980.

Dickerson, Dennis C., Out of the Crucible: Black Steelworkers in Western Pennsylvania, 1875–1980, Albany: State University of New York Press, 1986.

Grossman, James R., Land of Hope: Chicago, Black Southerners, and the Great Migration, Chicago: University of Chicago Press, 1989.

Hine, Darlene Clark, Black Women in White: Racial Conflict and Cooperation in the Nursing Profession, 1890–1950, Bloomington: Indiana University Press, 1989.

Lewis, Earl, In Their Own Interests: Race, Class, and Power in Twentieth-Century Norfolk, Virginia, Berkeley: University of California Press, 1991.

Rosengarten, Theodore, All God's Dangers: The Life of Nate Shaw, New York: Knopf, 1974.

Trotter, Joe William, Jr. (ed.), The Great Migration in Historical Perspective: New Dimensions of Race, Class, and Gender, Bloomington: Indiana University Press, 1991.

Chapter 7

Greenberg, Cheryl Lynn, Or Does It Explode?: Black Harlem in the Great Depression, New York: Oxford University Press, 1991.

Hutton, Elizabeth Turner, and Bunch, Lonnie G., Jacob Lawrence: The Migration Series, Washington, DC: Rappahannock Press, 1993.

Kelley, Robin D. G., Hammer and Hoe: Alabama Communists during the Great Depression, Chapel Hill: University of North Carolina Press, 1990.

Lewis, David Levering, When Harlem Was In Vogue, New York: Oxford University Press, 1982.

Lewis, Elizabeth Clark, Living In, Living Out: African American Domestics in Washington, D.C., 1910–1940, Washington, DC: Smithsonian Institution Press, 1994.

Locke, Alain, ed., The New Negro: Voices of the Harlem Renaissance, [1925] New York: Athenaeum, 1992.

Palmer, Phyllis M., Domesticity and Dirt: Housewives and Domestic Servants in the United States, 1920–1945, Philadelphia: Temple University Press, 1989.

Stein, Judith, The World of Marcus Garvey: Race and Class in Modern Society, Baton Rouge: Louisiana State University Press, 1986.

Trotter, Joe William, Jr., Black Milwaukee: The Making of an Industrial Proletariat, 1915–45, Urbana: University of Illinois Press, 1985.

Trotter, Joe William, Jr., Coal, Class, and Color: Blacks in Southern West Virginia, 1915–32, Urbana: University of Illinois Press, 1990.

Chapter 8

Carson, Clayborne, In Struggle: SNCC and The Awakening of the 1960s, Cambridge: Harvard University Press, 1981.

Carson, Clayborne, Malcolm X and the F.B.I., New York: Carroll & Grat Publishers, 1991.

Crawford, Vickie L., et. al., Women in the Civil Rights Movement: Trailblazers and Torchbearers, 1941–1965, New York: Carlson Publishers, 1990.

Harris, Michael W., The Rise of Gospel Blues: The Music of Thomas Andrew Dorsey in the Urban Church, New York: Oxford University Press, 1992.

Jackson, Walter A., Gunnar Myrdal and America's Conscience: Social Engineering and Racial Liberalism, 1938–1987, Chapel Hill, NC: University of North Carolina Press, 1990.

McDonald, F. Fred, Blacks and White T.V.: Afro-Americans in Television Since 1946, Chicago: University of Chicago Press, 1983.

Reeves, Martha, Dancing in the Street: Confessions of a Motown Diva, New York: Hyperion, 1994.

Terry, Wallace, Bloods: An Oral History of the Vietnam War by Black Veterans, New York: Random House, 1984.

Washington, James, M. (ed.), A Testament of Hope: The Essential Writings of Martin Luther King, Jr., San Francisco: Harper & Row, 1986.

Wilkins, Roger, A Man's Life: An Autobiography, New York: Simon & Schuster, Inc., 1982.

Chapter 9

Banner-Haley, Charles Pete, The Fruits of Integration: Black Middle Class Ideology and Culture, 1960–1990, Jackson, MS: University of Mississippi Press, 1993.

Hacker, Andrew, Two Nations: Black and White, Separate, Hostile, Unequal, New York: Maxwell Macmillan International, 1992.

Johnson, Haynes, Sleep Walking Through History: America in the Reagan Years, New York: W. W. Norton, 1991.

Morrison, Toni (ed.), Race-ing Justice, En-gendering Power: Essays on Anita Hill, Clarence Thomas, and the Construction of Social Reality, New York: Pantheon Books, 1992.

Rose, Tricia, Black Noise: Rap Music and Black Culture in Contemporary America, Hanover: Wesleyan University Press, 1994.

West, Cornel, Race Matters, Boston: Beacon Press, 1993.

Wilson, William J., The Declining Significance of Race: Blacks and Changing American Institutions, Chicago: University of Chicago Press, 1978.

INDEX

Page numbers in *italic* indicate illustrations or mentions in captions.

Picture Credits and Acknowledgments

With the exception of any items listed below, all the artifact photography was shot either by Don Eiler with the cooperation of the National Museum of American History, Smithsonian Institution, Washington, DC., or by Gregory A. Linder with the cooperation of the National Afro-American Museum and Cultural Center, Wilberforce, Ohio. The artifacts are credited below, either to NMAH (National Museum of American History) or to NAAMCC (National Afro-American Museum and Cultural Center), with collection numbers given when they are known.

The publishers are grateful to the Smithsonian Institution for the opportunity to photograph artifacts and offer thanks to Martha Morris, Lucy Greene, and the many curators, staff, and interns for all their help. A special thank you to Christopher Shaffer, Museum Consultant, who organized things so efficiently and whose contribution was vital to the project; thanks too to Peter Moen for several moments of inspiration. The publishers are also grateful to the National African American Museum and Cultural Center (NAAMCC) in Wilberforce for the opportunity to photograph their artifacts and offer thanks to the staff for all their help. A special thank you to Floyd Thomas, Jr. for his curatorial guidance and access to his own collections.

Additional thanks are offered to the following: New York University Press for permission to quote Sojourner Truth from Susan Mabee Newhouse's book; Dorothy Sterling for permission to quote Susie King Taylor from Dorothy Sterling's book *Speak Out in Thunder Tones*; Random House, Inc. for permission to quote veterans' reminiscences from Wallace Terry's *Bloods*; Alfred A. Knopf, Inc. of Random House, Inc. and Harold Ober Associates Incorporated for permission to reproduce 'I Too' and 'Dream Variations' by Langston Hughes; Alfred A. Knopf, Inc. of Random House, Inc. and Virago Press for permission to reproduce 'Still I Rise' by Maya Angelou.

In addition to the two principal sources, other individuals and museums helped with the project. Thanks go to Lysbeth B. Acuff, Chief Curator, Virginia Department of Historic Resources; Dr. Thomas Battle, Director of Moorland-Spingarn Research Center; Mrs Loretta Carter Hanes; John H. Motley; Sharon L. Pekrul, Curator of Collections, South Carolina Institute of Archaeology, University of South Carolina; Mildred C. Settle; and Alan B. Taylor. A very special thanks must go to the picture researcher, Kym S. Rice, of Maryland, who did a remarkable job in a short space of time.

All the organizations and individuals that supplied photographs or artifacts are credited here by page number and position, with reference numbers where known. For reasons of space, references have had to be abbreviated for both sources and positions. The principal photographic sources are: LC (Library of Congress); NA (National Archives); and RBUPI (Range/Bettman/UPI). The positions are indicated as follows: (T): Top; (B) Bottom; (C) Center; (TR) Top Right; (BR) Bottom Right; (TL) Top Left; and (BL) Bottom Left.

Endpapers: Solomon D. Butcher Collection, Nebraska State Historical Society, ref B983-1345; **Page 1:** NMAH (Division of Domestic Life, DL), ref 1990.0410.01; **2:** LCUSZC4-2329; **3:** NAAMCC/John H. Motley; **5:** NMAH (Political History, PH), see pages **166** & **173** below; **7:** LCUSZ62-22980; **8/9:** NMAH, neg 84-18675; **10:** LCUSZ62-30841; **11:** (T) NMAH (DL, on loan from the National Museum of Natural History, NMNH, Department of Anthropology), ref 66.5069, (B) LCUSZ62-068966; **12:** LCUSZ62-30839; **13:** NMAH (Division of Community Life: CL), clockwise from top left - 298252.56, 298252.37, 314,675.1, 281920.1, 298252.10, and 298252.8; **14:** (T) NMAH (DL, on loan from the NMNH, Department of Anthropology), ref 174811, (B) NMAH (DL), ref 1990.0410.01; **15:** (C) Cliche Ville de Nantes-Musees du Chateau des Dues de Bretagne, France; **16:** Wilberforce House Museum, Hull City Museums, Art Gallery and Archives; **17:** (L) LCUSZ62-106828, (R) NMAH (DL, on loan from the Moorland-Spingarn Research Center), ref MB9 E95; **19:** (T) Wilberforce House Museum, Hull City Museums, Art Gallery and Archives, (B) LCUSZ62-44000; **20:** LC; **21:** (T) LCUSZ62-2580, (B) Gibbes Museum of Art, ref 68.18.01; **22:** Maryland Historical Society (MHS), Baltimore, ref II.36; **23:** (T) LCUSZ62-26369, (B) MHS, ref 12.1.3; **24/25:** Library Company of Philadelphia, ref 1-6a; **26:** (T) LCUSZ62-56850; **26/27:** New York State Historical Association, Cooperstown, ref N-366.54; **27:** NMAH (Division of Political History, PH), ref 1980.523.1; **28:** Lafayette College Art Collection, Easton, Pennsylvania. Gift of Mrs John Hubbard; **29:** Historical Society of Pennsylvania; **30:** LCUSZ62-45; **31:** NMAH (DL), (scale) ref 309675.1, (ledger) ref 67,918; **32:** (T) NMAH (PH), ref C58324, (B) NMAH (CL), ref 1993.0507.01; **33:** The Menil Collection, Houston, Texas, ref 74-001 DJ; **34:** National Portrait Gallery/Art Resource (NPG/AR), New York, ref NPG.77.161; **35:** LCUSZ62-56336; **36:** (T) LCUSZ62-42044, (B) Delaware Art Museum; **37:** The Metropolitan Museum of Art, Rogers Fund, 1942, ref 42.95.15; **38:** NMAH, neg 84-15404; **39:** all items are on loan to NMAH (DL) - river bowl, ref 38CN7-1-254, and river jar, ref 3BK48-322, are courtesy of South Carolina Institute of Archaeology, University of South Carolina; the pipe and chamber pot are courtesy of Virginia Department of Historic Resources; the blue bowls, ref 44FX762/40, are courtesy of Mrs Loretta Carter Hanes; **40:** Valentine Museum, Richmond, Virginia; **41:** Anonymous loan to New Hampshire Historical Society; **42/43:** T.W. Wood Art Gallery, Vermont College Arts Center, Montpelier, Vermont; **44:** Georgia Historical Society; **45:** Chicago Historical Society, ref 1957.27; **46:** NMAH (CL), ref 291348.2; **47:** (T) Missouri Historical Society, St. Louis, ref 690B, (TR) NMAH, neg 94-6907, (B) NMAH (CL), ref 1989.0020.01; **48:** LCUSZ62-11341; **49:** (T) Louisiana State Museum, New Orleans, (B) NMAH (CL), ref 1990.0605; **50:** The New-York Historical Society; **51:** LCUSZ62-4204; **52:** Wilberforce House Museum, Hull City Museums, Art Gallery and Archives; **53:** The New-York Historical Society; **54:** Massachusetts Historical Society; **55:** North Carolina Museum of Art, ref CT4859; **56:** (from top to bottom) NMAH (DL), ref 75.44; NMAH (DL, on loan from the NMNH, Department of Anthropology), ref 174757; NMAH (DL, on loan from the NMNH, Department of Anthropology), ref 174756; **57:** Hampton University Museum, Hampton, Virginia; **58:** The Historic New Orleans Collection, ref 1960.46; **59:** LCUSZ62-107750; **60/61:** LCUSZC4-1388; **62:** Penn School Papers, Southern Historical Collection, University of North Carolina, Chapel Hill; **63:** (T) Bequest of Martha C. Karolik for the M. and M. Karolik Collection of American Paintings, 1815-1865, Museum of Fine Arts, Boston, ref 48.467, (B) LCUSZ62-13104; **64:** Valentine Museum, Richmond, Virginia, ref V86.32.5; **65:** (TL) Chicago Historical Society, ref 1904.18; (TR) Chicago Historical Society, ref 1955.197; (B) The Metropolitan Museum of Art, Rogers Fund, 1942, ref 42.95.18; 66: Wilberforce House Museum, Hull City Museums, Art Gallery and Archives; **67:** (T) Bequest of Martha C. Karolik for the M. and M. Karolik Collection of American Paintings, 1815-1865, Museum of Fine Arts, Boston, ref 48.461; (B) The Amistad Research Center, New Orleans, Louisiana; **68:** (T) NMAH (PH), clockwise from bottom left – 227,739.1837, 1994.0082.01, and 1977.0010.01; (B) LCBH8270-3247; **69:** (T) Peter Newark's Historical Pictures, (B) Massachusetts Historical Society; **70:** (T) LCUSZ62-1283, (B) LCUSZ62-40698; **71:** (T) NMAH (Archives Center, AC), (B) LCUSZ62-73349; **72:** Kym S. Rice; **73:** NPG/AR, ref NPG.76.101; **74/75:** LCUSZ62-22265?; **76:** LC; **77:** LCUSZ62-36240; **78:** The New-York Historical Society, ref 37628; **79:** (T) NMAH (PH), clockwise from the bottom - ref 265,500.4, 265,500.2, 265,500.5, and 265,500.3, (B) National Park Service, US Dept. of Interior; **80:** (T) LCUSZ62-24411, (B) LCB8171-383; **81:** (T) LCUSZ62-1288, (TR) Schomburg Center for Research in Black Culture, ref SC-CN-89-0313 (B) The Howard University Gallery of Art, Permanent Collection, Washington, DC; **82:** NMAH (Military History, MH); **83:** (T) NMAH (MH), (B) Montana Historical Society; **84:** (TL) NMAH (MH), ref 178781, (C) NMAH (MH), ref 1985.0612.01, (TR) LCUSZ62-175; **85:** (TL) NMAH, neg 93-5818, (TR) NMAH, neg 93-10495; **86:** LCUSZC4-1561; **87:** LCUSZ62-8461; **88:** (T) LCUSZ62-68959; (B) LCUSZ62-22105; **89:** Kym S. Rice; **90:** Floyd Thomas Collection (FMC); **91:** (TL) The Kansas State Historical Society, (TR) Western History Collections, University of Oklahoma Library, (B) RBUPI, ref F.9554; **92:** (T) NMAH (PH), ref 227,739.1899.M1, (B) LCUSZ62-31911; **93:** LCUSZ62-38149; **94/95:** LCUSZ62-62591; **96:** LCUSZ62-12511; **97:** (T) NMAH (AC), (B) LCUSZ62-43679; **98:** (T) Amon Carter Museum, Fort Worth, Texas, (B) NMAH (CL); **99:** (T) NMAH (CL), refs - (dish) 76,749, (tool) 23,405, (B) NA 42-SPB-18; **100:** (T) NMAH (CL), (B) NA 69-83-FB-272; **101:** (L) LCUSZ62-28040, (R) Georgia State Archives; **102:** LCUSZ62-134; **103:** all items from the John H. Motley Collection, except the flag (NAAMCC, donated by Bob Sattem), and the note (NAAMCC, donated by Omega Psi Phi Fraternity, Inc.), *Crisis*, sheet music and sword (all NAAMCC); **104:** NMAH (AC); **105:** (T) LCUSZ62-39784, (C) NMAH (AC), (B) NA 67-2224; **106:** (T) NMAH (CL), ref 1987.0072.01, (B) NMAH, neg 75-2984; **107:** LCUSZ62-507793; **108:** (T) NAAMCC, (B) LCUSZ62-80591; **109:** (T) LCUSZ62-87008; (B) Peter Newark's Historical Pictures; **110:** (T) LCUSZ62-25650, (B) NMAH (CL), ref 129.492 A-F; **111:** (T) RBUPI, ref BHW.7224, (B) NA 65-1871; **112:** (L) LC17401-16155, (R) NMAH (CL); **114:** (L) LCUSZ62-62590, (R) NMAH/Smithsonian, neg 91-490; **115:** NA; **116:** LCUSZC4-2426; **117:** LCUSZ62-51941; **118/119:** LCUSF34-40837D; **120:** (T) NAAMCC, (B) NA 165-WW-127-49; **121:** (L) NMAH, neg 4.2.169G, (TR) NMAH (AC), ref 480; **122:** RBUPI; **123:** NAAMCC; **124:** NMAH (CL); **125:** (T) NMAH (CL), (B) LCUSZ62-28020; **126:** NAAMCC; **127:** (T) and (C) both NAAMCC, (B) NA 62-4495; **128:** RBUPI, ref F-8548; **129:** (T) NA 306-NT-171.611c, (B) RBUPI, ref F.6689; **130:** RBUPI, ref F.8963; **131:** NMAH (CL); **132:** (TL) RBUPI, ref WJ.30, (TR) NMAH (PH), clockwise from bottom left - 1985.0106.284, LC.14, 1985.0106.135; **133:** (T) LCUSZ62-48264, (B) LCUSF34-31160; **134:** (T) LCUSZ62-36649, (B) Howard University Gallery of Art; **135:** (T) NAAMCC, (B) RBUPI, ref W.1525; **136:** (T) LCUSW3-11696C, (B) LCUSZ62-66161; **137:** (T) LCUSF34-25348, (B) RBUPI, ref F.8425; **138/139:** NMAH (CL); **140:** (TL) NAAMCC, (TR) NA 51-3076, (B) NMAH (AC); **141:** (TR) LCUSF34-25348D, (BL) LCUSZ62-4473D, (BL inset) NMAH (PH); **142:** (TL) NAAMCC, (TR) NA 51-193; **143:** clockwise from bottom left - NAAMCC, NA 50-9473, Floyd Thomas Collection, NA 49-6800; **144:** NMAH (CL), clockwise from bottom left - 1981.0123.8, 1981.0202, 1981.0129.4, 1981.0356.1, and 1981.0123.5; **145:** (T) National Baseball Library & Archive, Cooperstown, New York, (B) RBUPI, ref U927935; **146:** (T) NA 208-PMP-68, (B) NA 111-SC-189383-S; **147:** (T) RBUPI, ref F.8594, (B) Alan B. Taylor Collection; **148/149:** Alan B. Taylor Collection; **150:** Hampton University Museum, Hampton, Virginia; **151:** NA 80-G-469544; **152/153:** RBUPI, ref U1392070; **154:** RBUPI, ref U.56956L; **155:** (T) NAAMCC, (BL) NA 59-637, (BR) NA 63-5178; **156:** (TL) NAAMCC, (TR) NA 63-4059; **157:** RBUPI, ref U1305870; **158:** NA 67-3309; **159:** NAAMCC; **160:** (TL) NA 54-7563, (TR) NA 65-2835, (B) NMAH (PH), ref 282,806.1; **161:** (T) RBUPI, ref U1214991, (B) NMAH (DL); **162:** (T) NA 71-791, (B) NAAMCC; **163:** (T) NAAMCC, (B) NA 62-4482; **164:** (T) NA 67-3917, (B) LCU9-10380; **165**: NAAMCC - *Life* magazine reproduced courtesy of Katz Pictures, Charles Moore cover photograph courtesy of Black Star/Colorific; **166:** (T) all NMAH (PH), refs where known - (Emancipation March) 2559949.5, (Equal Rights) 1989.0486.21, (Jobs & Freedom) 1983.0592.07, (SNCC) 1978.0123.05, (SCLC) 1977.0737.62, (We Share the Dream) 1984.0447.03, (CORE) 1986.1040.205, (We Shall Overcome) 1986.1040.312, (B) NA 65-1456; **167:** (T) NA 63-3241, (B) NMAH (PH), ref 1994.0154; **168:** NA 69-131; **169:** (T) NMAH (AC), (B) RBUPI, ref U1689960; **170:** (T) NA 65-1457, (B) NA 65-3502; **171:** NA 66-1887; **172:** RBUPI, ref U1379406; **173:** (T) all NMAH (PH), refs are clockwise from 'June 8th Free Bobby' pin - 1977.0737.57, 1988.0661.54, 1984.1081.320, 1986.0666.353, (free all political prisoners) no ref, 279,881.5, 1985.0106.400, 1985.0106.308, (BL) NA 70-2165, (BR) RBUPI, ref U1610619; **174:** (L) all NMAH (PH), from top to bottom - 1988.0081.02, 310,546.2, 1988.0368.15, (R) NA 68-1314; **175:** (T) RBUPI, ref U1588581, (B) US Navy, ref 1138466; **176:** (T) NA 67-220, (B) NA 65-2171; **177:** (T) NAAMCC, (B) RBUPI, ref U1652892; **178/179:** RBUPI, ref R91052112; **180:** (T) NA 63-4458, (B) RBUPI, ref R91304122; **181:** (T) NA 71-973, (B) NA 72-5168; **182:** (T) RBUPI, UPI1725468, (B) Floyd Thomas Collection; **183:** (T) Mildred C. Settle, (B) NAAMCC; **184:** BFI Stills, Posters and Designs/Forty Acres and a Mule Filmworks; **185:** (TL) NA 72-1394, (TR) BFI Stills, Posters and Designs/Turner Entertainment Co., (BL) & (BR) BFI Stills, Posters and Designs/Forty Acres and a Mule Filmworks; **186:** (T) NA 66-1591, (B) NMAH (CL) , left to right - 1979.1020.03, 1991,0178.01, 1979.0622.01; **187:** (T) RBUPI, ref UPI1581985, (B) Floyd Thomas Collection; **188:** all from the Floyd Thomas Collection, (TL), (TR) & (BL) all reproduced courtesy of Marvel, © 1995 Marvel Entertainment Group, Inc. All rights reserved. Marvel Comics, Luke Cage, Black Panther and all other Marvel character's names and the distinctive likenesses thereof are trademarks of Marvel Entertainment Group, Inc. and are used with permission; **189:** (T) RBUPI, ref 85127075, (B) RBUPI, ref U2012414; **190:** (T) NMAH (Costume, C), clockwise from bottom left - 1984.1033.03, 1987.0739.6, 1984.1033.01, (dashiki) 1991.0135.2, 1984.1033.10, 1984.1033.05; (B) NMAH (C), ref 1991.0135.1; **191:** (T) NA 72-1300, (B) NA 72-1452; **192:** (TL) NAAMCC, reproduced courtesy of Antonio's Manufacturing, Inc., Cresson, Pennsylvania, (TR) NMAH (C), ref (headwrap) 1992.0456.1, (dress) 1989.0175.01; **193:** (T) NA 67-4530, (B) RBUPI, ref U90016010; **194:** (TL) RBUPI, ref U86098071, (TR) Redferns; **195:** (T) Redferns, (B) RBUPI, ref R95061057; **196:** (T) NMAH (CL), ref 1989.0175.01, (C) NAAMCC, (B) RBUPI, ref U85112065; **197:** (T) Floyd Thomas Collection/ Afrocentric Comic Books, (B) NMAH (C), clockwise from the pin - 1992.0604.1, 1994.0251.1, 1994.0251.3, 1994.0251.2; **198:** (TL) Floyd Thomas Collection, courtesy of Michael Simmons and Harlem Globetrotters International, Inc., (TR) Floyd Thomas Collection, courtesy of General Mills, Inc., (BL) RBUPI, ref U86098067, (BR) RBUPI, ref R92227098; **199:** RBUPI, ref 89261060. **201:** NA 86-G-5L-1; **208:** Floyd Thomas Collection.

Editor's notes

Every effort has been made to contact original sources for permissions. The selection and captioning of all illustrations in this book have been the responsibility of Salamander Books Ltd and not of the individual contributors.

The Joe Louis World Champion clock was manufactured by the United Clock Corporation, Brooklyn, New York, in about 1940. Joe Louis won the heavyweight boxing crown in 1937 and became the first black national sports hero when he scored a first-round knockout of the German Max Schmeling on 22 June 1838 – sweet revenge against the man who had been the first to defeat Louis in 1936. The 'Brown Bomber' held the championship for 12 years and defended it 25 times.